Dear friends,

We're so happy to welcome you to *Daily Guideposts 2021*. The book you're holding in your hand contains 365 inspiring, faith-filled reflections to bolster you on your faith journey. If you're new to *Daily Guideposts*, welcome to the fold! And if you are a longtime reader, welcome back!

This year, our theme "Faithful in Prayer" (from Romans 12:12, "Be joyful in hope, patient in affliction, faithful in prayer.") inspired our fifty writers as they experienced God's unending faithfulness through various moments in their life—from suffering through addiction to moving homes to leaning on God and each other in tragedy and loss and celebrating with one another in joyful times.

"Faithful in Prayer" is an instruction from Paul to the Romans. In this passage he urges us to stay close to the Lord. We discover more of God's presence and His own faithfulness when we continually bring our fears, worries, hopes, and dreams to Him.

The pages of this year's *Daily Guideposts* are alive with joy, wonder, fear, uncertainty, hope, pain, and love, as each writer seeks God's light in the joys and trials of their lives. Edward Grinnan tells us some sweet and funny stories about his golden retriever, Gracie, including one where she is lost (and then found!) in the Berkshire Mountains, which teaches Edward a whole lot about trusting in God in all times; Vicki Kuyper is reminded of the power of prayer when a bucket of water is poured on her head while traveling in Myanmar; Daniel Schantz realizes his God-imbued worth when he grows some beautiful zinnias for his granddaughter's wedding; God uses a wiggly toddler and a dance party to remind Ashley Kappel to follow the example of Christ at all times; Jacqueline Wheelock reflects on the true rest Jesus offers to us; and so many more.

This year, we are pleased to welcome new contributor Leanne Jackson to *Daily Guideposts*. Contributor Sharon Foster has returned this year and we are very glad to welcome her back. We say a fond farewell to Julie Garmon, with so many thanks for all she's shared with us and prayers and good wishes for her next chapter of life.

Six special series await you in this year's volume. Erika Bentsen shares the moving and heartfelt story of her father's last week of life; Lynne Hartke explores the spiritual lessons God teaches her as she enjoys the breathtaking beauty of the Grand Canyon; Patricia Lorenz brings us alongside her as she says goodbye to her beloved husband, Jack, and practices joy, even in widowhood; Patty Kirk honestly turns the lens on her own faltering heart in her series about prayer, "Struggling to Pray"; Roberta Messner celebrates Christian hospitality in her series about breaking free from addiction, "Open Heart, Open Home"; and our longtime contributor Elizabeth Sherrill writes movingly about losing her husband of seventy years and thriving even while experiencing grief and then blindness.

DAILY
GUIDEPOSTS
2021

Guideposts
Danbury, Connecticut

ZONDERVAN
BOOKS

ZONDERVAN BOOKS

Daily Guideposts 2021
Copyright © 2020 by Guideposts. All rights reserved.

Requests for information should be addressed to:
Zondervan, *3900 Sparks Dr. SE, Grand Rapids, Michigan 49546*

Zondervan titles may be purchased in bulk for educational, business, fundraising, or sales promotional use. For information, please email SpecialMarkets@Zondervan.com.

ISBN 978-0-310-35472-7 (hardcover)
ISBN 978-0-310-35474-1 (leather edition)
ISBN 978-0-310-35473-4 (large print)
ISBN 978-0-310-35920-3 (audio)
ISBN 978-0-310-35475-8 (ebook)

Acknowledgments: Every attempt has been made to credit the sources of copyrighted material used in this book. If any such acknowledgment has been inadvertently omitted or miscredited, receipt of such information would be appreciated.

Scripture quotations marked (AMP) are taken from the *Amplified Bible*. Copyright © 2015 by The Lockman Foundation, La Habra, California. All rights reserved. • Scripture quotations marked (BEREAN STUDY BIBLE) are taken from The Holy Bible, Berean Study Bible, BSB. Copyright © 2016, 2018 by Bible Hub. Used by permission. All rights reserved worldwide. • Scripture quotations marked (CHABAD) are taken from Chabad.org. All rights reserved. • Scripture quotations marked (CEB) are taken from the *Common English Bible*. Copyright © 2011 by Common English Bible. • Scripture quotations marked (CEV) are taken from *Holy Bible: Contemporary English Version*. Copyright © 1995 American Bible Society. • Scripture quotations marked (CSB) are taken from *The Christian Standard Bible*. Copyright © 2017 by Holman Bible Publishers. Used by permission. • Scripture quotations marked (ESV) are taken from the *Holy Bible, English Standard Version*. Copyright © 2001 by Crossway Bibles, a division of Good News Publishers. Used by permission. All rights reserved. • Scripture quotations marked (GNT) are taken from the *Holy Bible, Good News Translation*. Copyright © 1992 by American Bible Society. • Scripture quotations marked (GW) are taken from *GOD'S WORD Translation*. Copyright © 1995 by God's Word to the Nations. Used by permission of Baker Publishing Group. • Scripture quotations marked (HCSB) are taken from the *Holman Christian Standard Bible*. Copyright © 1999, 2000, 2002, 2003, 2009 by Holman Bible Publishers, Nashville, Tennessee. All rights reserved. • Scripture quotations marked (JPS) are taken from *Tanakh: A New Translation of the Holy Scriptures according to the Traditional Hebrew Text*. Copyright © 1985 by the Jewish Publication Society. All rights reserved. • Scripture quotations marked (ICB) are taken from *The Holy Bible, International Children's Bible*®. Copyright © 1986, 1988, 1999, 2015 by Tommy Nelson™, a division of Thomas Nelson. Used by permission. • Scripture quotations marked (ISV) are taken from the *Holy Bible, International Standard Version*. Copyright © 1995–2014 by ISV Foundation. All rights reserved internationally. Used by permission of Davidson Press, LLC. • Scripture quotations marked (KJV) are taken from the *King James Version of the Bible*. • Scripture quotations marked (MSG) are taken from *The Message*. Copyright © 1993, 1994, 1995, 1996, 2000, 2001, 2002 by Eugene H. Peterson. • Scripture quotations marked (NASB) are taken from the *New American Standard Bible*. Copyright © 1960, 1962, 1963, 1968, 1971, 1972, 1973, 1975, 1977, 1995 by The Lockman Foundation, La Habra, California. Used by permission. • Scripture quotations marked (NCV) are taken from *The Holy Bible, New Century Version*. Copyright © 2005 by Thomas Nelson. • Scripture quotations marked (NET) are taken from the *NET Bible*®. Copyright © 1996–2006 by Biblical Studies Press, L.L.C. http://netbible.com. All rights reserved. • Scripture quotations marked (NIRV) are taken from the Holy Bible, New International Reader's Version®, NIrV®. Copyright © 1995, 1996, 1998, 2014 by Biblica, Inc.® Used by permission of Zondervan. All rights reserved worldwide. www.Zondervan.com. The "NIrV" and "New International Reader's Version" are trademarks registered in the United States Patent and Trademark Office by Biblica, Inc.® • Scripture quotations marked (NIV) are taken from *The Holy Bible, New International Version*. Copyright © 1973, 1978, 1984, 2011 by Biblica, Inc. Used by permission of Zondervan. All rights reserved worldwide. www.Zondervan.com • Scripture quotations marked (NKJV) are taken from *The Holy Bible, New King James Version*. Copyright © 1982 by Thomas Nelson. • Scripture quotations marked (NLT) are from the *Holy Bible, New Living Translation*. Copyright © 1996, 2004, 2007 by Tyndale House Foundation. Used by permission of Tyndale House Publishers Inc., Carol Stream, Illinois. All rights reserved. • Scripture quotations marked (NRSV) are taken from the *New Revised Standard Version Bible*. Copyright © 1989 by the Division of Christian Education of the National Council of the Churches of Christ in the United States of America. Used by permission. All rights reserved. • Scripture quotations marked (RSV) are taken from the *Revised Standard Version of the Bible*. Copyright © 1946, 1952, 1971 by the Division of Christian Education of the National Council of the Churches of Christ in the United States of America. Used by permission. • Scripture quotations marked (TLB) are taken from *The Living Bible*. Copyright © 1971 by Tyndale House Publishers, Inc., Carol Stream, Illinois. All rights reserved.

Cover and interior design: Müllerhaus
Cover photo: Shutterstock
Monthly page opener photos: Pixabay
Indexed: Kelly White
Typeset: Aptara, Inc.

20 21 22 23 24 25 26 27 28 29 30 31 32 33 34 35 /LSC/ 20 19 18 17 16 15 14 13 12 11 10 9 8 7 6 5 4 3 2 1

As you travel alongside our writers this year, it is our hope that you have a year rich in prayer and that you experience God's faithfulness in a new way, in each small, daily moment of which our lives are made.

Faithfully yours,
The Editors of Guideposts

P.S. We love hearing from you! We read every letter we receive. Let us know what *Daily Guideposts* means to you by emailing DailyGPEditors@guideposts.org or writing to Guideposts Books & Inspirational Media, 100 Reserve Road, Suite E200, Danbury, CT 06810-5212. You can also keep up with your *Daily Guideposts* friends on facebook.com /DailyDevofromGP.

Going Digital? Especially for You!
Get one-year instant access to the digital edition of *Daily Guideposts* delivered straight to your email. You'll be able to enjoy its daily inspiration and Scripture anytime, anywhere, on your computer, phone, or tablet. Visit DailyGuideposts.org/DG2021 and enter this code: **prayer**.

JANUARY

Through him we have also obtained access by faith into this grace in which we stand, and we rejoice in hope of the glory of God.

—Romans 5:2 (ESV)

New Year's Day, Friday, January 1

Jesus Christ is the same yesterday and today and forever. —Hebrews 13:8 (NIV)

"May I help, Mom?" ten-year-old Isaiah asks. "You bet," I say. I hand him the rolling pin. We're making our traditional homemade ice cream for New Year's Day. The last of the Christmas candy canes, crushed to bits, will go on top.

Isaiah rolls the pin over the candy, hands small and strong. For a moment, I see my grandmother's hands, well-worn from loving well, curled over that same pin, rolling homemade noodles or crust for pecan pie.

It's the essence of New Year's Day—heart-holding what was dear but forging toward what will be.

Change is at the center of life.

I don't have to look far to witness it. My family is jumbled close over game boards and books, another tradition, but we're in a different home. A fire still crackles and snaps, but the hearth isn't the same. My bevy of boys still stretch over the sofa and chairs and they sprawl, lanky-legged, over the rug. But they are bigger. Shoulders broader. Voices deeper. It's a growing time. For them. For their daddy and me.

New plans. New goals. New territory. Fresh, bright squares on a crisp, calendar page.

My gut is to resist. To grapple life. To grip it with both hands. To tether time. Sameness brings security, and I long for that.

Isaiah's chatter is as steady as the clackety-clack of the pin. The boys razz one another and laughter booms. Music from the 1940s comes from vinyl. But even in the bustle, I hear my soul whisper, from that deep place where all I know about the Lord lives. Where truth is stored like Old Testament grain.

He is the security I need. He is concrete. He is constant.

And as we move into a new year, this praise becomes my offering.

Lord, I can find solace in change because You are steadfast! —Shawnelle Eliasen

Digging Deeper: Psalm 90:2; Malachi 3:6

Saturday, January 2

Give thanks in all circumstances; for this is God's will for you in Christ Jesus. —1 Thessalonians 5:18 (NIV)

I grew up in the age of *Leave It to Beaver* and *Father Knows Best*, which is another way of saying I'm no spring chicken. This realization hit home when my husband experienced a series of medical problems that started out with an infection in his spine following surgery.

The infection wasn't the end of his health issues, however. Wayne suffered a series of small strokes known as TIAs, plus heart issues that resulted in two stents in the arteries leading to his heart. It has been one thing after another, and he isn't the only one. While I might think I'm still in my thirties, my body raises all kinds of reminders that the years are accumulating.

I've started reading books to help me stay healthy both physically and also mentally. The list of advice offered makes sense, and I have been doing my best to make it all part of my daily routine. One of the essential factors I've seen mentioned multiple times is the importance of having an attitude of gratitude.

For years now I've kept a gratitude journal. Each morning I list five things for which I'm grateful. I've found that the more things I am grateful for, the more I have for which to be grateful. It's through my gratitude journal that I find myself looking for everyday miracles. They are all around me in the petal of a rose, in the laughter of one of my grandchildren, or in the gentle touch of my husband reaching out to hold my hand. It's true Wayne and I are aging, but with God at our side, we intend to do it well.

Lord, no matter how much change I encounter in my life, You are my constant, unchanging source of joy and strength. —Debbie Macomber

Digging Deeper: 2 Corinthians 9:11

Sunday, January 3

When I am afraid, I put my trust in you.
In God, whose word I praise, in God I trust;
I shall not be afraid. What can flesh do to me?
—Psalm 56:3–4 (ESV)

It had been cold and snowy in the Berkshires until a sudden warm front rolled in that January night, shrouding the old hills in a thick, velvety fog. I let Gracie out after dinner for her evening reconnoiter. I was poking the fire in the woodstove when I heard her barking rather emphatically out in the yard. I looked out the window. There she stood in the mist, turning a slow circle and sounding off into the gloom. A deep, chesty bark, assertive but not aggressive, slightly muffled, the effort lifting her front paws a bit off the ground with each volley. "What's got into her?" my wife, Julee, asked, joining me at the window.

"The fog," I said. "It messes with her night vision." Goldens have superb eyesight, even in the dark. But not tonight. She couldn't see past her own wet black nose.

"Should I go get her?" I asked Julee.

"No, leave her. She's just doing her job."

What a thought! Gracie was barking out warnings to any would-be intruders who might infiltrate her yard under cover of fog, warding off threats, letting the hills know she was on duty, keeping us safe. What a brave dog!

I wondered if I was that brave—brave when it counted, brave in my faith. I like to believe my faith is clear and unwavering, and yet there are times when I can't see my way, when my spiritual visibility is compromised by the fog of fear or doubt or regret. It is at those moments that I must stand in the dark and proclaim my trust in that unseen heaven.

"Gracie is too brave to let a little fog bother her," Julee said. I would be brave, too, the next time a spiritual fog found me.

When I grope and falter, when I fear and I doubt, lead me, Lord, through the gloom to Your eternal light.
—Edward Grinnan
Digging Deeper: Isaiah 41:10;
2 Timothy 1:7

Monday, January 4

Simon answered, "Master, we've worked hard all night and haven't caught anything. But because you say so, I will let down the nets." —Luke 5:5 (NIV)

I get so sick of praying sometimes. It seems fruitless, like talking at a rock concert.

I've been at a crossroads in my marriage. Again. I think he's spending too much money on poker. He thinks I'm overreacting. "It's nowhere near what we've spent on this move to Cleveland for your new job," he said. Ouch.

We have gone round and round like this. I've prayed for guidance, for courage, for a way out of the deep ruts of our resentments. How can we ever find common ground? Dear God, even a postage-stamp-size patch will do!

"I'm not getting any answers," I said to a friend.

"Keep lifting your face to the Light, even though, for now, you may not see," she replied.

I wanted to believe, so I followed her suggestion. I kept praying. I cast my net of need out into the vast, dark ocean, again. Slowly, out of the depths, bubbles of hope rose to the surface.

Not too long after, I realized God's indecisiveness *was* my answer. I still wanted my husband. Our marriage felt essential and necessary. I hadn't been acting like it was. In my telling him this, we found our common ground.

The net was filling with nourishment: hope, love, peaceful evenings, a quiet joy. They came when I set aside my doubts and petulant demands and, once again, lowered the net.

**God, thank You for the people in my
life who remind me to keep turning to You.**
—Amy Eddings

Digging Deeper: Luke 11:5–8;
Romans 5:1–5

Tuesday, January 5

Pray in the Spirit on all occasions with all kinds of prayers and requests....—Ephesians 6:18 (NIV)

Breathe in. Breathe out. Each tiny breath holds my full attention, as if it were something as awe-inspiring as the Grand Canyon at sunrise or as unexpected as a whale breaching from the ocean. And it is. Some things are just so miraculous, so impossibly wonderful, that you can't help but stare. A grandson, three days new, is one of them.

My cell phone sits on the table, set on silent. Email waits on my computer, unread. Deadlines are pushed back. Breakfast is forgotten. I cradle baby Oliver in my lap, and the warmth of his little body, not yet unfurled from nine months of life "on the inside," relaxes me more than a day at a spa. This is joy.

But it stirs up memories of the last time I simply sat and watched someone breathe. It was my mother, a little over a year ago, the night she died. I watched her breathe in, breathe out. Until she didn't anymore. That moment, and this one, feel so similar, so strikingly sacred.

When my emotions run deep, I don't have to remind myself to pray. God's Spirit does it for me. If I'm overwhelmed by joy, pain, grief, fear, or awe, offerings of thanks and praise, pleas for help, or longings too profound to be put into words spill out of me as effortlessly as conversing across the kitchen table with someone I love. What could be more natural than sharing the deepest moments of this life with the One who gave it to me?

Dear Lord, teach me how to pray more openly, passionately, and regularly—talking to You with the same ease I feel when I speak to anyone I love.
—Vicki Kuyper

Digging Deeper: Romans 8:26–27

I have seen something else under the sun: The race
is not to the swift or the battle to the strong....
—Ecclesiastes 9:11 (NIV)

Years ago, Frankie Valli and the Four Seasons had
a hit single, "Dawn, Go Away (I'm No Good for
You)." It was about this girl named Dawn, and there
was this guy, and...well, it's kinda self-explanatory
after that.

I'm thinking of that song right now as I watch
the sun rise. Unlike with Frankie, chronic insomnia
has made my last four (eight? twelve?) seasons pretty
miserable, and I don't have a hit single—or even a
sacrifice bunt. This explains why I'm awake at 5:00 a.m.,
raging at misfortune and doubt, searching for sleep,
searching for answers to life's issues, or both—and
preferably in that order.

But dawn insists on coming anyway, despite my
insomnia-induced protests. Turns out dawn is the
answer I'm looking for. Dawn is *always* the answer:
another day, another shot at redemption, another
chance to make me worthy of the next sunrise,
content at the next sunset.

Having a rough night? Having a rough season?
Don't deserve the dawn? Don't worry. You and your
rage against outrageous fortune will still be forgiven
and welcomed by the reassuring, awesome, blessed
gift of the brand-new day.

Lord, please make me a good steward of this day,
and please send me Your angel of rest tonight.
—Mark Collins

Digging Deeper: Ecclesiastes 7:11

Thursday, January 7

Set up road signs; put up guideposts. Take note of
the highway, the road that you take. Return, Virgin
Israel, return to your towns. —Jeremiah 31:21 (NIV)

I have read *Daily Guideposts* for many years. This is
a fond tradition for me. However, it is ironic that
I have not glimpsed the word *guideposts* within the
text of the Bible until today. This morning I read
Jeremiah 31:21 for the first time and the word
guideposts jumped off the page with new insight.

Becoming lost or disoriented on our life's journey
is a common experience for most people. As we
traverse adulthood we are forced to travel new paths.
We often fear we have lost our way, our perspective,
and our connection to God and each other. It seems
we have not seen a clear guidepost to give direction
in a long time.

What helps me find direction in my life is
listening to the stories of fellow travelers. My
primary mentors, guides, and teachers have been
men and women who told me their stories—their
trials, victories, defeats, fears, and hard-earned
lessons.

Perhaps our own story is the most helpful thing we can give to another person. To share those rare moments when a guidepost appeared on our roadside that sent us in new directions or connected us to paths long lost that led us home.

Today, in my heart I heard the old prophet Jeremiah speak an ancient word with new meaning: "Place for yourself *guideposts* so you won't get lost." Sharing personal stories with each other is how we create guideposts to lead us home.

Dear God, thank You for many people who have told me their story and placed guideposts on my path. Amen. —Scott Walker

Digging Deeper: Psalm 119:103–105; Proverbs 3:1–8

Friday, January 8

Let no one seek his own good, but that of his neighbor. —1 Corinthians 10:24 (NASB)

"Little Missy," our young grands call her. She's a small fine-boned beagle who belonged to a neighbor down our rural road.

I met up with Leroy and Missy often on my walks, pausing to give her a friendly pat. Then Leroy became ill—unable to climb the hill to our place where he and Missy chatted with my husband in the garage.

Within a short time Leroy was confined to bed. I checked on him and wondered what I could do to be helpful. The idea of walking Missy surfaced. Leroy, not one to ask a favor, seemed willing to accept my offer. His adult son who lived with him worked during the day. That left Missy curled on Leroy's bed with not much to do.

So began weeks of trekking down the hill, leashing Missy in the back entry—once she quit throwing herself at the door in excitement—and walking her in rain or snow or shine. On icy days I fastened cleats on my boots. If the grandchildren were over, they each wanted to be first to hold her leash.

Nose to the ground, off she'd go. I told the children she was "reading her book." We wondered what story it told. Leroy—not a talker—arranged a simple flower in a pot and a thank-you balloon for me. His gift spoke for him.

The January morning arrived when I went to walk Missy—and Leroy's room was empty. His son and I sat on his bed and remembered and cried. There was Missy, eager for her walk. We trudged through the snow and I thought about how glad I was Jesus said He came not to be served, but to serve (Mark 10:45).

When I think I can do nothing, I can do the something You show me, Jesus. —Carol Knapp

Digging Deeper: Micah 6:8; Galatians 6:2, 9–10; Colossians 3:23–24

Saturday, January 9

So keep your mind on Jesus.... Then you won't get discouraged and give up. —Hebrews 12:3 (CEV)

It was a cold January morning, so I cranked up the heat in my old home, wrapped myself in a blanket, and snuggled in my prayer chair. Sipping some steaming coffee, I glanced at my day planner, which was opened to yesterday's date— but none of my goals were crossed off! I groaned. *I fell into bed exhausted last night. What did I do all day?* I flipped back and wondered, *What did I do all week?* The only thing I'd accomplished had been distractions.

I flipped open my Bible and whined to God. *I'm so discouraged. Will I ever learn to focus?* Suddenly, a housefly, which must have been tucked away for winter hibernation, woke up from the heat. It flew around my lamp, nearly bopping me in the head. I swatted at it, but it dodged away.

Once again I read a couple of verses. *Bzzzz, bzzz, bzzz.* Warp speed, the critter skimmed past my nose and dove around the lightbulb in crazy spiraling circles. It looked like a fighter pilot on a bombing mission as he flew straight for the light. *Bam!* He crashed head-on and fell into my coffee! "Gross."

When I picked up my coffee cup to dump it, I had a strange thought. *Distractions are like that pesky fly; they discourage me and I end up tossing away my goals. It's time to focus on God and tackle my days with Him.*

13

The following week I consciously struggled to keep my thoughts on God, asking Him to lead me. Each day I whittled away at my goals.

Lord, help me stay tuned to You. Amen.
—Rebecca Ondov

Digging Deeper: Hebrews 3:1; 12:2

Sunday, January 10

Ask and it will be given to you; seek and you will find.... —Matthew 7:7 (NIV)

"If you find it, please call me," I said, hanging up. I'd left messages at church and our lunch spot in hopes of finding my lost diamond earring, which I'd noticed was missing from my earlobe when I got home that afternoon.

I felt guilty for losing such a costly earring, but it was more than that. Brian had given it to me for our five-year anniversary, just after Olivia was born, and it was her birthstone. I had hoped to give the earrings to her one day, and here I had lost one after only a few years! "Please help me find it," I prayed aloud.

I got everyone down for a nap, then was planning to head back to the church to look around when something caught Brian's eye. There, in the middle of our floor, was the earring with the back still on it. Somehow I must have dropped it before we even left the house that morning.

I let out a gasp and am pretty sure I kissed that earring when Brian handed it to me. The fact that he spotted it after hours of tiny feet running across our well-traveled floor made it even more of a celebration.

Something tells me my guardian angels were watching over that stud, making sure no one stashed the tiny treasure in a special place in their rooms or, let's be real, ate it. Instead, after a morning of routine, though wonderful, churchgoing, I found myself outwardly praising Jesus for helping me. Even though losing an earring isn't a huge deal in the scope of the world, it was a big deal to me.

Lord, thank You for being my helper and my guide in issues large and small. —Ashley Kappel

Digging Deeper: Psalm 63:7; 115:11

Monday, January 11

With trumpets and the sound of the horn make a joyful noise before the King, the Lord!
—Psalm 98:6 (ESV)

I lowered my trumpet from my lips and leaned back in my practice chair, disgusted. The notes of the piece "Arabesque" mocked me from my music stand. "Relax!" I said aloud, echoing what I knew my trumpet teacher would tell me. I willed my white-knuckled fingers to loosen their grip on the horn.

"Squeezing the thing will not make the sound come out any prettier," he'd say. If only it could.

I got scolded for being self-deprecating in my lessons, too. "It's holding you back," my teacher told me. I knew he was right. Yet I could not get past the belief that I'd never be truly skilled at playing the trumpet. Or anything else, for that matter.

Why oh why couldn't my fifth-grade self have picked a quieter instrument to learn? Then, decades later, I could've played comfortably in the back row of the community band, keeping all my mistakes and inadequacies safely to myself.

Sighing, I looked down at the horn I was holding—at its flared bell designed specifically for amplifying and projecting sound—and was struck with a realization. God had known exactly what He was doing when He placed this instrument in my young hands. He didn't want me living trapped within a spirit of fear. And He'd known, as only God can, that someday a trumpet would be what motivated me to learn to play boldly, loud mistakes and all. Bringing the horn back to my lips for another try at "Arabesque," I smiled. Trumpets aren't made for hiding comfortably and quietly in back rows. And neither, apparently, am I.

Thank You, God, for providing me with the tools and opportunities to overcome my weaknesses, so I can become the person You've made me to be.
—Erin Janoso

Digging Deeper: Joshua 1:9; 2 Timothy 1:7

Tuesday, January 12

GOING HOME: Preparing for the Journey

Before they call, I will answer....
—Isaiah 65:24 (NKJV)

"We have to save the orchard," I told my brother. The notion just wouldn't go away.

For almost a decade Dad had been doing less and less around the farm where Aaron and I grew up. The apple orchard was dying off. These varieties aren't found in stores; they were planted in the 1800s by a sea captain who homesteaded our farm. He made his fortune sailing to California, selling apples for a dollar apiece during the gold rush. Now only a few of the original varieties remained, and they were sorely in need of care. We needed to work fast to keep the heritage flavors alive. Neither my brother nor I could be home often enough to keep up with the farm. But when I mentioned rescuing the orchard to Aaron, the idea took hold and interest turned into action.

Within months my brother and his family moved into a second home on the farm, which had been built when my dad took care of his mom in her final years. My parents were thrilled. For a year Dad showed Aaron the ropes, and he tackled the projects Dad wasn't agile enough to do. I visited often. The farm was reborn. New trees grew from seeds and starts.

And then we discovered the real reason why God orchestrated Aaron's move. Dad, who had always taken care of himself with nutrition and vitamins, was taken ill. As the next week played out, it became vividly clear that God had brought Aaron's family there, at this exact time, specifically for the final care of Dad.

Lord, long before we knew, You knew. Faith is following Your will without question; You alone know what's around the corner. —Erika Bentsen

Digging Deeper: Psalm 36:7; 121

Wednesday, January 13

He said to him the third time, "Simon, son of John, do you love me?" Peter was grieved because he said to him the third time, "Do you love me?" and he said to him, "Lord, you know everything; you know that I love you." Jesus said to him, "Feed my sheep." —John 21:17 (ESV)

There are moments when the reality of living and working in a military community really jar your soul. One evening I received an email from the principal of our children's school. She explained that a parent whose children also attend our school was killed in action. It was sobering news to say the least; my heart wept for his wife and four small children.

In this small Christian school of military and nonmilitary families, news like this has strong and reaching effects. The care of our community for one another is a powerful, holy example of carrying others through tragedy. There were no words to console this family's loss, so care came in the form of hugs, household chores, and outings with friends. The community not only embraced and cared for this family, whose father made the ultimate sacrifice for his country, but the community also graciously hugged all the students extra tight. They took steps to ensure that a pastor and a social worker visited each and every class of students the very next day. The children were able to ask questions and share their thoughts and fears.

Just like Peter, we are all called to take care of one another because we love Him. This school community knew that whenever any member lives through tragedy, the tragedy is felt by everyone.

Heavenly Father, thank You for the precious gift of salvation. Help us to allow Your love to work through us so we may care for others in Your most holy name. Amen. —Jolynda Strandberg

Digging Deeper: Matthew 22:39; John 21:15–19; 2 Corinthians 1

Thursday, January 14

But a certain Samaritan, as he journeyed, came where he was: and when he saw him, he had compassion on him. —Luke 10:33 (KJV)

Smack! Confusion! Head pain! Despite nimbly walking the slick marble of the Acropolis and the steep steps of the Oracle at Delphi, I tripped over a small curb in Tinos, a holy island in the Cyclades of Greece. My friend Liz and a Greek woman in a black-and-white dress fished for tissues to mop my bloody head and hand. Liz, a trained physician's assistant, gently brushed hair back from my left eyebrow. "It's deep. You'll need stitches."

A passing car stopped and called an ambulance. Meanwhile, the nameless woman appeared with peroxide and a large bag of cotton. She wore no gloves, just dabbed my temple with gentle care. Liz continued to wipe blood from my head; the woman, from my hands. Soon, I could rise and sit in a chair in front of a small hotel. The woman gestured to me to move out of the sun to a seat under the canopy. Then she brought me a bottle of water. I never learned her name.

My black eye was a beauty, but my injuries weren't serious; Liz and I continued our vacation. Nonetheless, I continue to think fondly of Tinos as a holy island, not so much because of the Panagia Evangelistria Church, which pilgrims crawl to on their knees, but because one compassionate woman showed kindness to a stranger.

Lord of All, I find Your loving presence everywhere I go. —Gail Thorell Schilling

Digging Deeper: Exodus 2:22; Psalm 31:21; Matthew 25:40

Do not be overcome by evil, but overcome evil with good. —Romans 12:21 (NIV)

Recently, someone resurrected a perceived wrong I was to have committed two decades before. It was in a setting where I wasn't given the opportunity to defend myself. I felt wronged...defeated, as the accusation was so targeted, so personal.

As the days wore on, I found myself closing my heart to doing good for others. *That's people for you,* I would tell myself. *You try to help everyone, and* this *is the thanks you get.*

Then my laundry room was out of commission and I had to take a couple of loads of clothes to the Laundromat. I loaded my washers only to discover I was short eight quarters. The change machine was out of order, so I canvassed the aisles. "Do you happen to have eight quarters in exchange for two dollar bills?" I asked each person. I was met with blank stares and empty nods.

I expected as much, I muttered to myself as I retreated to my car to search for spare change. *That's people for you.*

But when I returned, there were two stacks of four quarters on top of one of my machines. Again, I canvassed the aisles, this time to identify my benefactor. And again, I was met with blank stares. This time, though, they were accompanied by sly smiles. Every single person vehemently denied helping me.

The kindness was targeted, and oh so personal. And in that moment, I understood. Every day, I have a choice as to which type of person *I* want to be.

My once-closed heart cracked open wide. I chose kindness.

**Dear Lord, help me to always choose Your way...
the way of love.** —Roberta Messner

Digging Deeper: Proverbs 31:12;
John 5:29; 1 Timothy 5:10

Saturday, January 16

You will be given a new name by the Lord's own mouth. The Lord will hold you in his hand for all to see.... —Isaiah 62:2–3 (NLT)

Last weekend, to celebrate my winter birthday, I traveled four hours by train to visit a nephew. How would I use the hours? I packed a novel and note cards. I slipped in a copy of the assigned Sunday Bible readings, one of them being Isaiah 62:2–3.

On an Amtrak quiet car, I turned to the Scriptures. *Lord, do you have a birthday message?* The Isaiah passage brought to mind a long-forgotten nighttime dream: decades ago—as a young professional unsure of my career viability, childless though my given name promised *life*—I'd woken, startled and puzzled by a "dreamland" announcement that my name had been changed to

Flower and Song. For a season, before slipping from my memory, the two nouns had heartened me.

Not until last week, praying to the click-clack rhythm of the rails, did I track a correlating, fulfilling, missional journey: Every spring I've planted porch boxes—petunias, marigolds, geraniums—that brighten the street. I've tended a rosebush. At a publisher's request, I've written a book about historic hymns. I've played piano for worship services. I've taught a neighbor girl to sing through her fears.

After the train ride, I felt more tangibly reminded of a Flower-and-Song grace. Behind my nephew's garage, I discovered—and we picked—six late-blooming roses. Then yesterday, back home, I happened upon a decades-old birthday note my dad wrote shortly before his death: whenever "you come home, you are like a rose" in the yard.

I've turned a calendar page. I'm a year closer to old age. Even in winter, God gets His message across. He's near. He's not silent. Do I listen?

Lord, help me remember and note a lifetime of graces—those I've given and received. —Evelyn Bence

Digging Deeper: Isaiah 55

Sunday, January 17

My brothers and sisters, you are believers in our glorious Lord Jesus Christ. So treat everyone the same. —James 2:1 (NIRV)

I sat on the couch with my husband's ninety-year-old grandmother and watched three men from a moving company carry her possessions out her front door. For the past few months, I'd helped her get ready to move to a retirement center near us. She'd given away, sold, and packed sixty-nine years of memories. Thankfully, church members and even the daughter of the elementary-school secretary where Mam Ma taught pitched in to help.

As the movers walked in and out, a new man entered. Long oily hair, scruffy beard, and big Coke-bottle eighties-style eyeglasses, a stained sweatshirt and jeans that looked like they'd not been washed recently. As he approached, Mam Ma smiled.

"I cleaned out that back shed. I think there are a few things that will bring some money," he said, not making eye contact with me.

Mam Ma and the man talked for a few minutes. As they did, the pungent smell of body odor wafted near, even though he stood ten feet away. Normally, in situations where I don't know someone and I'm not introduced, I introduce myself. This time I didn't bother.

The man left. Mam Ma turned to me. "That was Roger. He's my yardman and handyman."

I nodded. Mam Ma must have read my mind.

"When I taught first grade, I learned to treat all my students the same," she said with a faraway look in her eye. "I loved every one of them. And they loved me back."

I needed that lesson. I wished I had thanked Roger for helping Mam Ma.

Lord, I often look at the outside of people, but You look at the inside. Help me to be gracious, show no favoritism, and always love others like You and Mam Ma do. —Stephanie Thompson

Digging Deeper: Deuteronomy 10:17; 1 Samuel 16:7; James 2:9–10

Martin Luther King Jr. Day, Monday, January 18

There is neither Jew nor Gentile, neither slave nor free, nor is there male and female, for you are all one in Christ Jesus. —Galatians 3:28 (NIV)

Recently, my husband began coleading community discussions on racial unity in our growing city in Tennessee. At the end of one of these discussions, my husband's coleader invited audience members to share their personal experiences with race.

After listening through a few others' testimonies, I rose from my seat and walked to the podium. Accompanied by my thumping heartbeat and shaking hands, I shared my family's story as minorities in a largely homogeneous city. I spoke of vandalism at my son's middle school, with racially offensive words written on a wall in the boys' bathroom. I shared the day my husband

and I discovered similarly offensive words painted on utility boxes on our lawn in a neighborhood where we were the only African-American family. I recounted the fear that gripped me the night a police officer pulled over my college-age son as I drove nearby praying he would remember the safety protocol my husband and I had taught him.

As I shared story after story, I felt empathy from others in the room. I saw tears pooled in the eyes of a few. When I walked away from the podium, I was encouraged that our community had begun this conversation on race that would continue through future challenges we might face. I was hopeful that now we could face them together.

Near the end of his "I have a Dream" speech, Dr. Martin Luther King Jr. proclaimed these words, "Let freedom ring from Lookout Mountain of Tennessee." I believe Dr. King would be proud of this small community in Tennessee, filled with people of different races and cultures sharing, listening, and lamenting with one another.

Lord may we, Your children, continue to fight for unity, peace, and love. —Carla Hendricks

Digging Deeper: 1 Samuel 16:7; 1 Corinthians 12:13

Tuesday, January 19

GOING HOME: The Road Home
Let not your heart be troubled. —John 14:1 (KJV)

My heart knotted up when I learned Dad was in the hospital; he didn't trust his health to others. Leaving my husband to care for our ranch, I started the long drive to my childhood home. Two days before Dad admitted he was hurting, he'd suffered an immense rupture internally. Now infection filled his body. The moment the doctors said "inoperable," Dad knew it was time to go home—for good. They'd given him three days.

The five-hour drive felt like five years. Anger and fear gnawed at me. He was too young to die; his parents lived into their nineties. How could he be so stubborn as to not seek medical help sooner? Thoughts flayed me, spurred my foot to press harder on the gas. I was mad enough to give him what-for. But really, the doctors had merely confirmed that he'd diagnosed himself correctly. There was no cure for his condition. He'd known all along this was coming.

In everything he did, whether it was right or wrong, Dad always meant the best for us kids. He made his own decisions about his health, just like I do. Can I blame him for what I do myself? After all, I inherited my stubbornness from him. The way I figured it, he wasn't a perfect father and I wasn't a perfect daughter. It was a fair swap.

I eased off the pedal. No sense getting into an accident on the way there. If he passed away before I got there, it was okay. We'd had a great relationship throughout our lives; there was nothing left unsaid.

Lord, we are only human. We are headstrong and make mistakes. And yet You love us perfectly through our faults. Help us love one another even when our struggles and pain get in our way.
—Erika Bentsen

Digging Deeper: 1 Thessalonians 3:12; 1 John 4:18

Wednesday, January 20

Let the little children come to me, and do not hinder them, for the kingdom of God belongs to such as these. —Mark 10:14 (NIV)

As I walk up the subway stairs, the weight of my guitar case is heavy on my back. I'm still sleepy, and the long commute hasn't helped. After walking several blocks, I finally reach the door to the preschool. I know full well what's going to happen next. A class full of three-year-olds will abandon their toys on the rug once they see me. "Karen!" they scream as always, and race toward me with arms opened wide. They swarm my legs, struggling with each other for a space to give me a hug.

My guitar, still strapped to my back, doesn't feel as heavy as I reach forward to return their embrace. I no longer feel sleepy, and I'm ready to give them the same joy they give me. I sing their favorite songs as they dance and fill the air with bubbles. Together we shake the giant parachute and watch its colors go up and down.

On this day, I reach for an illustrated book of the song "What a Wonderful World." I sing the words as I show them the beautiful pictures. The song reminds me of my father, so my voice is filled with love. They sit mesmerized until the last note, and then I hear a sweet little voice say, "Good job, Karen."

One by one, they get up to hug me again, this time patiently taking turns. I know the song has moved them, and the reverence in their affection moves me as well.

How beautiful to experience how mutually we can touch the heart of another.

Lord, give me the heart of a child, that I may love purely, live joyfully, and give of myself openly.
—Karen Valentin

Digging Deeper: Matthew 18:4

Thursday, January 21

Who among the gods is like you, Lord? Who is like you—majestic in holiness, awesome in glory, working wonders? —Exodus 15:11 (NIV)

I hadn't seen Mary Ellen in eighteen months, so catching up on how her four kids were doing and updating her on my five took most of lunch. Then we chatted about stressed husbands and finally asked each other earnestly, "How are *you* doing?"

She was well, working full-time as a youth-ministry coordinator after fifteen years of homeschooling. When she parroted my inquiry with her own I said, "I'm okay, I guess. I think I need to get a job." I'd been a freelance writer and editor while raising kids, homeschooling, and dealing with seemingly endless family crises. Now with my youngest in high school, it was time for a change.

"What kind of work are you looking for?" Mary Ellen asked.

To be honest, this was the first time I'd voiced the idea. I replied, "Something with benefits! Beyond that, I don't care. I'd prefer to do something new. Not writing or mental health."

Mary Ellen perked up. "I had dinner with a friend last week, an attorney who is looking for an assistant. Want me to put you in touch?"

I shrugged and said, "Sure, why not?" I've always grown more by accepting what God throws in my path than by following my own desires.

Mary Ellen introduced me to her friend via email that afternoon. I interviewed the next Friday and started my job the following Tuesday. It happened so painlessly that it was hard to process: I'd forgotten it was possible life could go smoothly. Every day I ride the subway in a daze of thankfulness for the blessing of family health insurance, a steady income, and the opportunity to learn, serve, and grow in new ways.

Father, thank You for teaching me to see small miracles in everyday life before handing me a big one.
—Julia Attaway

Digging Deeper: Matthew 17:20

Friday, January 22

My flesh and my heart may fail, but God is
the strength of my heart, my portion forever.
—Psalm 73:26 (HCSB)

It's been a good week. I've gone to the gym
every day. I've completed several writing projects.
I've cranked through a ton of assignments at
work.

It's snowing outside. I know it's cold, but I don't
hesitate as I exit my car. I'm pumped up. Confident.
Proud that things are going so well for me.

My phone buzzes in my pocket, and I pick up.

"Logan," my mom says. Her voice trembles.
"Pray for Isaiah. He tripped and hurt his throat. He's
having a hard time breathing. We're on our way to
the emergency room."

I think of my little brother gasping for air, and
my body tenses.

"I'm praying," I say. "Keep me updated."

The phone clicks, and I'm alone. I exhale. The
cold turns my breath to visible vapor.

My fear flows free, displacing the confidence I
had a moment ago. I feel helpless. There's nothing
I can do for my brother. I'm entirely reliant upon
God.

I was arrogant before the phone call. I had
forgotten that I am powerless and God is limitless. I
had forgotten that every breath I take is provided by
the One who designed and formed me. I do nothing
on my own.

As I reach the door to my apartment, I begin to pray, "Lord, my brother is in Your hands—not mine. Please protect him."

An hour later, my phone rings again.

"Isaiah is going to be fine," my mom says. The calm in her voice is as reassuring as her words.

I inhale deeply. Then I give thanks to the God who fills my lungs with air.

Lord, remind me that in all I do, I am dependent on You. —Logan Eliasen

Digging Deeper: Matthew 6:26; Philippians 4:19

Saturday, January 23

But when I am afraid, I will put my trust in you. —Psalm 56:3 (NLT)

For over six months, my mother had put off having a necessary heart valve procedure. During this time, my family tried to convince her to make an appointment, but she avoided the topic at all costs. We became more and more concerned about her health as she was already having difficulty walking due to her heart. My mother is a woman of faith, but fear was getting the best of her. After a long struggle, she agreed to make an appointment for the procedure.

A few days before my mother's surgery, she voiced her concerns to me over the phone. She was worried about one of the risks—a stroke. I sought to calm her fears. All procedures have possible risks, I told her, but the chances of a stroke were less than 1 percent. I also reminded her that she had this procedure once before and was fine. Though she knew these were valid points, I could sense that she wasn't convinced. I then said, "Mom, this is more about trusting the Lord. Your life is in God's hands." Mom sighed, acknowledging she needed to trust the Lord.

On the day of the procedure, Mom was apprehensive, but she was hanging on to her trust in God. My dad and I gathered around Mom as we prayed together and thanked the Lord for His presence and care.

After the procedure, her face radiated peace and confidence despite her discomfort. A day later, she was discharged.

Lord, help us to keep our trust and confidence in You always. —Pablo Diaz

Digging Deeper: Lamentations 3:23; Romans 15:13

Sunday, January 24

...a time to keep, and a time to throw away.
—Ecclesiastes 3:6 (NIV)

The final sentence of a web article on de-cluttering the Marie Kondo way intrigued me: "If something in your house doesn't bring you joy, let it go."

My house contained one huge item that no longer brought me joy: the 1954 church-model Hammond organ and cabinet speaker I'd inherited from my grandma. When I was a child Grandma spent hours teaching me to play hymns such as "Wonderful Words of Life," "Down at the Cross," and my grandfather's favorite, "His Eye Is on the Sparrow." I loved playing, and I was eventually able to serve as organist for our small church.

But now the organ was showing its age. The finish was scratched from several moves. The electronic tubes it required were expensive and hard to find. The sound quality had diminished. The organ wasn't fun to play. Still, I had mixed feelings about giving it up. After all, it was a family treasure, albeit an annoying one! Besides, it was far too heavy for my husband, Don, and me to move, and potential buyers weren't interested unless we would deliver it.

Last January it was still sitting there when we had fourteen family members for lunch. As I looked around the room, I realized there were plenty of young, strong bodies to move the organ out of the house and into storage. I took a deep breath, said a quick prayer, and thirty minutes after the meal ended the organ was gone.

Four months later I replaced it with a small digital piano. And you know what? Those old hymns sound more wonderful than ever! I think Grandma would approve.

Lord, give me wisdom to discard possessions, attitudes, and actions that keep me from experiencing joy in my music, my home, and most especially in You. Amen. —Penney Schwab

Monday, January 25

**Then your light shall break forth like the dawn,
your healing shall spring forth speedily, and your
righteousness shall go before you; the glory of the
Lord shall be your rear guard. —Isaiah 58:8 (NKJV)**

The January evening was settling in like most. My
husband lounged in his favorite spot on the couch
with the television muted while he reviewed a
contract. The children were engulfed in lively chatter
at the kitchen table while I put finishing touches on
a simmering pot of spaghetti.

My cell phone buzzed in my pocket and I escaped
upstairs for privacy. I'd been expecting a call from
the radiologist about results from a biopsy that she
suspected was benign.

"I'm so sorry. It's cancerous," the doctor said,
her voice breaking the slightest bit. And with those
words, life as I'd known it took an unexpected and
alarming detour. I walked downstairs in a fog. Upon
seeing my tear-streaked face, my husband pulled me
into his arms. Words were futile and I could only
manage moans that felt like they'd escaped from my
soul.

A floodgate of emotions led by fear, anxiety, and
anger distressed me during the daytime and taunted
me at night. My only respite was meditating on

God's Word, so I did so relentlessly. Instead of allowing my thoughts to linger on a prognosis and treatments, I studied God's promises of healing daily.

After a surgical procedure and sixteen rounds of radiation therapy, I was given a clean bill of health. God's plans were for me to prosper and be in good health—my body and my soul. I'm grateful that my breast cancer diagnosis didn't define me, but it refined me: it's still part of my daily routine to read and declare the Scriptures, and I believe it always will be.

Lord, I accept Your divine healing for my body, soul, and mind. —Tia McCollors

Digging Deeper: Deuteronomy 33:25; Proverbs 3:24; 2 Corinthians 4:17; 3 John 1:2

Tuesday, January 26

GOING HOME: Lost and Found
If you had known me, you would have known my Father.... —John 14:7 (ESV)

Mom warned me that Dad had changed a lot in the past few days, but I'd driven across Oregon to see him after hearing he didn't have long to live. I dropped my suitcase and went to the back room in my brother's home where they had set up a bed for him. My eyes fell upon the face of a stranger.

Who was this frail, gray person? Eyes sunken, skin stretched tightly over an angular skull, a body barely making a bulge in the blanket. I hoped I hid my shock. We visited briefly. I found an excuse and bolted from the room. How could I not recognize my own father? Had I lost him already? I felt robbed.

I made myself go back. At first, I avoided looking at him, but then he started joking like old times. Those were his eyes with the laughter in them! That was his smile! There he was—it really was Dad. Gladness overflowed. We spoke easily of happy memories; nothing of the future—that hurt too much to consider—but there were countless good times to remember.

"I love you, Erika," he said, often. Time together was salve to both of our hurting souls. Dad didn't want me sad. He wanted to recover. He wanted to fight this infection with both barrels. He mostly wanted me to know how much I was loved. Helping him made our love for each other even stronger. Every moment with him was so precious, so valuable, so alive. I could scarcely believe I could find such sweetness and happiness in a time as dark as this.

Lord, my heart weeps for those who think they have no one at the end. Please reassure those who feel alone that You are beside them through it all. You are the light in the darkness. —Erika Bentsen

Digging Deeper: John 14:9; 1 John 4:16

Wednesday, January 27

BECOMING JUST ME AGAIN
Human Touch

Jesus reached out his hand and touched the man. "I am willing," he said. "Be clean!" Immediately he was cleansed of his leprosy. —Matthew 8:3 (NIV)

When Jack was diagnosed with melanoma in January, the entire year was filled with four surgeries, hospital stays, monthly doctor visits, and finally months when he was hospitalized, in rehab, then hospitalized again. What I missed most about not having my husband with me at home was holding his hand. We'd always held hands when we walked on the beach, at the movies, in church, and always at night just before we fell asleep.

I also missed his hugs. I remember the day during his illness that I decided I would stand up every time one of Jack's six children or any of my relatives or our friends came into the hospital or rehab room and give them a big bear hug. Once I set the precedent, it became automatic for all of us. Those hugs nourished me day after day.

I also decided that every day as I sat there in those various hospitals I would pull my chair up very close to Jack's bed and simply hold his hand even when we'd run out of things to talk about. For hours on end I was comforted by his big hand, often warm to the touch, cradling mine. I could practically feel my heart rate slow down each time I held his hand.

When my sister-in-law Linda visited from Kentucky, she insisted on giving me a back rub each evening. As she rubbed cream into my knotted shoulders, upper back, and neck muscles I could feel the worry and exhaustion leave my body just as those hugs and hand-holdings had done.

Heavenly Father, help me to put the hands of others in my own and to hug love into each person who needs it. Thank You for these arms and hands that can give as well as receive. —Patricia Lorenz

Digging Deeper: Matthew 8:14–17; Mark 5:24–34

Thursday, January 28

The Lord is my shepherd; I shall not want. He makes me to lie down in green pastures; He leads me beside the still waters. He restores my soul.... —Psalm 23:1–3 (NKJV)

I keep hearing about the importance of a morning routine—rituals repeated every morning to jump-start our days with disciplined focus that puts us on track for efficient use of our time. Many recommended routines go in order like this: time with Jesus, reading Scripture, and praying; quick exercise and stretching; followed by eating something nutritious for energy.

Mine, in my empty nest home, usually goes more like this: I let the dog out and stumble into the kitchen to make coffee, then feed my demanding dog and the equally demanding cat, sip my first cup of coffee as I put away some kitchen clutter, wipe off the counters, and water the wilting plant on the windowsill. I quickly check text messages to be sure nothing drastic happened overnight or find out whether somebody needs something from me right then.

It's a routine I call fuddling, my made-up word that's a combination of fiddling and muddling, which means putting things in order so they're not a distraction. By the time I pour my second cup of coffee and sit down at the end of the kitchen counter, my perch where I talk to Jesus in the mornings, I'm ready.

I reach for my Bible and open the computer to my Spiritual Reflections file where I journal my thoughts. My fuddling has been my early-morning physical and spiritual warm-up that prepares a place for me in the green pastures of my home, free from distractions, where the Shepherd restores my soul.

In the stillness of green pastures, You feed my soul with love and grace and guidance, no matter what time I get there. —Carol Kuykendall

Digging Deeper: Psalm 46:10; 2 Timothy 3:16–17

Friday, January 29

And my spirit rejoices in God my Savior.
—Luke 1:47 (ESV)

The phone rang too early to be good news. With Mom's name on the caller ID, I answered it anxiously. She paused before she spoke and I felt myself brace for whatever was to come.

"My computer," she said. "I woke up this morning and it's just a black screen. I'm sorry for calling so early."

Relieved, I said, "Sure. I'll be right over."

Mom's face brightened as I entered her home office. "I hope I don't need a new computer," she said.

I inspected the cords, pushed one of them in just a little, and turned it on. As we waited for it to boot, Mom opened the curio cabinet by the window and picked up one of her many Santa ornaments that she hadn't yet put away. "I love this one," she said. "What are you going to do with all these when I'm gone?" Mom isn't sick or anything. I guess she's just a planner. Her collection of vintage Christmas ornaments from years of collecting crowd the display case.

"They're worth a lot," she said. "What will happen to them?"

"Mom, my house is filled with knickknacks. You really think I'd part with your Santas?"

She smiled. The computer started up as good as new. "All is well," I said, and off I went, back down the street, grateful for the morning, for things going right, problems solved, and the decision I made on a whim all those years ago to move to my hometown, right next door to my mom.

Dear Lord, thank You for mornings like this
that help me to see how blessed I really am.
—Sabra Ciancanelli

Digging Deeper: Exodus 20:12; Psalm 133:1

Saturday, January 30

For in Him we live and move and exist....
—Acts 17:28 (NASB)

Now, what was that creative thought I had? I couldn't
seem to remember. *You'll have to show me, Lord, if
you want me to do something with it.* Then an email
arrived from a friend excited about a successful
project. The letter included a sentence of apology for
the "overuse of exclamation marks." There was my
lost thought—lit up like an exclamation!

I'd been thinking about personalities as
"punctuation." Some people know exactly who
they are. Personality with a *period.* My mother was
this way. From first grade she decided she would
become a nurse. She remained quietly determined
throughout her life.

Other personalities are *question* marks. Those
who are curious and ask lots of questions. And those
hesitant people who question themselves. I once
realized *I ask too many questions for the comfort levels
of some.* Questions can overwhelm, but they can also
nudge.

Then there are people who add an *exclamation*
point wherever they go. Excited, eager, filled with

42

enthusiasm! This personality creates a natural wake. I have a cousin like this. She wears bright colors. She brings joy. Others flock around her.

The "personality as punctuation" exploration leads me to Jesus. He made definite "I know who I am" declaratives. There are seven in John's Gospel, including "I am the good shepherd..." (John 10:11). Jesus was never unsure of His worth or actions or purpose, but He asked many questions—"Why are you afraid? Do you still have no faith?" (Mark 4:40). His life was an exclamation of healing and joy and confidence! The leaders of the day said, "Look, the world has gone after Him" (John 12:19).

I can trust Jesus with my temperament. His is the personality from which I can learn.

When I embrace You, Jesus, I embrace the best! — Carol Knapp

Digging Deeper: Proverbs 27:19; Luke 2:52; 1 Corinthians 2:10–12

Sunday, January 31

Rejoice in hope, be patient in tribulation.... —Romans 12:12 (ESV)

"Hey, Buck, what do you think penguins did to deserve that life?" John said, in his John Brooklynese.

I know this sounds like a strange conversation starter, but if you knew John you'd understand.

"Okay. I'll bite," I said, settling in for the verbal ride.

"Seriously, take a look at those guys. They basically live in a subzero blizzard, everything around is trying to eat them, the dads have to stand there protecting an egg while the mom walks a million miles for a beak-full of food to bring back..."

"Well...?"

But John, being John, was off to another topic.

But I was stuck on the penguins. Do you ever wonder the same? *God, what did I do to deserve this?*

It's interesting, the longer I walk with the Lord, the more wonderfully mysterious He becomes. Sometimes He blesses me when I least expect it. Sometimes I think I'm plugging along great and He leads me smack into a season of struggle. But, fair winds or storms, He is God. And He is *good.*

I've never stood in a blizzard protecting an egg. But there *have* been rough parts of the road, and it's been there in the valleys, in the darkest dark, that I've felt that warm arm around my shoulders and I've heard that heavenly whisper of love that never leaves or forsakes. Looking back, I wouldn't trade a mile.

And, now that I think about it, penguins actually look pretty happy. Maybe they already know something I'm learning every day—mountaintop or canyon, we have a Friend on the journey. And I'm so glad.

May the stars make me humble and the storms make me strong. Thank You, Lord, for the things that bring me closer to You. —Buck Storm

Digging Deeper: James 1:2; 1:12

JOYFUL IN HOPE

1 _____

2 _____

3 _____

4 _____

5 _____

6 _____

7 _____

8 _____

9 _____

10 _____

11 _____

12 _____

13 _____

14 _____

15 _____

16 _____

17 _____

18 _____

19 _____

20 _____

21 _____

22 _____

23 _____

24 _____

25 _____

26 _____

27 _____

28 _____

29 _____

30 _____

31 _____

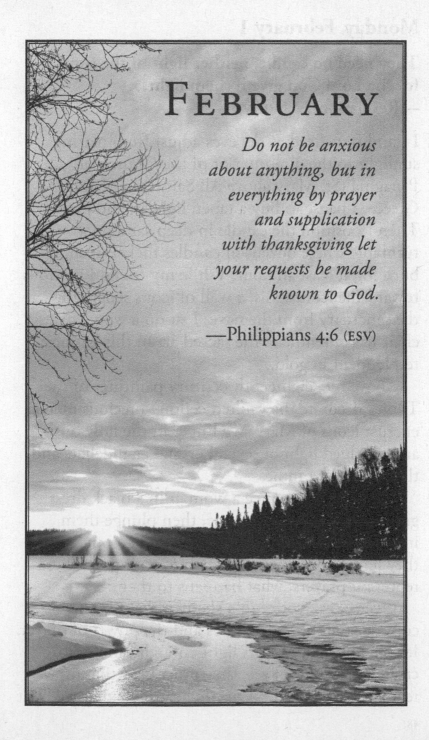

FEBRUARY

Do not be anxious about anything, but in everything by prayer and supplication with thanksgiving let your requests be made known to God.

—Philippians 4:6 (ESV)

Monday, February 1

They need no candle, neither light of the sun;
for the Lord God giveth them light....
—Revelation 22:5 (KJV)

I stand transfixed as my eyes adjust from blazing
sunlight to the dim interior of the Church of
Panaghia (St. Mary above All Saints) in Nafplio,
Greece. I pause to buy a taper, light it, and pray.
Then I position the candle in deep sand on a
turntable where dozens of candles flicker. It should
burn for at least an hour. While my friend Liz strolls
toward the iconostasis, a wall of icons separating
the sanctuary from the nave, I sit on a wooden
chair to contemplate the sacred art in this basilica,
resplendent in gold.

Above me, eighteenth-century paintings of the
Trinity decorate the vaulted ceiling; precious metals
encrust icons of Mary. We linger in the holy hush
and subdued light of several crystal chandeliers and
the twinkling candles.

As we leave, I notice a woman in a black dress
grasp several candles at once, then plunge them
into a bucket of water. They hiss and go out. And
they haven't even burned down to stumps! If these
represent prayers, what happens to them?

Over Greek coffee in a shady plaza, Liz and I
consider the snuffed candles and the power of prayer.
It's obvious that visitors light enough candles to
create a fire hazard; yes, they must be extinguished
regularly. And our prayers are heard whether we light

candles or not. Yet if each candle flame represents one earnest prayer…and many candle flames pose the threat of conflagration…Wow! What an awesome visual for the power of prayers!

Lord, may I never underestimate the power of prayer.
—Gail Thorell Schilling

Digging Deeper: Psalm 18:28; Job 18:6; Matthew 18:19–20; 1 Corinthians 14:15

Tuesday, February 2

GOING HOME: A Glorious Invitation
And if I go and prepare a place for you, I will come back and welcome you. —John 14:3 (BEREAN STUDY BIBLE)

The moment came at the end of a good day when my dad was in the best of spirits. I'd come a long way home to see Dad in his final days at my brother's home on my parents' farm. We'd spent days visiting and reminiscing. This had been Dad's strongest, most vibrant day since I'd been here.

Aaron, my brother, came over late to where I was staying with Mom. He just had to share the news: Dad had seen Jesus. He'd told Aaron, "He was right here in this room! He is here all the time. He loves us so much." Dad could hardly describe the magnitude of His love for us. Dad's face was lit from within. Aaron said Dad looked like a little boy at Christmas, not a dying old man.

49

Later that night, Dad told Aaron about glimpses of heaven. The beauty was indescribable in human terms; no words approached the glory he saw. Dad spoke of how eager he was to see his parents, and especially his brother. Dad became excited about what was to come. His body too became ready to release his soul. The food of this earth no longer appealed to him. He hungered for something else. He shifted from home care to hospice care.

The less he spoke, the more I clung to that vision of hope. The energy in the room changed. Jesus Himself was here! Heaven is for real! I could feel it! And Dad was on the doorstep, his hand already on the knob.

Lord, You love this world so much that You sent Your Son so that we may have eternal life. Bless Your Wondrous Name forever! —Erika Bentsen

Digging Deeper: John 3:16–21; 14:1

Wednesday, February 3

You are my defender and protector. You are my God; in you I trust. —Psalm 91:2 (GNT)

There is a retired army chaplain assistant who continues to serve, always ready as a deacon in our church—straightening altar linens, pouring communion cups, updating hymn number boards. Father Will, as he is affectionately known, also keeps me informed of veteran happenings and events throughout the region.

I wanted to honor Tech Sergeant (Retired) Dave Wilcox (aka Father Will) for his "Soldier for Life" dedication. I invited him to join me in attending the fifty-first Four Chaplains Day Banquet in Philadelphia. This annual event recognizes the February 3, 1943, sinking of the SS *Dorchester* off the coast of Greenland and the four chaplains who gave away their life jackets so that soldiers might live.

Parking for the dinner was unconventional. We found a spot on the street. After walking across the median, I stepped over a slight curb and onto the pavement. I then saw Dave—as if in slow motion—stumble, dizzily lose his balance, and land on the asphalt. As if he were a running back, he flowed with the tumble and came to a stop.

Citizens of the City of Brotherly Love helped Dave to his feet. Thankfully, though a bit sore and shaken, he was fine. We enjoyed the evening, though I silently prayed throughout that Dave would sustain no lingering injuries. A "Four Chaplains Spirit" of acceptance and unselfish love seemed present during the entire banquet.

Days later, I asked Dave about his experience. "Oh, you mean my 'circus act'? I followed advice learned long ago: 'Don't stretch your arms out, keep your knees bent, and roll with the fall.'" With gratitude I again quietly prayed, this time words of thanks to our ever-watchful God.

God our protector, we thank You for Your guarding us in all circumstances. Continue to guide us this day, and always. Amen. —Ken Sampson

Digging Deeper: Proverbs 30:5; Hebrews 6:19

Thursday, February 4

The Lord will watch over your coming and going both now and forevermore. —Psalm 121:8 (NIV)

It was the dead of winter in the Berkshires when I first noticed the signs: two missing pugs, their pictures side by side.

Posters for lost pets upset me. A picture makes it worse. An image infiltrates my mind of the poor frightened creature trying to find home. I think of how panic-stricken Julee and I would be if Gracie was missing. Just imagining Gracie lost makes my heart race. Maybe I should never let her off leash. Maybe I should never let her out of my sight!

I mentioned the missing dogs to my vet not long after. She said an ASPCA survey she'd read verified that more than 90 percent of lost dogs are found and nearly as great a percentage of lost cats.

That surprised me. My assumption had been far more pessimistic. So I asked an editor at our *All Creatures* magazine about lost pets. She reminded me we did an advice column on it once.

"Posters are great," she said. "They really work. Social media, too. Instagram, Facebook. That's why you should always have a good clear picture of your pet."

I rushed home and took a mug shot of Gracie. Several angles. "I'm surprised there's room on your phone for another picture of her," Julee said, laughing, so I explained. "Maybe," she said, "you should just say a prayer for the pugs and their owner and not get so freaked-out."

It was the solution I should have seen for myself, but as so often happens, my self-centered fears blinded me. What other problems in the world should I be praying for instead of turning from? I can think of a few.

Hey, Lord. Me again. Same old problem. Help me believe in Your protection rather than believing my fears. I know You watch over me. Please watch over those pugs. —Edward Grinnan

Digging Deeper: Psalm 91:1–16; 121:5–8

Friday, February 5

For the grace of God has appeared, bringing salvation for all people. —Titus 2:11 (ESV)

"I'd like you to have my bookcase," my friend Carol said. "When we move."

I wasn't sure I'd heard correctly. My expression told the tale.

"I can't take it with me," she explained. "And it would make me happy to give it to you."

I set my mug on the table. The coffeehouse hummed with conversation, but I struggled to find a word. I knew the bookcase. I'd admired it often. It was an antique barrister. Four shelves high. Dark, lovely wood. It had been in her family for years.

"What about your sons?" I finally asked.

"They don't appreciate old things. I know you love it. And I love you."

"Carol, I can't."

"Well, why not?"

Thoughts ran wild. *Because I love you, Carol, with my whole heart, but I'm often not a great friend. I scarcely have a moment to share. I forget important dates. I pray for you with all that I am, but then I get caught in the whirlwind of life and forget to check in.* "It's too special," I said.

"Nonsense." A smile broke wide over a face that I love. "You're special."

A week later, Carol's husband delivered the bookcase. He carried it, piece by piece, into our living room. Fully assembled, tall and regal, shelves stacked with volumes of old books, it brought character to our home. A year later, I'm still overwhelmed every time I look at it. To me, the bookcase bears more than books. It holds a message of grace: I didn't earn this gift. I couldn't have. My shortcomings were no secret, yet love was lavished.

Jesus, You brought me to a right relationship with the Father. I could not have earned it. Oh, what grace! Amen. —Shawnelle Eliasen

Digging Deeper: Romans 5:8; 11:6

For this reason I bow my knees before the Father, from whom every family in heaven and on earth is named. —Ephesians 3:14–15 (ESV)

My wife, Carol, and I drove to Connecticut for her uncle's funeral. He had died at the age of ninety-three. The service was lovely—clearly, he had been a pillar in the church. But the oddest thing was that sitting across the aisle from us was a fellow I knew from our neighborhood back in New York.

It was Jim and his wife, Jenny. Our kids had played together in Little League and I used to see him in the park when I did my morning runs. We would talk about everything as we jogged together. Our kids, our work, our families, what we were reading. He and Jenny had moved out of the neighborhood a couple of years ago and I hadn't seen him in a long while. Imagine my surprise to see them here at this funeral. How did they know the deceased?

At the passing of the peace I gave Jim a hug and explained that the man who had died, the man lying in the flag-draped coffin, was my wife's uncle. He looked quizzically at me and said, "He's my wife's uncle, too."

We didn't have time just then to figure out the connection. But when the service had ended, Jim and I were able to piece together exactly how our wives were related—by marriage—to the deceased.

Small world? It is indeed. I keep reflecting on the Bible passage that had been read at the service, "I am the Resurrection and the Life, says the Lord. Whoever has faith in me shall have life, even though he dies." It struck me how we are all connected, in life and death. We are God's family.

I give thanks, Lord, for the connections that bring all of Your children together. —Rick Hamlin

Digging Deeper: Proverbs 17:17; Mark 3:34–35

Sunday, February 7

And he said, "Your name shall no longer be called Jacob, but Israel, because you have commanding power with [an angel of] God." —Genesis 32:29 (CHABAD)

Torah study that day was a slog. Even though the session was only an hour long, the room was stuffy, a dying can light was blinking distractingly, and the text was full of antiquated laws that no longer had any relevance for our lives.

After about ten minutes, one of the other people said, "I really don't know what I'm supposed to get out of this."

I saw some others nodding, and since I had been wondering the same thing, I didn't speak up.

The rabbi said that sometimes he, too, was at a loss, but all our commentators had insisted over the centuries that every word in the Torah was there for a purpose, and it was up to us to engage with it.

So we kept trying to see what outdated, obscure rules might be trying to tell us. Suddenly, one of the people burst out, "This is an awful struggle!"

And someone else said, "Bingo!"

Then it was obvious. We were supposed to be finding this hard. We wouldn't be true to who we were in the world or in history if everything was easily grasped or if we simply accepted the *p'shat* (simple) meaning of the words.

By the time the session came to an end, we were all fully engaged, despite the fact that the previously bothersome conditions hadn't changed. And the rabbi, who hadn't needed to say anything for a long while, was grinning. I think I probably was, too.

Thank You for letting us struggle with Your teachings, God of Israel, and for Your understanding when we find it hard going! —Rhoda Blecker

Digging Deeper: Genesis 28:16; Job 8:7

Monday, February 8

A prudent person foresees danger and takes precautions. The simpleton goes blindly on and suffers the consequences. —Proverbs 22:3 (NLT)

It seemed like a great idea...

I'd recently learned how to make boxes out of two sheets of stiff paper. With Valentine's Day approaching, I was going to teach my newfound skill to four of our young grandchildren. I shopped for poster board, markers, heart stickers, and other Valentine glue-ons, then unloaded my red, white, and pink treasures onto our son and daughter-in-law's dining room table. The children eagerly gathered around.

"I need a yardstick," I said, thinking its longer length would make measuring the poster board cuts easier. Five-year-old Maddie quickly retrieved one. "First, you measure to the midpoint of the poster board and draw a line down the middle," I confidently instructed, proud that I, for once, had mastered a craft. I drew a long line to show them how, then lifted the yardstick from the paper. *Crash!* I had totally forgotten the retro bubble-glass pendant light that hung low over the table.

After we cleaned up the broken glass and moved to a safer spot, the Valentine boxes were created and were a big success. It only cost me a hundred and twenty dollars and two weeks of waiting for a new glass pendant light!

Lord, help me to think before I speak or act, and to consider the potential consequences of what I say and do. It's easy to rush into things and to pay the price later. —Kim Taylor Henry

Digging Deeper: Proverbs 14:16; 29:20

Tuesday, February 9

GOING HOME: Save a Place for Me

I will not leave you as orphans; I will come to you.
—John 14:18 (NIV)

Bing Crosby crooned softly as I sat with Dad in my brother's house sometime before dawn. Dad's favorite music—John Denver, Henry Mancini, The *Grand Canyon Suite,* among many others— ran nonstop in the background for the whole week once Dad came home from the hospital with an inoperable condition.

We all knew Dad was ready to go Home. He had seen Jesus Himself welcoming him several nights before. Since then we had taken turns keeping him company. The doctors had given Dad three days to live; this was day seven. I had stopped praying for healing and instead for a smooth transition. Dad hadn't spoken for over a day. He didn't eat or drink or respond to us at all. His time was close. I pressed a cloth to Dad's forehead, but it seemed like he was just a shell of who he was. He was still breathing, but was he in there anymore? I put my hand in his. Could he still hear his beloved music? Could he even hear me anymore?

"When you get to heaven, Dad," I whispered, "please be sure to save a spot for me."

I gasped when he squeezed my hand, surprised at the strength of his grip. Cool. Firm. Assuring. He'd be in heaven, ready to welcome me home one day.

Lord, Dad is in sight of heaven. Guide him Home
with Your love. You have prepared a table for him,
just as You will welcome all of Your children with the
comfort of Your outstretched arms. —Erika Bentsen

Digging Deeper: John 14:15–21

Wednesday, February 10

Walk with the wise and become wise.
—Proverbs 13:20 (NIV)

It was quite the talk, this little scandal in our
community. All the evidence pointed to the
person's guilt. I hadn't discussed it publicly, but
I'd thought it, too, just like everyone else. Well,
not everyone.

"I just have to believe that there's something
we don't know," my husband, Dwight, said when
someone brought it up to us.

I couldn't help but smile. Sweet Dwight, always
looking for the best in everyone. Always giving the
benefit of the doubt. But come on, it was so obvious!
What other possible explanation could there be?
This person wasn't someone we knew well at all,
but it was someone in a position to be held to a
higher standard. Someone who'd clearly betrayed the
community's trust.

A few days later, a family member called me.
"Remember what everyone was saying about that
scandal? Turns out there was more to it." It had, in
fact, all been a big misunderstanding. What everyone,

including me, had thought to be so obvious wasn't so obvious after all.

Oh, how quick I was to believe the worst of someone! And how ashamed of myself I felt!

And how not quick to say "I told you so" was Dwight.

I read somewhere that you become like the five people you spend the most time with. I pray that's true, because I hope one day to have a heart like my husband's: wise and full of grace...and always looking for the best in others.

Lord, as David wrote in Psalm 51, "Create in me a clean heart...and renew a right spirit within me."
—Ginger Rue

Digging Deeper: Psalm 1:1; Titus 1:15

Thursday, February 11

For God has not given us a spirit of fear, but of power and of love and of a sound mind.
—2 Timothy 1:7 (NKJV)

"Grandpa, please! Just tell me!" our fourth-grade grandson, Logan, pleaded.

My husband, Chuck, sat at the kitchen table helping Logan with his homework. "How do you make an equivalent fraction?" Chuck said. The subject was math, and the problem was converting a word problem to a math equation, which Logan had been studying in school.

"I don't know!" Logan moaned, writhing in his chair. "Please help me!"

"I am helping you," Chuck said.

It seemed what Logan really wanted was for Chuck to give him the answer instead of figuring out the problem himself. He knew Chuck could do it faster and better. But we knew Logan needed to know how to do the problem if he was going to learn the lesson.

The situation reminded me of the lesson I learned when I was laid off. Like Logan, I wanted God to snap his fingers and instantly provide another job. But He didn't, and I had to do the work—write the résumé, look for job openings, schedule the interviews, and be open to possibilities God had for me. The process took longer than I wanted, and several opportunities fell through, but when the right door opened, I knew which position I should take.

Once Logan figured out he had to do his own work, he started listening to Chuck's hints about how to find the answer. And not only did he find the right answer, but he also learned how to get it.

In the same way, God helps us by giving us what we need to work things through for ourselves so we can learn how to handle life's challenges.

Lord, thank You for giving us a mind that can work out life's problems. And thank You for providing us with just enough help to succeed. —Marilyn Turk

Digging Deeper: Exodus 3–4

I praise you, for I am fearfully and wonderfully made. Wonderful are your works; my soul knows it very well. —Psalm 139:14 (ESV)

I'd never lost a friend before. Not like this. This wasn't a drifting apart caused by changing schools or moving. This was a rending break, a splintering of bonds I'd considered sacrosanct. To make it worse, I believed the breach was caused by a terrible misunderstanding that honest conversation could heal. But nothing I said or did helped. I had to accept that my friend's regard for me was gone. I was desolate.

The loss sent me into a tailspin. Who was I without this treasured relationship? I found myself tongue-tied in social situations, constantly second-guessing what I thought to say. Maybe it wasn't interesting after all. Did people secretly roll their eyes whenever I walked into the room, wishing I'd leave again? I didn't know. I felt paralyzed—unable to trust my judgment.

I confided my heartache to my brother, and it was his reply that proved a turning point for me. "Erin, you are strong enough to weather this," he told me, with conviction.

Strong? What an odd word choice. I'd never felt weaker. But his words stayed with me as we talked about the danger of allowing other people's opinions to determine our self-worth. I'd struggled with that for most of my life. But suddenly, the habit's harmful consequences crystallized into real understanding. The internal voice telling me I'm not good enough is a deceiver that wants me to feel fragile, weak. The truth is, I am a child of God, infinitely valuable in His eyes. Through Him, I'll always be strong enough—just as He made me to be.

Lord, when I'm tempted to worry over the approval of others, help me remember—I am Your creation and therefore valuable just as I am.
—Erin Janoso

Digging Deeper: Luke 12:6–7

Saturday, February 13

On the third day a wedding took place at Cana in Galilee. Jesus' mother was there, and Jesus and his disciples had also been invited to the wedding.
—John 2:1–2 (NIV)

I was surprised and excited when Robyn, my grandson David's fiancée, asked me to be part of the group helping her choose a wedding dress. I looked forward to spending time with my daughter-in-law Patricia and meeting Robyn's mom, grandmother, and one of her sisters.

When I shared my news with a friend, however, she rolled her eyes. "You are in for an experience! Haven't you ever watched *Say Yes to the Dress?*" I'd never seen it (and still haven't), but she shared a couple of horror stories and cautioned, "Prepare for an exhausting day. And don't expect your opinion to matter."

Although I tried to put her comments behind me, I was a bit apprehensive when Patricia picked me up to drive to the bridal shop. I needn't have worried. The day was cold and blustery, but the atmosphere inside was warm and friendly. Robyn had a price range and stuck to it. Her only request was "no ruffles." She tried on five dresses. After asking all of us for input, she modeled two of the dresses again and sent pictures to her dad, granddad, and sisters who were in Nebraska. After considering all of our opinions, she chose a lovely, simply cut white satin with a row of buttons down the back. We all agreed: it was the perfect dress.

We adjourned to a Mexican restaurant for a late lunch to conclude an enjoyable day with a bride-to-be who has a beautiful and caring spirit. Beyond a doubt, the upcoming marriage was off to a good start.

Jesus, You blessed the wedding in Cana with
Your presence. Please bless David, Robyn,
and other soon-to-be-wed couples with
Your presence in their celebrations and lives.
—Penney Schwab

Digging Deeper: Proverbs 18:22; Isaiah 62:5;
Matthew 19:4–6

Sunday, February 14

For this is the love of God, that we keep his commandments. —1 John 5:3 (NKJV)

It has always bothered me that the apostle John defines our love for God as "keep His commandments." That seems so legalistic, so unromantic.

My wife's birthday falls next to Valentine's Day, so I just get her one card and gift to cover both days. She is steering away from sweets, for health reasons, so as I wander through the store, I'm looking for something else that might please her. When I get to the frozen food aisle, I come across some frozen okra and asparagus, two of her very favorite foods. On impulse I buy one of each and pick up a pretty card on my way out of the store.

I wrap the vegetables in colorful paper and hide them in the freezer. When Sharon comes to breakfast the next morning, she lights up at the sight of a card and a package. She looks over the mushy card, then picks up the frosty package and begins tearing it open. I brace myself for her reaction to a gift that contains no chocolate.

To my surprise, she lets out a squeal of delight. "This is perfect, Danny! Two of my favorite foods. I can get several meals out of these, and I won't feel sinful eating them, like I would with chocolate." She gives me a hug, to my relief.

Do I have a great wife, or what?

As I ponder the apostle's words, "This is love, that we keep His commandments," I can see now that my obedience is like chocolate (or asparagus) to Him. It shows that I love Him more than I love myself. If that's not romantic, what is?

God, thanks for telling us how to please You, so we don't have to guess. —Daniel Schantz

Digging Deeper: Exodus 19:5; John 15:14

Presidents' Day, Monday, February 15

Whatever you do, work at it with all your heart, as working for the Lord, not for human masters.
—Colossians 3:23 (NIV)

Cleaning out my desk, I came across a picture of Air Force One. The picture brought back an extraordinary experience from my Air Force years. President Jimmy Carter visited the area where I was stationed, and he flew in and out of the base where I served. I was the base fuels officer, and Air Force One required refueling during the visit.

I ordered the preferred fuel for Air Force One, and the day the fuel arrived, I commented to the delivery driver, "Looks like a new tank truck!" The driver, also looking sharp in new shirt and trousers, said, "Yes... doing our best for the president." The refueling operators who refueled Air Force One a few days later performed flawlessly. And fuel was only one of many areas of support provided by base personnel. Everyone involved performed with excellence. After all, each one was *doing their best for the president.*

It was exciting to be part of something in direct support of the president of the United States. The picture I have of Air Force One still reminds me of what total commitment, unified teamwork, and precise execution looks like when everyone involved works at it with all their heart—as if working for the Lord.

Today, as we honor our past and current presidents, I must ask myself, "How can I do my best for the president today?" How can you? One thing we can all do every day is pray for the president.

Dear God, help us to pray daily for our president to be guided by Your wisdom and strengthened by Your presence to govern in Your truth.
—John Dilworth

Digging Deeper: Proverbs 16:3; 1 Corinthians 10:31

Tuesday, February 16

GOING HOME: A Father's Legacy
Come now; let us leave. —John 14:31 (NIV)

Dad left us in the cool quiet of a winter's morning. I walked through the replanted section of his apple orchard. I felt no stronger than the spindly saplings, fragile inside their protective fencing. Low clouds sifted through the forest on the solemn hills overlooking the farm, cradled into its valley. A kiss of moisture in the air brushed tears on my cheek. It was early on the eighth day after Dad's internal rupture. It was a miracle that he lasted that long. And of this precious final week, I wouldn't trade a single moment.

My heart ached as if pierced by a thorn. But there was undeniable sweetness mixed with the sadness. Dad left us with the greatest gift a father could ever leave his children: faith rooted as deeply as the ancient apple trees from which these saplings were born.

The true importance of life isn't the concerns of this earth. The problems and goals that loomed so large over me had dwindled to nothing. Dad spent his entire life living his faith, being an example for his kids. Riches, cars, mansions; no earthly thing really matters. Sowing seeds of faith and letting them grow; that's our purpose. The end of life as we know it isn't an end at all. Dad's journey was proof enough. The seeds of faith he planted in us makes it undeniable that heaven is right there waiting for each of us.

Thank You, Lord, for parents who raised my brother and me in a faith-based home. Thank You for the inspiration to pass this Good News to those coming behind us, so they, too, are confident that You will gather us all together to be with You. Just like the apples from these spindly saplings that we will someday harvest from Dad's orchard.
—Erika Bentsen

Digging Deeper: Mark 8:36; Galatians 6:7

Ash Wednesday, February 17

Then I proclaimed a fast there...that we might deny ourselves before our God. —Ezra 8:21 (NRSV)

Outings with our godsons frequently include ice cream, popcorn, or some other sticky treat. When they were little, they didn't mind me cleaning them up with a wet napkin, but now that they consider themselves practically men at nine and ten, they don't want to be "babied." So I started keeping Wet Ones in the car for self-swabbing. Last week when the oldest, R.J., finished an ice-cream cone, I handed him an unopened packet with a flourish.

Moments later I heard an outraged cry from the backseat, "Hey, that hurts!"

He had a small cut on his hand, and the astringent in the cloth had stung. I turned to find him regarding me with a look of hurt surprise that did not match the tough-guy persona he'd assumed since his last birthday.

I remembered this today on Ash Wednesday when a bit of the ash from the cross the priest made on my forehead fell into my eye. It stung! *Hey,* I wanted to cry to my Father, *that hurts!*

Then it occurred to me that maybe it's supposed to. Maybe it's supposed to sting when we confront our humanity, failures, and sins, as we do on Ash Wednesday. Maybe applying ashes *should* smart a bit to motivate us for the work we need to do to prepare for Easter, that indeed we are dust and unto dust we shall return. Maybe that "sting" is a reminder that no matter how grown-up we think we are, we still can't clean up our own messes without God's help.

Father, wake me from the dust of complacency to better appreciate Your majesty and forgiveness.
—Marci Alborghetti

Digging Deeper: Esther 4:1–4; Jonah 3:1–10

Thursday, February 18

"I will not offer to the Lord my God sacrifices that have cost me nothing." —2 Samuel 24:24 (GNT)

I like to observe Lent as a way to prepare my heart for Easter. Sacrificing something I'm used to doing or having each day reminds me of Christ's sacrifice on the cross. Typically, I choose a food or activity to set aside. Each year, I encourage my husband and daughter to forgo something they love, too.

"I'm giving up desserts and sugary snacks for Lent," I announce proudly as we eat dinner around the kitchen table a few evenings before the forty-day remembrance begins. I hope my boldness inspires them.

"Oh, you should give up coffee," sixteen-year-old Micah quips. "You love it more than I love soda, and that's what I'm doing."

My husband, Michael, snickers under his breath.

I frown. "Sweets are harder," I protest. "I only have coffee in the morning." I elaborate on how we should search our hearts and ask the Lord to guide us to a sacrifice that brings us closer to Him.

At 6:15 a.m., I slap my alarm. *I need coffee.* The thought startles me. Is coffee really the first thing I think about? Perhaps I'm in denial about my relationship with java, after all.

I love a robust cup with delicious flavored creamers. Deep down, I'm not sure if I can break up with my beloved for forty days. And to be honest, I don't want to. It's a huge challenge. Something I definitely can't do on my own.

That's why you must. The thought sizzles in my mind.

I go into the kitchen and pour a big glass of ice water, eager to tell Micah that I'm taking her advice—giving up something I love, for something I love more.

Lord, I'll need Your strength to keep my Lent promise. Open my eyes to understanding Your suffering and selfless love as I go without my much-loved morning brew. —Stephanie Thompson

Digging Deeper: Proverbs 21:2; Matthew 6:21

Friday, February 19

And the peace of God, which transcends all understanding, will guard your hearts and your minds in Christ Jesus. —Philippians 4:7 (NIV)

Since I began my adult walk with Christ, I became keenly aware of people and their actions. I began to notice that here were people placed in my path who showed me God's love and light, wherever I went.

My forever friend, David, always relied heavily upon his faith to get through the challenges of high school and college. While I wallowed in my worries, David moved through similar concerns with a confidence that I couldn't understand. But I knew that he prayed regularly and went to Mass diligently. There was something different about David. I suspect it was the Christ in him.

A coworker, Jackie, who was solidly walking along with God in her life, once asked why I didn't go to church regularly. To her, it was a simple question. To me, it was a turning point. I didn't have a reason for not attending church, except that I hadn't yet found one that I wanted to join.

After caring for twenty toddlers all day, Andrea, my son's preschool teacher, spent her evenings caring for her elderly and infirm parents. Nevertheless, she came to work, lovingly cared for children, sang them to sleep, and kept them smiling, even when they missed their mommies. I visited Andrea once at her home, observed her caring for her parents, and saw all her love. I love the Christ in her.

Each of these friends offered me clear proof about how putting God first and relying upon Him can propel you through life's challenges. When I saw the Christ in Andrea, Jackie, and David, I knew that I wanted that peace in my own life.

Heavenly Father, thank You for the people who follow You, whom You so strategically place in our lives to offer us tangible examples of how to be better disciples. —Gayle T. Williams

Digging Deeper: Psalm 125:4; Ezekiel 20:19

Saturday, February 20

Don't fret or worry. Instead of worrying, pray.
—Philippians 4:6 (MSG)

"C'mon, Sunrise." My golden retriever dove into the powdery snow. I knew that a walk with Sunrise into the outdoors winter wonderland would help calm my nerves. I was facing a situation at work where I needed to have a confrontation in order to achieve a resolution.

Instead of relaxing, I fretted as Sunrise bounded across the field. Suddenly, she dropped and chewed on her feet, trying to dislodge the snow that had wadded between her pads. Then she was up and running. So were my thoughts. I scripted what I would say...and then what I thought they'd say.

Sunrise plopped into a drift. She whimpered as she gritted her teeth and pulled at the snowballs. By the time I had waded up to her, she raced off, and so had my inner dialogue.

The snow poofed as Sunrise fell to the ground. With her teeth she yanked, then yipped in pain. I checked her hind foot. The warmth of her pads had melted the snow into icicles with jagged edges that stabbed her every step. "Oh, Sunrise, the farther you ran, the worse this got." In my heart I heard, *Just like you.* The more I'd fretted, the sharper the edges of my thoughts had become. They'd grown from uncomfortable to painful in a matter of minutes.

After I'd dug out the ice, we headed back. Sunrise stopped several times to clean out her feet, and I cleaned out my heart by chatting with God. His answer was simple. In my confrontation, I was to just state the facts, no emotions, and ask how we could move forward. *Of course, how simple.* And it worked.

Lord, Your answers are always the solution. Remind me to ask You first, instead of fretting. Amen.
—Rebecca Ondov

Digging Deeper: Matthew 6:25–33; 1 John 5:14

Sunday, February 21

Well done, good and faithful servant....
—Matthew 25:21 (ESV)

Sometimes I'm envious of my friend Anne, who is quick to compliment a good deed, a Sunday dress, a tasty dessert. My parents challenged me to attain high standards but rarely commended me for achievements. I learned to value the positive but look for and point out the negative. This may have made me well suited for my editorial career: nudging writers to polish their prose. But it stunted my ability to affirm the efforts and attributions of others: the beautiful, the creative, the well done.

My envy of Anne will get me nowhere unless I use it to emulate her relational skills. So last week I called her. "Anne, you're so good at complimenting people. But it doesn't come naturally for me. Any tips?"

She hesitated, then said, "If you see something, say something. Positive, that is."

So obvious. So easy. "I can remember that." It's taken conscious effort, but I have.

Wednesday I praised a neighbor girl for carrying grocery bags for an elderly acquaintance. Thursday I noted a friend's fashionable jacket. Friday, by email, I complimented a school chorus teacher on his concert lineup—such redemptive selections. Saturday—a friend's birthday—I raised a toast, naming qualities I admire: her generosity and low-key wisdom. Today, Sunday, I'll soon drive to church. During the service, I'll pause to thank God for His faithfulness. I'll also listen carefully for a quiet voice—the Spirit's quiet whisper: *well done.*

God, help me to see—and name—the positive qualities and excellent efforts I see in others.
—Evelyn Bence

Digging Deeper: 1 Thessalonians 3:6–13; 1 Timothy 5:1–2

He gives strength to the weary and increases the power of the weak. —Isaiah 40:29 (NIV)

Addiction can affect anyone, even those who come from loving, faith-filled homes. My mother-in-law, Nereida, raised her nine children with love and took them to church every Sunday; yet three of her children became involved with drugs. In addition, her husband, a Korean War veteran and hardworking man, battled alcoholism.

When her oldest son was in his early teenage years, Nereida worried he was using drugs due to his erratic behavior, but she wasn't certain. One afternoon while praying for an answer, she sensed God was directing her to search a specific spot in the apartment, and when she did, she found drug paraphernalia. This revealed what she feared most. It was the beginning of a long journey as others in her family soon followed in his footsteps.

Though times were hard, Nereida never lost her faith or stopped loving, praying, and caring for each member of her family. She turned to prayer and found strength and hope in God's promises and her church community. And when she lost her husband and three of her children to addiction-related causes, she stayed strong in her faith and leaned on her church family for support.

Eventually, one of her children was able to break free from drugs and alcohol. He is now a deacon at his church and a witness that God answers prayers. Today, at eighty-eight years old, Nereida is grateful to God for her loving, drug-free family. When talking to others who are in a similar situation to what she went through, she tells them, "Never give up. Keep your faith in God. Find support."

Lord, deliver those who battle addiction and strengthen their loved ones. —Pablo Diaz

Digging Deeper: Psalm 29:11; Romans 4:20

Tuesday, February 23

GOING HOME: A Testament in Tears
But that the world may know that I love the Father.... —John 14:31 (KJV)

Mourning doesn't come easy to me. I'm not the type to carry tissues as I go about my day. Unique to me or not, the mantra "cowgirls don't cry" is alive and well in my life. I make sure to be stoic and strong in every situation. When discussing the death of my father with others, I brush over my feelings. I can do it. I can, that is, until I speak of his seeing Jesus welcoming him Home. My joy peaks, and then tears follow.

All through the final week of his passing as I went home to be with my father and my family, I stayed strong—mostly. I could talk about the facts, but if someone asked how I was doing, I broke down. Everything I've read says that openly mourning a loved one's loss is supposed to be okay. And yet I don't want to show anyone else that side of me. Tears show weakness, right?

Weeks after the fact, I was telling a friend about Dad's passing. Tears erupted and wouldn't stop. I was mortified and apologized. "No." Bunne stopped me with a hand on my arm. "Tears make you real. Don't be ashamed that you're human. He is definitely a man worth mourning. Tears are a testament to what a great dad he was."

Thank You, Lord, for Dad—a dad who did his best to make sure I was brought up with a solid foundation of faith in Christ. Thank You for a dad who raised me with an awareness of You. Thank You for a dad who shared Your life with me from the start. Thank You for being with him at the end of this life and on into the next. —Erika Bentsen

Digging Deeper: John 14:27; Colossians 1:23

Wednesday, February 24

The Lord hears when I call to Him.
—Psalm 4:3 (NIV)

My husband, Lynn, and I stood alone in silence, waiting for the elevator. We'd just left his neuro-oncologist's office where the doctor reviewed Lynn's latest test results.

We had hoped to see healing in his brain tissue damaged by cancer and radiation treatments nearly fifteen years ago, losses that robbed him of some memory and balance functions. For the past three months, Lynn had been traveling from Boulder to Denver on a combination of buses and light rail five days a week for a total of sixty hyperbaric treatments. He was surrounded by many people's specific prayers for healing that would give him back some of what he'd lost.

The tests didn't show much difference, and we felt discouraged as we began the hour-long drive home. What could we tell all those who'd been praying so specifically that his results would show improvement?

As I drove, Lynn began pointing out the landmarks he'd seen from his regular commutes to the hospital. He also described how bus passengers readily helped other less able passengers, and the kind bus driver whom he'd thanked with a gift on the last day of his treatment.

Suddenly, the test results didn't matter so much. Here were Lynn's improvements. His recall of the landmarks; recognizing the kindness of strangers; his can-do courage to keep going, even in wet, cold weather. And his problem-solving confidence when he failed to get off the train at the right stop. Prayers weren't answered the way we specifically prayed, but the positive side effects of the experience were clearly evident. Good results!

Lord, even when things don't turn out the way we pray, You are still at work. Help us recognize those blessed side effects. —Carol Kuykendall

Digging Deeper: Matthew 7:11; 21:22

Thursday, February 25

So I recommend having fun, because there is nothing better for people in this world than to eat, drink, and enjoy life. That way they will experience some happiness along with all the hard work God gives them under the sun.
—Ecclesiastes 8:15 (NLT)

Impulsive. That's my sixteen-year-old daughter. Micah's playful, lighthearted, and all about fun. The more spontaneous, the better, as far as she's concerned. Not me. I'm a planner. In fact, I joke that the only way I can tolerate spur-of-the-moment activities is if they're scheduled. I strive to be less predictable, but I often fall short.

When Micah got her driver's license, she was pumped about tooling around town, picking up friends and doing whatever she wanted. My husband and I explained that wasn't how it would be. We intended to keep her on a familiar route until we could see she was responsible.

"You can only drive to school, work, and then straight home the first few weeks," he told her.

Micah was disappointed, but obliged.

On her second day of driving, I'd finished at the grocer's a few minutes before dismissal at her school. I called to say I'd follow her home to see how she was doing. "Stop for an Icee?" she begged.

I agreed. Following in the car behind, I thought about our dinner in the grocery bags.

At the convenience store, Micah told me she wanted a slice of pizza. She'd talked before about how much she liked it, but I had already planned dinner.

I gazed at the display case. Besides individual slices, they had whole pizzas. I grabbed a big square box and met wide-eyed Micah at the checkout.

Months later, Micah still raves about the time Mom got convenience-store pizza for dinner.

Lord, never let me become so rigid that I miss opportunities to spontaneously show love.
—Stephanie Thompson

Digging Deeper: Ecclesiastes 3:12; Romans 12:9–10

Friday, February 26

BECOMING JUST ME AGAIN
Real Help
I will give them an undivided heart and put a new spirit in them; I will remove from them their heart of stone and give them a heart of flesh.
—Ezekiel 11:19 (NIV)

After my "Hunka Hunka Burnin' Love" was hospitalized with stage IV melanoma, I marveled at the creativity of family and friends. Instead of the traditional gift of flowers (thank goodness for that because there is no space in any intensive-care hospital rooms for bouquets), innumerable people blessed us with lively visits. All six of Jack's children, who have full-time jobs, managed to be in his hospital room every minute I wasn't there and often when I was. My children, sister, brother, in-laws, and cousins from out of state bought airline tickets so they could visit Jack.

Other ways of showing love emerged. My sister gave him a foot rub. His children set up the hospital TV so Jack could watch his favorite sports network. His daughter made him his favorite homemade asparagus soup. And the prayers, oh my goodness, the prayers. My requests on Facebook for prayers spiraled out into the world exponentially and I daresay there were millions of prayers being said for my sweet husband.

Even I received care that touched my core. Friends brought me home-cooked meals. My sister did my laundry and organized my kitchen shelves. My neighbor picked up my trash and left groceries in my refrigerator.

I learned that flowers, gifts, and cards are not necessarily the best things for a sick person. Instead, taking the time to visit even for ten minutes, having tender conversations, giving gentle hugs, and saying prayers often touch the core of not only the patient, but the disease itself.

Jesus, You didn't hand out things to people on Your way; You gave Yourself, Your time, Your wisdom, and Your infinite love. Keep teaching me ways to give to others. —Patricia Lorenz

Digging Deeper: Philippians 4:4–7; 10–14

Saturday, February 27

If I say, "Surely the darkness will hide me and the light become night around me," even the darkness will not be dark to you; the night will shine like the day, for darkness is as light to you. —Psalm 139: 11–12 (NIV)

I could hear the silverware clinking. My parents were in our kitchen making us dinner, and the silverware coming out meant the table was being set and it was almost ready. But I wasn't ready. I was in our master bathroom, standing in front of the mirror with tears running down my cheeks. I heard my two-month-old son cry in the main room, to which I heard my husband's voice, "I'm coming, buddy."

I had spent too many moments of motherhood in this bathroom, half in a secret state of sadness and half in a state of confusion. I hardly recognized myself these days in the mirror. I couldn't understand what had happened to me after my son's birth. Postpartum depression tried to steal all the things I thought would be amazing about becoming a mother. It tried to destroy my relationships by convincing me I should hide it. The shame of that sadness was the heaviest part.

I leaned forward, putting my palms flat on the bathroom sink, staring into my eyes in that mirror. My life felt bleak, dark. "Jesus, why have you not come to help me?" I prayed.

There was a knock on the bathroom door. "Dinner's ready," came my husband's voice.

It was in that moment I felt Jesus respond: *Have you heard Me knocking? I've been waiting for you to open up and give this battle to Me.*

"Everything okay?" My husband was back. I opened the door with tears still drying on my cheeks. I knew I could never be outside Jesus's love and light, so I finally had the strength to tell my family the truth.

Jesus, thank You for shining light into our darkness.
—Desiree Cole

Digging Deeper: Deuteronomy 28:7;
2 Thessalonians 3:3

Sunday, February 28

A friend loves at all times, and a brother is born for a time of adversity. —Proverbs 17:17 (NIV)

My daughters and I were enjoying a trip to the mall during a recent trip to visit with family. We tried on jeans, bought a couple of wedding and graduation gifts, and concluded our visit with treats—a cinnamon bun for one daughter, a smoothie for the other, and an acai bowl for me. All was well with the world until we arrived at our minivan. I reached into my bag for the van keys, but they were nowhere to be found.

My heart sank as I assessed my current situation. We were thousands of miles away from home with our second set of keys hanging in our laundry room. I instructed my daughters to remain near the van, figuring I could conduct a more thorough search without them worrying and asking questions. I reentered the mall while lifting up a quick prayer, then retraced my steps, searching dressing rooms and store shelves and questioning mall employees to see if anyone had turned in my lost keys. I even called mall security, thinking perhaps I had dropped them in the middle of the mall.

I couldn't find the keys anywhere.

I called my husband out of desperation as I returned to the girls. Within fifteen minutes he arrived and parked. Together we entered the mall to search one more time. This time I wasn't alone—I had help with me, my husband and our girls. After only a few minutes my oldest daughter ran up to me wearing a huge smile. She'd found the keys! I was thrilled and reminded that challenges are best overcome with prayer... and with an army of loved ones.

Thank You, Lord, for the army of believers You have blessed me with, especially my family.
—Carla Hendricks

Digging Deeper: Proverbs 27:17; Ecclesiastes 4:9–12; Matthew 18:20

JOYFUL IN HOPE

1 _____

2 _____

3 _____

4 _____

5 _____

6 _____

7 _____

8 _____

9 _____

10 _____

11 _____

12 _____

13 _____

14 _____

15 _____

16 _____

17 _____

18 _____

19 _____

20 _____

21 _____

22 _____

23 _____

24 _____

25 _____

26 _____

27 _____

28 _____

MARCH

Only fear the Lord and serve Him
in truth with all your heart;
for consider what great things
He has done for you.

—1 Samuel 12:24 (NASB)

Monday, March 1

"Have I not commanded you? Be strong
and courageous. Do not be afraid; do not be
discouraged, for the Lord your God will be with
you wherever you go." —Joshua 1:9 (NIV)

I became obsessed last year reading about a particular
arctic fox who made an impossible journey of
2,175 miles, mostly across open sea ice, leaving her
home in Norway in search of a more advantageous
environment to mate and raise her young. Scientists
point to changes in climate as the reason for her epic
trek. But I believe there was more at play.

Initially, researchers in Norway attached a pink
satellite transmitter to the young vixen to study her
local migration patterns. Boy, were they surprised
when she ended up in Canada! According to the
pink tracking device, in one day alone she traveled
a mind-boggling ninety-seven miles. The scientists
were sure she must have been scooped up by a boat
until they realized there was no ship traffic that far
north in the frozen Arctic Ocean. Eventually, the
transmitter petered out and the little fox vanished
into the vast wilderness of remote Nunavut. One
stunned researcher called the trek a miracle.

What I found truly miraculous was that God could
imbue this wondrous creature with such courage,
stamina, and determination for her to undertake a
perilous odyssey for the sake of her future offspring.

We too are divinely endowed with courage and
determination, for the times in life when we are

called on to do more than we think we can do. But often, in our fear, we forget; we believe we are weak and that God has abandoned us. You might claim the fox was driven by the energy of millions of screaming genes driving her to a better breeding ground. I think God had a bigger hand in it.

Father, I know You have prepared me for the journey of life with its ever-changing landscape. Help me to find the courage of the little fox when I need it most. To draw on the strength that is Yours. —Edward Grinnan

Digging Deeper: 1 Chronicles 28:20; Psalm 119:105

OPEN HEART, OPEN HOME
The Front Door

Lord, I love the house where you live, the place where your glory dwells. —Psalm 26:8 (NIV)

In the wee hours of that cold March morning in 2018, I lay on my back on the hardwood floor of my old log cabin, moving my legs in a frantic circular motion like I was riding a bicycle. Then I flew up and down the attic stairs, followed by furious rounds of deep knee bends and jumping jacks.

After the twenty-five years that I'd been taking a high dose of OxyContin for excruciating nerve pain, my new doctor at the pain management clinic had prescribed a different medication. He assured me I would not go through withdrawal, but that was exactly what was happening.

There's a name for it: dope sick. It was the worst kind of misery I'd ever been through, even after thirty-four complex surgeries to remove tumors inside my head. After I had two grand mal seizures, I phoned the pain clinic and begged them to admit me to the hospital. "If we hospitalized everyone in this town in withdrawal, ma'am," they said, "we wouldn't have room for the flu patients."

"This town" was Huntington, West Virginia, the opioid capital of the United States. A city in crisis, just like me. I'd lived here all of my sixty-four years, but I didn't feel welcome anymore. It was then I made the most difficult phone call of my life. I called my friend Sue and pleaded for her to help me.

Sue didn't say, "Let me run the vacuum," or "I'll need to buy some groceries." She only said, "Oh, honey. Come now." When that big, paneled door swung open and I saw my friend's face in the lamplight, it was the Lord's presence I felt.

Dear Father, thank You for welcoming me home.
—Roberta Messner

Digging Deeper: Isaiah 58:7; 1 Timothy 5:10

Wednesday, March 3

DISCOVERING GOD IN THE GRAND CANYON: Walking in Hope and Faith

I will instruct you and teach you in the way you should go; I will counsel you with my loving eye on you. —Psalm 32:8 (NIV)

We almost didn't go. With eight inches of new snow expected at the Grand Canyon, along with strong winds, we were tempted to stay home in the Phoenix area and enjoy the local sights. But our friends Charlotte and Raymond, visiting from Canada, had this one chance to see one of the Seven Wonders of the Natural World. So we bundled up our snow gear, rented a four-wheel-drive vehicle, and arrived five hours later to a handwritten sign at the pay station at the entrance to the national park: No Refunds for Bad Weather.

"We can go to our hotel or hope for a break in the clouds," my husband, Kevin, said.

"The canyon," our friends declared.

Decision made, we parked near the visitor center and walked to a scenic viewpoint. Undeterred by the low-hanging clouds, our friends snapped photo after photo. Suddenly, the sky opened behind us, exposing the famous rocks.

"Thank you, Jesus," Charlotte breathed, peering over the edge. She repeated her gratitude many times during the next few hours as we walked the Rim Trail, capturing photos of the breathtaking views, a herd of elk, and a friendly mountain chickadee.

Only at the end of the day, when we were stumbling back to our vehicle, did the predicted snow begin to fall. We drove in blizzard conditions to the hotel. Grabbing our suitcases, Charlotte wondered, "What if we had stayed home?" We would have missed the beauty of God's creation.

Jesus, may my fear of uncertainty not keep me from experiencing today's adventures. —Lynne Hartke

Digging Deeper: Psalm 143:8; Proverbs 3:5–6

Thursday, March 4

DISCOVERING GOD IN THE GRAND CANYON: Through Fresh Eyes
Sing to God, sing in praise of his name, extol him who rides on the clouds; rejoice before him—his name is the Lord. —Psalm 68:4 (NIV)

Nearly five million people visit the Grand Canyon each year—to take photos of the panoramic views, to catch the change of color on the rocks at sunrise or sunset, or to hike a few miles on the dusty trails, dodging the steaming piles of dung from the ever-present, plodding pack mules.

Most people only make it to the Grand Canyon once in their lifetime, so, when our friends Charlotte and Raymond asked to go with us, we quickly agreed, eager to serve as tour guides to our state's most famous destination.

While there, we decided to enjoy the views on the Rim Trail. We shuttled to the Trailview Overlook and proceeded to three more points: Maricopa, Powell, and Hopi. Through the eyes of our friends, we saw the canyon again with fresh eyes and felt the beauty of the place seep into the deepest corners of our overworked souls.

Rounding a corner, Raymond was the first to see them—seven elk, their five-hundred-pound bodies barely hidden by the underbrush. We caught our breath as a young doe stretched out her black, shaggy neck to nibble on the low-hanging branch of a nearby tree, unconcerned by our presence. Backing away, we boarded the shuttle, chatting about all the beautiful creation we had seen.

At our final shuttle stop, we found ourselves in agreement with a carved wooden sign posted near the canyon edge: *Sing to God, sing in praise of his name, extol him who rides on the clouds; rejoice before him—his name is the Lord. Psalm 68:4* (NIV)

Thank You, God, for leaving a testimony of Your greatness in Your created work. —Lynne Hartke

Digging Deeper: 1 Chronicles 16:30–31; Psalm 100:1–4

DISCOVERING GOD IN THE GRAND CANYON: New Layers of Memories
Your faithfulness continues through all generations; you established the earth, and it endures.
—Psalm 119:90 (NIV)

My husband and I, with friends Charlotte and Raymond, stepped onto the Trail of Time, an interpretive trail at the Grand Canyon that focused on the various rock layers and the immensity of the geological time span. A blizzard the night before had blanketed everything in white.

We passed a boulder of the oldest rock layer in the canyon, the Elves Chasm gneiss, a predominantly gray stone that was as old as the magma of the earth, followed by Rama schist, a rock cut and brought to the rim from the very depths of the canyon. Although I was surrounded by time measured in geology, my mind was not on ancient history.

"Do you remember when we came with all four kids? We hiked the Nature Walk and the kids pressed their noses into ponderosa pines to capture the vanilla scent?" I said. "And how about the time Zach hiked at age ten and it was over a hundred degrees?"

As we walked forward into time, passing boulders of granite and Awatubi limestone, I reminisced about other trips: of backpacking toddlers, entertaining them with fruit snacks and Goldfish crackers, and a decade later, of encouraging grumpy teenagers up the unyielding switchbacks.

Kevin interrupted my reflections. "We've never seen the canyon after eight inches of fresh snow."

We snapped multiple photos of the famous landscape framed by overhanging tree limbs, laden in white. Kevin grabbed a branch, and a cascade of snow fell down Charlotte's face. After the laughter, the only sounds were our footsteps making fresh layers in the paths of our collective memories as we created stories to be told another day.

No matter the season, Lord God, open my eyes to
discover the beauty of Your faithfulness today.
—Lynne Hartke

Digging Deeper: Deuteronomy 7:9; Psalm 33:4

DISCOVERING GOD IN THE GRAND CANYON: Witnessing Today's Beauty

Furthermore, tell the people, "This is what the Lord says: See, I am setting before you the way of life and the way of death." —Jeremiah 21:8 (NIV)

"The wind!" complained my friend Charlotte, the only words she could utter before we simultaneously turned our backs on the penetrating gale that lashed around Hopi Point at the Grand Canyon.

"How long until the guys join us?" she asked, zipping her maroon jacket to her chin.

I glanced at my watch. Our husbands had decided to walk to the viewpoint rather than grab the shuttle as Charlotte and I had done. "At least another ten minutes." I pulled on my gloves.

She nodded and stepped toward the guardrail to take photos of the panoramic view, her dark hair whipping in all directions.

Unphased by the March temperatures in the low twenties, a lone raven soared over the abyss, a distinct black silhouette against the rock layers. I lifted my camera, hoping to witness its famous acrobatic tricks as one of the only birds capable of flying upside down, but this raven was more interested in a short flight near the canyon rim before landing with a four-foot spread of his wings. With a flick of a wedge-shaped tail, he hopped over to the garbage can, searching for a tourist handout.

I had seen the souvenirs at the visitor center highlighting this prominent canyon bird. But no man-made rendition did justice to the gleam of black feathers in the flickering sunlight as he pounced on a paper bag with his all-black claws.

Finding no food, he gave a low gurgling protest, before launching off the railing. The air currents propelled him again to soaring heights above the canyon.

Dear Jesus, it's so easy to be distracted from the soaring heights by the daily tasks of survival. I don't want to miss today's beauty. Help me choose wisely.
—Lynne Hartke

Digging Deeper: Deuteronomy 30:15–16; John 10:10

Sunday, March 7

OPEN HEART, OPEN HOME
The Family Room

"You are welcome at my house," the old man said. "Let me supply whatever you need. Only don't spend the night in the square." —Judges 19:20 (NIV)

Sue carried the paper sack holding the few clothes, medications, and toiletries I'd tossed inside into her family room. "I knew you'd be too weak to climb the stairs to the guest room," she said, "so I've set up a makeshift bed on the sofa for now."

For now, I marveled. *She's in this with me for the long haul.*

I was shivering from the cold when I entered the cozy space warmed by the logs crackling in the fireplace. Still, my body jerked, crying for more of the prescribed pain medication that had been taken away. Silently, I mouthed the word *Jesus,* pleading for Him to be with me in this new place where my body aches were now ten times worse than with a bad case of the flu.

As Sue tucked a vintage patchwork quilt around me and propped a tapestry pillow under my head, every dearly chosen object became a welcome mat.

But I was so terrified, embarrassed, and ashamed; I couldn't make eye contact with the caretaker of my comfort. Undeterred, Sue parked a chair at the end of the sofa and began massaging my jerking legs, willing them to be still so I could at long last get some rest.

As my body succumbed to the healing power of physical touch and caring, my eyes took in the buttery yellow walls that now seemed to wrap their arms around me. This wasn't a mere room; it was a sanctuary. I had more amenities than anyone could dream of. Most of all, I was safe.

T. S. Eliot was right: the hospitality of home—it's where we start from.

Dear Jesus, in the hands of this earth angel, I have never felt so cared for. How can I thank You?
—Roberta Messner

Digging Deeper: Matthew 25:40; Romans 12:13

Monday, March 8

Instead of worrying, pray. Let petitions and praises shape your worries into prayers, letting God know your concerns. Before you know it, a sense of God's wholeness, everything coming together for good, will come and settle you down.
—Philippians 4:6–7 (MSG)

I recently read the account of the disciples distressed over the atmospheric blast buffeting their boat. They woke Jesus, who quickly addressed the raging wind and waves: "Quiet! Settle down!" (Mark 4:39 MSG). The storm stopped.

This translation of Jesus's words caught my attention. "Settle down." I first heard the phrase from my mom, admonishing us young siblings when too much unfocused energy spun through the house.

Last week I noted a basketball coach advising his scrambling high- school team: "Settle down."

On Saturday—when attending an anxious neighbor girl at a medical lab appointment—I resolutely instructed: "Settle down."

"Settle down," I whispered this morning, talking to myself—claiming God's power—while behind the wheel and approaching an intimidating elevated highway I try to avoid. But today's demanding schedule limited my options, so there I was, driving with white knuckles and clenched jaw. As I repeated the phrase, its message engulfed me with grace. I could envision angels flanking my front bumpers, steadying the car, calming my overstimulated nerves, guiding my way.

Lord, I look to You. Please settle my anxious spirit.
—Evelyn Bence

Digging Deeper: Matthew 8:23–27; Mark 4:35–41

Tuesday, March 9

For I satisfy the weary ones....
—Jeremiah 31:25 (NASB)

Even though my generation of Americans usually work fewer hours per day than the generations that preceded us, fatigue remains a major health issue in America. As a college professor, I often notice that my students are sleep-deprived. I, too, am a night owl and resist going to bed before midnight. The next morning I often wonder why I am tired. Most of us need more nourishing sleep than we are getting.

One of my best friends is my old recliner chair in my home study. Secluded on the second floor,

I often plop down in this worn chair with book in hand, soft music playing, and within minutes am fast asleep. An hour later, I usually wake refreshed and ready to grade papers. It is amazing what a good nap or siesta does for me!

Yesterday as I sat in my recliner, I opened my Bible to the prophecy of Jeremiah. As I read the story of a tired and disheartened prophet, I heard the old sage reflect, "For I [your God] satisfy the weary ones and refresh everyone who languishes. At this I awoke and looked, and my sleep was pleasant to me" (Jeremiah 31:25–26 NASB).

Sometimes we need to lie back with Jeremiah and rest in the Lord. It is all right if your prayers and meditation usher you into a deep state of rest, reflection, or sleep. God is one who refreshes our souls with His presence and brings strength to the weary.

Father, thank You for the gift of a gentle nap, a quiet reflection, a quiet time with You. Amen.
—Scott Walker

Digging Deeper: Psalm 23; Matthew 11:28–30

Wednesday, March 10

BECOMING JUST ME AGAIN: Procession of People

Remain faithful even when facing death and I will give you the crown of life—an unending, glorious future. —Revelation 2:10 (TLB)

The week before Jack died I was exhausted and feeling more inadequate by the minute. He'd been under hospice care at home for over a week, and even though I bombarded the hospice nurses with phone calls about how to do this and that, I was over my head. Jack's six wonderful children helped out in the evenings, but I was alone with him all night and most of the day.

When the visiting nurse taught me the four-step process to administer morphine to my husband, my blood pressure shot up high enough that I had to start taking blood pressure medicine for the first time ever.

Then on Sunday, one week before he died, Jack had thirteen visitors and an anointing of the sick by two monsignors. Two neighbors, Al and Skip, brought Jack his favorite drink and the three friends shared laughs, memories, and stories about past golf games. Because it was a weekend, three of Jack's children were there helping throughout the day. Two of his high-school-age granddaughters came and made him smile. His twin brother, Bud, and Bud's wife, Kathy, shared family happenings and sat quietly with him while I took a short nap.

The procession of people visiting my husband calmed me down and helped me see that I had more resources than I ever imagined. By the next weekend the hospice nurses were there twenty-four hours a day. When one of them suggested we say prayers aloud over Jack, four of us said the Our Father and the Hail Mary. The last line of the Hail Mary prayer is "Holy Mary, Mother of God, pray for us sinners now, and at the hour of our death. Amen." At that very moment Jack took his last breath.

> **Lord, thank You for all those who step in when I can't do it alone. Now let me be the one to reach out to others.** —Patricia Lorenz

Digging Deeper: Isaiah 57:1–2; Hebrews 2:14–18

Thursday, March 11

When the Lord heard your complaining, he became very angry.... —Deuteronomy 1:34 (NLT)

"You've got to be kidding me," I mumbled under my breath as I stood in line at the grocery store. At the best of times, I'm not a patient person. And on this day, even less so. I was late to meet friends, and Wayne was waiting in the car for me. The store was busy, so I chose the shortest line. I quickly discovered why no one else had chosen this line. The woman in front of me looked like she was feeding the Third Infantry. After all her groceries had been scanned, she opened her huge purse and started digging out coupons. I groaned in frustration. Could this get any worse? It did. After the coupons had all been scanned, she dug through her massive purse a second time and pulled out her checkbook. Who writes checks these days? Frozen with frustration and impatience, I tapped my foot and clenched my jaw.

That's when it hit me. For years I've been striving to live a life of gratitude. Yet I found it far too easy to grumble, to moan and groan about the injustices placed upon me. It was as if I needed to balance my attitude of gratitude with something about which to complain. Like the Israelites Moses led through the desert, I looked for reasons to be discontent. Immediately, I paused, drew in a deep breath, and released my frustration and whispered a prayer, asking God to forgive my attitude.

As I stepped forward and placed my few items before the cashier, she smiled at me and said, "Thank you for your patience."

Lord, when I think of all the ways You have blessed me, I am overwhelmed. Help me to keep my focus on You and not on the frustrations of life.
—Debbie Macomber

Digging Deeper: James 1:2–3

Friday, March 12

The Lord is near to all who call on him, to all who call on him in truth. —Psalm 145:18 (NIV)

My youngest two boys host a magic show. They wear hats and capes from the costume trunk. A blanket curtain stretches across the arched doorway. Grandparents and the brothers are here. Lonny and I sit close and nibble popcorn our sons sold for twenty-five cents.

"Now a coin will appear in this bag," ten-year-old Isaiah says. He pokes his hand into an empty velvet pouch.

Twelve-year-old Gabriel waves a wand.

There's magic mumble and a coin in the bag!

We clap like mad and the boys bow. Ask and receive. Goodness flows from the wand. I think about this as the magicians prepare the next trick.

I used to look at prayer this way.

Back then, my needs were simple and the turnaround was fast. It seemed a whispered prayer brought a prompt response. A desirable outcome. An answer would appear like a toy rabbit in the bottom of a hat.

Then life got tougher.

We worked through infertility. Miscarriage. Health issues and the heartbreak of a broken child. Our prayers became pleas, and the answers weren't wave-of-a-wand swift. Sometimes the answer looked different than we wanted it to. Sometimes the answer was "no." Often the answer was "wait." But I learned that prayer is so much more than an immediate solution. It's hearing the Lord speak through His Word. Or it's strength surging from the Spirit when our own is gone. Or the comfort of His presence when we cry *Abba Father* and know, despite our circumstance, that we're safe and secure. Suddenly, a worn deck of cards is fanned near my face. "Pick a card, any card," Gabriel says. I do.

A magician works his magic, but I know a sweeter thing.

Thank You, Lord, for Your intimate care. Amen.
—Shawnelle Eliasen

Digging Deeper: Job 22:27; Psalm 17:6

Saturday, March 13

But whoever lives by the truth comes into the light, so that it may be seen plainly that what they have done has been done in the sight of God.
—John 3:21 (NIV)

I generally think of prayer as something I do with my eyes closed. That's how I do it at home or sitting on the subway on my way to work. But recently I was at a museum, the Pennsylvania Academy of the Fine Arts in Philadelphia, and in one skylighted room with magnificent art on the walls, my eyes lingered over an old favorite, *Nicodemus* by the American artist Henry Ossawa Tanner.

Here was Nicodemus the Pharisee meeting with Jesus at night—for fear of being seen with Jesus in broad daylight. I thought of how fear can get in the way of faith. Maybe darkness can be a blessing at times, giving me the chance to go where my daylight self would rather not.

In the painting Jesus is infused with light. Some of it comes up the stairway to the rooftop where He and Nicodemus are sitting. Some of it comes from Jesus's own luminous presence. The bearded Nicodemus leans forward and I could imagine his bewilderment when Jesus tells him,

"Unless someone is born anew, it's not possible to see God's kingdom."

Later in the Gospel of John it is Nicodemus who defends Jesus against the Pharisees and then brings seventy-five pounds of myrrh and aloe to Jesus's burial site. That nighttime visit changed him. I could imagine it all happening from the picture I was seeing.

I got up from the bench, taking the images of the painting with me. It had spoken to my mind's eye and I hadn't closed my own eyes at all.

God, I bask in Your love and light so that I might spread it and bring more love and light into this world. —Rick Hamlin

Digging Deeper: 2 Corinthians 5:17; 1 Peter 1:23

Sunday, March 14

Because you relied on the king of Aram and not on the Lord your God... You have done a foolish thing, and from now on you will be at war. —2 Chronicles 16:7, 9 (NIV)

Soon to celebrate my golden anniversary in Hawaii, I was dancing inside my own four walls. I'd been praying about an arthritic kneecap, and though it was the doctor who'd injected my knee, it was the Great Physician who had answered my prayer. Today my knee felt like a thirtysomething's, so I strutted in front of my husband as we laughed like newlyweds. But how long would it last?

As I'd too often done, I began nitpicking the good results, allowing sour projections to blunt my blessing and turn my praise into withering doubts. Like King Asa in 2 Chronicles who allowed negative anticipation to cause him to forget his strong Deliverer and turn to a secular leader for security, would I dismiss my God-orchestrated victory in favor of the old next-shoe-to-drop trick?

A recent Bible study, which referenced Emily P. Freeman's phrase found in *The Next Right Thing*, came to mind, its emphasis on choosing "the next *right* thing." Initially, King Asa did "what was good and right in the eyes of the Lord." Yet when confronted with a hard challenge, he doubted, seeking help from a secular king and causing God's seer to declare, "From now on you will be at war." Would I, too, insult my Savior by forgetting His perfect record of faithfulness and spiraling down into the next worry? No. My heart would stubbornly praise my God.

I thought of the Lord's "new mercies" I receive each morning. Either I could fight to keep them front and center, or, like Asa, I could set myself up for the perpetual "war" of fear and doubt. Not today. This day, I would anticipate the next *good* thing.

Lord, help me to always look forward to Your goodness. —Jacqueline F. Wheelock

Digging Deeper: Psalm 27:13; Jeremiah 32:40–41

Monday, March 15

OPEN HEART, OPEN HOME: The Kitchen
Give me a sign of your goodness, that my enemies may see it and be put to shame, for you, Lord, have helped me and comforted me. —Psalm 86:17 (NIV)

I woke to the smell and sound of coffee brewing in the nearby kitchen. For the first time in days, the thought of drinking a cup of it appealed to me. "Is that you stirring?" Sue called out. "Bryan and I are getting ready for some breakfast. Come join us."

I smoothed the jeans and sweater I'd slept in and headed to their heart of the home. Bryan offered his chair, which he insisted was the best seat in the house. Then as Sue handed me a fragrant mug of coffee in a lovely floral stoneware mug, he added, "I'm so glad you came to *our* place, Roberta."

Because Bryan experienced short-term memory loss from Alzheimer's, he repeated those words seven times. Each offering of hospitality was sweeter than before. Especially when he added, "You can have my recliner anytime you like." No one could have gotten more beautiful words in one sentence.

I glanced around the table and noticed we were all enjoying coffee from charming yet mismatched cups. No grand gestures or pretense here. Just the simple sharing of what they had.

When my stomach growled, Sue asked if I might like a piece of raisin toast. "We always have it with butter and apricot fruit spread." So that's what I had, too. Never had I tasted anything finer.

Food served up around a worn-and-wonderful, blue-and-white porcelain-topped table. Food for the family of God. A symbol of His perfectly imperfect goodness to me in the tender mercies of this household.

I was fast losing heart, Lord, but then I found Your goodness in this land of the living.
—Roberta Messner

Digging Deeper: 1 Chronicles 16:34; Psalm 145:9; James 1:17

Tuesday, March 16

Let my teaching fall like rain and my words descend like dew, like showers on new grass, like abundant rain on tender plants. —Deuteronomy 32:2 (NIV)

I turned on the windshield wipers, then eased my minivan slowly down our concrete driveway. As I searched right, left, and behind for walkers, joggers, or small children, I was startled at my clear view through the gray drizzle. It looked as if each raindrop was a lens.

That's strange, I thought, *the exact opposite of that bright sunny day!*

That had been a dazzling summer noon. I'd squinted through my sunglasses at the light bouncing painfully off every shiny surface. I'd searched the glare for dogs or people, anything moving. Reassured, I slowly backed into the street. I slammed on the brakes when I felt a bump. Heart hammering, I opened my car door to look behind me. There was a tan car parked opposite my driveway!

I got out to examine both cars. I found no scratches on my bumper, but a small dent in the sedan's rear door. Resolutely, I rang my neighbor's doorbell. I called my insurance company and confessed again.

I thanked God no one was hurt. But how had I missed an entire car? Maybe it was all that light.

I thought of other sunny days—new babies, exciting vacations, satisfying work, dear friends. And the rainy days, lately, with my husband Dave's cancer diagnosis.

Many days Dave and I are overwhelmed by his pain, or struggling to decipher his latest test, or worried about an oncology appointment. But once the predicament passes, Dave declares, "I am overwhelmed by the support of so many loved ones!" Our relatives, friends, and coworkers are wonderful blessings we see clearly and appreciate.

Maybe raindrops do sharpen the view.

Thank You, Lord, for blessings hidden in difficult days. —Leanne Jackson

Digging Deeper: Exodus 18:8; Romans 8:35

St. Patrick's Day, Wednesday, March 17

Each one should test their own actions. Then they can take pride in themselves alone, without comparing themselves to someone else, for each one should carry their own load. —Galatians 6:4–5 (NIV)

Olivia came home on St. Patrick's Day from school gushing about how her friend had a leprechaun visit their house. "He made a big mess in glitter and even"—she dropped her voice to a whisper—"peed green in the potty and didn't flush."

Part of me loved it. What imagination! The other part of me groaned inside. Would she be sad that no leprechaun made a mess in our kitchen?

Every month, it's something new to navigate. Do I lean into Santa and *The Elf on the Shelf*, or pull back to keep the simple glory of the tree and the story of Jesus's birth? Do the tooth fairy and Easter bunny bring toys and more, or a single gold coin and a basket with candy?

I used to worry about how these choices would impact my children, but then I realized that I was doing the very thing I remind them not to do: comparing myself to others.

I can't know what's going on at someone else's house. Maybe it was a regular week with an awesome mom, or maybe it was a week when that mom needed a win. We often talk about how Jesus called us to love each other, not to judge or compare our actions with others, and motherhood has been a constant reminder to me that I need that lesson as much as my kids do.

I may never be the mom whose tooth fairy leaves handwritten notes, or maybe one day I will, but either way, I can choose my own path and traditions for my kids as well as celebrate the mom next to me who is navigating her own path as well.

Jesus, help me remember that the only standard for my life is You. —Ashley Kappel

Digging Deeper: Proverbs 14:30; 1 Thessalonians 4:11–12; James 3:16

Thursday, March 18

We take captive every thought to make it obedient to Christ. —2 Corinthians 10:5 (NIV)

I carefully lowered my waterproof boot into the tray of disinfectant. Tightly grasping a handrail (undoubtedly designed with aging adventurers like me in mind), I did a one-footed decontamination dance. Briskly moving my foot up and down between rough bristled brushes, I attempted to eradicate any hitchhiking debris I might have inadvertently picked up while exploring the frozen shoreline. Who knew my cute, leaf-print boots could harbor such potential danger? I certainly didn't. At least, not until I traveled to Svalbard, a remote archipelago in Arctic Norway.

A seed, a trace of soil, a stray insect, an unseen microorganism transferred from one shore to another . . . that's all it would take for an invasive species to invade a fragile ecosystem. I certainly didn't want to be the source of an Arctic Armageddon! So I scrubbed my boots diligently every time I left the ship and as soon as I stepped back on board.

It wasn't lost on me that while I was conscientious about protecting one of God's miraculously crafted ecosystems, I wasn't nearly as diligent about safeguarding the easily compromised territory of my own mind and heart. How often have I found myself caught up in a gossip fest? Watched a television program where the level of sex or violence made me squirm with discomfort? Rationalized exaggeration instead of calling it out for the lie it is?

One wayward "seed" has the potential to compromise the spiritual landscape of my life. If I truly want my heart to reflect God's own—and I do—I need to seek out God's best and turn my back on anything less.

Dear Lord, give me the strength, courage, and resolve I need to turn away from anything that may prevent me from becoming the person You created me to be.
—Vicki Kuyper

Digging Deeper: Romans 12:1–2; Ephesians 4:22–24; Philippians 4:8

Friday, March 19

Take the stumbling block out of the way of My people. —Isaiah 57:14 (NKJV)

The sunrise is sweet, as my wife, Sharon, and I roll north on the freeway, listening to "oldies" on the radio. Traffic is very light at this early hour.

As I come over a rise, I see something scattered across the road ahead. I stand on the brakes and pull off on the berm to check it out. The road is littered with construction debris that has fallen from a truck: blocks of wood, wallboard, nails, sheet metal, broken glass, bricks.

I bound out of the car.

"Danny!" my wife shrieks. "What are you doing?"

"Got to clean this up before someone gets hurt!"

While Sharon watches for traffic, I dash back and forth, heaving trash off to the side of the road. At last the road is clear.

Sweaty, exhausted, I climb back into the car just in time for a row of cars that comes whizzing by, unaware of the danger they were in.

As I pull back onto the road, I am thinking of all the people who have cleared obstacles for me on the road of life. People like my parents, who guided me through the tumultuous teenage years, plus schoolteachers and youth leaders who taught me to recognize dangers ahead.

The words of John Newton come to mind: "Through many dangers, toils, and snares, I have already come; 'Tis grace that brought me safe thus far, and grace will lead me home."*

The world is a dangerous place, and so I pray:

Thank You, Lord, for protecting me on the highways of life; show me how I can clear the road for younger lives who come after me. —Daniel Schantz

Digging Deeper: John 11:9; 1 Corinthians 8:9

* "Amazing Grace," by John Newton, third stanza

Perhaps the Lord will see (the tears of) my eye, and the Lord will return to me good instead of his curse on this day. —2 Samuel 16:12 (CHABAD)

My friend Dawn came at once when I told her the vet was on her way to put my greyhound, Anjin, down. Anjin had been failing for the past month, but as long as she was not in pain, I refused to consider euthanasia. But that morning she was telling me the time had come.

I wish I could have gotten another greyhound, but Anjin's illness had shown me I could not lift an eighty-pound dog. I was putting Anjin's toys back in the toy basket when Dawn said, "I know a Silken Windhound that needs to be rehomed."

Silkens are like half-size greyhounds with longer hair and the same couch potato personality. I said yes without asking any questions.

Dawn brought her over the next day. Her call name was Halle, and she was seven years old, a former champion who had had a bad experience. I resolved that what was going to happen to her now was pampering and safety.

It took a couple of weeks for her to trust me enough to sleep pressed up against my shoulder. After that, Halle quickly understood that the yard was hers now, and she lay pressed against the house or the back door on the days when the sun came out. She and the cat soon developed a respectful detente.

In three months she became territorial, barking at strangers and guarding the space, the way Anjin had done. I still missed Anjin, but Halle was a gift, just as Dawn had known she would be. I was infinitely grateful for both of them.

You know me so well, God of All Creatures, and You made sure I got the right dog—and the right friend.
—Rhoda Blecker

Digging Deeper: Psalm 55:18; Proverbs 17:17

Sunday, March 21

On that day I will gather you together and bring you home again. —Zephaniah 3:20 (NLT)

I don't believe in coincidences.

Scattered over the map, my husband, David, and his four siblings rarely get together. So when his brother, who lives in France, planned a trip to Colorado several months in advance, all of them, save one, made plans to come as well. The one who couldn't plan to attend was their sister Pat, who lived in Texas and who, for seven years, had been battling early-onset Alzheimer's.

The big reunion day finally arrived. The remaining four siblings were together at lunch when a phone call from Pat's husband came in. Pat had passed away.

It had been sixteen years since David and his brothers and sisters had been together. Yet, on the day of their sister's passing, there they were with each other, to comfort, to mourn, to reminisce. That evening at dinner, we all toasted Pat and said a grateful prayer to our gracious, all-knowing God.

Father God, You alone know all things—what was, what is, and what is to be. Thank You that even in the most difficult times, we can depend upon Your great compassion, love, and grace.
—Kim Taylor Henry

Digging Deeper: Lamentations 3:22; Psalm 36:5

Monday, March 22

STRUGGLING TO PRAY: Sometimes I Just Can't Pray

We do not know what we ought to pray for, but the Spirit himself intercedes for us through wordless groans. —Romans 8:26 (NIV)

My husband, Kris, had a heart attack this spring. Shortly after we went to the emergency room, they wheeled him off for surgery.

You might guess I was in constant prayer from that moment onward, but I'm ashamed to say I wasn't. I couldn't pray at all.

Our church pastor came at six the morning of the surgery. Kris was being prepped, and I was trying to keep out of the way of technicians shaving his chest and nurses in green masks fiddling with his IVs. We three held hands, and Pastor Mike prayed. I said amen at the end, but only out of politeness. With so much happening, I was too agitated to actually pray.

What's wrong with me? I wondered after they wheeled Kris away. I chatted with Mike and my boss for hours in the waiting room. A friend took me out to dinner and I recounted everything that had happened. But I couldn't utter or even think forth a word to the One I depended on for Kris's recovery, my salvation, everything.

After that first day, whenever I thought of praying, I fell asleep. A lifelong bad sleeper, I've never slept so deeply, immediately, or well as at Kris's bedside: through meals, nurses replacing IV bags and taking blood, doctors visiting, machines beeping.

You're worse than those disciples at Gethsemane, I accused myself: *your flesh weak, your spirit nonexistent.*

But the rest I was getting—so restorative in those hard days of worry!—felt so blessed. And God promises rest to those who love him. Evidently, despite my inability to pray, God attended to not only Kris but also me, restoring me with sleep.

Thank You, Father, for accepting even my failed prayers. —Patty Kirk

Digging Deeper: Matthew 11:25–30

Tuesday, March 23

OPEN HEART, OPEN HOME
The Bathroom
The greatest among you will be your servant.
—Matthew 23:11 (NIV)

Withdrawal from medically prescribed opioids proved to be a journey with many detours: physical, emotional, and spiritual. Two days later, I was once again riding the bicycle to nowhere, crazier than before, like a hamster on a never-ending wheel. *Where in the world* are *you, God?* I asked. *I'm going to end up in the loony bin.*

I did everything I could to shut out the world. Yet overwhelming anxiety took over my body, mind, and heart. My spirit became a big black hole as a voice inside my head taunted, *You're going to be like this forever, Roberta.*

I began to eat again, but my digestive system didn't cooperate. Humiliated, I made a mess of the black-and-white tile floor in Sue's adorable bathroom. When I asked for a bucket and some Mr. Clean and Lysol, though, she insisted I was too weak to clean it up. "Let me take care of it," she insisted. "You just try to get some rest, honey." As a nurse, I never flinched about doing the messy work, yet I found it so hard to let someone do it for me now.

Before I came to this wonderful home, I had begun to lose faith in people. I'd served my hometown as a registered nurse for over four decades, but the care I'd tried to extend didn't seem to be there for me. That was before my eighty-three-year-old friend with her arthritic knees welcomed me into her home and cleaned that bathroom. I saw that true, God-centered hospitality isn't just fragrant candles and fluffy towels. Sometimes it's the gritty details of life, like mopping a floor for a weary friend, offered up as if to Jesus Himself.

Hospitality is made of small moments in Your service,
Lord. Help me to one day pass it along to others.
—Roberta Messner

Digging Deeper: Mark 10:45; John 12:26;
Galatians 5:13; Hebrews 6:10

Wednesday, March 24

**Then the King will say to those on his right,
"Come, you who are blessed by my Father, inherit
the kingdom prepared for you from the foundation
of the world." —Matthew 25:34 (ESV)**

My mom loves nothing better than to give gifts to
my daughters. Mother grew up one of nine children
in rural Mississippi, and money was tight. But as
a lifelong hard worker who's a whiz with money,
she now likes to spoil her granddaughters. She can't
understand why it makes them uncomfortable.

But I can. I remember my Big Daddy giving me a
dollar now and then. I always felt bad taking it. I didn't
understand that it made him happy to treat me. All I
knew was that I loved Big Daddy with all my heart,
and I never wanted him to think it was because of the
dollar he pulled from his pocket. Although he died
more than thirty years ago, I still treasure the memories
of sitting on the porch with him, the smell of his pipe
tobacco, the feel of my cheek against his soft shirt.

Sometimes when I think of all that my heavenly
Father has given me, I feel the same pang of
conscience I felt when Big Daddy gave me a dollar.

I don't want to be the person Satan accused Job of being—faithful only because there's a hedge around me. When we sing "Mansions over the Hilltop" during worship, I squirm, knowing that God has already given me more than I deserve. I don't want to go to heaven because there's a mansion there... I want to go so that I can feel the warm embrace of my Lord.

Lord, You see my heart. Please know that I love You for who You are and not just the things You give me. I just want to be wherever You are. —Ginger Rue

Digging Deeper: John 14:2; Revelation 21:4; Hebrews 13:5

Thursday, March 25

It is more blessed to give than to receive.
—Acts 20:35 (NIV)

This year I will celebrate my twenty-fifth year in the investment business. That means I have been helping people with financial decisions longer than half of my life.

The scope of those decisions runs from putting aside money for a child's education to planning for retirement and deciding how to pass an estate from one generation to the next.

Serious business for sure, for each client whom I'm privileged to serve, as I measure a range of considerations and put a lot of careful thought into each individual's needs.

There's an extra dimension in these meetings that might surprise those who don't know me well. Like a whisper in my ear as I sit across from those who are planning how to spend their money, I hear my grandmother Bebe remind me, "Don't ever forget, Brock, you can never outgive the Lord." That's when I bring up the possibility of philanthropy, which in its simplest form is sharing what one has with others.

I have come to believe that in the investment business, this is the most important module of all. For those who are blessed enough to afford it, properly giving money away can be as rewarding as anything else in their lives. There are numerous studies that attest to this truth. There are researchers who have spent great sums of money reaching this same conclusion.

It doesn't surprise me that Bebe's words strike true as a guide to even the most important analyst. That's why her few simple words will always be the bedrock of any truly successful investment portfolio that I create.

Father, I constantly see the rewards that come to those who give freely. Thank You for my grandmother who lived this lesson and passed it on. —Brock Kidd

Digging Deeper: Ecclesiastes 11:1; Matthew 10:8

Friday, March 26

My counsel for you is simple and straightforward: Just go ahead with what you've been given.
—Colossians 2:6 (MSG)

Several years ago in spring, when my daughter was three, she and I were walking down the sidewalk near our house. She paused to pick a dandelion, knowing that I like dandelions. I'm one of those people who tells their kids that dandelions are flowers, not weeds. She handed it to me with what seemed like aplomb.

I took the dandelion from her with a big smile on my face. "Thank you!" I said. But I guess my reaction was a bit over-the-top with praise and excitement—a dad trying to encourage his little one—because she then looked at me and said quite drily, "It isn't a present. It's just a flower."

At all of three, she'd already learned something important that I, now at fifty-three, often forget. Praise—pats on the back—doesn't connect us as much as walking and sharing do. I fall into this with God, imagining that God is liking what I'm up to. I do what I think God will "like." I imagine God approving my little deeds. But it's the walking and sharing—living what I've been given—that matter.

May I live today what I've been given.
—Jon M. Sweeney
Digging Deeper: Psalm 119:104–105

Saturday, March 27

For Christ also suffered once for sins, the righteous for the unrighteous, to bring you to God. —1 Peter 3:18 (NIV)

I stepped gingerly onto the wooded path between our cabin and the neighboring farm, testing the snow. Would it still hold me? In one hand, I carried a bucketful of kitchen scraps for the farm's chickens. In the other arm, I balanced a stack of borrowed books I was returning and a dozen empty egg cartons. A little unwieldy but it should be fine, I thought. It was only a short walk.

And it was fine. For the first step. But then I took the second. I'd no sooner thought, *Snow's soft* than my left foot and half my leg disappeared down into the snow. The tower of egg cartons and books went tumbling. I tried to gain purchase with my right foot so I could heave myself back up. But when I shifted my weight, that leg post-holed down, too. "Ugh!" I yelled to the trees. I would've stamped my foot in frustration if both hadn't been encased by snow. This half-mile walk was going to take all morning! What I wouldn't give for the hard-packed snow we'd traversed on this trail all winter.

Wait. What was I thinking? Had I seriously just wished away the approach of spring? Just because I didn't want to deal with the temporary difficulties the warming temperatures brought? If it stayed frozen, this walk would be easier than it was now, for sure. But it would also mean spring wouldn't come, with all its beautiful blessings. Flowers. New leaves. Warmth. And an entirely snow-free walking path.

How often, I wondered, did I miss out on life's gifts simply because I wished away the discomfort that preceded them?

I know You care more about my character than You do my comfort, Lord. Help that be my priority too.
—Erin Janoso

Digging Deeper: Romans 5:3; James 1:2–3

Palm Sunday, March 28

JOY COMES IN THE MORNING
Experiencing His Forgiveness

Those who went ahead and those who followed were shouting, "Hosanna! Blessed is the one who comes in the Name of the Lord!" —Mark 11:9 (NRSV)

I struggle with forgiveness. Not only with forgiving others, especially those close to me, for hurting me, but also with feeling God's forgiveness. I *believe* He forgives me, but I can't always let myself *feel* His forgiveness.

This Lent I decided to work on forgiveness. I prayed daily for someone I needed to forgive. Some days, I confess, especially if the hurt was fresh, I prayed sincerely for the person but without much confidence in my ability to completely forgive. Now reviewing my prayer list at the end of Lent on Palm Sunday, I face a stark realization. Everyone I tried to forgive probably felt that I'd hurt them as much as I felt they'd hurt me! If asked, they might just say that I needed their forgiveness.

It wasn't that way with Jesus. When He entered Jerusalem on that first Palm Sunday, almost everyone in that adoring crowd would soon need His forgiveness. Peter, who gleefully helped Him onto the donkey, would deny Him three times. Judas, part of the parade, would betray Him. The apostles, basking in His glory, would abandon Him. The crowds would ignore Him, some even screaming for His crucifixion.

But unlike me, Jesus had done nothing to hurt those who would need His forgiveness. Quite the opposite: He'd done everything to save them, us. Yet He rode on, greeting them, knowing they'd turn on Him, knowing we'd continue to sin against each other and Him, already forgiving, always forgiving.

Jesus, when forgiveness is hard, let me remember what it cost You to forgive me, so that I could live to forgive others. —Marci Alborghetti

Digging Deeper: Matthew 21:4–17; Luke 7:36–50

Monday, March 29

When my anxious thoughts multiply within me, Your consolations delight my soul.
—Psalm 94:19 (NASB)

It was the simplest epiphany.

A thick icicle hung from the porch eave above the front steps. I knocked it down so it wouldn't fall on anyone in the unpredictable March thaw. A waft of whimsy prompted me to bring it in and prop it on the kitchen windowsill. I posted a photo on social media asking, "How long can I keep this crystal lady on my nature shelf?"

A friend replied, "It's gonna make a natural lake for your shelf."

An idea was born. I set it in a bread pan to melt. How much water was really in that icicle? I poured the liquid in a glass measuring cup.

A second photo showing the measuring cup said, "And if the recipe calls for one medium icicle you know that's ¾ cup!"

I was surprised by how small the puddle was for the size of the icicle. I learned water expands by 9 percent when frozen. No wonder the icicle seemed more than it was.

That's when my epiphany occurred. Problems can seem threatening, like icicles spiking from the eaves. Anxiety expanding them. I'd recently had some heart arrhythmia and I understood how worry could increase a problem.

Jesus called those who are "heavy laden" to come to Him for rest (Matthew 11:28). My icicle experiment showed me if I will bring my weighted burdens "inside" to the warmth and love of God's care, what seems overwhelming can be reduced to a manageable measure.

Lord, keep reminding me of the icicle lesson—how problems lessen when I place them with You.
—Carol Knapp

Tuesday, March 30

OPEN HEART, OPEN HOME
The Guest Room
**The Lord is my shepherd, I lack nothing.
—Psalm 23:1 (NIV)**

On the ninth night of my hospitable care at Sue's home, I retreated once again to the cozy guest room at the top of the stairs. I snuggled under the time-loved double wedding ring quilt and basked in the details of the bed-and-breakfast-worthy quarters. By the light of the *Gone with the Wind* lamp, I found dearly familiar passages in the Bible on the bedside table. My surroundings were like something from a dream, a portrait of peace. I needed nothing else.

Finally, I drifted off to sleep. The next morning before the sun was even up, I heard a magnificent arpeggio on the downstairs piano and Sue singing the words in her rich alto to the nineteenth-century Easter hymn "He Arose." Each word was a prayer I knew was reaching heaven for me.

> *Up from the grave he arose;*
> *with a mighty triumph o'er his foes;*
> *he arose a victor from the dark domain,*
> *and he lives forever with his saints to reign.*

He arose! He arose!
Hallelujah! Christ arose!

In the blackness of my own opiate-withdrawal world, I'd forgotten that Easter was coming. I repeated the hope-filled words to that classic song in my heart. Soon, I heard a weak, crackling sound. It was me! I was singing, too. A song from the very depths of my soul.

Oh yes, Jesus ... it's Eastertime at last. Because of You and the gracious hospitality of these friends, I lack nothing. I am going to make it.
—Roberta Messner

Digging Deeper: Matthew 6:26; 11:28;
Philippians 4:19

Wednesday, March 31

The earth is the Lord's and all it contains.
—Psalm 24:1 (NASB)

Nature and I share a friendship going way back. Back to lying in my sleeping bag in a tent as a child, listening to the wind whoosh in the pines.

Romans 1:20 speaks of God making Himself known "since the creation of the world ... through what has been made." Nature is God's conversation with me.

A lone wild rose growing in a secluded woodland glade—blooming so lovely with no one to see—once spoke these words, *Be that hidden person of the heart with... a gentle and quiet spirit, which is precious in the sight of God* (1 Peter 3:4). I began calling wild roses "hidden hearts of the forest."

The gurgling creek near our house with its little waterfalls spilling over the rocks carries Jesus's promise, "He who believes in Me... 'From his innermost being will flow rivers of living water'" (John 7:38 NASB).

A maple leaf I picked up because it was marred by holes—at a time when my life had holes of its own—held a message of hope. As I twirled it against the sky, a glimmer of sun shone through its torn places. I heard, *These aren't holes—they are windows to something new.*

It seems God often sends a timely message through His natural world. What joy one night—as I considered an idea I'd read about "naming" God in a personal way—to suddenly see a meteor flash across the sky. And with it the instant thought, *God of my Surprise.*

The language of His creation is one God has set before us for all to know.

Lord, I treasure Your "God-speak" in our intimate nature talks. —Carol Knapp

Digging Deeper: Job 12:7; Isaiah 40:6; John 1:3; Colossians 1:15–17

JOYFUL IN HOPE

1 _____

2 _____

3 _____

4 _____

5 _____

6 _____

7 _____

8 _____

9 _____

10 _____

11 _____

12 _____

13 _____

14 _____

15 _____

16 _____

17 _____

18 _____

19 _____

20 _____

21 _____

22 _____

23 _____

24 _____

25 _____

26 _____

27 _____

28 _____

29 _____

30 _____

31 _____

APRIL

If you abide in me, and my words abide in you, ask whatever you wish, and it will be done for you…As the Father has loved me, so have I loved you. Abide in my love.

—John 15:7, 9 (ESV)

Maundy Thursday, April 1

JOY COMES IN THE MORNING
Come as You Are

He took His place at the table, and the apostles with Him. He said to them, "I have eagerly desired to eat this Passover with you before I suffer." —Luke 22:14–15 (NRSV)

When my uncle Elliot died, he'd been sick for decades, ravaged by colitis and the stress that exacerbated that illness. Still, he was funny, acerbic, and sharp-witted. In basketball terms, he knew how to throw an elbow. The most uncharacteristic thing he did, and now I realize it was for stress reduction, was paint-by-numbers. His most uncharacteristic painting was a depiction of the Last Supper. A lavish, lively, color-drenched masterpiece, it showed the apostles seated, leaning forward, listening intently to Jesus.

It's an image that remains fixed in my mind's eye, as much for the picture as for the painter. My uncle was no churchgoer. He barely made it to weddings and funerals. He avoided crowds, and spent more of his life than we would know in discomfort and pain.

But when he sought comfort, he sought it in that image, that idea, really, of Jesus spending His last moments with His apostles.

That night He washed their feet, established in them the Holy Eucharist, and perhaps most importantly to my uncle, made them into a community. Jesus knew that just as He would soon suffer alone, so would each of them in the coming days and years suffer alone.

My uncle saw what I've come to see in the Last Supper: a place next to Jesus for everyone who at some point suffers alone. There was a community for Uncle Elliot at that table; there is for each of us.

Lord, remind me that I am—that we all are— welcome, anytime, any way, at Your table.
—Marci Alborghetti

Digging Deeper: John 17:6–25; Acts 2:37–47

Good Friday, April 2

JOY COMES IN THE MORNING
Gratitude for His Sacrifice

And about three o'clock Jesus cried with a loud voice, "Eli, Eli, lema sabachthani?" that is, "My God, my God, why have you forsaken me?"
—Matthew 27:46 (NRSV)

Years ago, my husband, Charlie, and I started keeping a gratitude book. Each day we write about one thing for which we are thankful. Sometimes it's inconsequential, like seeing baby swans paddling along behind their parents in the cove across the street. Other days it's important, like a new work contract or vacation. This year, as the Lord has guided us through a number of health and financial challenges, we've decided to start each daily note with Thank You, God, for...

I've noticed that in Charlie's script, "God" often looks like "Dad." It reminds me of how much we expect from our fathers, and how much more we expect from our heavenly Father. Jesus had an expectation of His Father, and even in perfect obedience, the human Son who hung on the cross was briefly and agonizingly disappointed in that expectation.

"My Dad, my Dad, why have you forsaken me?"

Is there a more wrenching moment in the Gospels? Is there any passage in Scripture that more painfully describes the anguish of feeling separated from God, our Father? And yet Jesus felt this terrible rending, not as we do—because of our own sins as adopted children, but because the Father was willing to be separated from His true Son, the Beloved, to save us from spending our lives apart from Him.

Thank You, Father, for sacrificing Your only begotten Son to keep the rest of us from being misbegotten, so that we, too, could call You Dad. —Marci Alborghetti

Digging Deeper: Isaiah 47:18–19; John 10:14–18

Holy Saturday, April 3

JOY COMES IN THE MORNING
Awaiting His Arrival
And so, because it was the Jewish day of Preparation, and the tomb was nearby, they laid Jesus there. Early on the first day of the week, while it was still dark, Mary Magdalene came to the tomb. —John 19:42, 20:1 (NRSV)

I pulled back the curtains on Holy Saturday morning to reveal a gray, misty day.

Perfect!

In my family we are obsessed with weather. We judge the prospect of a holiday by the weather that ushers it in, particularly on Easter weekend when so much of Jesus's passion and Resurrection unfolded outdoors.

My father expects cold rain on Good Friday because that's the most dispiriting weather for him, and he feels the world should be dispirited on the day humankind crucified our Lord. My mother wants a clear, bright Easter Sunday because that's the kind of light that should greet the risen Jesus.

I want Holy Saturday to be bleak, a muted day of mourning. While offering respite from the brutality of Jesus's suffering and death, Holy Saturday is still a day of uncertainty and grief.

I'm always surprised to see people up and about on Holy Saturday, shopping, cooking, gardening. I think of it as the day we should pull the covers over our heads and consider what it is like to be entombed by our sins, as Jesus was. And at sunset on every Holy Saturday, if I had my weather way, there would be a reddening sky in the west to remind us that clearing is about to begin, that in a few short hours, the Son will rise.

Lord, let me meditate on Your great sacrifice as I await the joy that comes in the morning.
—Marci Alborghetti

Easter Sunday, April 4

JOY COMES IN THE MORNING
The Gift of Everlasting Life

Then he opened their minds to understand the
scriptures, and he said to them "Thus it is written,
that the Messiah is to suffer and to rise from the
dead on the third day, and that repentance and
forgiveness of sins is to be proclaimed in his name
to all nations, beginning from Jerusalem."
—Luke 24:45–47 (NRSV)

The baby was tiny, dressed in white lace, a little
headband with a small silk flower around her bald
head. She didn't make a peep when the baptismal
water was poured on her forehead, and she kept her
eyes focused intently on the pastor who held her
tenderly. After introducing her to the congregation
this Easter morning, he strode over to the large white
cross now festooned in flowers with a victorious
white sash and raised her dramatically over his
head to the cross. Everyone in church gasped for a
moment, and then cheered.

What a triumphant way to celebrate the Lord
walking out of that cave on the first Easter!

And how very appropriate since the first time
Jesus emerged from a cave was as a tiny infant
Himself. His birth cave, a stable in Bethlehem,

was just a few miles south of His tomb cave in Jerusalem. He emerged from that birth cave as a fragile, vulnerable, hunted refugee met by an adoring audience of shepherds. He emerged from his death cave as the Everlasting Good Shepherd. A bright star led kings to that birth cave. He was the Morning Star, King of Kings, when He left that death cave.

We give each other temporal gifts to mark His miraculous birth in the first cave. He strode out of that second cave, our ever-living gift of everlasting Life.

Jesus, Lord, live in me always, so that someday I may rise to You. —Marci Alborghetti

Digging Deeper: Luke 1:68–75; 2:25–35

Easter Monday, April 5

JOY COMES IN THE MORNING
The Rest of the Story

But there are also many other things that Jesus did; if every one of them were written down, I suppose that the world itself could not contain the books that would be written. —John 21:25 (NRSV)

We were watching part 2 of *King of Kings*, the great film of Jesus's life. We'd seen the first half yesterday on Easter and now watched while Jesus, horribly flogged, mocked, and brutalized, carried the cross. We view this movie every year, and it's always hard to witness this part. Charlie paused the movie, turned to me, and said, "I bet it has a happy ending."

I gave him a look, but had to suppress a smile. It was one of those moments between two people who know and love each other that has several meanings. Charlie is ridiculously optimistic, and no matter how bleak a film or television show is, he always predicts a happy ending. Always. We could be watching *Titanic*—we could be *on* the *Titanic*—and he'd assure me that all would end well.

Now he could predict a happy ending to the one seemingly devastating movie he knew actually had one. He was also comforting me, knowing that these scenes always hurt my heart. But most endearingly, he was addressing the little letdown I feel after Easter. I intensely experience Lent's long repentant waiting, Holy Week's triumphs and agonies, Holy Saturday's expectant vigil, and finally Easter's joy. In the days after, I feel a bit lost.

Charlie was reminding me that the happy ending isn't over in one light-filled Son-rise. That's the whole point of Easter: the happy ending *isn't* an ending. It's a beginning, one we can freshly, joyfully experience daily. Because He is *still* risen! He is always risen! Indeed! Alleluia!

Jesus, Rise in my heart, my life every day, every moment. —Marci Alborghetti

Digging Deeper: Acts 1:1–11; 26:8–23

Tuesday, April 6

Jesus said to her, "I am the resurrection and the life. Whoever believes in me, though he die, yet shall he live." —John 11:25 (ESV)

Everything about Easter says "Spring!" The flowers that decorate the church, the cherry blossoms, the azalea buds, the Easter lilies (doesn't that say it all?), the eggs we color, the chicks that hatch, the bunnies we cuddle. Martin Luther once said, "Our Lord has written the promise of the resurrection, not in books alone, but in every leaf in springtime." So it was a bit of a surprise to celebrate Easter in South Africa this year, where it was autumn, not spring.

We were visiting our younger son, Tim, who was spending ten months in a monastery there, working at the school the brothers had started. The setting was beautiful, in the rolling hills outside Grahamstown. If I noticed any blooming flowers they were proteas, not lilies. The climate is mild, not unlike Southern California, but the season was clearly headed toward cooler days, not longer, warmer ones. In the chill before dawn we got up to light the Paschal candle and made our way to the chapel, the rising sun coming in the window just as we all exclaimed, "The Lord is risen... the Lord is risen indeed."

It made me reconsider the images we use as we try to comprehend the message of the Resurrection. It is indeed rebirth but not quite like the rebirth of spring. Inherent in the glories of spring are the cycles of the season. The buds will turn into fruit that we eat before the leaves turn gold and red and fall off and the birds go into hibernation only to return in the spring as the buds come out on the trees again, a cycle that repeats itself again and again. On the other hand, Jesus came out of that tomb never to return.

"Alleluia," we sang in the sunlit chapel with proteas on the altar. "Alleluia." Easter is here forever, for always, never to leave.

Every day of the year is Easter season with You, Lord. Alleluia. —Rick Hamlin

Digging Deeper: Romans 6:5–6; 1 Thessalonians 4:14

Wednesday, April 7

From the lips of children and infants you, Lord, have called forth your praise. —Matthew 21:16 (NIV)

"You know, we don't have to take Logan with us to sunrise service. His dad is here, so he can stay. We'll come back and get him for church," my husband, Chuck, said. "He doesn't pay attention to the service anyway."

True, for the first time in three years, we could leave our nine-year-old grandson behind when we went to Easter sunrise service at the beach. Logan's dad wouldn't be going, so he would be home with Logan.

I shook my head. "No, we're taking him. He might not be with us next year, so we have to take him while we can."

Logan's dad planned to move soon and take Logan with him. After six years of living with us full-time, Logan would be living with his dad. Part of me wanted that to happen. The other part wasn't so sure. His dad wouldn't teach him the same values we did, one of them attending church.

On Easter Sunday, we bundled Logan up for a chilly predawn service and drove twenty minutes to the beach. We set out chairs, and Logan sank into his, covering up with his blanket. The music began, the praise and worship team sang, and the crowd gathered. The sky grew light as the sun peeked over the horizon, warming the worshippers while waves gently kissed the sand. Logan slid out of his chair and played in the sand while the minister delivered the Easter message. Afterward, we packed up and went home to change for our regular church worship.

When Logan came home from school the next day, he said, "I told my teacher what Jesus said when He came out of the grave. 'Ta-da!'"

The minister at the beach had told that story the day before. And Logan was listening.

Thank You, Lord, for the opportunity to share You with our grandchildren. —Marilyn Turk

Digging Deeper: Matthew 18:3, 5; 19:14

Thursday, April 8

Trust in the LORD with all your heart and lean not on your own understanding; in all your ways submit to him, and he will make your paths straight. —Proverbs 3:5–6 (NIV)

It's been raining for weeks. Our yard is too wet to mow. The ground is mushy, the lawn overgrown. My husband can't stand to see it this way—with nothing to do but wait. "Rain, rain, rain," he grumbles.

The first day without rain, even though his feet sink with every step to the garage, he takes out the driver mower. The engine runs for about ten minutes and cuts out. I look out the window and see he's stuck in big muddy ruts down by the catalpa tree. Slipping on my shoes, I go out to help him. He puts it in reverse, and I lean over and push and push until the mower is freed.

As I walk back inside, I think of one of my favorite Dr. Peale sermons about a sign in upstate New York on an old dirt road that read something like Choose Your Rut Carefully. You'll Be in It for the Next 25 Miles.

I look at the window as the engine revs. The rider mower is splattered with a thick layer of mud. Tires spin on the deep, growing groove, but it's no use— he is stuck again. Our kind neighbor drives his four-wheeler over and rescues him.

Out the upstairs window, I see the big muddy ruts trailing through the long grass and say this prayer:

Lord, when I stop forcing what I want and trust Your timing, I avoid life's ruts. —Sabra Ciancanelli

Digging Deeper: Romans 12:1–2

Friday, April 9

GOD, your God, will cross the river ahead of you.
—Deuteronomy 31:5 (MSG)

My second-grade daughter slammed into the back of
a parked car on the side of the road. It happened while
we were riding our bikes home from baseball practice
one afternoon. One moment we were riding and
chatting about what was coming next in the day, and
the next moment she turned her head just for a second
and lost sight of where she was in the lane. *Boom!*

I screamed and jumped off my bike. Fortunately,
it was a quiet backstreet and there were no cars
around. I left my bike wherever it landed, in the
middle of the street, and ran to her. She was in a
heap on the ground, crying.

"Oh, Daddy!" she said. Every parent knows what
it is like to hear those words. You would lift a car off
the ground to help your child at that moment. All I
had to do was quickly see that she had a small scrape
but otherwise looked okay. I helped her to her feet.
Then sat her on my lap, still in the middle of the
quiet street.

"Why?" she said, still a bit stunned. "You turned
your head for a moment, honey. It's okay. Sometimes
we turn our heads. Sometimes we hit a car. I think
you're okay."

Bad things happen to us, sometimes, and it's no
one's fault, not even our own. God is there at those
times, too.

You are my hope today, God, my Protector, and my
Comfort, all at once. —Jon M. Sweeney

Digging Deeper: Deuteronomy 31:6

Saturday, April 10

**If we confess our sins, he is faithful and just to
forgive us our sins and to cleanse us from all
unrighteousness. —1 John 1:9 (NKJV)**

There was nowhere to hide. Water poured in by
the bucket- and bowlful. Stuck in the back of a
slow-moving pony cart in rural Myanmar during
Thingyan (a three-day water festival to welcome in
the new year), I found my only defense was to smile,
cover my camera, and try my best to keep the tainted
water out of my mouth. I wasn't wholly successful on
any count.

Granted, it was over a hundred degrees. Being
soaked from the tip of my toes to the top of my
graying head wasn't wholly unappreciated. Neither
was the fact that every man, woman, and child who
participated in the frenzied dousing (many wearing
water tanks on their backs to feed their oversize
plastic water cannons) was trying to do me a favor.
They believed the water would wash away my past,
including any evil in my life, and assure me of
blessings in the coming year. What a wonderful gift!

What these kindhearted people didn't realize
is that God had already bestowed this gift on me.
My sins are forgiven, and I find myself blessed,

year-round—without the waterworks. All I have to do is pray. So that's what I did. With every bowl of water poured down my back or playfully tossed into my face, I thanked God for all He's doing and has done for me. (I also thanked Him for water-resistant mascara and that we'd bypassed the street where revelers were using fire hoses!)

Dear Father, thank You that forgiveness, and a fresh start, are always just a prayer away. —Vicki Kuyper

Digging Deeper: John 4:7–14; Psalm 103:12; 2 Corinthians 5:17

Sunday, April 11

OPEN HEART, OPEN HOME
The Front Porch
He is not here; he has risen!... —Luke 24:6 (NIV)

I poured myself a mug of coffee and found my way out to Sue and Bryan's front porch.

Yellow and white daffodils had pushed through the once-barren soil and were now in glorious bloom. Just then, Sue appeared at the door. "Come and look at these dogwoods," I said to her. "They're neon pink this year."

"They've always been that color, honey," she answered with a chuckle.

"Not in my old world," I told her. "With my senses dulled from the opioids, they've always been the color of cotton candy."

Taking in all of the beauty around me, I felt a shiver of anticipation. Hope. The power of the Resurrection. The worst of my withdrawal from medically prescribed opioid pain medication was over. It was as if I were experiencing the miracle of spring's rebirth, of Easter, for the very first time.

There were inner voices, but they were different now. Encouraging, promise-filled ones. *You're going to make it, Roberta. But you aren't going to merely survive. This time you're going to thrive. And that new medication? It's going to keep relieving your pain.*

Sue found a seat at the bistro table by the swing and passed me a plate of raisin toast. I inhaled its comforting aroma; it would always symbolize a new beginning for me. I felt suddenly energized. Strong. Confident. Joyful. Where was all of this coming from? I had hardly been able to ask God for help, so it couldn't be the result of anything *I* had done.

The answer came from deep within: ten days of gracious, biblical hospitality had reconnected me to God. And it had made me honest and transparent with myself. I was ready to face the world.

When folks open their hearts and homes, Lord, miracles happen. I will never stop thanking You.
—Roberta Messner

Digging Deeper: Matthew 28:5–6; John 11:25–26; 1 Peter 1:3

He changes times and seasons; he deposes kings
and raises up others. He gives wisdom to the wise
and knowledge to the discerning.
—Daniel 2:21 (NIV)

I'd treated myself to a whole hour on my knees in
my garden. No cell phone or computer. No right or
wrong way to do it. No deadlines. I inhaled, letting
the bright greens, cheerful yellows, and soothing
blues quiet my thoughts.

I dug compost into our clay soil, smiling at
the analogy my friend JoAnn had given me that
morning. I had called to apologize that I could
not continue to help her with a volunteer project
at church. I felt as if I were letting her down, as I
always do when I say no.

JoAnn's gracious response stayed with me. "Your
life is not a marathon, it's a relay. You carry the baton
for a while, then pass it to the next person. You aren't
intended to carry it forever."

I divided a heavy clump of hostas to share with
my neighbor. I thought back a dozen years to when I
had struggled with saying no to a different volunteer
opportunity in another church. That friend,
Melinda, had told me, "I figure when I say no, it
opens the door for someone else to say yes." Passing
the baton.

I surveyed my garden, admiring the now-tidy
hosta bed and picturing the other plants I'd like to
move or share. The older I become, the more I give

up expecting to do everything, and do it right now! More good things will be done in this garden by its next owner. After I pass the baton.

Dear Lord, in what other areas of my life are You nudging me to take up, or pass, the baton?
—Leanne Jackson

Digging Deeper: Genesis 1:11–12; Ephesians 4:16

Tuesday, April 13

Do everything without grumbling or arguing, so that you may become blameless and pure, "children of God without fault in a warped and crooked generation." —Philippians 2:14 (NIV)

We were all looking forward to spring break as a time to relax and recharge as a family. I booked a beach house and planned a low-key week of ice cream, sand castles, and easy dinners at home.

"It looks like it's going to be windy," my mom said the week before we headed out. "And maybe a little cool." I brushed it off. A little wind couldn't stop us!

But it wasn't a little wind. It was sustained wind of twenty-five miles per hour for three days straight with temperatures topping out in the fifties. Every so often one of the kids would attempt to go outside, only to be nearly knocked down by the wind. When Beau, fifteen months old, ventured out, he held on to the hair on his head, fearful it would blow clear off.

I would love to say I handled this well, but no, I pouted. In short, I was grumpy.

The last day, I realized that my kids had not complained at all. While I simmered, frustrated that our vacation had been ruined, they had spent the time being loved on by grandparents, playing games, and reading books. Of course, I had done all that as well, but let's just say my attitude was not what it should've been.

I'm continually reminded by my children to be in the moment and grateful for what I have right here, right now. This vacation was intended to recharge all of us emotionally and physically, but it renewed and restored my soul instead.

God, thank You for three tiny reminders that I need to be grateful for all that I have, even if it wasn't what I asked for. —Ashley Kappel

Digging Deeper: Exodus 16:2–10; Philemon 1:7

Wednesday, April 14

When you pray, go away by yourself, all alone, and shut the door behind you and pray to your Father secretly, and your Father, who knows your secrets, will reward you. —Matthew 6:6 (TLB)

The beautiful junior-Olympic-size swimming pool across the street from my condo was one of the main reasons I moved to Florida in 2004. I don't swim neat-looking laps or even normal swim strokes.

No, I swim willy-nilly, flinging my arms and legs in dozens of different directions. I'm in that giant pool by 8:30 a.m. every day almost always by myself, swimming and exercising my limbs, torso, back, and feet in every imaginable crazy movement. Then at 9:00 a.m., Monday through Saturday, I join a water aerobics class where we twist, bounce, stretch, do jumping jacks, skiing motions, leg and arm kicks, lifts, and an amazing array of other body workouts.

Some mornings in the winter I'm there when it's fifty degrees out and raining. The water temp is always eighty-five degrees, so who cares if it's raining? I'm already wet. The point is, I'm there, I feel deliciously free and powerful in the water, and my body, my artificial knees, my mind, and my soul thank me for taking the time to do this every day.

The best part of my daily swim habit is when I'm in the pool alone and I say my morning prayers. As I swim in a big rectangle I praise God for being almighty, ask God for what I need including forgiveness, intercede for others by asking God for what they need, and thank God for what He has already done for me. The important thing is that these water prayers have become a daily habit, one I hope to keep well into my nineties and beyond.

Lord, as I age, give me the stamina and determination to keep this body moving and shaking and the prayers flowing. —Patricia Lorenz

Digging Deeper: Matthew 6:1–15; Psalm 66:16–20

Know ye not that ye are the temple of God,
and that the Spirit of God dwelleth in you?
—1 Corinthians 3:16–17 (KJV)

On this day two years ago, the majestic Notre Dame
Cathedral in Paris burned in a spectacular fire,
causing anguish to millions who revered the Gothic
building and the faith it stood for. Now I hear the
groan of heavy equipment, the thunk of metal on
stone. A yellow excavator rotates its claw arm amid a
pile of rubble two blocks from my home. *St. Peter's
Church! Gone!* My heart cannot absorb so much loss.

Though St. Peter's was not my church, I feel a
deep sadness that yet another sacred worship space
has been demolished. My friend's son was baptized
there and my optometrist, married. Nor is that the
only church to disappear in my town: Sacred Heart
Church downtown was deconsecrated and converted
into condos a few years ago. Where are the faithful
who once gathered within these buildings?

Everywhere!

It's time to remind myself that the church is—
and always has been—a community of believers,
not a building. Jesus Himself taught outdoors and
in homes; worship within dedicated structures
came much later. And though the buildings provide
shelter, often exquisitely beautiful and inspiring, the
heart of a church beats in its living members' hearts,
not in the stained glass and stones. Even as I mourn

the destruction of sacred spaces, I sense that God—who cannot be contained—is very near.

Spirit of God, dwell in me. —Gail Thorell Schilling

Digging Deeper: Acts 7:48; Romans 8:9; Ephesians 3:10; 1 John 4:12

Friday, April 16

The Lord replied, "My Presence will go with you, and I will give you rest." —Exodus 33:14 (NIV)

I soak in the sun as two seagulls squawk at each other, fighting over bread on the sand.

I lift my head from the blanket, a motherly instinct. But these two are not mine. There is no squabble between two brothers to referee. My two sons are back in New York City as I visit my parents in Florida, a rare time away from my parenting duties.

I lie back down, squinting at the sun, then close my eyes. I listen to the waves crashing gently on the shore, and feel the heat of the sun and the cool breeze of the wind on my skin.

My hands press down into the sand, feeling its powdery texture on my fingertips. In some faraway land, I am a woman busied by responsibilities, someone preoccupied with worry and a to-do list that never seems to end. I am here, there, and everywhere with children in tow, traveling in cars, buses, and trains. I'm the one who makes meals and beds and sometimes peace when her children squawk like seagulls fighting over bread on the sand.

But here I am none of those things. By the sea, I'm reminded that I just am.

Lord, I am so many things to so many people. Thank You for those moments when I can simply just be.
—Karen Valentin

Digging Deeper: Psalm 23:2–3

Saturday, April 17

But they refused to pay attention; stubbornly they turned their backs and stopped up their ears.
—Zechariah 7:11 (NIV)

The sun had descended, the air grown cold, as I slipped into the hot tub at our neighborhood pool— my reward for swimming laps. A little girl, I'll call her Katie, stood by the tub, towel-less in a dripping swimsuit, arms clutched, teeth chattering, entire body vibrating. "Come on in. It feels wonderful and will warm you up," her father coaxed from inside the tub. Katie frowned and shook her head.

Katie's father repeated his invitation. But Katie was adamant. She would *not* go in. Her pale white skin was taking on a purplish cast. Her small body continued to shudder. "I promise you," her father tried again. "It will feel so good." Katie was not convinced. "You're turning into a Popsicle," he observed. Katie stood her ground.

How early our fears take hold of us. How soon we become stubborn. Rather than venture into unknown waters, we stand, miserable, our choice remaining with the familiar, regardless of its folly or even danger. "Come to me," says our heavenly Father. "Trust me. My way will be best for you." Too often we remain in place, too obstinate to submit.

Lord, when my actions have left me cold and shivering, may I surrender to the warmth of Your welcoming arms and the wisdom of Your ways.
—Kim Taylor Henry

Digging Deeper: 2 Kings 17:14; Isaiah 30:8–9; 41:10

Sunday, April 18

My heart is in anguish within me; the terrors of death have fallen on me. —Psalm 55:4 (NIV)

My dad will be dead three years in April. I still miss him as acutely as I did that first year we were without him. But those first twelve months were especially poignant. Every day was a day when I could say, "A year ago, Dad was alive."

In July, I thought, *A year ago, Dad was probably picking tomatoes from the garden he always planted along the side of the house.* Winter had me thinking about how, a year ago, he was refilling the bird feeders near the patio for the blue jays, cardinals, and juncos.

As the days marched steadily toward that first anniversary, I felt the loss of my dad deepen. The span of time between when he was last alive and this present moment grew with every passing minute. And now, three years out, there's no longer a mere three hundred and sixty-five days between me and his voice or his hug. He's no longer merely absent. My dad is forever and ever dead.

I think about this, and about dying, and I'm afraid of becoming nothing, of disappearing like that. I've spent all my life trying to be noticed, from the playground monkey bars ("Hey, Dad, look at me!") to the radio airwaves. Eternity, that Big Eraser, is unmoved.

But God is not. He's counted every hair on my head; He's got my dad in the palm of His hand, I'm sure of it.

In Psalm 55, the psalmist goes on to say, "I would hurry to my place of shelter, far from the tempest and storm." That shelter is prayer, where I ask God for more faith, more trust, less fear, in forever after.

God, ease my fear of death, so I can be more present to You and to others today. —Amy Eddings

Digging Deeper: Psalm 55:5–8; Luke 12:4–7; John 14:27–28

Monday, April 19

"Look, I am about to die," Esau said. "What good is the birthright to me?" —Genesis 25:32 (NIV)

Our dog Cookie isn't much of a barker. When she wants something, she whines until I more than likely give in. So when I heard her barking outside in the yard one day, I knew something was up. I went out to investigate.

Cookie had found herself what she supposed to be a treasure: a turtle! As big as a soup bowl! It must've been moving when she discovered it, and I guess she reasoned that if she barked loudly long enough, her prize would reemerge from its shell. "Be careful what you wish for," I told her. "You're asking for a big snap on the snout!"

I picked the turtle up and lifted it out of Cookie's reach. She barked all the more loudly, then whined as if to say, "But I really, really want it! Please, please, pleeeease let me have it!"

Despite her pleadings, I took the turtle outside the fence and released it. Cookie seemed to feel pretty betrayed, but she forgave and forgot quickly (dogs are so much better at that than we humans are).

A minister once told me that there's no such thing as an unanswered prayer; it's just that sometimes, the answer is no. I thought of this as I cuddled my pup, wondering about all the things in my life that I'd ever asked God for that, had I gotten, would have been not at all what I'd bargained for.

Father, You know what we need…and what we don't. Thank You for answering our prayers, even when Your answer is no. —Ginger Rue

Digging Deeper: Numbers 11:4–6; John 12:27

STRUGGLING TO PRAY: Forgetting to Pray

When the bow is in the clouds, I will see it and
remember.... —Genesis 9:16 (ESV)

I just got off the phone with my sister Sharon.
"Don't forget to pray about Tom's radiologist visit
tomorrow. He's really upset about it," she said.

"I won't," I told her.

But I know from experience I'll probably
forget.

Forgetting is one of my biggest prayer struggles. I
say I'll pray, then forget. I even forget to pray about
my own big worries, a kind of prayer I call "pray-
worrying." Typically, I forget the prayer part and just
flat-out worry.

I know: I should keep a list. Problem with lists,
though, is that I lose them. Or forget I ever wrote
them. Lists also seem superstitious, like if I don't
pray what's on the list, whichever way I want it
resolved won't happen.

Which gets at a scary question looming beneath
all my prayer-worries: what, exactly, is prayer? A way
to orchestrate what I want? Surely, God knows that
already—and also, more importantly, He knows
what I need. He has my best interests at heart. And
He doesn't forget.

Or does He? After the flood, He put a rainbow in
the sky as a reminder—to *Himself*—of His promise
never to destroy the world with a flood again.

My husband says prayer, like remembering the Sabbath, is for us, not God. If so, what would my prayer be for Tom, for me, for everyone I pray for?

That we'd go fearless into God's keep. And that God, being God, would make things turn out for the best.

Let, oh, let thy will be done, Lord. —Patty Kirk

Digging Deeper: Genesis 9:1–17; Jeremiah 29:1–14

Wednesday, April 21

Then he said to Thomas, "Put your finger here; see my hands. Reach out your hand and put it into my side. Stop doubting and believe." —John 20:27 (NIV)

In some cultures scars are thought to be decorative, but not in the United States.

My friend Kimberly is writing the story of her life. But, like with most of us, there are things she doesn't want to divulge. She is a childhood survivor of domestic abuse, repeated visits by the police who, she says, did nothing to stop beatings by her mother's boyfriend. She survived, married her high-school sweetheart, and then gave birth to an autistic daughter who died young of a tragic heart attack. What she's been through is a lot for anyone.

She asked me for some advice as she began writing.

"Show your scars," I encouraged her.

This is hard-won wisdom I had to learn myself. When I first began writing, I had a vivid dream. I dreamed that I was clothed in a long black dress, with long sleeves and a high collar. But a voice of authority in the dream chastened me, "Show your scars."

It was terrifying to me to think of revealing to other people things that shamed me, things I wanted to hide—like a sexual assault that I hadn't even told my parents about.

Suddenly, in the dream, I was dressed differently; my arms and legs were visible. I was covered with dreadful raised scars all over my body.

I was so ashamed to reveal these scars. Their presence reminded me of pain I had endured. Then, in the dream, the scars began to morph together, creating beautiful patterns. "It is your scars that make you beautiful," the voice of authority comforted me. "When people see your scars, then they know their wounds can be healed."

Lord, thank You for scars. Help us to see the beauty You bring, even out of our tragedies, and give us courage to show others our scars. —Sharon Foster

Digging Deeper: Isaiah 61:3, 7

Thursday, April 22

He will not suffer thy foot to be moved.
—Psalm 121:3 (KJV)

We are on a family holiday in Mexico and David, Charles, and I have escaped the fancy resort for a long walk down the wild beach.

"Wear your shoes," David warns, "the sand is hot."

Charles, eight at the time, and I laugh. "We'll walk along the water's edge," we say, leaving him to the beach.

The sand is blistering as we run down to the surf and splash along. Then, as we wade around a giant pile of ragged rocks jutting out into the water, the waves grow ferocious. And suddenly we are trapped between an unrelenting surf and deadly rocks.

The waves are hitting us hard as I grab Charles, praying that I can get him to a higher place before we're crushed against the rocks. I know we can die here.

"God," I call.

And then I see it. There is no doubt. God has put it there. It is a tiny pool of sand, carved into the razorlike rock.

"Put your foot there and climb," I cry to Charles. And then I yell, "David!"

In an instant Charles obeys and David's hand is there from above, pulling him to safety.

I'm alone now. The waves crash toward me, picking me up, throwing me into the rock, then pulling me down deep into the whirling sand, filling my mouth, my nose, my ears.

And then the voice: *Grab hold of the rock.*

Hurled forward, I find a ridge with my hand.

Hold on. Hold on, the voice says.

Then David's yelling, "Reach up!"

As the next wave roars, I let go, reach up, and, scraped, bruised, and bleeding, am pulled to safety by David's sure grip.

Father, I called and You answered with a foothold in the rock. Knowing this is everything. —Pam Kidd

Digging Deeper: Job 5:11; Psalm 118:5

Friday, April 23

Take my yoke upon you and learn from me, for I am gentle and humble in heart, and you will find rest for your souls. —Matthew 11:29 (NIV)

The thunder started with a small rumble, but the shaking of the house only grew stronger as the seconds passed. I was rocking my four-month-old son back to sleep after he woke at 1:00 a.m. His eyes were starting to close, his grip around my finger loosening, and he slipped into a deep sleep. I couldn't bear to put him back into bed yet.

Since he was born, I haven't wanted to miss a second of his life, even when I was running on no sleep.

The walls quaked again as I looked over at a small salt lamp plugged into his wall. It furnished the room with an orange glow, which was cast across his cheek. Something about that orange hue caused me to really gaze at my son. Here was this tiny boy, who often fought sleep as much as I did, now in my arms, dreaming with a small grin.

The scene brought me back to a dream I'd had earlier in the week. I was in a cabin with a woodstove burning in one corner of the room. It created that same orange glow. I wandered around the cabin, exhausted from the weight of my thoughts these days: frightened my son was going to forget me if I was gone for too many minutes; fearful I'd do something wrong that I should have learned before he arrived; embarrassed by my failure to breastfeed. In the dream, my eyes met with Jesus's tender gaze and I stopped moving. "It's time to let go of all this fear by giving it to me. It won't let you rest, but I will."

Jesus, show me when I'm carrying too much. Help me to keep handing my burdens over to You. And help me to find rest for my weary soul. —Desiree Cole

Digging Deeper: Psalm 23:2; Jeremiah 31:25

Saturday, April 24

Create in me a clean heart, O God, and renew a right spirit within me. —Psalm 51:10 (ESV)

It was finally getting warm enough—and dry enough outside—to clean the windows. I got out the Windex and a roll of paper towels and went to work.

I like to tell myself that cleaning anything— like doing the dishes or vacuuming the floor—is satisfying work because it delivers real results. Over the winter the windows had accumulated plenty of grime from the salt strewn on the roads on icy days, from the dust and dirt of cars going by and the smoke fumes from the boiler. I was looking forward to a cleaner view of the first buds of spring.

I squirted the outside of the windows first, then wrapped my hand around and wiped them clean. To my surprise the glass still looked dull. No sparkle, none of that shine.

Then I closed the windows and did the inside. More elbow grease and wiping. I was amazed at what a difference it made. You could see the beautiful spring day on the other side of the glistening glass, the sun on the lawn, the light on the trees, almost as if you were in it. I hadn't realized how dirty the windows were on the inside.

A pertinent Bible verse came to mind: "Woe to you, scribes and Pharisees, hypocrites! For you cleanse the outside of the cup and of the plate, but inside they are full of extortion and rapacity. You blind Pharisee! First cleanse the inside of the cup and of the plate, that the outside also may be clean" (Matthew 23:25–26).

Washing windows is sort of like working on the soul. Lasting change happens from inside out.

Lord, help me scrub all the grime from inside me, all the anger, resentment, envy, pride, and let me shine.
—Rick Hamlin

Digging Deeper: Psalm 26; 1 Corinthians 13:12

Sunday, April 25

So then, as we have opportunity, let us do good to everyone, and especially to those who are of the household of faith. —Galatians 6:10 (ESV)

I scribbled a note in my bar exam prep book, then flipped the page. I had around a thousand more to turn before I took the test.

My ten-year-old brother, Isaiah, was sitting next to me at the dining room table. He was using my phone to check for online garage sale listings.

"Logan!" he said. He stood up, and the table shuddered. "Star Wars action figures! A bunch of them! Can we go to this sale?"

I grabbed my phone before he could drop it. Then I looked at the listing.

"Buddy, that sale is in Macomb," I said. "That's almost two hours away."

I watched the excitement slip from his face.

"Oh," he said. "I didn't know."

I considered my itinerary for the day. I still needed to listen to a couple of hours of online lectures. They had fill-in-the-blank worksheets to accompany them. I could stay home and finish my work. But God had given me a unique opportunity to pour into my brother.

"I'll make you a deal," I said. "If we go, would you mind listening to my lectures with me? You'd have to fill in the blanks on my worksheets when I ask you."

Isaiah grinned. "I'll grab a pen," he said.

A few minutes later, I was driving and Isaiah was riding shotgun. We were both learning about contract law. But I was also learning to take every opportunity to invest in others.

Father, help me use my time to draw closer to others.
—Logan Eliasen

Digging Deeper: Philippians 2:3–4; 1 Peter 4:10

Monday, April 26

I press toward the goal for the prize of the upward call of God in Christ Jesus. —Philippians 3:14 (NKJV)

I've lived in a metropolitan area for over half my life, but I'm truly a country girl at heart. I woke up to deer on the lawn, caught fireflies at dusk, and have come in contact with my share of nature. I relish the five-and-a-half-hour drive from Georgia to my North Carolina hometown. It's an opportunity to reflect on my past and to contemplate future goals.

I was headed up I-85 for an annual family visit, and as usual I was contemplating life. *I'm behind,* I thought. I hadn't accomplished as much as I'd hoped. There were ideas that hadn't seen the light of day, unfinished projects, things that I'd intended to achieve that I hadn't scratched the surface of. Things were going slow—sometimes from my own volition, but often because—let's face it—things don't always go as planned.

While visiting my parents, I headed to the grocery store, and as I rounded a curve, I noticed that the cars ahead had slowed and were cautiously veering into the oncoming lane in an attempt to dodge an obstruction in the road. It was a turtle, unbothered by the whisk of cars. In fact, on my return trip from the store, the turtle was still making its slow way across the road.

As silly as it may sound, I realized it's okay to be the turtle. I could stay on course and move at the pace God has set for me. Moving forward—however slow—is still progress.

Lord, help me not to be anxious, but to stay on the course You've set for me. I want to find comfort in knowing that Your timing is perfect. —Tia McCollors

Digging Deeper: Proverbs 5:1–2; 19:21; Ecclesiastes 3:11

Tuesday, April 27

In all your ways acknowledge him, and he will make straight your paths. —Proverbs 3:6 (ESV)

Hi, everyone, Gracie speaking, Edward and Julee's golden. I've spoken here before, with Edward's help, but only when I have something important to say. So here it is: *I love mud!*

If there is mud, I will find it. When I find mud, I will flop in it. I can't resist the temptation. I want to be a good dog, I really do, but mud always wins. Is that really such a bad thing?

However, I am not allowed to enjoy my mud. I am swiftly taken to a public bathing facility for dogs where Edward lures me into a tub by deceiving me with liver treats. I cannot resist liver treats. So unfair! I am subjected to a complete hosing down and washed with something called "oatmeal shampoo," which doesn't taste anything like the oatmeal I am familiar with.

Then comes the horrible blow dryer. I do everything to escape it. I will flee to a corner of the "spa" area. Edward will pursue me, waving the weapon, but the floor is wet and sometimes he falls down. At that point workers in the store will come and restrain me. And I thought they were my friends! At least I am given more liver treats.

Finally, they more or less give up and I am allowed to dry naturally. This can take some time. I'm told I give off an odor in this interim, but people shouldn't talk.

My humans do something they call praying, and I have overheard them pray that I resist the temptation of mud. I hope those prayers work because *I hate baths*.

Father, Gracie may not know better when it comes to mud, but I understand that we humans must resist temptation in all forms if we are to honor You. Please help keep me on the righteous path today and out of the metaphorical mud. —Edward Grinnan

Digging Deeper: Matthew 26:41; 1 Corinthians 10:13

Wednesday, April 28

And we know that for those who love God all things work together for good, for those who are called according to his purpose. —Romans 8:28 (ESV)

"Jolynda, share your *why* with us—why do you do what you do?" asked a colleague at a recent conference. Big question! In that moment it was hard to easily sum up the path of my calling, but I immediately knew it started simply. At twelve, I met this little old lady. I couldn't understand a word she said with her heavy accent. But she was holiness, mercy, and grace. I know her as inspiration, and you may know her as Mother Teresa of Calcutta. I knew instantly I wanted the grace she exuded, and so I started my path.

Like everyone's, my path has been at times muddled and confusing. Remembering my "why" reminds me the paths laid out by the Lord can be meandering, joyful, and scary; His paths are often filled with grace, but not without tears and challenges.

As I recalled the specific calling to religious education that I live, I remembered the many other calls I answer: mother, wife, friend, and daughter. So often we tend to align divine calling with work done for and with the kingdom of God directly. The truth is, divine calling comes in many forms, and we answer our calls in many ways. As we experience and embrace our faith, we come to understand God's intent for our lives. The Lord calls each of us continually, and often in order to embrace our call, we must take a leap of faith and trust God's timing and ability to equip us to live out our calling, our "why."

Father, Author of our soul, bestow in me a listening heart and a courageous body that I may answer Your call more fully and embrace Your holy purpose for me. Amen. —Jolynda Strandberg

Digging Deeper: Psalm 17:3; Proverbs 19:20–22; Luke 4:42–44

Thursday, April 29

For God hath not given us the spirit of fear; but of power.... —2 Timothy 1:7 (KJV)

Leaving our ranch is about the last thing we want to do, but with my husband's job relocation, we have to move. Will we find a place we'll like? Do we have to sell our cattle? Fear looms so large over me that I'd bet it has snow on its upper peak. I have to get outside where I can pray without a ceiling in my way. I saddle Jack. With BlueDog at our heels, we climb through sage and pines, but I scarcely notice. I've packed my problems along with me. Worry only escalates.

A hawk's scream startles me. It screams again, upset. Two little blackbirds dive at the red-tailed hawk, driving the predator away from their hidden nest. The hawk is a giant compared to the blackbirds, but in nature, attitude trumps size. Hmm. Couldn't my fifty-pound BlueDog direct an entire herd of twelve-hundred-pound cows without so much as a single nip? How often had I run from an angry wasp smaller than my fingernail? The Bible overflows with encouragement for strength against towering odds. What about Esther, a bitty woman, outwitting the powerful Haman? And David creaming Goliath?

I take a deep breath. How often has God left me without a solution? Never. How often has God turned something that seems horrible into something better than I could ever imagine on my own? Always. I'm asked to trust Him in this. If God has decided to plant us in a new place, then bring it. I'm going to give Him glory all the way.

My chin lifts. Well, Big Problem, is that the best you can do?

Thank You for making me brave against my giant. You alone can make the impossible not just possible, but a spirit-lifting adventure. —Erika Bentsen

Digging Deeper: 1 Chronicles 28:20; Deuteronomy 4:31; Joshua 1:9

Friday, April 30

He spreads the snow like wool and scatters the frost like ashes. —Psalm 147:16 (NIV)

I stared out the window at an opaque gray sky. The very late-season snow was falling fast. Just yesterday, my young daughter and I were delighting over the green chives she'd spotted pushing up through the brown mud. What welcome harbingers of the long-awaited spring!

But now everything was frozen under another deep layer of winter. The scene felt as bleak as my mood. The night before, my husband and I had quarreled bitterly. Old wounds reared their ugly heads, and weaponized words like "you never" and "you're always" flew. We both knew better and were past stooping to those lows. Or so I'd thought.

Turns out I'd been silly to think spring had finally arrived. And I'd been a fool to think we would ever rise above our flaws.

Donning my jacket, I stepped out onto the deck. The cold bit at my cheeks as I looked up at the tall spruce trees surrounding the cabin. It was so quiet I could hear the whispers the snowflakes made as they hit the ground.

Slowly, a peace enveloped me, quieting my churning mind. I made my way over to where we'd found the chives and pushed the snow aside. There they were, as bright and green and full of life as they'd been the day before. They'd been protected from the bitter cold by the same layer of fluffy white snow I'd been so upset about.

As I turned to go back inside, my heart felt lighter. Maybe last night's quarrel wasn't as grim as it'd seemed either. After all, my husband and I, and our marriage, were covered by a protective blanket of our own: God's love. With Him in our corner, we could weather any storm.

The protections You provide come in so many different forms. Thank You, God, for the reminder that Your love is with me always. —Erin Janoso

Digging Deeper: Psalm 121; Romans 8:31

JOYFUL IN HOPE

1 _____

2 _____

3 _____

4 _____

5 _____

6 _____

7 _____

8 _____

9 _____

10 _____

11 _____

12 _____

13 _____

14 _____

15 _____

16 _____

17 _____

18 _____

19 _____

20 _____

21 _____

22 _____

23 _____

24 _____

25 _____

26 _____

27 _____

28 _____

29 _____

30 _____

MAY

*...let the hearts of those who
seek the Lord rejoice.*

—Psalm 105:3 (NIV)

And to this people you shall say: "Thus says the Lord: Behold, I set before you the way of life and the way of death. —Jeremiah 21:8 (ESV)

I was looking forward to the wedding but feared it would be a bittersweet experience. Lynn, the widow of my dear friend Charley, was getting remarried. I was so pleased for her, really thrilled. She'd been an extraordinary caregiver for Charley in his long struggle with ALS. Charley spent the last two years of his life in a hospital bed set up in their living room with round-the-clock care—and his family nearby.

Or at least streaming in and out, watching videos, playing games, singing songs. Lynn and Charley had two sets of twins. They were five and two years old when he died. But that was the whole point of him being in that hospital bed in the midst of their lives. They would know their dad after he was gone. And he knew them.

It had been seventeen years now since his passing—had it really been so long?—and those kids were adults now and we, his old college buddies, had a few more gray hairs on our heads. We celebrated Lynn's wedding to a wonderful man named Tom. We also remembered Charley. We sang, we danced, we ate, we prayed.

At the end of the weekend I realized why it was not a bittersweet experience at all. How glad I was to be there. To have that chance to say to Charley's kids, in between the dancing and eating and laughing: "Your dad would be so proud of who you are today." Each of them had fulfilled the promise that he must have seen in them as they scurried around his bed. In each of them I saw a bit of him, very much alive.

Dear Lord, may I treasure this life and honor it, never forgetting those who have passed. —Rick Hamlin

Digging Deeper: Ruth 2:20; John 5:24

Sunday, May 2

This is eternal life, that they may know You, the only true God, and Jesus Christ whom You have sent. —John 17:3 (NASB)

I first saw Pioche, Nevada, in our road atlas as a small white circle along US Highway 93. A good overnight destination before pushing into Las Vegas to visit friends. At least I hoped it was. I knew nothing except the Motherlode Motel could offer us lodging.

We arrived on a spring Sunday evening to find the motel barely off the pavement winding into the sleepy town with the notorious Wild West history.

We were directed to the Ghost Town Art & Coffee Co. for dinner. A repurposed 1880s blacksmith shop. Wooden planking on the floor. Walls covered in superb metal creations. The owner and artist's worktable part of the ambience. And a tasty pulled pork sandwich.

The next morning I strolled along the highway to an old bench in front of the historic brick Lincoln County Courthouse (I'd learned surprisingly the county has no traffic lights) and watched the sun rise across the valley. A man walking a magnificent Irish wolfhound–malamute mix named Caesar stopped briefly to chat.

I contemplated all I'd discovered since seeing that unfamiliar dot on the map. Pioche had substance because I had spent time there. I'd personalized it. I knew it now. And quietly, like the town, I thought of God's invitation to "Be still and know that I am God" (Psalm 46:10).

God makes Himself known in His created world, in His Word, in Jesus—who has "explained Him" (John 1:18). If I want to know God I need to spend time—to have conversation—to seek the place He is. He is not hiding. I just need to go to Him.

Thank You, God, for Your message in a map.
—Carol Knapp

Digging Deeper: Jeremiah 9:24; John 14:7; 1 John 4:8

Monday, May 3

Ask and it will be given to you....
—Matthew 7:7 (NIV)

My writing life was languishing. Each day brought distractions, chores, errands, appointments. Writing, what I wanted to do, kept being pushed to the side, something I would get to "tomorrow."

I prayed, "Lord, if you agree I should write, please remove the distractions and lead me to take the time."

Then my husband convinced me to go on a vacation—not just a short break, but a five-week cruise with lots of sea days. On other cruises, sea days had been so filled with activities I'd never even had a chance to read a book, let alone try to write one. When would I ever get time to write?

The cruise was on a smaller ship than we were used to. On board, I looked over the paltry list of activities and complained to my husband about how little there was that interested me. I tossed the daily schedule aside and huffed, "Looks like a whole lot of sea days with absolutely nothing to do!" I continued to grumble until it hit me. Not only did I now have time to write with no distractions, but I had a gorgeous and peaceful place in which to do it.

I positioned my laptop, gazed at azure sunshine-flooded depths, thanked my awesome God, and to the rhythmic swoosh of ship through waves, began to type.

Lord, how many other prayers have You answered that I need only open my eyes to see?
—Kim Taylor Henry

Digging Deeper: Psalm 66:19–20; 120:1

For if they fall, one will lift up his friend, but woe to the one who falls and has no second one to lift him up. —Ecclesiastes 4:10 (CHABAD)

The basket of kriah ribbons was very unusual. At every other Jewish funeral I'd attended, only the immediate family wore the black pin-on ribbons to tear in an expression of grief.

At my husband's funeral, my grandson and I would have been the only ones to participate in the kriah tradition, so I asked Mother Catarina if she would like to join us. She pinned a ribbon on her habit as I was pinning mine on my shirtfront, and we tore them at the same time. As I ripped mine, I felt a breaking of the buildup of grief and began to cry.

But I could never feel that way at the funeral of a stranger, which I was attending only to support a friend whose cousin was being buried.

I didn't take a ribbon from the basket, and I noticed that most other people didn't either. I couldn't help wondering what the point was. As the funeral went on, I tried to think about the reasons for having so many kriah ribbons available when there was only one member of the family there to grieve.

Slowly, it occurred to me that my friend didn't want to grieve alone, didn't want to be the single person there with an outward sign of the loss. I remembered how grateful I was that my grandson and Mother Catarina shared the experience with me. On my way out of the cemetery, going to the memorial luncheon, I took a ribbon from the basket and pinned it on. I understood that sometimes being a friend involved standing in for family that wasn't there.

As You gave me others to hold me up, O Lord, You taught me to pass Your blessing along to others.
—Rhoda Blecker

Digging Deeper: Lamentations 3:32; Isaiah 61:2

Wednesday, May 5

And pray in the Spirit on all occasions with all kinds of prayers and requests. With this in mind, be alert and always keep on praying for all the Lord's people. —Ephesians 6:18 (NIV)

I would imagine that many praying folks seek out particular places and postures where they commune with the Lord: kneeling on the floor next to their beds, while seated in a special chair in a quiet room, or perhaps in a special dedicated "prayer closet."

Me? Some of my best praying is done in the shower. It's there that I keep a waterproof list of names of people to pray for. The list typically includes about fifteen names, including members of my church's prayer list, family and friends, neighbors, or just about anyone in need of prayer who crosses my mind.

I'm able to think clearly in the shower. Those thoughts may include the day to come or a laser focus on the lives of my husband or sons. Perhaps it's the soothing sound of the water splashing and echoing off the tile. Maybe it's the much-needed solitude, which is such a departure from a hectic day.

But what really inspires me is seeing the names of those family members and friends listed on that waterproof pad. It helps me to remember, reflect, and target my prayers to those who need them most. I often add names to the list, which may come from my church bulletin, through chats with friends, or by reading a particularly moving or concerning story in a newspaper or magazine.

My shower prayer list may not be as traditional as some other prayer reminders, but it works for me. And if this list encourages me and empowers me to lift up others, as God has commanded, then it's a powerful piece of paper indeed.

Heavenly Father, help us to always follow Your direction to pray for others, as we pray for ourselves.
—Gayle T. Williams

Digging Deeper: James 5:14–16

Thursday, May 6

"For I know the plans I have for you," declares the Lord, "plans to prosper you and not to harm you, plans to give you hope and a future."
—Jeremiah 29:11 (NIV)

When my son Brandon came in second in the nation for his level in power tumbling, I was bursting with pride. I proudly shared the news and his pictures on social media and the response was overwhelming.

Yet along with congratulations for Brandon, messages were there for me as well. Many friends and family knew about my long commutes twice a week from New York City to New Jersey for practice. They understood how expensive tuition and competitions were for my two boys and the hours I worked in their gym in exchange for a small discount. Brandon's win was the culmination of all the sacrifices, financial burdens, and hard work.

In the eyes of family and friends, I was a hero, a supermom, a great role model. But weeks before he was awarded the silver medal at the nationals, I had already made the decision that I needed a break. I'd already wrestled with my own guilt and feelings of letting my kids down.

Now I wondered if I was letting down others who are watching my journey. I responded personally to a friend who texted his praises, and told him what the plan would be for this year—less intensive training, no competitions, and working on increasing my income so I can take this on again at some point with less stress.

"This encourages me even more," was his response. "I know you are making the right choice." His words quieted my renewed doubt and confirmed that no matter how hard these decisions are, my intentions will always be to do what's best for my family.

Lord, help me remember that even when it doesn't seem that way, You are always choosing Your best for me. —Karen Valentin

Digging Deeper: 1 John 4:18

Friday, May 7

I wait for the Lord, my whole being waits, and in his word I put my hope. —Psalm 130:5 (NIV)

I was forced to use a messaging app when a friend began using it to communicate with me. When I downloaded and opened the app, I was surprised to find not only the message I was expecting, but also a message from Diana, whom I had worked with many years ago in Argentina. I was stunned to see that Diana had sent the message to me nine years before.

I sent Diana a reply explaining the long delay and wondered if I would hear back from her. Each time I picked up my iPhone, I caught myself looking for a message from her. She hadn't gotten a reply from me in almost a decade and I was expecting an instant message from her! Diana did respond the next day and we exchanged several more messages, catching up on family, work, and other happenings.

As I thought about the absurdness of my impatience, I wondered, *Am I the same way with God's responses to my prayers?* Too often I am slow to ask for God's help until an issue becomes a bigger challenge. And when I truly do surrender something to Him, I find that a new insight or next step comes to mind—often not the total solution but all I need in the moment to move the situation forward. What a reassurance that God is helping me and will provide additional direction in His time—even when I want an instant answer. He always has.

Thank You for Your patience, God. Help us bring our needs to You when we see them coming and then wait patiently for Your response. —John Dilworth

Digging Deeper: Psalm 130:1–2, 6; Isaiah 40:31

Saturday, May 8

Let us then with confidence draw near to the throne of grace, that we may receive mercy and find grace to help in time of need. —Hebrews 4:16 (ESV)

Thunk. Thunk. Thunk.

I forced open my eyes, checked my phone: 6:02 a.m. I noticed Gracie, my golden retriever, peering at me with concern. "Not again," I groaned. The crazy robin was back, on a Saturday morning no less.

That spring a robin had been hurling himself at our windows. At first I felt sorry for him, but after he became obsessed with our car, not so much. In between assaults on the windows he would perch atop our black SUV, which was now, as a result, turning white.

Thunk. Gracie whined. "What do you want me to do?" I asked her. "You're the bird dog."

Once the hour was decent I called our longtime vet. "Is this robin suffering from some sort of avian madness?" I wanted to know.

"Just confused," Dr. Phillips said. "This is mating season."

"It wants to mate with my car?"

Dr. Phillips laughed. "He's protecting his patch from competitors. He sees his reflection in your window and thinks it's a rival. It will be over once he identifies a mate and transfers his efforts to guarding the nest. Besides, how many times in life have you banged your head against the wall trying to make something happen?"

I hung up. She had a point. The robin and I weren't so different. Except I knew better than to keep banging. Presumably, I knew when my efforts were fruitless and I had to turn my will over to God. And yet it didn't always happen so quickly. I turned to God only after I was too dizzy to go on. I could cut this poor, overeager robin some slack.

I whistled for Gracie. "Come on, girl! Let's go to the car wash."

So many times, Lord, have I tried to force my will on situations far beyond my control. Teach me to ask for Your help first, not last. —Edward Grinnan

Digging Deeper: Psalm 13:5; 37:5

Mother's Day, Sunday, May 9

We give thanks to God always for all of you, constantly mentioning you in our prayers, remembering before our God and Father your work of faith and labor of love and steadfastness of hope in our Lord Jesus Christ. —1 Thessalonians 1:2–3 (ESV)

"Look at this one!" My sister pointed to a photograph. It was my grandmother Kerttu, standing next to what appeared to be a frozen river, wearing a furry cap and holding a pair of snowshoes.

We sat there for hours, poring through the stacks of photo albums that had been stored for decades in my great-aunt's closet. We pointed out our favorites, laughing as we recognized "that smile she always made when she was laughing" or "that glimmer in her eye that lasted until the very end."

Tears began to stream down my face and I looked up at my sister and saw a similar dampness in her eyes. It felt so good to remember who my grandmother actually was.

The end of my grandmother's life had been less than wonderful. Her mind deteriorated into confusion with Alzheimer's as her will became stronger, and to be honest, it was hard. I didn't always enjoy spending time with her. In fact, I often dreaded it.

When she passed away, I felt a sense of relief. Relief followed by guilt and shame that lasted until that afternoon at my great-aunt's house with those photo albums.

On that day, I was able to remember my grandmother for who she was, the wonderful, spunky, and smart woman who had taught me how to pick blueberries, how to make apple cider, how to pray unceasingly.

The woman I loved dearly and will one day see again, fully restored.

Jesus, thank You for our mothers, the ones who gave so much and who are so loved. Amen.
—Erin MacPherson

Digging Deeper: Psalm 77:11; John 14:1

Monday, May 10

"And on this rock I will build My church...."
—Matthew 16:18 (NKJV)

Finally, my puppy, Zeke, was old enough to go to the popular dog park down the street known as a community of dog people who come together on common ground because they love dogs. What a perfect place to learn to play nice and interact with other dogs and their owners.

On our first day, Zeke zoomed off to introduce himself to the closest dog. I followed, and the woman who owned the dog smiled. "What's your dog's name?" she asked as my dog zealously jump-danced around her dog. "Zeke," I answered, "for Ezekiel, a prophet in the Bible who brought hope to his people." Awkward silence.

"Dixie's not playful." She gestured toward her dog. "She just loves to watch."

Zeke was already on to the next dog who responded to his jump- dancing and off they went, chasing each other in huge circles. "Bolt loves to run," the owner said proudly. We chatted briefly as Zeke tried to entice another dog to run, but that dog growled and nipped at Zeke.

"Berkley, no!" the dog's owner reprimanded. "He's always gotta be the alpha dog," he apologized.

After a few more dog interactions, I called Zeke, thankful he heard my voice and came running because he knew he belonged to me. As we headed to the car, I thought about the nature of communities. The dog park is a community of people who come together because they love dogs, just like my church community comes together because we love Jesus. Yet within both communities, the people and dogs are uniquely different. Both are good places to learn to play nice and interact with others.

Lord, may I appreciate the diversity of people who come together in our communities.
—Carol Kuykendall

Digging Deeper: Psalm 119:73; 139:13–16

Tuesday, May 11

Even youths grow tired and weary, and young men stumble and fall. —Isaiah 40:30 (NIV)

My friend Tonya lost her son a few years ago. I use the word *lost* because I cannot bring myself to say, "Steve died," because Steve was a popular high-school junior, and those people aren't supposed to die. Truth is, we didn't lose Steve; he's always in the same place, with his name carved into a stone marker in case we forget, but we never, ever will.

Steve and Tonya had talked about opening a restaurant after Steve graduated. Tonya went ahead with the plan, in part to honor her son. It's a hoppin' place, often frequented by Tonya's many, many friends.

One friend confided in Tonya that her daughter was expecting a child, but without the benefit of marriage. This upset Tonya's friend a great deal—the shame, the embarrassment of it all, how she hadn't raised her daughter that way...

...until Tonya couldn't take it anymore. "Do you know what I would do to have a grandchild?" Tonya asked. "That would mean I have my own child back. I would give up everything for just a chance to hold that baby in my arms."

Tonya's friend was properly mortified and apologized profusely. "Don't be sorry," Tonya said. "Be grateful."

And that means I have to correct myself, twice: We didn't lose Steve, and he's not beneath a stone marker. He is still with us, his memory a blessing. We can choose to feel lost—lots of reasons for that— or we can locate ourselves in this moment, bearing witness to a grieving mother, bearing witness to life in all its chaos, feeling sorrow amid endless and holy and divine joyfulness and gratitude.

> **Lord, may we always be counted among the communion of saints, both here and in heaven.**
> **—Mark Collins**

Digging Deeper: Isaiah 40:28–31

Wednesday, May 12

Are not two sparrows sold for a penny? Yet not one of them will fall to the ground outside your Father's care. —Matthew 10:29 (NIV)

The back porch door was only open for a few seconds, but that was time enough for a half-grown robin to fly down the hall and into our laundry room. The poor bird frantically circled the room, wings beating hard. I knew it was scared, but what to do? I tried capturing it in a large towel, but couldn't get close. Trapping it in the corner with my broom didn't work, either.

My husband, Don, squeezed through the door. "Stop trying to catch it!" he said. "When the bird tires it will land on a shelf and I'll get it." A couple of minutes later, that's what happened. Don picked the robin up, carried it outside, and watched it fly to the nearest Bradford pear tree.

I hate to admit it, but I'm a lot like that bird. My initial reaction to unsettling news or a troubling circumstance is panic. I rush around and try to fix things that don't need fixing or aren't my business. Often my hasty "solutions" to problems often don't even make sense, like the time my granddaughter Olivia was driving alone and had a flat tire ninety miles away. My plan was to go pick her up, but Don said, "Why not call a garage to fix the tire?" I did, and Olivia was back on the road in forty-five minutes.

These days I'm trying to remember that robin when I receive bad news or encounter stressful situations. With God's help, I'm learning to take a deep breath, stay calm, wait awhile, and trust that He will provide appropriate help in every situation.

Lord, You have told us to learn from the birds of the air (Matthew 6:26). Let it be so in my life. Amen.
—Penney Schwab

Digging Deeper: Isaiah 41:10; Matthew 6:25–27; James 5:7–8

Thursday, May 13

He heals the brokenhearted and binds up their wounds. —Psalm 147:3 (NIV)

This has been a year of celebrations—graduations, weddings, and new beginnings. During the month of May, my immediate family celebrated four graduations within three weeks, with my husband earning a master's degree, my son an undergraduate degree, one daughter graduating from middle school, and my other daughter from elementary.

It's been a fun, exhilarating whirlwind. So it struck me as very strange when I felt increasingly tired and withdrawn after my son's college graduation. Several extended family members had traveled to join in the festivities, yet all I wanted to do was retreat to my bedroom, close the blinds, and take a long nap.

Excusing myself from the group, I did just that, but realized fatigue wasn't the issue. Being surrounded by extended family was wonderful, but two people were missing: my deceased parents, who were both lifelong educators and often spoke of the importance of the next generation's pursuit of higher learning. I knew if they were alive, they would have moved mountains to join us that day as we celebrated our oldest child's milestone.

As the years accumulate since my parents' passing, grief has become an ever-present friend that visits me at the least expected moments. It is constant and intermittent, certain and unpredictable. Oftentimes, when I expect to experience low moments of grief, I am okay. Other times, when I expect to feel joy and celebration, grief clings to me like the muggy air of a hot summer day. I have learned to continue moving forward, sharing my grief openly and honestly, remaining focused on pouring into family and friends with whom I continue to share life.

Dear Lord, help me to grieve with hope, believing that You are close to the brokenhearted.
—Carla Hendricks

Friday, May 14

Finally, brethren, whatever things are true,
whatever things are noble, whatever things are
just, whatever things are pure, whatever things are
lovely, whatever things are of good report, if there is
any virtue and if there is anything praiseworthy—
meditate on these things. —Philippians 4:8 (NKJV)

Sweat ran down my back in rivulets as the hot
afternoon sun made yard work difficult. I was
weaving a lattice of bendable decorative boards
through a metal fence.

Finally, I arrived at a part of the project I'd been
dreading—a grapevine I had planted several years
ago. It had never borne fruit, and Margi and I talked
about removing it, but I held out hope. Over the
years, the vine had wrapped through the fence I was
working on. Now I had to remove some branches to
finish my project.

I got out my pruners and reluctantly cut several
branches. As I untangled the freshly pruned branches
from the fence, I made a painful discovery. I found
six clusters of tiny grapes clinging to the branches.
The grapes were small, but the clusters were big. Yet,
in one of the more questionable moves as an amateur
gardener, I had just lopped them off. My heart sank.
The goodness was there, but I just hadn't seen it.

Just like life, I thought. So many times, there is beauty and goodness and abundance in my life, but I'm too focused on other things to see them. I let the negatives and the labor and the problems hide the gift of fruit.

Before snipping another branch, I made careful inspection. I found half a dozen more clusters on the vine. When I looked carefully for the good, I found it. That hot sun had given us homegrown grapes, and they were delicious.

Heavenly Father, tune my heart to see Your goodness and grace every single day. Amen. —Bill Giovannetti

Digging Deeper: Psalm 121:1

Saturday, May 15

Wait on the Lord: be of good courage.
—Psalm 27:14 (KJV)

Our table for eight at the Veterans Appreciation Breakfast included all branches of the armed forces. We gathered as guests of the Hospice of Orange & Sullivan Counties. Awareness of end-of-life volunteer services to veterans was the theme.

I sat next to Russ, our table's sponsor. "I was in the coast guard for four years in the early eighties," Russ remarked when asked about his military branch. "Coastie service is not as dramatic as the other branches, yet their mission is valuable."

I mentioned my appreciation for the coast guard, based on my experiences while stationed in

Washington, DC, and on later Guideposts ministry visits. I also told of a recent obituary of former US Coast Guard Petty Officer Third Class Andrew Fitzgerald.

On February 18, 1952, Fitzgerald volunteered with three other guardsmen stationed at Chatham Lifeboat Station, Massachusetts. Their mission was to rescue merchant seamen from the broken 503-foot tanker *Pendleton* located in freezing seas some twenty miles off the coast.

Braving sixty-foot swells, and soaring and plunging waves, and executing a rising and falling dance, lifeboat *CG-36500* rescued thirty-two of the thirty-three seamen from the broken bow. Some rank the saving as the "greatest small-coast rescue in the history of the coast guard."

Russ immediately told me of a tanker rescue mission he, too, was a part of. Saving merchant seaman off the Carolina coast, and seeing the disabled tanker sink stern-up, remain most memorable experiences in this coast guard veteran's service.

I left the breakfast honored to have shared the meal with these other veterans. I left also thankful for all those who, this day, protect and keep us safe.

Gracious God, our provider, today we are grateful for military veterans and for our armed forces members who this moment selflessly serve around the globe. Amen. —Ken Sampson

Digging Deeper: Deuteronomy 31:6; Hebrews 11:34

Sunday, May 16

In their hearts humans plan their course, but the Lord establishes their steps. —Proverbs 16:9 (NIV)

I breathed in. The mountain air was thin but pure. My dad paused to look out over the Colorado landscape. The view was stunning: deep green trees and dark gray rock. For just a moment, the grandeur pulled me from my thoughts. I was waiting to hear back from two recent job interviews. I was uneasy not knowing what direction my life would go in the coming months.

As we resumed ascending the dirt path, the terrain began to change. Fragmented rock surrounded us. The trees here were scraggly; they had fought for their turf. I looked ahead. The trail ended in about a dozen yards.

"This was a shorter hike than I expected," I said.

My dad shook his head. "I've been on this trail before. Keep going."

I kept walking, but I knew my dad was mistaken. The trail came to a clear halt ahead. The path was surrounded by rocks. Even so, I walked to the end of the path.

"Are you sure you remember this trail?" I asked him.

"Look to your right," he said.

I did. And I saw what I hadn't seen before. Among the jumbled mess of rocks was a set of stones. They were small, flat, and regularly spaced. The staircase they created was only visible at this angle—at the end of the dirt trail.

As I followed that new path upward, I thought about my career. There was no way to know what job position I would end up in. I had to trust the Lord to guide me. And though I didn't yet know where I was headed, I did understand He had set a path before me.

Lord, help me to trust You to guide every aspect of my life. —Logan Eliasen

Digging Deeper: Psalm 23:1–3; 32:8

Monday, May 17

"Which of these three do you think was a neighbor…?"
—Luke 10:36 (NIV)

My fifteen-year-old came in looking unexpectedly solemn. His demeanor was odd. It was a gorgeous spring day, one of the first he'd been out on the water at his sailing program.

"Hey, Buddy, how was sailing?" I asked.

"Good," he mumbled.

"You don't look good. Something happened," I replied cautiously. "What's up?"

There was a long silence. "I did a good thing," he said at last.

I let that hang in the air before asking, "What?"

There was silence. Then, "Me and my friend Mehrob talked someone out of jumping onto the tracks at the Twenty-third Street Station."

I tried to process that bombshell. A year earlier I'd been on a subway platform when someone leaped in front of a train, and the shock resonated through my life for months. That my teenager had almost had the same experience was sobering. I barely knew how to respond.

"How did you know the person was going to jump?" I eventually asked.

"He was sitting near the edge of the platform, inching forward, talking to himself."

I nodded slowly. "Were you able to get help?"

"Yes, after the train pulled in we told the conductor, and they didn't let the train leave until EMTs arrived," my son said.

He walked into his room, leaving his supper uneaten. I let him go.

I tried to sort out my chaotic emotions. There was fear, confusion, and concern swirling in there. It took a bit of sifting to figure out that I wasn't exactly proud of my son, but thankful: that he had noticed a need, stepped forward, and did what was needed.

Jesus, in the midst of messy and scary things, guide my heart to compassion. —Julia Attaway

Digging Deeper: 1 Corinthians 12:27

Tuesday, May 18

STRUGGLING TO PRAY: Middle-of-the-Night Prayers
Jacob woke up and said, "The LORD is here!..."
—Genesis 28:16 (GNT)

I have what sleep experts call "sleep maintenance insomnia": waking most nights after a few hours, unable to return to sleep. I've tried all the experts' tips—to no avail. A noise, a rise in humidity, a bathroom trip, or an upsetting dream wakes me, and I'm lying there sunk in my current worries or a writing project for hours, sometimes till dawn.

Eventually, I remember God is there, too, and start to pray, but soon I'm back in those worries and projects.

Lately, though, I've started conversing with God more strategically by praying the prayer Jesus prescribes: "Our Father, who art in heaven…" There's a snag, though. You'd think the familiar words would slide mindlessly through my consciousness like so many sheep and bear me back to sleep, but, alas, that never happens.

So I reframe the words to sound more like myself and maybe actually mean them. Who uses words like *art* and *hallowed* anymore, anyway? Altering the Our Father in this way invariably starts me thinking about each word individually, beginning with *Our*.

Our as in *whose?* I ask myself, as I'd ask in the margins of a student's paper upon encountering any other pronoun without an antecedent. Scrutiny of *Our* takes me to all my human sisters and brothers who share this Father: my beloved daughters and husband and friends, my students and colleagues, my biological siblings. That eventually gets me thinking about all the people in my life I don't generally think of as related to me or in any way beloved. Not enemies, exactly. Just those who irk me or whom I'd prefer not to share a meal with or generally avoid.

I don't know if thinking about them is what puts me to sleep. Hours later, though, when morning is pinking up beyond the window, I wake rested.

Father, use even my sleeplessness and self-centeredness to bring me to You. —Patty Kirk

Digging Deeper: Psalm 4

Wednesday, May 19

BECOMING JUST ME AGAIN: New Widow Goes to Spain

Some of these people have missed the most important thing in life—they don't know God. May God's mercy be upon you. —1 Timothy 6:21 (TLB)

Two months after Jack died I received a phone call from my cousin Jerry, a Catholic monsignor who was planning a pilgrimage to Spain and Lourdes, France, with his siblings and their spouses. Four other people from his parish were also planning to go, but unfortunately two of them had to back out at the last minute. Jerry was offering me and a friend the chance to take their place, all expenses paid.

My head was spinning. Could I get ready for a twelve-day trip to Europe in two days? I'd have to cancel a number of things on my calendar. But then I remembered my philosophy of life that had kept me going for years, "Never say no to an opportunity unless it is illegal or immoral."

There were five happily married couples on that trip. At first seeing those happy couples holding hands everywhere they went made me miss Jack even more. But then we talked to hikers along the El Camino, the famous five-hundred-mile hike in northern Spain, and I discovered many were single people, some even widows like me.

We walked in the evening candlelit procession at Lourdes. As we proceeded with over a thousand people, I felt like part of the whole. My new widow status seemed to evaporate; I was simply Pat, a much-loved cousin, friend, and fellow traveler.

On that trip as we fifteen pilgrims soaked in history, culture, daily Mass, exotic foods, ancient sights, and more laughs than you can imagine, my aching widowed heart became whole as my beloved cousins and new single friends helped me realize that I am me, a whole person, not just half of a couple.

Father, help me to be me, the whole person You want me to be. —Patricia Lorenz

Digging Deeper: 1 Corinthians 16:5–8; Galatians 5:22–23

Thursday, May 20

Blessed be the God and Father of our Lord Jesus Christ, who has blessed us in Christ with every spiritual blessing in the heavenly places. —Ephesians 1:3 (NASB)

May 20, 1972, is my "spiritual birthday." That's the day I fell to my knees and surrendered my heart to Jesus. I can't begin to imagine what my life would have been like if I hadn't taken that step toward faith.

This spiritual awakening came about when a Christian neighbor had invited me to attend a Bible study class with her. I'd grown up in the church, sat in the pew every Sunday, and heard the gospel preached, but it was more of an obligation than anything meaningful. This was different. This was life-changing. This was powerful.

From the moment I became a Christian, my life changed. I changed. I became fascinated with the Word of God, absorbing Scripture like it was the oxygen required to breathe. When I did, my mind opened to new possibilities.

I might never have had the courage to pursue a writing career if it wasn't for God's love and encouragement. He was the one who planted the desire in my heart from the time I was a youngster. Me, be a writer? Me, write books? I wanted to remind God I was in the fifth grade before I learned to read. I was a creative speller, and my English grades were nothing to brag about. As many arguments as I put forth, He responded with a simple request. He asked me to trust Him to fulfill that dream. To set aside my doubts, my fears.

So, on May 20 I can look back and thank Jesus for coming into my life and be forever grateful to the neighbor who saw a young woman with a spiritual hunger and issued a simple invitation.

Lord, Your provision and faithfulness have sustained me. I praise You for going above and beyond anything I could ever think or imagine.
—Debbie Macomber

Digging Deeper: Matthew 19:26

Friday, May 21

He that dwelleth in the secret place of the most High shall abide under the shadow of the Almighty.
—Psalm 91:1 (KJV)

Sitting in the yard of my century-old log cabin that May afternoon, I sketched the herb garden I'd planned on, once that stand of old honeysuckle bushes was removed. Just then a darling dark-haired boy appeared. I recognized him and the younger version trailing behind as the brothers from the ranch house beside me.

Breathless from playing out-of-doors, Brandon spoke up. "Mrs. Messner," he said, "would it be okay if we used the path between those two bushes to ride our bikes? We'd like it for our secret place."

"Yeah," chimed in Paul. "Nobody'll be able to find us there."

I studied the area they spoke about. There *was* a gap between two of the honeysuckles, though it took the imagination of youngsters to see it.

"Sure," I heard myself say, bidding farewell to the proposed spot for my garden. "You boys go right ahead, and have yourselves a great time, too."

For several summers, the two of them disappeared daily to whatever was behind those bushes. They were always smiling and scheming. Then one day, their family moved away to a new life. I missed their joyful banter and wondered what had happened to them.

Whenever I glimpsed those old honeysuckle bushes, I asked God to be with them. "Make your heart their forever secret place," I would ask.

Then one afternoon, I ran into their mother while shopping. "They're teenagers now," she said wistfully. "Facing all the things kids deal with today. Pressures from peers and society. Social media. Bullying. Drugs and alcohol . . ."

I told her about my prayers. Now more than ever, I'm so glad Brandon and Paul have God's secret place, his love and protection.

Lord, thank You for Your tender love and care, Your protection from trouble, and Your songs of deliverance. —Roberta Messner

Digging Deeper: Exodus 33:22; Psalm 32:7; 139:15

Saturday, May 22

**A cheerful look brings joy to the heart.
—Proverbs 15:30 (NLT)**

I followed the tag sale signs to the yard dotted with belongings. A woman, her son, and her mom greeted me from behind a card table. It was late afternoon and on first glance it seemed that things had been pretty picked over.

"There's more inside," the woman said. "Mom's moving closer to us to assisted living." Her son, about ten, leaned into his grandmother and she put her arm around him.

I quickly looked inside, but I didn't need a couch or a coffee table, so I went back out. I was about to walk to my car when I saw a cute little frog planter. It was weathered—the coloring on the top of head and hands had worn off—but cute. Beside the frog was an old concrete angel statue that had once played an instrument that had broken off. I couldn't decide if I wanted one, both, or neither, but a little voice said, *Take both,* so I did.

I went over to pay for them.

"Yay!" the boy yelled out. "They're staying together! They're staying together!"

"That's Angie and Fred," the mom explained. "John named them when he was little. They've always been in Mom's garden. He really hoped they'd find a home together."

After paying for them I was in my car when I heard, "I knew they'd go together!" the boy shouted. "Friends stick together!"

Angie and Fred live on my front porch—right next to each other—beautiful best friends, no worse for the wear.

Heavenly Father, thank You for the power of the stories of our lives that can turn worn belongings from strangers into special sentimental tokens of love.
—Sabra Ciancanelli

Digging Deeper: Psalm 118:24; Proverbs 15:13–15

Sunday, May 23

Freely have you received; freely give.
—Matthew 10:8 (NIV)

Serving on my hospitality team at church fills me
with purpose and joy. When the invitation to help
with the Pentecost luncheon reception landed in
my inbox, I quickly volunteered to bring fruit and
do the flowers, my favorite. This would be a major
celebration to feed about 175 guests and honor both
those confirmed and those being received into the
church. Even our bishop was coming.

I shopped the day before the event and found
watermelon, grapes, and strawberries, very fresh and
reasonably priced. The grocery store flowers were
another story. I wanted red and white for Pentecost,
but found no carnations, an inexpensive bloom.
The cheapest red flowers were small Peruvian lilies,
dainty, dark red, but hardly dramatic. Well, mixed
with white Peruvian lilies and baby's breath, they
would do. Then I spotted gorgeous, lipstick-red
roses for ten dollars a bunch; with baby's breath, they
would make perfect focal points on the long tables in
the large hall.

Suddenly, the extra ten-dollar total seemed too
much along with all the fruit. I clenched. I argued
with myself for two or three minutes, but I still
couldn't do it. No roses this time.

The next day, the dark red and white bouquets
looked pretty on the serving tables; one person even
complimented them, but I know I could have done

better. God has been generous with me. I need to do likewise.

Gracious God, forgive me when I lapse into cheapskate mode. I'll be more generous next time.
—Gail Thorell Schilling

Digging Deeper: Psalm 37:26; Malachi 3:10; Luke 6:38

Monday, May 24

And the King will answer them, "Truly, I say to you, as you did it to one of the least of these my brothers, you did it to me." —Matthew 25:40 (ESV)

I have found that university graduations exude both hope and relief: hope for the future and relief at having finished the academic requirements. My son Justin graduated this past spring from LSU Health Sciences Center. With almost a thousand graduates, it was a long morning. Aside from seeing Justin walk across the stage, the other highlight of the ceremony was the graduation speaker.

The graduation speaker was an alumnus and a physician. It was a captivating speech on many levels, but when he mentioned he was sharing a story called "The Face of Jesus," my attention was fixed. Jesus is not usually mentioned at state university graduations. The speaker shared with this group of new dentists, medical doctors, nurses, and allied health professionals the importance of seeing the face of Jesus in those served in the health-care field. He described the harrowing circumstances in which they will find themselves—tired, irritated, shorthanded, treating patients with self-inflicted illness, and depleted of compassion. He explained in those inevitable moments, it is essential to see the face of Jesus in patients; each patient is someone's parent, spouse, child, or friend. How profound!

Now, whenever my compassion is lacking, I try to see the face of Jesus in the person next to me, whether it's at work, at home, or out in the world, and give everyone reverence, care, and love.

Dear Lord, help us to see Your face in the face of our family, of our neighbors, and of those we come into contact with. May we honor You in the care we bestow upon others. Amen. —Jolynda Strandberg

Digging Deeper: 1 Kings 8:50; Isaiah 55:1–3; Matthew 9:35–37

Tuesday, May 25

On the glorious splendor of your majesty, and on your wondrous works, I will meditate.
—Psalm 145:5 (ESV)

Downshifting into third gear, I sighed as we continued to lose speed. My husband, daughter, and I were on our way from Alaska to Montana, where we spend our summers. This detour through Canada's Jasper National Park was meant to be a fun and scenic diversion. But the steep mountain grades were proving hard on our poor, heavily loaded minivan. "Come on, you're almost to the top," I said aloud to the van. I added a muttered "sorry" to the line of headlights in my rearview mirror.

Over and over again, as we'd climbed one pass after another, vehicles stacked up behind us. I'd pull onto the shoulder to let them by when I could, but sometimes that space wasn't available. It never failed that, at the first opportunity, sometimes even on a double yellow line, car after car would zip around us, eager to be rid of the obstacle we presented to their progress. We'd often catch up to the same cars stopped at the next overlook, their occupants busily snapping pictures of the view. After they'd gotten their photos, they'd pile back into their vehicles and zoom off again. "They're missing it," six-year-old Aurora had even said once, as we'd watched a car pull away.

She was right. The overlooks where we stopped were breathtaking, no doubt. But, as in life, the bulk of this drive's beauty was happening between the big stops along the way. It occurred to me suddenly that our heavy, slow vehicle wasn't a burden at all. It was a gift. An opportunity to slow down and take in God's masterpiece surrounding us.

The glory of Your creation is exquisite, God, but it is so easy to rush through life. Thank You for the times You slow me down. —Erin Janoso

Digging Deeper: Psalm 95:4–5; Isaiah 40:28

Wednesday, May 26

Because of the LORD's great love we are not consumed, for his compassions never fail. They are new every morning; great is your faithfulness.
—Lamentations 3:22–23 (NIV)

I'm in my car and my mind races. There are only two weeks left this school year and then this fall my son, Solomon, will be entering his senior year. There are lists of things we need to do, exams he needs to take, and he still has got to schedule his driver's test—so much to do and still my heart both wanting and not wanting this next milestone that will come whether I'm ready or not.

I spot a school bus ahead. *Ugh.* I timed my afternoon quick trip to the store completely wrong. I'll be stuck behind the bus dropping off kids for the next five miles.

The lights flash and a little girl gets off the bus and hugs her mom. Half a block ahead a boy gets off and runs to the doorstep as his mom watches from the window. I think of all the days I've waited for Solomon, anticipating how his day went, hoping for the best.

I decide to go a different way and turn down a lonely road. Ahead, a deer darts across and I come to a full stop in time to see a tiny fawn, just a baby, and then another cross. They catch up to their mom, who waits by the thick brush. When she sees they've made it, she disappears into the woods, trusting her babies will follow in her footsteps.

Heavenly Father, thank You for showing me letting go is a necessary part of love—and because of You I trust all will be fine. —Sabra Ciancanelli

Digging Deeper: Proverbs 22:6; Matthew 6:34

Thursday, May 27

But blessed are your eyes because they see, and your ears because they hear. —Matthew 13:16 (NIV)

It was a quiet afternoon. I was sitting on the couch in my living room, listening to a worship song that had been stuck in my head all morning. I kept turning up the volume. The singer's voice was filling up the whole house with its melody.

I looked out the window as the singer's words about Jesus's beauty were saturating the house. A storm was starting to blow in and the trees began to sway back and forth from the sudden burst of wind being pushed through the neighborhood. It was almost as if the song was seeping from the spiritual realm into our physical world, and the trees could feel Him, even outside that room. They were dancing for Him.

I started to wonder: Do we naturally put barriers up about where and how Jesus can permeate? What if that worship song wasn't so randomly stuck in my head when I woke up this morning? What if Jesus planted that song so I could see and hear Him enter our realm today? In that powerful moment, as I sat on the couch and listened to that song, I was reminded that there is nothing that separates us from Him.

> Jesus, whisper a melody in our hearts that helps us
> see You move through places we never thought
> were possible. —Desiree Cole

Digging Deeper: Job 13:1; Proverbs 20:12

Friday, May 28

From his fullness we have all received grace upon grace. —John 1:16 (CEB)

Grant, my second-born son, is moving out. He attended a local college, so departure was delayed, but he graduated this week. Now it's time for him to fly. He isn't going far—a few hours. I'll miss the daily living, though. Sharing talk and avocado toast before school and Sleepytime tea after work. The way he sings aloud and jokes with his brothers until they're all half wild. Grant makes life rich.

"Need any help?" Gabriel, my twelve-year-old, asks Grant. Together they move T-shirts from drawers to boxes. My youngest, Isaiah, helps, too, stacking books and framed photos in straight, neat rows. I watch from Grant's bedroom doorway. I admire the easiness among brothers—the banter and the boyhood.

Soon, the house will be quieter.

I've experienced this before. We launched our oldest son, Logan, years ago. I know I'll find traces of Grant all over. Shoes left in the pottery crock by the door. Favorite foods on shelves. The empty place where he parked his car.

Empty places.

Hard as we try, we can't run from them. Kids grow up. Life changes. Physical emptiness feels like an emptiness of the soul. But the Lord offers a filling from the fullness of His grace. Abundant, immeasurable grace—the kind that makes one's cup overflow.

"Hey, Mom. Can you grab another box from the garage?" Grant asks. His smile warms me.

I can help my son leave, because I know that my Father will help me, too.

Lord, I invite You into my empty places. Please fill me. Amen. —Shawnelle Eliasen

Digging Deeper: Psalm 16:11; Romans 15:13

Saturday, May 29

There is a time for everything, and a season for every activity under the heavens.
—Ecclesiastes 3:1 (NIV)

"There's a turtle in the garage!" my grandson Logan announced.

"There are two turtles in the backyard!" he said the next day.

All over social media, people in the area were talking about turtle sightings. Why were there so many turtles?

Springtime, with its warmer weather and blooming flowers, is also egg-laying season for turtles. These reptiles come out of their ponds and search for places to lay their eggs, no matter how far they must go or whose yard it is. Their God-given instinct tells them it's time.

Coincidentally, it's the time people come out of their houses to enjoy the warm weather, so when my husband, Chuck, asked if I wanted to go fishing on Saturday, I wasn't surprised. We hadn't used the boat for eight months. Even when the weather is nice, we often don't have time to enjoy boating and fishing because Logan has soccer games or Scout activities that take precedence.

So when Chuck asked that weekend in May when Logan had no activities, I dreaded telling him I had a meeting that day. I could hear the disappointment in his voice when he said, "No problem. We'll go next week." But I knew we already had plans for the next week.

I felt I needed to go to the meeting. But then I thought about the fact that my husband and I had not shared one of our favorite activities together for a long time. I realized the meeting could go on without me. My God-given instinct told me being with my husband and grandson was more important this time.

Lord, please help me make time for what's most important. —Marilyn Turk

Digging Deeper: Ecclesiastes 3

I will both lie down in peace, and sleep; For You
alone, O Lord, make me dwell in safety.
—Psalm 4:8 (NKJV)

I have trouble falling asleep sometimes, probably
because in the quiet darkness, I often start thinking
about troubling things. Recently, I started doing
something different that's helping.

No spiritual rocket science here. I just practice
gratitude, in bed, in the dark.

Here's my routine: I usually read a little before
turning out the light and getting comfy under
the comforter. (I love that it's called a "comforter.")
Then I begin a quick review of the goodness that
surrounds me at that moment and in my day that is
ending.

Like last night, my first thankful thought was for
my husband, who was peacefully asleep next to me.
Then for the feel and smell of the clean sheets I put
on our bed that day.

Next, I remembered a moment in church
that morning when I looked around and saw so
many people I know and feel known by. I know
their stories; they know mine, which brings such
comfort. I also saw people I didn't yet know whose
stories will stretch me and bring new life into our
community.

Finally, I thought of the fresh ripe red strawberries
in our refrigerator. They are in season now and I love
how they look and how they tasted today.

These are ordinary things and ordinary moments that might easily be taken for granted but they become sacred and comforting when I recognize God's presence in all that is good. I thank Him, which is a good way to end the day.

Then I fall asleep filled with gratitude rather than worries.

Lord, acknowledging You as the faithful Giver of all goodness in my days helps me sleep peacefully.
—Carol Kuykendall

Digging Deeper: Genesis 28:16; Psalm 46:1

Memorial Day, Monday, May 31

I urge, then, first of all, that petitions, prayers, intercession and thanksgiving be made for all people—for kings and all those in authority.
—1 Timothy 2:1–2 (NIV)

It was Memorial Day morning when I sipped my coffee and watched the Internet load on my computer. My blood pressure spiked as I scanned the political headlines. *I can't believe what is going on!* For the next several minutes, I ranted and complained.

Shaking my head, I clicked on a veteran's inspirational story. When I finished reading it, my thoughts swirled about the huge price he'd paid for my freedom. My mind skipped through others that had willingly sacrificed: my father, a World War II veteran, who after his seventeenth birthday shipped off to the South Pacific and became disabled; my mother, who assembled submarine carburetors on an assembly line before she went to school to become a cadet nurse; my brother-in-law, who was career military and would go on hardship duties for a year at a time, leaving my sister behind, eventually becoming disabled; and stories of so many friends who had served.

Then a foreign thought struck me. *What price have I paid?* My stomach turned as I remembered how much I complained. Other than voting, I hadn't done much else. Why? I was busy. *Is busyness a reason to stand by? What price am I willing to pay?*

Taking out a sheet of paper, I started a list: 1) pray every day for our leaders; 2) honor our veterans with a thank-you and pray for our servicemen and women; 3) instead of complaining, help those who are working toward a solution; 4) pray some more.

Lord, give me witty ideas of how I can help our nation remain the land of the free and the home of the brave. Amen. —Rebecca Ondov

Digging Deeper: 1 Timothy 2:8; Proverbs 21:1

JOYFUL IN HOPE

1 _____

2 _____

3 _____

4 _____

5 _____

6 _____

7 _____

8 _____

9 _____

10 _____

11 _____

12 _____

13 _____

14 _____

15 _____

16 _____

17 _____

18 _____

19 _____

20 _____

21 _____

22 _____

23 _____

24 _____

25 _____

26 _____

27 _____

28 _____

29 _____

30 _____

31 _____

JUNE

But you, when you pray, go into your inner room, close your door and pray to your Father who is in secret, and your Father who sees what is done in secret will reward you.

—Matthew 6:6 (NASB)

In the beginning God created the heavens and
the earth. The earth was formless and empty, and
darkness covered the deep waters....
—Genesis 1:1–2 (NLT)

After three days visiting large cities in South America,
our cruise ship had four sea days—nothing but
water as far as our eyes could take in, and farther. I
sat on our cabin's balcony and watched the ocean.
What a contrast from the bustling, jostling, beeping,
swerving traffic (vehicular and human) we'd just
experienced. I'd enjoyed being immersed in a foreign
culture, but now it felt wonderful to be surrounded
by the vast, undisturbed peace on which our ship
was merely a dot.

The cities had been interesting and exciting,
but they had unsettled me. The ocean "stilled
and quieted my soul" (Psalm 131:2). The cities
showcased the fleeting, striving busyness of man.
The sea spoke eternity and majestic calm. As I was
watching it, all man-made tension left me. Ageless
omnipotence reigned and I sensed, as in Genesis 1:2,
the Spirit of God hovering over the surface of the
waters.

**Thank You, Almighty God, for enveloping the flurry
of our daily life in the cocoon of Your creation.**
—Kim Taylor Henry

Digging Deeper: Psalm 46:10; 107:29–30

Wednesday, June 2

Serve the Lord with gladness; come before His presence with singing. —Psalm 100:2 (NKJV)

For weeks our church bulletin contained the same announcement: "Joy Club each Wednesday afternoon. Helpers needed!" For weeks I ignored the request. The Christian after-school program was important, but I doubted I had the energy and patience to keep up with thirty to forty-five kids ranging in age from preschool through fifth grade.

But no one else volunteered. Maybe God was calling me. So I went the Wednesdays I could. I doled out cookies and sandwiches, listened to kids say Bible memory verses, and helped clean up. But I wondered: was I really helping these children learn about Jesus? Sometimes my main accomplishments were mopping up spilled juice and breaking up shoving matches. I certainly wasn't feeling the joy!

The last session of the school year featured a program for parents. Rehearsal was a disaster. Kids whispered their Bible verses and screamed the song lyrics. They elbowed each other and ignored instructions on displaying the signs they'd made to accompany some of the songs.

But everything changed when they walked into the sanctuary. They sang enthusiastically, especially on "I Have the Joy, Joy, Joy." The memory verses were perfect. Everyone knew the Lord's Prayer—in fact, eight of the children prayed it in German (the language many speak at home) as well as English.

From conversations with parents afterward, I was confident that many children had gained heart knowledge of Jesus.

I'd learned something, too: joy is sometimes moments of pure elation. But it can also be the quiet satisfaction that comes from obeying God's call to help, even when that obedience is reluctantly given.

Lord Jesus, thank You for the joy that comes when I say yes to serving others. —Penney Schwab

Digging Deeper: Matthew 21:28–31; Luke 18:15–17; Hebrews 12:1–2

Thursday, June 3

Jesus replied, "No one who puts a hand to the plow and looks back is fit for service in the kingdom of God." —Luke 9:62 (NIV)

"I'm just really going to miss kindergarten," Olivia said as we wrapped up her last week of school. Field day, a disco dance party, and awards ceremonies were packed into the remaining hours of the last week of school, and when the final bell rang releasing everyone for summer, it broke her heart.

Olivia has an incredible gift. She's all in on what's right in front of her, which is great, except when what's right in front of her is so amazing that she can't imagine anything will ever get better. She can be nostalgic for the present, and I can say she definitely gets it from her mama.

227

"What about first grade?" I asked. "They won't have all the things I love," Olivia replied, tears spilling over onto her already damp cheeks.

"If you go back to kindergarten, you're going to work on the things you already know," I reminded her. "Wouldn't you rather go to first grade and learn new things?"

Her eyes brightened as she realized that there was more out there for her, greater things to experience and to learn. As she scampered off to play, I reflected on how I should absorb my own words. What was I so stuck in that I was afraid to move on for fear that the next thing might not be as good? Where in my life did I need to spurn the safety of routine and look for new lessons and adventures?

Lord, stretch me so that I may find more of You to love. —Ashley Kappel

Digging Deeper: Isaiah 43:18–19; Jeremiah 29:11

Friday, June 4

The light shines in the darkness, and the darkness has not overcome it. —John 1:5 (NIV)

Last night I walked the dog around the house. The moon hid behind a blanket of clouds, so it was darker than usual. Nights like this, I stay close to the porch, away from the shadows and things that might go bump or make the dog turn his head abruptly and stare at things I can't see—which freaks me out a little.

It had been a long day filled with mishaps and work conference calls, and I wanted to move this short walk along so that I could go back inside and go to bed.

"Come on, Soda," I said. A slight warm breeze blew in from the south and he pulled forward, heading into the darkness.

"Okay, just a little ways," I said. For some reason, I let him lead. We walked down the hill, away from the house, where the shapes of trees were a hint darker than the sky. I was about to turn back when a burst of light caught my eye—and then another and then another.

Fireflies! The first ones of the season! They twinkled around us, like magic. I stood in awe. The brilliant flashes sparking a deep nostalgic joy, bringing a passion deep from the depths of my childhood up to the surface. Had we stayed by the house I would have missed this stunning display that lifted my spirit in a heartbeat.

Heavenly Father, thank You for showing me that Your beauty and magic are all around me—especially when I have the faith to go beyond my fear.
—Sabra Ciancanelli

Digging Deeper: John 12:36; James 1:17

Saturday, June 5

Pay attention to the ministry you have received
in the Lord, so that you can accomplish it.
—Colossians 4:17 (HCSB)

Over several years, I've made maybe eight labor-
intensive papier-mâché piñatas, satisfying the
persistent requests of a neighbor girl who anticipates
any occasion that might land her candy: her own
birthday, her sister's, her cousin's. And two weeks
ago, she—and then her mother—asked if I'd make
two for the younger sister's upcoming birthday.
"There's supposed to be one piñata for the girls and
one for the boys. You know, pink and blue. Please,
Miss Evelyn."

Two for one event? Though it seemed excessive,
I said yes, wanting to help give the girl a bang-up
birthday. I concocted a flour-water glue. On a
balloon frame, I pasted layer upon layer of torn
newspaper strips. One piñata formed. Then the
time-consuming second.

Now the ugly ovals had to be prettified. "Lord…"
Before I mumbled a tired complaint, the Spirit planted
an idea. Hadn't the church missions committee
discussed the value of families solving their own
problems, claiming ownership of solutions? I spoke to
the neighbor mother. "Would you like me to teach you
how to decorate the piñatas?"

"Okay." So on Saturday morning, supplies in
hand, I knocked on their door. Once I demonstrated
how to cut and snip pink tissue paper streamers,

everyone in the family pitched in, layering fringe upon fringe, from bottom to top. A few days later I returned to applaud their show-and-tell of the blue version completed in my absence. I took pictures. I praised the product.

I returned home satisfied with and grateful for a mission accomplished. A party prepared. All they'll need is . . . the candy.

Lord, show me the best way to serve my neighbors.
—Evelyn Bence

Digging Deeper: 2 Corinthians 9:8–15

Sunday, June 6

And now that I am old and gray, don't forsake me. Give me time to tell this new generation (and their children too) about all your mighty miracles.
—Psalm 71:18 (TLB)

My four-year-old granddaughter, Shea, leaned over the dinner table and looked me straight in the eye. "Mimsy, when I grow up, I want to be just like you!" she announced with a giggle and a grin.

Taken aback, I was momentarily speechless. All I knew for certain was that this was undoubtedly the best compliment I'd ever received. A little unsure of how to respond, I decided to go with lovingly lighthearted. "And, Shea, when I get little, I want to be just like *you!*" I replied, giving my granddaughter's shoulder a loving nudge.

Shea laughed and rolled her eyes. "Silly Mimsy. You're not going to get little. You're just going to get older and older and older!"

There's nothing like a good dose of truth from a child to help keep life in perspective. If God chooses to grant me more days on earth, my only option is to grow old. That makes aging a gift— one that not everyone receives. So, what should I do with a gift given to me by Someone I love? Show my gratitude by using it well. That includes trying to pour as much of God's love into my grandchildren's lives as possible, as I continue to celebrate every passing day, and every wrinkle life may bring my way.

Dear Father, thank You for grandchildren and the blessing of living long enough to enjoy them!
—Vicki Kuyper

Digging Deeper: Proverbs 16:31; Isaiah 46:4

Monday, June 7

Sin is not ended by multiplying words, but the prudent hold their tongues. —Proverbs 10:19 (NIV)

My intense, emotional seventeen-year-old scored a public health internship for the summer. I'm thrilled...and also concerned. She has had enough difficulties that not succeeding would be devastating.

But my concerns are mine, not hers. Sharing them is unlikely to do any good. This is my fourth go-round with an almost-adult, and I suspect she would hear my (probably valid) concerns as negative. I have also been made aware I am not omniscient. So I stick to my maxim: you can't always make it better, but you can always make it worse. In this case, that means keeping my worries to myself.

Parenting is not exactly as I envisioned it in my young-mom days. My fantasy of family life sorely underestimated the extent to which the free will of my offspring, God's will, and my husband's and my strengths and weaknesses would interact. The result is a decidedly mixed bag, and I'm only in charge of part of the mix.

The good news is that this has forced me to focus on what *is* in my control. I've had to recognize my hot buttons as mine, to manage my feelings, to concentrate on how to act instead of react. These things have taught me greater patience and fortitude, restraint and humility. All good.

So it's not as difficult to restrain myself from voicing my opinions as it might have been a decade ago. If my daughter can pull off the internship, fantastic—I'll be impressed! If she staggers, I will help her find her balance (if she will let me). And if she falls, we will figure things out from there.

Jesus, keep my eyes steady on what I can do, rather than on what I can't. —Julia Attaway

Digging Deeper: Proverbs 18:21

Tuesday, June 8

He fills my life with good things! My youth is renewed like the eagle's! —Psalm 103:5 (TLB)

Not long after I had both knees replaced on the same day, I started to feel like a caged bird, doing most of my rehab inside my condo. One day I asked my daughter visiting from California to take me to the nature park a few blocks away. We walked slowly to the area where a number of wild birds are caged because of permanent injury. That was the first time I took a close look at Sarge, a large stately American bald eagle. Unfortunately, Sarge was born with a feather disorder that makes her feathers brittle. She can't hunt or fly, so she has lived in captivity since 2014.

During the next three years as my knees healed, I visited Sarge often. One day I sat and talked with the man in charge of all the birds at the turtle park. I learned that many of Sarge's visitors are patients from the veterans' hospital.

He told me about the many injured military men and women who visit Sarge, who sometimes ask to put on a handler's glove so they can hold her. They're hurt, she's hurt. They form a bond and keep coming back and eventually get to work with Sarge as an educational leader at nursing homes, schools, and veterans programs, providing tens of thousands of people with the opportunity to get to know America's symbol of freedom up close and personal.

Sarge taught me the importance of reaching out to others. I'm drawn to people who have had knee replacements, curious as to how their healing is going. Once I tell them I had both knees done on the same day, they're eager to share their own story.

Lord, let me to reach out to those whose bodies may be failing and who need encouragement.
—Patricia Lorenz

Digging Deeper: Ezekiel 17:1–10; Isaiah 40:27–31

Wednesday, June 9

Be submissive to one another, and be clothed with humility... —1 Peter 5:5 (NKJV)

My wife and I hop off the tour bus and trudge toward the big red barns in the middle of the pasture. We are here to see the famous Budweiser Clydesdales, pastured just outside Boonville, Missouri.

These huge draft horses from Scotland are jaw-dropping beauties. Weighing over two thousand pounds each, they stand six feet to the saddle area, with another four feet of neck and head. Their lower legs are covered with white "feathers" that hide their massive hooves.

"They eat about fifty pounds of hay a day," our tour guide says, "plus about ten pounds of grain." She hands me a horseshoe, and it's the size of a dinner plate and weighs about five pounds.

"These animals cost about as much as a luxury car," she continues, "if you should want to own one."

I raise my hand. "What makes these animals so valuable?"

She smiles, as if she has heard the question before. "It's because they are so manageable, so submissive. They are gentle giants and not easily spooked. They can march in noisy parades or carry small children safely, for equine therapy."

On the bus ride home, I thought about the guide's words. "They are so manageable…submissive… gentle." What if they were not? I wondered. What if they were stubborn as mules or as violent as bucking broncos? Then all that strength would be wasted, even dangerous.

Then I thought about myself, at six-one and two hundred and thirty pounds. I am strong from a lifetime of hard work, but if I don't obey my Master, I will be of little worth to anyone.

And so I pray:

Lord, teach me to be submissive, so that my strength will be useful to others. —Daniel Schantz

Digging Deeper: Hebrews 13:17

Thursday, June 10

You intended to harm me, but God intended it for good to accomplish what is now being done, the saving of many lives. —Genesis 50:20 (NIV)

This month eighty-six years ago, an alcoholic doctor in Akron, Ohio, named Bob miraculously got sober. His sobriety date—June 10, 1935—is considered the birthday of Alcoholics Anonymous. He stopped drinking as a result of a conversation with a stranger, an out-of-work stockbroker from New York named Bill.

Bill, who had stopped drinking six months earlier, spoke of his humiliating and demoralizing powerlessness over alcohol. Drinking had led him to steal from his wife's purse, lose promising business deals in the midst of the Depression, and think of suicide.

Dr. Bob leaned in as Bill told him his alcohol problem was a deadly, progressive disease. The doctor had never heard that before, but it made sense. So, too, did Bill's solution: admit you're licked and throw yourself upon the mercy of a loving and powerful God who can do what you can't.

This story moves me because it begins with deep, black-bottomed pain. I sure don't want this pain to come to me. I give my days a "good" or "bad" rating based on how successfully I am able to avoid it. But, like with Bill, out of my own demoralizing tussles with crushing problems came a desire for mercy, which has always led me closer to God.

Bill and Dr. Bob and the experience of millions of recovering members of AA remind me that good can, with God's grace, come from bad. The scars of my sins are mine to bear and God's to heal, but yours, perhaps, to identify with and take solace from.

God, I offer You my pain, so that You may put it to good use to help others. —Amy Eddings

Digging Deeper: Job 38:25–27; 42:2–4; 2 Corinthians 4:17

Friday, June 11

Give thanks in everything, for this is God's will for you in Christ Jesus. —1 Thessalonians 5:18 (HCSB)

The light ahead changed from yellow to red. I tapped my brake pedal and came to a smooth stop. That feeling was unfamiliar to me. I was used to coming to grinding, uneven stops.

Which is why I'd had my brakes repaired that morning. At a cost of five hundred dollars. Half the market value of my 2005 car.

I'm conscientious about my spending. I wait to make major purchases until I find a sale. I pack my lunch instead of eating out. So I was irritated at having to drop so much cash on a car repair.

As I sat at the intersection, I looked across the street. A man shuffled down the sidewalk. His long gray hair was tangled. His jeans were several sizes too large. He pushed a shopping cart stuffed with worn clothes and empty aluminum cans.

Although he and I were on the same street, we were in alternate worlds. My foot pushed down on a set of five-hundred-dollar brakes. He pushed everything he owned in front of him.

Looking at the man, I felt ashamed of my complaining. I had grumbled about paying for a car repair when I should have been thankful that God blessed me with a vehicle. I had been focused on what I lost instead of considering all I had.

The man rounded the corner. By the time the light turned green, he was gone. But he left me with a change of heart. I was now appreciative of God's blessings. And I had a desire to share those blessings with people in need.

Father, thank You for providing for me even when I am undeserving. And help me to mirror Your spirit of generosity. —Logan Eliasen

Digging Deeper: Psalm 69:30; James 1:17

Saturday, June 12

So teach us to number our days, that we may get a heart of wisdom. —Psalm 90:12 (NIV)

The morning sunshine glinted off the snowcapped peaks that rimmed Lake Como as Teri and Jesse paddled their kayaks along the shoreline. It was our girls' day out to rest and have fun. But my kayak barely moved as I deeply dug the paddle into the water and strained to pull it toward myself, trying to catch up. Bobbing behind my boat was an eleven-foot-long driftwood log that I was towing. I'd discovered it on our shore-lunch break and thought it'd be perfect for decorating my yard. But that was two miles of paddling ago, and I regretted tying it behind me.

Only one more mile to go. Each time I dipped a paddle in the water, my arms burned. Teri and Jesse were nearly out of sight. I took a deep breath. *Maybe I should just quit.... But I'm not a quitter.* I fought my thoughts, tugging the log the whole way.

When we beached our kayaks and I pulled the log onshore, my heart sank. That log really wasn't unique or very pretty. It looked like all the other driftwood logs that lined the shore by the launch. I shook my head. I'd taken a perfectly great day to relax and made it into a lot of work. I was so determined not to quit that I paid too high a price for something I really didn't want.

After we loaded the kayaks into our trucks, it took two of us to lift the log into mine. I pulled away from the boat launch wondering what other unimportant things I was lugging around in my life.

Lord, reveal to me what is important, so that I don't waste my time being busy and working on things that don't matter. Amen. —Rebecca Ondov

Digging Deeper: Psalm 144:3–4; Proverbs 3:13–16

Sunday, June 13

He guides the humble in what is right and teaches them his way. —Psalm 25:9 (NIV)

I'm on the back porch of our new home and I'm missing the yard of our old home. Our Victorian was surrounded by century-old trees, lilacs, hydrangeas, ferns, ivy, and peonies. I look over this young yard, barren but for grass. I try to appreciate the creative opportunity, but I miss the scent and predictability of blooms and the familiar green life that felt like friendship.

"Hey, Mom," ten-year-old Isaiah says, "want to see if this floats?" He springs from the floor to running legs, carrying a boat he made from Popsicle sticks and a foam tray. Soon he's at the back of the yard where a creek, the bed stippled with rocks, cuts along our property. My son crouches like only a child can and places the boat in the water. It floats, but it doesn't glide. The rippling water grabs it. It veers into rocks and ends up stuck at the side. Isaiah sets it straight, but it's like a game of pinball. The boat won't stay on course.

Isaiah fishes the boat out of the water and disappears into the trees on the neighbor's side of the creek. When he returns, he has a long stick. Now when he places the boat in the water, he walks alongside. He guides the boat with his stick.

It's on its way!

Maybe I need help moving forward, too.

Where there is loss, there is grief. I've been stuck in grief for a long time. I'm hitting against memories, safety, security, and love that skims idolatry. I can't move forward on my own. Until now, I haven't had this understanding. Until now, I wasn't ready.

Isaiah continues to captain his boat, and I begin to pray.

Lord, guide me as I move from grief toward healing.
Amen. —Shawnelle Eliasen

Digging Deeper: Isaiah 30:21; Psalm 32:8

Monday, June 14

Preach the Good News.... —2 Timothy 4:2 (NCV)

It has changed my life! I am so much happier and more content. It's been so wonderful that I can't wait to tell everyone I know about it.

I should be talking about the saving power of the gospel, but unfortunately, I'm talking about my vacuum cleaner. It really is a marvel: cordless, lightweight, a pivoting head, and an easy-to-empty, bagless canister. I'd seen it in the store for a while but never dreamed I'd fork over the money to buy one. Then, last Christmas, I had a coupon on top of a store sale, a gift card, and some spending money, and there I was...smack-dab in the middle of vacuum heaven! It's been everything I'd hoped and more.

When I found myself talking to yet another friend about my new toy, I joked about how I'd been telling everyone, "I'm like a vacuum evangelist!" And that's when it hit me. The owner of the vacuum cleaner company, if he'd met me, would probably have said, "Well done, good and faithful servant. You've helped us sell a lot of vacuums."

Wow.

A preacher once told me that I should put myself on what he called the "Ten-Thousand-Year

Plan"—that is, try not to focus too much on things that won't matter ten thousand years from now.

I thought of this in regard to my floors. Ten thousand years from now, no one will know how almost effortlessly clean they've become. In fact, ten years from now... or even a week from now... no one will care! Only what I've done for the Lord will matter.

Lord, help me to focus less on day-to-day trivialities and more on the Ten-Thousand-Year Plan!
—Ginger Rue

Digging Deeper: Matthew 25:21; Mark 16:15

Tuesday, June 15

And may your hearts be fully committed to the Lord our God, to live by his decrees and obey his commands, as at this time. —1 Kings 8:61 (NIV)

Each day of my grandmother's ninety-five years began with reading the Bible and prayer. It was a practice that she began as a child—it was required by her parents—and it became a habit that she never relinquished.

Since my grandmother lived with me, I was privileged to view her daily prayer position: sitting in her mahogany-brown rocking chair in her bedroom, sunlight streaming over her right shoulder, with her large-print King James Bible with gilded pages perched on her lap. Her lips whispered the words she read, as she rocked gently to the rhythm of the verses. Her dedication and commitment to the Word resonated with me then and lives with me still, more than thirty years after her death.

I've always longed for this kind of commitment to reading and studying the Word, and thanks to two sisters in Christ and a web-based Bible site, I'm getting there! Nearly every day for the past several years, we three women—living in New York, Massachusetts, and North Carolina—jointly read devotions and Scripture, and trade thoughts on what messages God is sharing with us. Not only have these readings heightened my accountability to God, but this practice also encourages my commitment to my two prayer partners.

At long last, and thanks to technology and a love of Christ planted in me by my grandmother, I'm finally making progress in my Christian walk. And I am so very thankful.

Dear Lord, thank You for all the ways and methods that You have made available to us so we may become more learned about Your Word. May we use them wisely, to edify Your teachings. —Gayle T. Williams

Digging Deeper: 2 Chronicles 6:19; Psalm 119:103–105

Wednesday, June 16

The God of all grace . . . will Himself perfect, confirm, strengthen and establish you.
—1 Peter 5:10 (NASB)

"I feel like I'm pushing the envelope," my husband, Terry, told me, dreading a potential third spinal fusion surgery—this time a double fusion. Each surgery had helped, but more kept going wrong. Now stairs were increasingly difficult and he was in constant pain.

During this decision-making time we flew to Alaska to care for our five grandchildren for ten days. To ease his fear I suggested he see the same surgeon on the Kenai Peninsula who had looked at the scans for his first surgery. Our daughter—a registered nurse in the community— had requested those films for a second opinion.

We had never met the Alaska physician—but were incredibly grateful to him. When he had looked at Terry's original spine scans, he had urged consultation for a growth he noted on a kidney. Terry had a cancerous kidney removed before it caused other damage.

This surgeon not only fit Terry into his schedule, but also ordered an MRI and squeezed us in for a follow-up appointment. He concurred with the planned surgery—it was tricky, he said, but it could be done.

When he learned the surgery would be in Spokane, Washington, he mentioned he had a good friend living there, whom he'd taught in medical school in Chicago, who had just been up visiting. Later in the visit I happened to drop the name of Terry's Spokane surgeon. The physician exclaimed, "That's my friend!"

Terry's anxiety toward his next surgery left him. God's steadying hand was clearly visible in this unlikely bridge.

Yours, Lord, are the true skilled Physician's hands.
—Carol Knapp

Digging Deeper: 1 Chronicles 16:11; Psalm 16:8; Isaiah 41:10

Thursday, June 17

Above all, keep loving one another earnestly, since love covers a multitude of sins. —1 Peter 4:8 (ESV)

"Good morning, Celery," my son Solomon says in the doorway of my home office.

My kids started calling me Celery as a joke years ago and it stuck. Just the other day in the grocery store a man asked a clerk, "Where's the celery?" and I turned the way you do when you hear your name, making my kids laugh.

My dad would never have allowed me to call him anything but a proper parent name. When I was a defiant teenager and only saw him once or twice for a few hours each year, I started calling him Father. It had a formality and distance that reflected our relationship, and a bonus was that this fact wasn't lost on him.

Father's Day is approaching and it's always been a hard day for me. In my twenties I tried hard to mend things. I'd write honest letters. He'd write long letters back and we did reach a place where we had a future, and yet the past was still there—an abyss of hurt feelings.

My dad's death was a painful, lonely loss in ways I won't go into, only to say there was a single moment in our last conversation of complete forgiveness, where every wrong vanished because I knew I was about to lose him. All the scars of injustice and wounding memories fell away and all I was left with is what bound us together in the first place. All that remained was love.

"I love you, Dad," I say out loud, to send it out into the air, into the day, and up to heaven.

Dear Lord, thank You for guiding me back to love.
—Sabra Ciancanelli

Digging Deeper: John 15:9–10; Ephesians 4:32

Friday, June 18

If I rise on the wings of the dawn, if I settle on the far side of the sea, even there your hand will guide me, your right hand will hold me fast. —Psalm 139:9–10 (NIV)

Handing me a pocket card handwritten with the words above from Psalm 139, my mom said, "Remember, wherever you go God is always with you." I was on summer break before my junior year of college and leaving to fly to San Francisco to visit my sister Carole and her family.

That was my first major trip and those words became a life verse for me. I love the imagery that *rising on the wings of the dawn* and *settling on the far side of the sea* creates in my mind. And I cherish the promise that even on the *far side*, God is there.

Through the years, I have enjoyed traveling to some far side places in our world. One of the most remote was to see the glaciers in Patagonia, Argentina. At the time, the almost two-hundred-mile trip from Río Gallegos was mostly over gravel roads followed with a boat trip the next morning through fields of icebergs to the glaciers.

It is easy in such places, surrounded in majestic beauty, to sense God's hand. And my awareness of His presence is especially strong when I am far from home and all that is familiar. But *far side* moments also occur at home—when I am struggling with a situation that has taken me to the outer edge of my comfort zone. No matter what place I have been to—geographically or situationally—the words on the card my mom gave me years ago have always proven true. God is with us, guiding and helping—wherever we are!

Dear God, thank you for promises from the Scriptures that we stake our lives to and for Your faithfulness to fulfill them. Amen. —John Dilworth

Digging Deeper: Psalm 34:4; Isaiah 41:10; Matthew 28:20

As every man hath received the gift, even so minister the same one to another, as good stewards of the manifold grace of God. —1 Peter 4:10 (KJV)

I recently completed Education for Ministry certification, a lay program to enrich the background in Christian tradition and to help identify paths of service. Though several of my classmates discerned vocations during the four years of study and entered seminary, I did not. Instead, I continue serving as I always have done: providing hospitality, singing, writing, and listening, which some call Ministry of Presence. Humble offerings, indeed.

I keep thinking I should be doing more, but schedules never align for me to join medical missions or relief efforts. Volunteering at the Homeless Resource Center didn't seem to tap my oddball skill set. Nor vestry—I doze off during long meetings. I pray continuously for God to help me find my paths of service.

Perhaps God's challenge for me is to discern ministry relationships in ordinary, everyday life. So I reflect:

I led a spiritual writing seminar—and the participants said I helped them to release their stories, some decades old. My ghostwriting helped refugee friends tell their stories, too.

A friend chatted at length during coffee hour. As we parted, she said, "Every time I talk with you, I feel so much better!"

Just yesterday, our choir director, whom I think of as a daughter, said, "I see you and feel like I'm with my own mom!"

So I keep doing what I'm doing, inspired by Jesus's observation: "Whoever is faithful in very little is also faithful in much" (Luke 16:10 CSB). Maybe one day I'll be called to a more visible or dynamic ministry. In the meantime, I'm using and developing God's gifts to me.

Loving Lord, let me ever discern Your still, small voice as You guide my lay ministry.
—Gail Thorell Schilling

Digging Deeper: Romans 12:6–7;
1 Corinthians 12:4;
1 Timothy 4:14; Revelation 2:19

Father's Day, Sunday, June 20

Do not withhold good from those to whom it is due, when it is in your power to act. —Proverbs 3:27 (NIV)

A friend invited me to a concert performance of a musical I remembered well, although it's probably not on most people's hit list, *The Happy Time* by that venerable team of Kander and Ebb, better known for shows like *Cabaret* and *Chicago*.

The Happy Time had its out-of-town premiere in Los Angeles at the then newly built Music Center.

I was an eleven-year-old kid who loved listening to recordings of musicals, but they usually opened thousands of miles away, on Broadway. Here was one that was happening a short freeway ride away. I just *had* to see it. I had to go to that show. I must have been pretty insistent because my dad took me to it, just the two of us, and I got to watch Robert Goulet perform. Live. Onstage.

Sometimes it's not for many years—we're talking almost fifty years here—that the power of a gift and the giver's generosity really registers. At that revival, as I was listening to the score, one of the actors sang that poignant song that Goulet premiered, "I Don't Remember You." *I do remember,* I thought. All at once I was that stagestruck eleven-year-old. I thought about how busy Mom and Dad were back then, how money could be tight raising us four children, how Dad himself wasn't particularly enamored of Broadway musicals.

But he loved me. That was enough. That was everything. Loving someone means knowing what they love, understanding what makes them truly happy. That was the lesson of a lifetime.

Father God, we give thanks to the fathers in our lives and the gifts they gave us. Even if it takes years to account for all of them. —Rick Hamlin

Digging Deeper: Deuteronomy 16:17; Luke 6:38

Monday, June 21

STRUGGLING TO PRAY: Is There a Right Way to Pray?

I tell you, you can pray for anything, and if you believe that you've received it, it will be yours.
—Mark 11:24 (NLT)

I've always felt inadequate as a pray-er. Certainly, I don't pray as well—or as much or as creatively—as other believers I know.

My husband, for example, talks to God first thing each morning and last thing each night. At length.

"What do you talk about?" I've asked.

"Oh, just stuff going on," he says.

"How do you remember to do it?"

"How can I forget?" is his reply.

Various friends' "prayer lives," as they call them, are equally impressive. One drinks tea with God every morning, setting out a steaming cup for Him in her breakfast nook. Another takes prayer walks on trails around her property. Once she prayed for our respective towns by lying down on the trail, one arm extended toward my town, the other toward hers.

Various prayer experts I've sought out promote similarly inventive practices: speaking Scripture aloud, just listening, singing. I've tried them all, hoping to experience prayer as an indispensable, exciting part of my day, as vital to me as it clearly is to them. Some methods, like singing, connect me more, but I never feel truly *with* God as with a flesh-and-blood person. My "conversations" feel at best one-sided, at worst, fictional.

I wonder if others' prayer practices might result from frustrations similar to mine—that God isn't audible or visible or tangible, as humans are. After all, God doesn't actually drink the tea my friend puts out. Maybe prayer is simply our feeble human yearning to experience him even so.

That notion comforts me—especially given Jesus's disciples' similar worries about prayer. He gave them a template but also reassured them that whoever asks receives, whoever seeks finds.

Father, accept as prayer even this groaned desire to pray better. —Patty Kirk

Digging Deeper: Luke 11:1–11

Tuesday, June 22

And Moses said unto God, Who am I, that I should go unto Pharaoh, and that I should bring forth the children of Israel out of Egypt? —Exodus 3:11 (KJV)

Recently, a successful friend of mine spoke to me openly, admitting to a lifelong struggle. Multigifted, he's nonetheless plagued with never quite feeling on par with his colleagues. The confession stung. Little did he know he was looking into a mirror, for often when God singles me out to complete a task, I quail, balking when my heart longs to embrace the call. "Who, me?" I ask. "Who am I to tackle this pharaoh?"

253

The crippling thought of *I'm not good enough* threads the biblical witness. When God commands Moses to lead the Hebrews out of Egypt, Moses asks, "Who am I that I should go unto Pharaoh?" while later Gideon, whom God chooses to battle for the soul of Israel, complains that he is the least of his clan. King Solomon admits, "I am but a little child" who knows not "how to go out or come in," even as the soon-to-be-queen Esther wonders if she is up to the task of saving her people.

Twenty-first-century believers who question their gifts are simply versions of their spiritual forebears. In modern times, we call this low self-esteem, but could it be that the first half of that hyphenated word, *self*, is often the culprit? Is it mostly a prideful stubborn dependence on self that scares and thwarts believers?

We have an option. We can latch onto the truth that we did not choose ourselves. It is Jesus who chooses us. It is not what we esteem ourselves to be. It is what the Lord has already chosen us to be and do.

Lord, grant me the strength to ignore self-absorption and do what You've chosen me to do.
—Jacqueline F. Wheelock

Digging Deeper: Jeremiah 1:6–8; Psalm 31:1; John 15:16

Wednesday, June 23

And God is able to bless you abundantly, so that in all things at all times, having all that you need, you will abound in every good work. —2 Corinthians 9:8 (NIV)

I was soaking in the bath the first time I heard it, a weird animal sound, a crackling that I couldn't quite place. A rattling above my head in the eaves or maybe behind the window shutters. I got quiet and it did, too; I waited, but the commotion ended, so I forgot all about it.

A week or so later, I glanced out the bathroom window just as a black bird flew into our house. From my vantage point, that's exactly what I saw and heard. A bird flew not above, but into our house.

Grabbing my robe, I went down the stairs, out the back door to the side of the house. Sure enough, a cover from one of the attic's vents had come off sometime in the winter and an opportunistic starling had made itself a nest. And so it seemed there was nothing for us to do, at least not until later in the year.

For over a month now, I've watched this bird bring twigs and stringy things (I'm guessing worms) into its nest in the small vent in our attic. I cringe thinking about the mess it will leave behind after its babies fly the coop, but for right now, honestly, it is a joy. I sit in the bathroom and watch it take off and land the way that people used to watch planes at airports.

Witnessing a starling soar from its nest is like seeing a miracle. Effortlessly, it glides into the air, right into life, and I feel free, changed, inspired, ready for the day.

Heavenly Father, thank You for the surprises in life that change my perspective and fill me with wonder.
—Sabra Ciancanelli

Digging Deeper: Isaiah 14:14; 40:31

Thursday, June 24

Love one another the way I loved you.
—John 15:12 (MSG)

The Priority Mail two-day delivery box arrived on our front porch as a real surprise. With expectancy, we opened the Butter Maid Bakery container.

Inside was a "Handmade with Love" genuine kolachi roll. To see the word kolachi was to recall savory kitchen aromas of my mom's dessert baking. Her yeast-dough kolachi-with-prunes, still warm from the oven, topped with real butter, remains a culinary highlight of my youth.

Immediately upon opening the box, we sliced off pieces from the large log-shaped roll. After warming it for thirty seconds in the microwave, I placed a forkful in my mouth. Ah...the first bite was a taste of Mom's Minnesota Czech kolachi recipe, appetizing and delicious.

My wife's sister and brother-in-law sent these lip-smacking treats. Few have supported us more in our thirty years of army life than Jan and Bill. Over the decades, their thoughtfulness, wise counsel, and encouragement have made a real difference.

Though unknown to them, the package arrived just before my Mom's birthday.

In my exuberance over the back-home kitchen flavor, I researched the web, found the vendor, and had kolachi roll treats express-delivered to my two brothers and sister. The occasion honored the memory of our mother.

"The dough tastes like Mom's!" came a happy face, thumbs-up emoji text from my sister. "The Kolachi Roll you sent us in Mom's memory was out of this world! Thank you! She would have loved it!" was another written response.

Sharing the love. Multiplying the joy. Isn't this what a life of faith is all about?

All-loving God, we thank You for those You've graced us with, who offer encouragement, inspiration, and hope. Amen. —Ken Sampson

Digging Deeper: Matthew 6:30; John 15:11–15

Friday, June 25

See to it that no one comes short of the grace of God; that no root of bitterness springing up causes trouble. —Hebrews 12:15 (NASB)

The cement truck was on the way and I was looking down at a stubborn root that threatened to delay the entire patio project. The thing had to be eight inches thick. I was convinced it was made out of some space-age compound of steel and rubber. I swung the ax, but it just bounced off. Ax to handsaw, handsaw to chain saw—the horrible sprout just laughed at me, comfortable right where it was.

Isn't that the way with roots? Some give up easy, some are hard to pull. And the longer we leave them, the bigger and more intractable they get. Bitterness, anger, fear, envy. They sprout from a lot of different

257

"trees," but all have one thing in common—unless we successfully remove them, it's impossible to lay a good and firm foundation for the future work God has for us.

Have you struggled with impossible roots? Don't worry; most of us have, me especially. But there is good news! I can say with the experience of years that we have something infinitely greater than a chain saw. Rest your arms, let go of the ax, raise the white flag. Then watch *God's love* start to dig away at those roots.

Thank you, Jesus—that big old backyard root is finally gone. And so are a few dozen that tried their best to choke my heart.

I am free.

And, hey, the patio is in and the sun is out. I think it's time for a barbecue.

Search me, God! By the power of Your love, remove anything in me that might keep me from Your perfect plan for my life. —Buck Storm

Digging Deeper: Psalm 139:23–24;
2 Corinthians 5:17

Saturday, June 26

Not with our forefathers did the Lord make this covenant, but with us, we, all of whom are alive today. —Deuteronomy 5:3 (CHABAD)

I've watched a lot of Bar and Bat Mitzvahs over the years. I don't remember whose was the first I saw—perhaps a cousin. When I was growing up, women did not get a synagogue ceremony, so I never had one of my own. In Los Angeles, Keith and I belonged to a *chavurah* (extended family) and celebrated with the other members of the group when it was their kids' turns. I got used to being a spectator for someone else's family's rite of passage.

Then I was asked to become the Jewish grandmother for a previously unknown family where I live now in Washington, because they wanted a third generation on the bimah during their oldest son's Bar Mitzvah. After I'd spent enough time with the family, I agreed.

But it wasn't until I was actually standing on the bimah that I felt the weight of thousands of years of tradition setting onto my shoulders as I took the Torah from the rabbi to pass along to Michael's parents. I could picture it so clearly that for a moment I wondered why my knees weren't buckling from the heaviness of the responsibility. I cradled the Torah for a second or two and then gave it to Michael's dad and mom. As I did, I realized how thoughtless I'd been in just accepting the honor they were offering without thinking about what it really meant.

They were trusting me to help them bring Michael to something important—not just to them, but to God. I had tears in my eyes as I joined the procession through the congregation. And I didn't wipe them away.

Help me to hold up the weight of Your words, Lord, as well as to uphold them. —Rhoda Blecker

Digging Deeper: Exodus 24:4; Deuteronomy 32:7

Sunday, June 27

Let each of you look out not only for his own interests, but also for the interests of others. —Philippians 2:4 (NKJV)

I've always earmarked money for the causes that touch my heart—scholarship donations for students, a monthly contribution to a Christian broadcasting station to support faith-based content. My habit had become to give from my purse, but not of my time. So when a friend spearheading a community service project asked me to join, I hesitantly agreed.

On a Sunday afternoon following church service, I gathered with a group of ladies to try my hand at transforming pillowcases into dresses and shirts for Haitian children in need. Most of the women were adept at stay stitching, finishing seams, maneuvering elastic bands, and handling the sewing machines with ease. Being a novice, I took on the job of securing embellishments with straight pins.

While we worked at our appointed sewing stations, I relaxed into the meditative work—I asked God to bless the work of our hands. As we shared our life's stories and daily struggles, I marveled at how the fabrics of our lives were so similar and how common threads wove our lives together.

This experience has changed how I serve others. Once it meant delivering dinner to neighbors grieving the loss of a loved one. Other times I've watched the children of an exhausted mother, and filled the gas tank of an elderly person with limited income. Since that Sunday with pillowcases, I'm often reminded how small sacrifices of my time impact the lives of others and at the same time change my life for the better.

Lord, let me be the extension of Your hands and Your love to those in need. Bless even the smallest acts, so that Your love can be experienced and shared to those who need it most. —Tia McCollors

Digging Deeper: Psalm 9:9; Proverbs 11:25; 19:17

Monday, June 28

Let all that you do be done in love. —1 Corinthians 16:14 (ESV)

As our long wars have wound down and the troops have finally come home to their communities and families, many face personal battles that could last for years, even a lifetime. Traumatic brain injury, moral injury, amputations and physical impairment, post-traumatic stress disorder—all are the scars of battle that many military personnel and their families carry. We can't forget them now that they have returned to the country they defended so selflessly.

I often think of my uncle Vince when he returned home from World War II. Unlike his two older brothers, he was never quite the same. He was a successful civil engineer but was not particularly ambitious despite his abilities. He never married, lived alone, and mostly kept to himself. He took his vacation every October so he could watch the World Series, back when the games were played in the afternoon. His garrulous bothers loved to tell stories about the war (all three were part of the D-Day invasion). Vince never did.

I remember a kind and quiet man with gentle eyes. My mom had a soft spot for her little brother and told me he went to Mass every day. She took extra care with Vince, as if she knew he suffered. I know she prayed for him. A chain smoker after he returned from the war, Vince died before he could retire.

Today we would suspect that Vince struggled with PTSD. If only we knew then what we know now. That the mental and emotional wounds of war are grievous and require the same therapeutic attention as physical wounds. Because it is love, love for the wounded soldier, that is most critical. And that is something we can all give.

Lord, love heals the wounds of the mind and spirit. Let me keep all the warriors who have sacrificed so much in my prayers today. —Edward Grinnan

Digging Deeper: John 13:34–35

You will seek me and find me, when you seek me with all your heart. —Jeremiah 29:13 (ESV)

My friend Alice brought home a kitten from the local shelter. Alice named her kitten Suzanne, an adorable tabby with folded ears.

Suzanne very quickly felt at home with Alice. And since Alice is British, I'll repeat what Alice told me one month in: "I'm this kitten's mum!"

One night, Alice had some friends over for dinner. Before sitting down, I asked where Suzanne had gone. "I've locked her in my bedroom," Alice explained. Alice was worried that one of her guests might be allergic to cat fur.

Midway through dinner, we heard a *crash* upstairs. Alice ran to investigate. "My cat seems to have bumped a lamp," she said, upon her return. Fifteen minutes later, we heard another crash. Alice ran upstairs again to investigate. Lamp number two had hit the floor.

We all realized, then, what was happening. This not-so-simple kitten knew where she wanted to be, and knew how to get her human friend's attention!

I am in need of Your attention today, God.
I'll do what I have to do to be with You!
—Jon M. Sweeney

Digging Deeper: Song of Songs 8:6

Wednesday, June 30

But our bodies have many parts, and God has put each part just where he wants it. How strange a body would be if it had only one part!
—1 Corinthians 12:18–19 (NLT)

Among many blessings of living out in the country is the ability to see an abundance of wildlife. A number of wild turkeys roam our neighborhood, with adorable chicks, called poults, following along. They help keep down the bug population, so our neighborhood appreciates them.

As I watched a small flock of turkeys make their way across the open field behind our house, something grabbed my eye. There was the mother, followed by four light brown poults, all pecking and foraging as they went. But it was a flash of white that caught my attention. At first, I thought another species was following the little flock. Upon closer inspection, I saw that it was a pure white poult. A pure white turkey.

I have now seen them most days for a couple of weeks. The poults are indistinguishable from each other, except for the one sporting all-white plumage. I've since learned these are quite rare in the wild. I wonder what this little one's brothers and sisters think. *Why are you different? Do you really fit in? Why are you here? You don't belong with the rest of us!*

As I sat in the early morning hours, sipping coffee, and watching these noble birds, God whispered to my heart. In his family, we all fit in. We all count. We all are equally beloved and equally precious in God's sight, no matter what everybody else thinks.

Thank you, little white turkey friend, for reminding me that it's our differences that make us beautiful.

Lord, give me Your heart to see the beauty in the infinite variety You've woven into Your awe-inspiring creation. Amen. —Bill Giovannetti

Digging Deeper: Galatians 3:28

JOYFUL IN HOPE

1 _____

2 _____

3 _____

4 _____

5 _____

6 _____

7 _____

8 _____

9 _____

10 _____

11 _____

12 _____

13 _____

14 _____

15 _____

16 _____

17 _____

18 _____

19 _____

20 _____

21 _____

22 _____

23 _____

24 _____

25 _____

26 _____

27 _____

28 _____

29 _____

30 _____

JULY

The Lord is near to all who call on him,
to all who call on him in truth.

—Psalm 145:18 (NIV)

Thursday, July 1

**All the ways of a man are pure in his own sight, but the Lord weighs the spirit. Commit your work to the Lord, and your plans will be established.
—Proverbs 16:2–3 (ESV)**

It was just a little puddle next to the driveway.

At first, we thought it was remnants from the cold, rainy spring we had. But then the sun came out and the ground dried out and began to crack everywhere except the area around that little puddle.

A few weeks later we got a water bill and it was a bit higher than normal. We weren't concerned, but we did call a plumber to check for a leak. He didn't find one, and instead suggested that we have the water company replace the meter.

They did. The puddle stayed. The next water bill was even higher.

We justified it. It had been a very rainy year. And sometimes groundwater just sits under the surface. Then came a water bill that was a hundred dollars over our normal average and suddenly all of our justifying and explaining and rationalizing seemed silly.

Twelve hundred dollars, twenty-eight hours, and a rented jackhammer later, we found the leak, huge and spurting, about six feet into the middle of our driveway.

It's fixed now. The puddle has finally disappeared, and the driveway has been patched. Every time I drive over that slightly discolored section of the concrete, I am reminded not only of how a tiny leak can cause huge damage, but also of how easy it is to rationalize it away.

Just like our sin. It may seem tiny, but over time, it wears away at what Jesus intends for our lives. And if we keep explaining it away, that tiny leak becomes a flooding stream that can cause a lot of damage.

Father God, reveal to me my struggles when they are just small leaks, before they become gushing fountains. —Erin MacPherson

Digging Deeper: Psalm 119:25–29; Isaiah 40:28–31

Friday, July 2

How good and pleasant it is when God's people live together in unity! —Psalm 133:1 (NIV)

"Oma, would you help me set up a lemonade stand?" my nine-year-old granddaughter texted one summer afternoon. I was home alone savoring the solitude to finish a project. So I wrestled with my answer—for about two seconds. There's just something about a lemonade stand.

I knew Peyton was home alone with her older brother and sister who'd outgrown the lure of a lemonade stand. "I'll come right over," I texted back. Soon, we'd made a huge sign, gathered supplies, and carried a small folding table down the driveway to set up shop in the shade on their neighborhood street. Two kinds of lemonade and some plastic cups. Nothin' fancy. Peyton set the price at a dollar a cup, with free refills. *Inflation!* I thought, remembering her mom's lemonade stands a generation ago. Peyton was here for the earnings; I was here for the memories.

Her first customer was a burly man in a construction truck.

"My kids used to have lemonade stands," he said, handing over a couple of dollar bills.

A biker zoomed by. "I'll be back!" he yelled, and soon reappeared. "Went home to get money. I can't pass up a lemonade stand."

The mail delivery vehicle stopped. "I love lemonade stands," the driver said, sipping her pink lemonade and telling us about her life as a mail carrier.

Others stopped—more workers, a teenager learning to drive, neighbors with their kids.

The last customer was a man on his way home from work. "There's just something about a lemonade stand," he said wistfully as he handed Peyton a five-dollar bill. "Keep the change. And thanks."

Lord, You are the powerful Creator of the universe and tender Shepherd who gathers generations and neighbors together at a simple lemonade stand. Thank You. —Carol Kuykendall

Digging Deeper: Luke 10:27; John 15:11

Then God said, "I am giving you a sign of my covenant with you and with all living creatures, for all generations to come. I have placed my rainbow in the clouds. It is the sign of my covenant with you and with all the earth. —Genesis 9:12–13 (NLT)

Eagles have played a significant role in my life. My maiden name is the German word for eagle, and while I had always been aware of this, it didn't affect me one way or the other until after my parents died.

When our oldest daughter, Jody, was married on the beach on a perfect summer's day in mid-July, two eagles suddenly appeared. As she stood exchanging her vows with Greg, the eagles flew overhead and circled them. I reached for Wayne's hand and whispered, "That's Mom and Dad."

Later at a cousin reunion, I experienced another eagle occurrence. As I was cleaning up after our get-together, I found an eagle feather in the yard. We'd lived in that house for over twenty years, and I'd never once found anything related to an eagle. Again, I felt, it was my parents' way of letting me know they'd been enjoying listening in to all the fun and laughter.

After Wayne and I sold our Florida home and were seeking to purchase a beach house, we looked at many properties. I knew we'd found the right one when we learned that two eagles had a huge nest in one of the trees close to the house. In my eyes that was a sure sign—this was the home for us.

Over the years God has given me several signs, but here's what I've found that I need to remember most. While signs are often a comfort and a gift, they all point back to the giver: our loving heavenly Father, who comforts and reassures us.

O Lord, open our eyes to the signs You place in each of our lives. May we never forget that they all point back to You and Your love for Your children.
—Debbie Macomber

Digging Deeper: Isaiah 43:2

Independence Day, Sunday, July 4

Have we not all one father?... —Malachi 2:10 (KJV)

Last week, I put my newspaper down on my desk and groaned out loud. "If I read one more disappointing story about our political system, I will lose my mind."

My assistant, Jeannine, walked by my office and rolled her eyes.

"The Fourth of July's coming up," she says, leaving a space for me to fill.

I grew up in a political family. We worked hard for good candidates, who we felt reflected our beliefs as expressed in Matthew 25. They didn't always win, but they always left us proud.

As a child, I remember seeing Tip O'Neill and Ronald Reagan smiling at each other over a drink at the end of the day, their civility trumping their political differences.

At that moment, my mailbox dinged. "You are invited to an Independence Day Celebration" danced across the screen in red, white, and blue letters. I scanned down and saw that the event was being held by several friends, both Democrat and Republican.

Earlier, my mother had told me about a neighborhood in east Tennessee that was planning their twenty-eighth annual Fourth of July parade. Politically mixed, they would be decorating bikes, scooters, strollers, wagons, and riding lawn mowers for a grand procession of music and singing as they traveled to the annual barbecue on the town square.

And down in rural Alabama, where my family has had a cabin for three generations, 452 American flags will be set along Highway 411, flying proud in memory of local veterans who gave all for our country.

In all of this, God seemed to be reminding me that the pulse of America was beating strong in its people. Today, hope surrounds me as I bow my head and pray:

Father, You tell us that we are Your children, Your family. Move us past strife and bring us together to realize the dream of America for all. —Brock Kidd

Digging Deeper: Genesis 13:8; John 13:34

Monday, July 5

Do not boast about tomorrow, for you do not know what a day may bring. —Proverbs 27:1 (NIV)

The Pacific island country of Vanuatu lies eleven hundred miles northeast of Australia. My husband and I spent a day there on one of its islands, admiring lush, brightly blossomed foliage, glass-clear waters, tumbling streams, emerald grasses, and white sands. We passed wind-twisted trees, roots dangling fringelike from their limbs, and coconut-laden groves. Schoolchildren acknowledged us shyly as they walked the roads we drove. An islander dozed in a hammock. A woman washed clothes on a rock while children swam in the sun-drenched river in which she stood. Laundry-filled lines undulated behind rough-hewn houses. Locals waved, nodded, and smiled. I bought a small carved wooden Rom dance statuette. The Rom dance is a local traditional dance portraying good vs. evil. That day we had indeed seen good.

Three days after we left Vanuatu, it was hit by a Category 5 cyclone with winds over a hundred and sixty miles per hour. Ninety percent of its buildings were damaged or destroyed. Sixteen islanders were dead, over thirty-three hundred left homeless.

I was struck hard by the contrast between the good and the evil, how both are a part of all our lives. I ran my fingers along the silken wood of my Rom dance statuette, carved by someone I had felt lived a life much different than my own. But the cyclone had opened my eyes to a larger truth. Regardless of where and how we live, we are, every one of us, doing our own Rom dance, a dance between wonders and trials, good and evil.

Lord, my heart and prayers go out to the brave people of Vanuatu and all who suffer tragedy. May we all remember that though our lives may differ, we are all fellow journeyers in this vast, unpredictable, yet amazing world. —Kim Taylor Henry

Digging Deeper: Ephesians 2:19; 4:4–6

Tuesday, July 6

"For I know the plans I have for you," declares the Lord, "plans to prosper you and not to harm you, plans to give you hope and a future." —Jeremiah 29:11 (NIV)

I was seventeen the first time I visited New York City, hitchhiking one summer from Michigan with a schoolmate after promising our parents we'd take a bus. My first impression was mixed.

I was overwhelmed—not unpleasantly so—by the sheer intensity of New York, its relentless energy and teeming humanity, its crowds and traffic. My friend had lived in Manhattan previously, and he took me on the roaring subway speeding under neighborhood after neighborhood, to Central Park and Morningside Heights, to St. Patrick's Cathedral. He introduced me to Patience and Fortitude, the proud stone lions who guard the entrance to the New York Public Library, a veritable cathedral in its own right. My neck was crinked from gazing up at the soaring glass and steel office towers lining Third Avenue.

It was like walking onto a movie set, a great, sweeping Hollywood epic about a living, breathing metropolis. The undisputed center of the world. Maybe this is why there was a nagging unreality about New York to my young, suburbanite eyes. Where were the two-car garages? The rolling lawns? The Weber grills? The backyard swing sets? That night, trying to fall asleep amid the cacophony of bleating taxis twenty floors below, I asked, *How can people actually live here?*

Fifteen years after that first visit I found myself working in one of those skyscrapers on Third Avenue writing for a magazine I'd barely heard of called *Guideposts* and living in Manhattan. I've lived here ever since, way longer than I have lived anywhere else. New York is not just where I live, it is home, both to my family and my work.

God has a way of showing you where He wants you to be. I never dreamed at seventeen that my future was being revealed to me.

God, thank You for planting us where we are meant to grow. —Edward Grinnan

Digging Deeper: Psalm 37:5; Isaiah 26:3–4

BECOMING JUST ME AGAIN
Stages of Grief

**Although God gives him grief, yet he will show
compassion too, according to the greatness of his
loving kindness. —Lamentations 3:32 (TLB)**

After Jack's funeral I made long lists of things that
needed to be done. Every inch of my big dining
room table was covered with papers. Sympathy
cards, thank-you cards I had to write, Jack's unpaid
medical bills, his bank statements, utility bills, notes
about removing his name on this and that, papers
from his desk. It was a sad, lonely task.

Some days I felt so alone that I was sure my
health would disintegrate and I would die in a few
years. But then the next day I'd be in the pool doing
my water aerobic exercises and I'd feel so happy and
free that I wanted to shout for joy. Then I would
immediately quash that feeling with a big pile of
guilt. I'd say to myself, *You're a grieving widow, knock
off the happiness.*

Then a letter came from hospice explaining
that some of the common feelings after the death
of a loved one include feeling numb, stunned,
confused, disbelieving, relieved, calm, grateful,
tearful, out of control, ready to move on, empty,
lonely, and focused on the past. *Oh, dear God, yes!*
That explained all the mixed-up feelings I'd been
having. At least I knew I wasn't going crazy. That list

helped me understand that it was perfectly normal and smart to accept not only the sad feelings but the positive ones as well.

One thing is certain. I believe with all my heart that Jack is in heaven doing a happy dance because I am moving forward, content, sleeping well, exercising, doing things with my friends, traveling, and anxious to experience all that life has to offer.

Lord, give me the daily grace to know that even though I miss Jack terribly I need to be positive, happy, grateful, and moving forward.
—Patricia Lorenz

Digging Deeper: 2 Samuel 19:1–7; Psalm 73:21–26; Hebrews 12:12

Thursday, July 8

Lord, You have heard the desire of the humble; You will prepare their heart. —Psalm 10:17 (NKJV)

I've lived on this street for decades and have seen a generation of children grow up. Some still live here, like Cynthia, now approaching thirty. Last weekend I saw her in her yard grilling fajitas. "Before you douse the coals, can I char a few hot dogs?"

"Sure, Miss Evelyn."

We chatted. I pointed to two diseased trees in front of my apartment. "They're marked for cutting."

"I noticed. I remember," she said knowingly. Late one afternoon twenty years ago, she and I had watched men in a cherry picker finishing a day's work—having chopped a big maple down to a naked trunk. I sobbed as they reduced it to a short stump. Twice in the next week, Cynthia came by to ask a specific question. "Are you still sad about the tree?"

We both recollect my distress. Since then, several other trees have been removed. My heart clings to four old oaks that harbor squirrels and songbirds—and sometimes a preying hawk—outside my second-floor home-office window. But now the two closest to me are marked for removal. This time blue ribbons tied around the trunks give fair warning. I can prepare for the loss. By commiserating with neighbors. By praying for grace. By appreciating the leafy sights and sidewalk shadows while they're still at hand. By anticipating an expanded view of the wide sky. By asking management if they could plant a sapling—maybe two.

Lord, when a loss seems inevitable, help me prepare my heart for a hopeful future. —Evelyn Bence

Digging Deeper: Jeremiah 29:11–14

Friday, July 9

If we live, we live for the Lord; and if we die, we die for the Lord. So, whether we live or die, we belong to the Lord. —Romans 14:8 (NIV)

It was early one summer morning when my wife and I received a call letting us know that our dear friend and past coworker, Oneida, had passed away from cancer. This news took us by surprise and deeply saddened us. It had been a while since we last saw Oneida, but thankfully we both had the pleasure of working with her at different organizations. She was truly an amazing person.

Prior to working at Guideposts, Oneida was diagnosed with and eventually overcame cancer. With all that she had been through in the past, she blessed us at the organization with her upbeat spirit and love for life. However, shortly after Oneida left the organization her cancer returned. She had been cancer-free for eight whole years, but sadly was forced to fight the battle yet again.

As hard as times were, Oneida never let her cancer get the best of her. She continued to build the Living Waters Retreat and Conference Center and serve at her local church while undergoing chemotherapy until her health got much worse. Up until the end, Oneida stayed positive and prayerful and continued to hope for a miracle.

At the funeral, her husband, Mike, shared stories about Oneida. He recalled how Oneida began painting rocks and writing words on them that meant a lot to her. He stated that he never gave these rocks much attention until one day he paused to look at them. One rock in particular that stood out to him said Worshipping You as I Wait. Even though she was in great pain, Oneida never stopped worshipping God.

Lord, teach us to worship You in our most difficult times. —Pablo Diaz

Digging Deeper: Psalm 103:1; Philippians 1:20

Saturday, July 10

Do everything without grumbling or arguing.
—Philippians 2:14 (NIV)

"The heat is driving me crazy!" I complained to our grown daughter, Katelyn. The continual blast of temperatures over a hundred degrees—a normal occurrence in Arizona summers—had been relentless, wearing me down.

"Everyone at work was complaining about the weather, too," she agreed, detailing the guests who came to the hotel where she worked at the front desk. "And we were servicing the pool today, so people were not happy."

"We could go to the mall."

She grimaced. "Too crowded."

"We could play a board game. I did that as a girl during a blizzard."

Snowed-in days during my childhood in rural Minnesota had meant endless games of Monopoly. My siblings and I had fought over Park Place and Boardwalk, while our mom had made chicken noodle soup and grilled cheese sandwiches and Dad had shoveled a path out to the barn. Sometimes we had bundled up to go sledding before returning to rub frostbitten faces and drink cups of hot chocolate.

Katelyn interrupted my nostalgia. "I've never seen a blizzard."

"What! How is that possible?" I went through her twenty-six years in my mind, incredulous at the thought. She had been born in Arizona, but we had traveled often to the Midwest to visit her grandparents. Had we missed all the bad weather? How could something so prominent in my childhood memories not even exist in hers?

Katelyn shrugged. "We live in a desert." She walked into the kitchen, pulling cream and eggs from the fridge. "Want to make homemade ice cream?"

Jesus, help me release my grumbling and discover homemade-ice-cream goodness in my current reality.
—Lynne Hartke

Digging Deeper: Ephesians 4:29; Philippians 4:8

Sunday, July 11

For the jar of flour was not used up and the jug of oil did not run dry, in keeping with the word of the LORD spoken by Elijah. —1 Kings 17:16 (NIV)

Our family spent the day on a small lake. The water glinted and glimmered as my husband, Lonny, and two sons skimmed the surface in a canoe. Sixteen-year-old Samuel and I climbed onto a paddleboat that was tethered to the dock. Soon, we were loose—moving backward in an arc and then toward family.

The sky was robin's-egg blue and rich with peace. I closed my eyes and the sun warmed me soul-deep, but suddenly Lonny's voice was jarring. "Head back," he shouted. "Sam, take Mom in now!" His arms waved like a madman's.

Sam and I shrugged, but we sputter-whirred back. We wondered what was up, though not for long. Lonny shared as soon as we were all firm-footed on the dock.

There were snakes in this lake. Lots of them. And Lonny understood my fear.

"I didn't want you to go wild and fall in," he said. I may have, but Lonny provided for me.

That day the provision was protection, but he provides many things. Encouragement. Support. Hands-on help. I know he's always ready to reach into my life.

This provision, though human and slight in comparison, offers a glimpse of God's love.

Recently, I've learned to cling to Him as Provider: A circumstance with a son is difficult, and I can't see how things will work out. But God meets my every need. Not always in the way I expect, but like with the oil and flour in the widow's jars, there's always provision. It's always enough.

We left the lake and picnicked on rustic tables a safe distance away. I didn't expect slithery visitors. But if they came, I'd be okay.

Lord, You are my faithful Provider. Amen.
—Shawnelle Eliasen
Digging Deeper: Psalm 34:10; 81:10

Monday, July 12

But whoever drinks the water I give them will never thirst. Indeed, the water I give them will become in them a spring of water welling up to eternal life.
—John 4:14 (NIV)

My morning devotion was pocked with wondering if I would ever be totally free from dry mouth caused by allergies and chronic congestion and their attendant sleeplessness. Indulging myself at the table of an extended pity party, I wondered how Jesus could say, in the scene where he meets the woman at the well, that I would never thirst again. Silly of me, I knew. I understood the spiritual implications, but I was thirsty for the outdoors, the fragrance of honeysuckles and roses, normal breathing.

Then, as He is wont to do, the Spirit infused the words Jesus spoke centuries ago, the hope of that "spring of water welling up to eternal life" plumbing a new depth in my soul. Jesus was not promising me the proverbial "rose garden" experience. I'm not guaranteed an earthly existence minus the annoyance of mouth-breathing. Yet His Spirit never quits. He is always there "welling up," nudging us back from despair toward the bliss Jesus has prepared for us. Paul puts it aptly in 2 Corinthians 4:8 (NIV). "We are hard pressed on every side . . . perplexed but not in despair."

Even if we don't understand how, the all-capacious Spirit of the Living God rushes into the dry places reimmersing us into Himself. Delighting us. Refilling us—so that the inner spirit is renewed day by day. Suddenly, I saw myself, dry mouth and all, full of the glorious moisture that only God supplies, setting the tone for a lovely summer's day.

Holy Spirit, continue to water my soul with hope and understanding. —Jacqueline F. Wheelock

Digging Deeper: Isaiah 12:3; 55:1; John 6:35

Tuesday, July 13

You shall love the Lord your God with all your heart, with all your soul, and with all your strength. —Deuteronomy 6:5 (NKJV)

I was upstairs waiting for my husband to return home. He'd been away for a few days to care for his mother post-surgery, and both the children and I missed him tremendously. A short time before his expected return, I heard a deep voice downstairs talking to my daughter. I announced his arrival to my youngest, who was sprawled across my bed reading. He sprang to his feet, nearly tumbling over himself as he sprinted downstairs.

To both of our surprises, the deep voice was actually my son's. He'd recently turned thirteen, and overnight it seemed as if his shoulders had broadened, the pudgy childlike face had transformed to a more mature and lean countenance, and we now stood eye-to-eye. His voice and physical stature weren't the only things changing.

As the years ticked by, he'd have to bear more responsibilities. He'd make decisions without parental insight and be presented with situations that would test his faith. Life would take him down paths that would bring him to a crossroad. Would he veer toward the path that was illuminated by God's light?

I watched as my oldest son popped leftovers in the microwave; then he looked over his shoulder with an assuring smile and that silly look that always makes me laugh. We spoke no words between us, but God already knew the unspoken yearning of my heart. Not only for him, but for all of my children— that His Word and His way be the guiding force in their lives.

Like with Samuel, let my children not only grow in stature, but in favor with the Lord. Let the words and teachings that have been planted in their lives take root and bear good fruit. —Tia McCollors

Digging Deeper: Proverbs 19:20; 1 Corinthians 13:11

Wednesday, July 14

He shall be like a tree planted by the rivers of water, that brings forth its fruit in its season, whose leaf also shall not wither; And whatever he does shall prosper. —Psalm 1:3 (NKJV)

"Why do they call it a weed whacker," I said to Margi, "when I'm the one who gets whacked?" She laughed as I peeled off my flannel shirt, splattered with burrs and the residue of chopped-up weeds. Our three-acre property is set in a verdant valley. Home to wildlife and wildflowers, with rolling hills beside us and purple mountains in the distance, our little plot of land couldn't be prettier.

Nor could it be a better host for weeds. Invasive species, like star thistle, had proliferated after our wildfires. It was my chore to weed-whack them into oblivion. I took every precaution for the all-day job. Eye protection, face protection, hat, earplugs, high boots, jeans, leather gloves, and a long-sleeved shirt. It had been a long while since the last time I attacked them.

Normally, I enjoy yard work, but not this time. The temperature hit triple digits and the sun was relentless. Clothed head to toe, I was a hot mess. I was a mess in my heart, too. I'd been letting discontent take root. I fretted over unanswered prayers, the demands of life, and a schedule I let get away from me.

I was glad to be finished with the weeds. "It's a lot easier when I don't let them grow this big," I said.

My wife nodded as she helped me pull my boots off. "Isn't it that way with everything?"

Her words touched my heart. I'd been letting weeds grow in my spirit, and it was time to get to them before they got too big.

Lord, teach me to tend every day the garden of faith, hope, and love in my soul. Amen. —Bill Giovannetti

Digging Deeper: Hosea 14:5

Thursday, July 15

If anyone, then, knows the good they ought to do and doesn't do it, it is sin for them. —James 4:17 (NIV)

Nothing gets my dander up like expectations. I don't like it when I think I'm being pressured to do certain things or act a certain way.

I tend to buy gifts and birthday cards at the eleventh hour, for example. I tell myself I'm resisting crass consumerism, but what I'm really doing is fighting the expectation to show my appreciation and love. My soul gets really pinched and narrow like this.

I remembered this in a daydreamy moment on the elevator in my apartment building. (For once, I wasn't preoccupied with my smartphone!)

I was thinking of my sister. She never seemed to get used to my husband and me moving to her hometown in rural Ohio, to a house just one mile from her family's place. She'd forget to include us in her children's birthday parties. Weeks would go by and I wouldn't hear from her until I picked up the phone.

When the chance came for me to take a job in Cleveland, a hundred and fifty miles away, I didn't hesitate. Family ties certainly weren't holding me back, I thought.

But in the elevator, a moment of grace: *Nobody likes being told what to do.*

I had all sorts of expectations for how my sister and I were going to be, how we were going to act. She had to have felt that. Siblings that we are, she reacted just like I would have.

My heart fizzed with love for her and compassion for the both of us. And with gratitude for those moments when we put aside our endless distractions to let God have His say.

God, what do You want me to know about myself today? I'm listening. —Amy Eddings

Digging Deeper: 1 Kings 19:11–12; Ephesians 5:1–3; James 2:8

Friday, July 16

Then he said to his disciples, "Why can't you trust me?" —Luke 8:25 (MSG)

I fidgeted as I sat in the veterinarian clinic with Sunrise, my golden retriever, waiting for the doctor to come into the room. Blood ran from Sunrise's right ear, down her golden coat, and pooled on the floor. She had ripped it open on some barbed wire fence and it wouldn't stop bleeding. I gently touched her ear and cooed, "The doctor will get you fixed up." I wished my own problems could be fixed so easily. I was facing a major decision, which I had prayed about. Just when I thought I had received the answer, I'd begin to doubt and spiral backward.

Sunrise wagged her tail as the veterinarian walked into the room, but when the doctor reached for her ear, she turned her head. No matter how the doctor tried, Sunrise kept her ear out of reach.

Frustrated, the doctor stepped back at the same time I thought of a solution. Sunrise's right ear was next to me. I reached down and gently flipped her ear flap to the left side of her head, the side the doctor was on. The doctor easily examined the ear—Sunrise thought it was me touching her ear.

I grinned. "She wouldn't let you touch it because she didn't trust you." With those words, my heart ached. I had some trust issues, too. My doubts about my decision were the result of not trusting God.

In time, Sunrise healed and so did I. By investing time with God and recounting His faithfulness toward me, I committed to trust Him.

Lord, thank You for Your faithfulness. Amen.
—Rebecca Ondov

Digging Deeper: Psalm 40:11; 57:10; 100:5

Saturday, July 17

Can any one of you by worrying add a single hour to your life? —Matthew 6:27 (NIV)

"Testing will begin in one minute."

I looked down at my bar exam, then up at the clock on the wall. The seconds passed slowly. My heart beat fast. This was the first of four test sessions. My career hinged on the next two days.

"You may begin now."

I broke the test seal and began reading the first essay question. I underlined, circled, and highlighted.

After analyzing the question, I began to type an answer on my computer.

The essay was difficult, but I had studied hard. Words spilled from my mind and onto my computer screen. Then that screen went black. My insides lurched. My vision blurred. I flagged down the IT representative.

"My laptop crashed," I said.

"I'll try to get it back up and running," he said.

I rubbed my face. The room was filled with the clicking noise of keyboards—people moving through exams while I stood stuck. I felt trapped.

What was I supposed to do?

I took a deep breath. Fixing the laptop was out of my control. It was in God's hands now. But I was responsible for how I reacted. I could drown in fear and continue to lose more time, or I could move on and start analyzing the next essay question.

I lifted a prayer that my laptop would restart. Then I lifted my pencil.

I read through the next question, outlining an answer in the margins as I worked. Soon, the IT rep put a hand on my shoulder.

"You're good to go," he said. I thanked him, then resumed typing. Whether I would finish in time was in question. But whether I would lose time worrying was not.

Lord, help me control my worry when all else is out of my hands. —Logan Eliasen

Digging Deeper: Philippians 4:6; 1 Peter 5:7

Sunday, July 18

Let not mercy and truth forsake you; bind them around your neck, write them on the tablet of your heart. —Proverbs 3:3 (NKJV)

It was a warm Sunday afternoon and I was walking across 125th Street from the train station to the subway that would take me back to our apartment in Upper Manhattan. The sidewalks were busy with a Sunday afternoon mix of tourists, churchgoers, and shoppers. I paused at an intersection where a man with a walker was trying to get up the curb. "Can I help you?" I asked.

"Yes," he said. He gestured toward the walker. Together we pushed and he got up on the sidewalk. Good deed accomplished. I was ready to head on my way, but then he asked, "Can you push me to the supermarket?"

"I'm going the other direction...," I'd started to say until my better nature got the better of me. "Sure."

He maneuvered around to sit in the seat of the walker and I pushed, trying to avoid the bumps in the uneven sidewalk (who knew there were so many?). We got to the supermarket. I pushed him up a slight ramp and in the door. Couldn't have been easier. "Thank you," he said, shaking my hand. "Can I buy you something? I can use my food stamps."

I stood there stumped. That he would want to use his limited means to help me was beyond belief. I stumbled around for the right words, probably not grabbing the right ones, then headed home. "Sometimes," I said to my wife, Carol, trying to explain the whole thing, "the kind thing you think you are doing is nothing compared to the kindness that comes back."

Lord, let me be always open to the opportunities to serve. —Rick Hamlin

Digging Deeper: Acts 9:36; Galatians 5:22–23

Monday, July 19

For the Lord is good and his love endures forever; his faithfulness continues through all generations. —Psalm 100:5 (NIV)

I am experiencing some sadness this year as I write this devotion. Each summer for the past ten years I have rented a cottage at Mexico Beach, Florida, for a "writer's retreat." During this special summer break I have written devotions, book chapters, and short essays while my wife, Beth, and our grandchildren played on the beach. Late in the afternoon I rode my bike for miles along the coastal highway, soaking in the coastal beauty. These days at Mexico Beach have been a special time for our family.

However, last year Hurricane Michael roared across the Gulf of Mexico with Category 5 winds, and the little coastal hamlet of Mexico Beach literally disappeared amid the storm's fury. The cottage that we rented was totally destroyed. Our favorite restaurant was washed away. People lost their homes and livelihood. It will take years for the little community to rebuild.

And so today as I write these words in the sweltering Georgia heat and gaze at a muddy river, I yearn for an "Eden in the past." Yet I am reminded to be thankful for life, for safety, for family, and for the fact that the privilege of writing and sharing stories cannot be blown away by the ravages of weather or time. Times and circumstances change, but God's truth is constant.

Dear God, help me—and all those affected by Hurricane Michael—to feel the warmth of the sun on my back, to see the glint of light in the heavens, and to feel the joy of You blowing softly on my face. Amen. —Scott Walker

Digging Deeper: Isaiah 40:8; Psalm 119:2; Mark 13:31

Tuesday, July 20

STRUGGLING TO PRAY: How to Pray When I've Lost Hope

For where two or three gather in my name, there am I with them. —Matthew 18:20 (NIV)

An old friend was diagnosed with terminal cancer. When I went to see her, I learned that somehow, though a professing Christian and lifelong churchgoer until the past decade, she'd forgotten or never understood or perhaps never accepted the most fundamental Christian teaching. As we talked, it became clear she considered herself such a bad person that God couldn't possibly want her with Him in heaven. When anyone around her mentioned salvation—or, really, anything about God—she got mad and changed the subject.

If I wanted to help her, I decided, I couldn't evangelize. But I could pray.

And I tried to. But how do you pray for someone whose situation seems hopeless?

I couldn't pray for healing. That clearly wasn't going to happen. She was getting sicker before our eyes as the cancer moved from organ to organ. I wanted to pray for peace, but I couldn't imagine any peace for her besides what she was rejecting.

My worst impediment to prayer was the conviction that I should be *doing* something, not "just praying," as I thought of it. I should be convincing her, comforting her with the only message that could help her.

In the end, all I could muster was this weak, unprayable grunt of faith: that God still loved her and waited close by, eager to wrench her from the cave of misery she'd backed herself into to accept His embrace.

And that's what He did. In a final moment of consciousness, barely able to speak, much less resist those around her, my friend suddenly joined us in the Lord's Prayer.

Not reflexively or reluctantly but fervently. I could tell from her face she meant each word.

Thank You, God, for staying with us and hearing even our unprayed prayers. —Patty Kirk

Digging Deeper: John 14

Wednesday, July 21

He is your praise. He is your God, who has done for you these great and terrifying things that your eyes have seen. —Deuteronomy 10:21 (ESV)

Bill and Iris, my neighbors, just love butterflies. They take vacations in places where rare butterflies can be easily spotted. They buy butterfly books. They have butterfly photographs on the walls of their dining room. They cultivate flowers in their garden that attract certain species.

Recently, they responded to a mail order offer to purchase a box of one hundred butterfly larvae. These arrived one day on their doorstep. With great excitement, they opened the box, followed the instructions, and watched these larvae prepare to become butterflies. A few weeks later, the larvae were ready to go.

Bill and Iris opened the box with anticipation. Bill had his phone set to video the moment.

But at the very moment when the butterflies flew into the air in Bill and Iris's front lawn, a flight of swallows—they live in nests under a bridge of a river just down the road from Bill and Iris's home—swooped into view, diving and gliding as they do, and in just a few seconds, those one hundred young butterflies were gone.

Iris screamed. Bill kept filming, and as the swallows left their view, Bill's camera found itself resting on Iris's face. Her scream had turned to a look of wonder, and even a smile. "Wow!" you can hear her saying to Bill at that moment. We can't begin to understand the ways of creation.

You tell me I am fearfully and wonderfully made. Today, I know that means that I cannot understand myself the way You understand me.
—Jon M. Sweeney

Digging Deeper: Psalm 139:14-15

Thursday, July 22

Ask the Lord your God for a sign, whether in the deepest depths or in the highest heights.
—Isaiah 7:11 (NIV)

This morning, I was in the middle of talking to myself, grumbling actually, or you could say I was praying out loud about a troubling worry, when *Aha!* came in through the window.

Aha! Aha!

We have an unusual crow around the neighborhood. His call is different than the rest.

Aha! Aha! he exclaims as if he just struck gold.

My mom lives next door and she mentioned this oddball crow to me last year. She said it liked to perch right outside her bedroom window every morning and caw this intriguing *aha.* "When you hear that crow's *aha* first thing in the morning, you know it will be a good day!" Mom said.

I thought she was exaggerating until I heard it for myself.

Aha! the crow cawed.

Only my day seemed anything but good with a bunch of worries and challenges ahead. Getting up, I followed the *ahas* out the front door. I spotted the crow on the bare dead branch at the very top of our black walnut tree.

"I see you," I said to the crow.

Aha! he cawed back.

"What are you thinking about?"

Aha!

I laughed to myself, thinking, *Am I having an* aha *moment?* The crow took flight and I watched him land on a pine tree in the distance. *Mom was right,* I thought. *It just might turn out to be a good day after all.*

Heavenly Father, thank You for taking me away from worry and into the moment. —Sabra Ciancanelli

Digging Deeper: 1 Samuel 14:10; Matthew 12:38

Friday, July 23

For I am persuaded that neither death nor life, nor angels nor principalities nor powers, nor things present nor things to come, nor height nor depth, nor any other created thing, shall be able to separate us from the love of God which is in Christ Jesus our Lord. —Romans 8:38–39 (NKJV)

Our family had spent an afternoon at the movies, watching the latest installment of a nostalgic cartoon from their childhood. On the way out, my daughter, Josie, realized she had lost her sunglasses.

After a quick search of the theater, we found nothing. My son and I volunteered to see if she had left them in the car. Sure enough, they were in the backseat, and soon we were headed home. With one in college and one almost in college, it was a rare treat to have our whole family together.

Josie turned the conversation spiritual. "What if I lost God?" she said. "Or what if God lost me?" We quickly realized she wasn't joking. With a tender conscience and a spiritually attuned heart, her sense of security with God had been a long-running question mark.

Margi asked, "Josie, do you actually think you're like God's sunglasses and He's forgetful like you, so He forgot where He put you?"

She laughed and shook her head. "No, but what if it happened?"

Her younger brother, Jonathan, teased her. "Right, Josie. You're the only person in the whole world that God forgot about."

I asked Josie to pull out her phone, open her Bible app, and read Romans 8:38 and 39. As she read the verses aloud, we could see a sense of peace wash over her. "Honey, if God keeps His Word, what is that verse telling you?"

"It's telling me God never loses His sunglasses," she said. "Or me!" She paused and finished. "Dad, I guess we could call this a Theology of Sunglasses!"

Gracious God, how grateful I am to rest secure in Your grip forever. Amen. —Bill Giovannetti

Digging Deeper: John 10:27–29

Saturday, July 24

The Lord is my strength and my shield; in him my heart trusts, and I am helped; my heart exults, and with my song I give thanks to him. —Psalm 28:7 (ESV)

Our old farmhouse fronts two acres. I wouldn't trade it, but it makes for a lot of time on the mower. And let me tell you, it's a tough old piece of grass. I'm convinced our yard grows rocks and old tools—even tractor parts. Every year, by fall, I get all the junk dug out only to have spring offer up a whole fresh crop of rusty memories.

This year's happy surprise is old wire fencing. Have you ever run over wire fence with a mower? It starts with a boom, then a happy screeching sound. You smell smoke. Then you spend the rest of the day pulling wrapped steel out of your mower blades while the dandelions laugh.

My daughter-in-law loves mowing. She was headed for the yard.

"Hey, Sarah," I said, "why don't you wait a few weeks till I can make sure all the rocks are out of the grass?"

She smiled. "Ah, Buck, have a little faith."

I listened for the crash, but all I heard was her singing over the engine noise.

I mowed the following week, cringing and waiting for inevitable collision. Guess what? It came.

I guess *life* is a tough old piece of grass, too. And when we look for it, trouble rarely fails to show. It crashes in with a boom and a screech. But the Master Gardener showed me something through Sarah.

Have a little faith, Buck, He says.

I've decided to take it to heart. The grass is high again and I'm gassing up. Tomorrow might bring plenty of clouds. But today I'm going to put in my earbuds, crank up the music, and enjoy the sun.

Lord, I lay it all at Your feet, knowing there isn't anything You can't handle. —Buck Storm

Digging Deeper: Isaiah 40:31; Philippians 4:6–7

Sunday, July 25

For our citizenship is in heaven....
—Philippians 3:20 (NASB)

When my mother took her final breath I was flooded with wonder. I kept softly repeating, "She's there. She's there."

The Bible gives us a beautiful vision of heaven, and tells us that Jesus's desire is for those who believe in Him to be where He is. I trust the truth of this glorious place Jesus calls home.

So why do I sometimes feel afraid of leaving life on this earth? I defended my fear to Jesus saying, "This world is what I know. It's familiar." The words were barely out when I felt an answer, *No, this world isn't what you know. It's me in the world that you know.*

Jesus—and His promises, power, and presence—have been with me from childhood when I gave my life to Him. Even when I have chosen to go my own direction, I am never separated from Him. His voice calls to me (John 10:4–5, 14).

If Jesus is who I know in this world, then joining Him in heaven is not something to be feared. It is something to eagerly await. Like the memory I have of my first cross-country train ride.

I stood beside the track in the middle of the night, gazing intently down the line. Suddenly, a light shone around the bend. The train was coming straight toward me. It began to slow. My heart was on fire. I thought, *This is my train, and it's stopping for me!* I could not wait to get on—to see where it was taking me.

This is how I want to be when the "glory train" stops for me. Unafraid, eager. Ready to see where it is carrying me. Excited to meet my Savior, whose love I have returned all my life.

All aboard! Jesus, make me ready. —Carol Knapp

Digging Deeper: John 14:2–4; Colossians 3:1–4; Revelation 21:1–4

Monday, July 26

And ye shall hallow the fiftieth year, and proclaim liberty throughout all the land unto all the inhabitants thereof: it shall be a jubilee unto you;

and ye shall return every man unto his possession,
and ye shall return every man unto his family.
—Leviticus 25:10 (KJV)

In the last years of his life, my father's interest in
genealogy grew. This past year, I searched to learn
more about land my great-grandfather acquired
about two decades after the end of the Civil War.
Rather than enjoying the journey, I was feeling
overwhelmed. Then I got an email forwarded from
Daily Guideposts's offices.

It read, "I became acquainted with Sharon Ewell
Foster through *Daily Guideposts* and just finished
reading her book, *Abraham's Well*." The email was
from a woman named Sandra who believes that we
share white ancestors in common.

How unusual! I'd left genealogical clues at the
back of Abraham's Well, hoping that it might find
its way to Native American relatives, but did not
consider the possibility that white distant relatives
might find me, as it is highly unusual for the
descendants of slave owners to acknowledge kinship
bonds with descendants of slaves.

"I am glad you are in my family," she wrote to
me on Facebook. She has sent me pictures. She has
already completed a DNA test. We are discussing
the possibility of a reunion of sorts. The thought
is exciting and troubling at the same time, as we
move forward to confront our shared past. My hope
is that out of past enslavement, I might learn new
information from our shared family tree that will
help us forge a brighter tomorrow.

Lord, bless Sandra for her courage and generosity. God, help us to acknowledge the past and envision glorious new days ahead. Help us to remember and acknowledge that You have made us all one family.
—Sharon Foster

Digging Deeper: 1 Samuel 18:18; 1 Corinthians 12:13; Ephesians 3:14–15

Tuesday, July 27

Teach us to number our days, that we may gain a heart of wisdom. —Psalm 90:12 (NIV)

I read the text message in disbelief. My new friend had suddenly passed away. A beloved wife and mom of four young daughters. A woman who had just relocated to my city and joined my church. A thirty-eight-year-old woman who didn't know she had a heart condition.

Once the news sank in, I searched for footprints of our short friendship. Through teary eyes I read the few text messages we had exchanged. My husband and I had discussed inviting her family over, but I had delayed the invitation. We were busy, tired, and my house was a mess. When I finally invited them over via text message, they were traveling and unable to visit.

I read my last message, wishing them a great trip and extending our invitation until they returned home. I was stunned by my last words shared with her. "No worries," I'd written. "We have plenty of time to have you over."

I read those words over and over again, aware that I did not have plenty of time to show her and her family hospitality.

Since my friend's passing, I have been intentional in doing the important things in life. I try not to put off sharing coffee with my close friends. I prioritize long road trips to attend milestones like weddings and graduations of extended family members. More than ever, I realize how short life can be and how brief our time to nurture relationships with others really is. I have committed to do what needs to be done today, because tomorrow is not promised.

Dear Lord, help me number my days and carry an urgency for the people and purposes You have placed in my life and heart. —Carla Hendricks

Digging Deeper: Psalm 39:4; James 4:13–17

Wednesday, July 28

"I will cause all my goodness to pass in front of you...." —Exodus 33:19 (NIV)

Sometimes it seems like a plague, this constant presence of technology and nonstop children's programs on TV. Even our youngest child, David, seems lost in games and stories that are ever ready on his iPad.

My dad recently commented that on an hour-long walk through one of our downtown parks, every person he met was looking at their smartphone rather than taking in the beauties of the day.

Sadly, I have to admit that there's no easy solution to this phenomena. From college-age Harrison on down, all my children are pretty much addicted to their devices. Even a family campaign to monitor our screen time left me doubting.

"Father," I found myself praying, "show me how to bring back some of the good and simplicity I remember from my childhood."

His answer came as I was perusing a jumbled table of knickknacks at a neighbor's garage sale. There it was, a complete DVD set of the old TV series *Little House on the Prairie*. My mind raced back to the times my mom, dad, Keri, and I gathered to watch the weekly adventures of the Ingalls family, living with little but happy nonetheless.

So began our "little House" nights. Soon, we were caught up in the adventures of the Ingalls. We knew all their names, suffered their defeats, and delighted in their successes. Our children were seeing how to be happy without stuff, and Corinne and I were reminded of the importance of family time.

We were all made better by our visits to "the prairie," something that really came home to me the day I looked out the window and saw the girls in the backyard, screens forgotten, creating a pretend playhouse under a big shade tree.

Father, thank You for showing us your goodness.
—Brock Kidd

Digging Deeper: Psalm 33:5; Philippians 4:8

But my eyes are fixed on you, Sovereign Lord.
—Psalm 141:8 (NIV)

"What do you see when you close your eyes?" I asked a friend.

She paused. "Nothing. Isn't that the point?"

"I see the back of my eyelids," I said, and then explained that I've spent a lifetime closing my eyes to shut out the distractions of the world around me, when I prayed or wanted to think more deeply, and of course when I went to sleep. But recently, instead of staring into nothingness, I've tried to really focus on what I see, and often I see starry patterns on the back of my eyelids. Especially at night in darkness.

I wondered if anyone else sees the same thing, so I did some research. Turns out, there's a scientific reason we might see twinkling patterns when we close our eyes in darkness. It has to do with phosphenes, the electrical charges the retina produces, which cause the visual sensation of stars. They can also appear when we gently rub our closed eyelids.

I've continued my own personal experiments with what I see on the back of my eyelids, in darkness and light, and it's become a spiritual practice for me. I close my eyes when I pray or simply want to sit in silence, and I focus patiently, as if I'm looking through my eyelids at a 3-D picture. Sometimes images begin to form, especially when I place my fingertips on my eyelids. Like when I'm thinking about Jesus, His face often appears.

Of all the screens available to me, I've come to especially love the one I carry with me on the back of my eyelids.

Lord, You intend us to use our bodies to praise You in worship, to kneel, to raise our hands, and surely to see You when we close our eyes. —Carol Kuykendall

Digging Deeper: Hebrews 12:1–2; 2 Corinthians 4:18

Friday, July 30

Nothing in all creation is hidden from God's sight. Everything is uncovered and laid bare before the eyes of him to whom we must give account. —Hebrews 4:13 (NIV)

I sat at my assigned table at the company picnic, name tag on, and thought about what I would say when it got to be my turn for the breaking-the-ice exercise. Each of us was to share two truths and a lie. Then we were to go around and guess which was which.

As soon as I heard the instructions, my mind jumped from one possibility to another. *How much should I share? What secrets do I reveal to my colleagues?* Our truths are just as revealing as our lies, and then what people guess is also telling.

I looked down at the blank page and realized I was overthinking this whole getting-to-know-you game that was supposed to be fun. Playing it safe, I wrote about driving across the country, having a twin sister, and living in France. Everyone guessed my lie correctly, most likely because my face is an open book, but something about the game wouldn't leave my mind.

On the drive home, I kept coming up with things I wished I said, things that might have gotten a laugh or possibly have been believed. My mind wandered until it occurred to me that no matter how well we think we know one another, the only One who truly knows us—inside and out, secrets and all—is God. I hadn't thought about that truth in a long time, if ever. And that is a beautiful thing—to be known and loved just as you are, right now.

Heavenly Father, You know me better than I know myself, and You love me and I am blessed.
—Sabra Ciancanelli

Digging Deeper: Psalm 44:21; 69:5

Saturday, July 31

Keep your heart with all vigilance, for from it flows the springs of life. —Proverbs 4:23 (ESV)

I walked down the stairs, breathing in the aroma of cinnamon and vanilla, my stomach grumbling.

"Good morning!" My friend Rachel smiled. A group of my friends was spending a much-needed weekend away together at Rachel's beach house, and the French toast casserole baking in the oven was the perfect culminating meal to a wonderful, refreshing weekend.

Rachel pulled the steaming pan out of the oven and went to the fridge to grab a bowl of fruit while the rest of us gathered around the table.

"Oh no!" Rachel looked at us wide-eyed from behind the refrigerator door.

We all walked over to her and she held up a box of cream cheese. "This is the cream cheese I bought to make this casserole for the weekend. I must have accidentally used an old package that had been sitting in the fridge when I made the casserole last night."

Since it was a vacation house that wasn't always used, old groceries often sat in the back of the fridge unnoticed. We found the used box of cream cheese in the recycling bin. The cream cheese she had used in our breakfast was more than a year past its expiration date.

We looked at what was once a promising breakfast, and our hearts sank. Blueberries shimmered on the top, and warm pecans were sprinkled across the bread. It was beautiful, but inedible.

We had cereal for breakfast, along with a wonderful reminder of how important it is to guard our hearts against the evil, rotten things that poison our world.

Lord, fill my heart with things that are good, true, and beautiful today. Amen. —Erin MacPherson

Digging Deeper: Deuteronomy 11:16; Philippians 4:7

JOYFUL IN HOPE

1 _____

2 _____

3 _____

4 _____

5 _____

6 _____

7 _____

8 _____

9 _____

10 _____

11 _____

12 _____

13 _____

14 _____

15 _____

16 _____

17 _____

18 _____

19 _____

20 _____

21 _____

22 _____

23 _____

24 _____

25 _____

26 _____

27 _____

28 _____

29 _____

30 _____

31 _____

AUGUST

Look to the Lord and his strength;
seek his face always.

—1 Chronicles 16:11 (NIV)

Sunday, August 1

Awake, north wind, and come, south wind! Blow on my garden, that its fragrance may spread everywhere. —Song of Songs 4:16 (NIV)

Perhaps it was her red hair that first caught my eye. The woman's strawberry blonde tresses reminded me of my own, before my auburn strands had faded to a fine silver gray. Or maybe it was the tile-roofed villa behind her, its arched windows stirring memories from the year I studied abroad in Tuscany. Then again, it could have been how the woman—eyes closed—drew the delicate pink rose toward herself, which brought to mind a certain garden outside of Paris where the ombré of the rosebushes subtly shifted from softest blush to lipstick red along a walking path. Just like the red-haired woman in *the Soul of the Rose* painting, I'd closed my eyes in the garden that day, drinking in the scent of the flowers that surrounded me. Whatever the reason, I'd connected with this particular painting the very first time I saw it.

Now here it was again, calling out to me from an overcrowded shelf at an antique shop. It was just a small print, displayed in a carved ebony frame. I turned it over to view the price tag. Six bucks. The red-haired lady was coming home with me.

The only explanation I can provide is that artwork, like *The Soul of the Rose*, beckons my own soul toward connecting with the divine. There's something sublime about this creative act, the attempt by imperfect yet inspired individuals drawn to follow in the Father's footsteps to create something from nothing—whether they recognize the original Source of their call or not. Art orchestrates its own unique form of worship within me. Hallelujah!

Glorious Creator, thank You for the beauty and creativity You've woven into this world, including the souls of Your beloved children. Amen.
—Vicki Kuyper

Digging Deeper: Jeremiah 32:17; Romans 1:20; Ephesians 2:10

Monday, August 2

But I trust in your unfailing love; my heart rejoices in your salvation. —Psalm 13:5 (NIV)

I am a devoted player of online brain and memory games though I get little joy from it, even when I outperform the norm for my age. It's more like heavy physical exercise, punishing rather than pleasurable. And if my performance slips... watch out!

Like the other day. I was intensely focused on a game that tested memory and cognition. Not only did I fail to perform at the level I had previously attained, but my score suffered with each new round.

"I'm losing it," I complained to a friend. Soon, I would need help remembering my own name. Which isn't as silly as it sounds. My mother and both her sisters, as well as one of their brothers, all died of Alzheimer's, as did their father, my maternal grandfather. And today several of my older cousins show signs of early cognitive decline. Don't tell me that's not scary.

"You know my family history," I snapped at my friend when I thought I detected a covert eye roll.

"Look," he said, "maybe so. Maybe you're doomed. But why live that way if you don't know? Besides, a positive attitude is probably as good for your brain as those crazy supplements you take and all those online brain tests. Really, dude. Chill."

I brooded over my friend's callous—in my mind at least—response to my cognitive crisis until I remembered something about my mom when she was in the final stages of Alzheimer's. She'd forgotten just about everything but not her prayers, not her favorite hymns that you could still entice her to hum.

Might I not put a little more faith in God than I do in online brain games? After all, no disease can destroy faith, but faith can destroy fear. *Chill, dude,* I told myself.

Lord, as I face an unknown future—for the future is unknown to all but You—help me to lean on my faith and not my fears. —Edward Grinnan

Digging Deeper: 2 Timothy 1:7; 1 John 4:18

Tuesday, August 3

Let your light so shine before men, that they may
see your good works, and glorify your Father which
is in heaven. —Matthew 5:16 (KJV)

I'm again culling my personal library. My goal:
one of six bookcases empty by the end of the
week. I want a tighter, targeted collection that will
nourish my better self. I see and choose to keep
a slim volume, *Let Your Life Speak,* intending to
read it again sometime. I pick up a hefty history of
Christianity. Because it's remained unread on the
shelf for decades, I anticipate an easy discard. But I
open the book, and the prose and photos draw me
in, chapter upon chapter. Uncharacteristically, I put
everything aside and I read for a whole day, intrigued
with how the Christian faith has been interpreted
and lived out over the span of two thousand years,
by martyrs, conquerors, buttress builders, zealous
crusaders, political players, reformers, fearful serfs
and slaves, persecutors, saints, colonizers, hopeful
worshippers, and generous mercy-bearers.

So many paradigms at different times. On
the book's last page, the author acknowledges
Christianity's wide range of representations. Can
they all be rooted in the same text and tradition? Yes,
he says. As I place the book on a low shelf of keepers,
I ask a more personal question: Where would I fit
on such a wide spectrum—in my younger days and
now with more maturity? Glancing higher up, I read

the spines of "saved" titles randomly standing side by side. *Clinging: The Experience of Prayer; All Things Considered; Listening to Your Life; A Song Called Hope; Wishful Thinking; A Passion for the Impossible.* Taken all together, I say they "let my life speak."

Lord, help me to exhibit a faith that glorifies You.
—Evelyn Bence

Digging Deeper: Matthew 5:13–15;
Philippians 2:15–16

Wednesday, August 4

Be still, and know that I am God. —Psalm 46:10 (KJV)

"What happened to your legs?" my brother Davey teased, noticing marks on my legs caused by laser spot removal treatment.

"I was attacked by a pack of wild Chihuahuas," I answered, making him laugh his trademark laugh that shook his body and made me happy.

As I spent the day with Davey, who was soldiering through cancer treatment, we talked awhile and reminisced. Then he looked at my husband, David, and said, "I've been thinking about how we used to fish together. I'd like to do that again."

"Ah," David answered. "Let's set a date. I'll hire a guide and line up a fishing boat."

"No," Davey said wistfully, "I'd like to just go and sit in the old boat and fish and talk, you know, just be together."

Two days later a phone call: "Come now," my niece cried.

We gathered Brock and Keri and began the frantic drive to Chattanooga.

"There's so much he wants to do," I said from the backseat.

After a divorce and years of estrangement, he was back with his first wife, Carol, looking forward to remarriage, enjoying his two grown daughters.

David was on the phone with Carol. "Let's do the marriage now," he said. So as the four of us sped toward Chattanooga, David and Carol and Davey were on speakerphone making a wedding happen on the spot.

By the time we arrived, Davey could still smile, but he could no longer speak. He had come full circle, surrounded by all the people he loved. There was a peace in the completeness of his life.

It took a year for the marks on my legs to fade away. Remembering my brother's last laugh, I was sorry to see them go.

Father, in all You have given us, help us remember "to just be." —Pam Kidd

Digging Deeper: John 1:4–5; Romans 8:24

Thursday, August 5

Men ought always to pray, and not to faint. —Luke 18:1 (KJV)

Prayer is a mystery to me. I have friends who seem to have dramatic answers to their prayers all the time, but seldom do I see an obvious answer to my prayers.

So why do I pray? I pray because "I can't not pray." I pray for the same reason I breathe, sigh, groan, walk, talk, sing, laugh. Without the release that prayer gives me, my anxieties and frustrations would soon reach dangerous levels.

If I had to make an appointment with a doctor every time I was troubled, I would have long ago bankrupted the entire health-care system, singlehandedly.

But prayer? No appointment necessary. No paperwork, and no copay. I just open my heart to the Great Physician, wherever I am: on the riding mower, working under the car, or speeding down the freeway.

I know, prayer is no substitute for professional counseling, but the act of praying is healing to me. I can "divulge" things to God and know that He will keep my confidences. I can "wrestle" with God before I yield to His will. I can "brag" to him about my achievements without being accused of pride.

I'm okay with the mystery of prayer. I don't have to witness answers to my prayers to know that they have been processed. I trust God to do what is best, on His timetable.

To me, prayer is less like putting coins in a vending machine, and more like a very powerful cell phone, built into my head, that can reach heaven on a moment's notice, without dialing, and with unlimited minutes. I don't know where I would be without this Heavenly Phone.

Hello, God, it's me, Danny. Thanks for that incredible sunrise this morning. Catch You later, bye.
—Daniel Schantz

Digging Deeper: Psalm 32:3; 55:22

Friday, August 6

I will remember the deeds of the LORD; yes,
I will remember your miracles of long ago.
—Psalm 77:11 (NIV)

"Two weeks from Friday. Hold the date," my husband, Lonny, said.

"Why?" I asked.

"Can't say."

He smiled the smile I've seen for thirty years, and time was shed. I stood there like I was twentysomething again. Swept away. From a dirty kitchen with boys and noise and coffee grounds on the floor.

Soon, we'd gather around the table with our sons for "dinner and dash"—the divide and conquer that had become our lifestyle. A baseball game, swim practice, and taking a son to work. But the promise of this date, the joy it brought, grew in my soul.

In our early married years, we'd been stuck in a destructive cycle that robbed our relationship. We created chasms that broke deep and left us standing on opposite sides of voids that were difficult to cross. More recently, we'd fought long and hard again but this time united on a battlefield for the well-being of our child. We'd held each other through sweet days and dark days. We held on through highs and lows. Through tangles and ties. Through life and breath.

And the Lord was in it all. In the center. Sustaining. Strengthening. Gifting us with grace, more than enough, more than our hands could hold.

Date night came and there was a convertible ride, dinner from my grandmother's picnic basket, and a spot on the river where the water hit the bank like a heartbeat.

"I love this night," I said. "Thank you."

Lonny pulled me close. His face was stubbly and my head rested on his shoulder. Frogs croaked and the sky painted pink.

If I ever doubt the Lord's presence, I need only look back to where He's been.

Father, when I look behind and see You, I'm brave to move ahead. —Shawnelle Eliasen

Digging Deeper: Deuteronomy 6:12; Isaiah 46:9

Saturday, August 7

The heavens declare the glory of God; the skies proclaim the work of his hands. —Psalm 19:1 (NIV)

"Who's up for a family hike?" our son Derek asked the group one morning at the mountain cabin where all eighteen of us gathered for a long weekend together. "I found an easy hike to a great lake less than an hour away. We leave in thirty minutes."

Enthusiasm was contagious as cousins talked reluctant cousins into going, and soon the hikers gathered, ten kids and five adults ranging in age between five and over sixty-five (me!). I was thankful for Derek's leadership as off we went in the beauty of God's creation. That's why we come to these Colorado mountains!

About twenty minutes and two steep hills later, the youngest hikers were done and turned around with a mom to go back and make cookies.

The rest of us trudged on. For the first hour we were good, but nearing the end of the second hour, enthusiasm waned. "Gather some flat rocks for skipping on the lake," Derek encouraged, promising it was "just around the next bend." It was not. The sun was hot and we were running low on water. Finally, we came into a clearing and there was the "lake," all dried up into a small muddy puddle, enclosed by a high wire fence with No Trespassing signs and an explanation that this man-made lake is filled when needed as a source for making snow on the surrounding ski runs. The kids threw their skipping rocks on the ground in frustration and Derek's sisters began unmercifully teasing him about his misjudgment.

What's the happy ending to this story? Our photos of the kids as they stood at the fence, reminders of a shared family memory that gets better with each retelling.

Lord, I'm thankful that our difficult times often become our best family stories. —Carol Kuykendall

Digging Deeper: Genesis 1:31; Proverbs 10:12

Sunday, August 8

Jesus replied, "What is impossible with man is possible with God." —Luke 18:27 (NIV)

When my boys were three and five years old, we climbed a mountain together until we reached the top. I was coming out of my grief from divorce and getting into the swing of single motherhood. I needed a challenge, a physical metaphor for what I'd just been through.

My boys and I would conquer this mountain no matter how difficult, and we would continue to triumph through the difficult times together. They seemed to breeze through it, running like ninjas up the steep trail as I huffed and puffed behind them. But when we reached the summit, I felt victorious and strong. I was prepared for life without their father.

Eight years later we climbed another mountain. This time, there was someone else with us on the trail. My ex-husband and I had climbed an uphill battle ourselves, learning to forgive, listen to each other, co-parent our boys, and create a new friendship. This was a mountain I'd had no expectations of conquering, but here we were, the two of us, on a family outing with our boys.

Again, this time the boys breezed through the climb, their father leading the way. I huffed and puffed behind as they encouraged me to keep going. The four of us reached the top. I felt just as victorious as that first summit so many years ago. This time, we looked down into the valley as a family, but my thoughts were the same: *Look at how far we've come. Just imagine how much higher we can go.*

Thank You, Father, because you grieve with me in the valleys, walk with me as I press forward and upward, and stand with me in victory when I reach the top.
—Karen Valentin

Digging Deeper: Colossians 3:13

Monday, August 9

Where shall I go from your Spirit? Or where shall I flee from your presence? If I ascend to heaven, you are there! If I make my bed in Sheol, you are there! —Psalm 139:7–8 (ESV)

My three-year-old niece, Beth, stormed into my house, wearing a purple glitter unicorn backpack and mismatched shoes.

"Hi, Beth, what are you doing?"

"I'm moving into your house, Auntie. I'm not in my family anymore." She put her hands on her hips and scowled.

I gave her a hug. "Why are you not in your family anymore?"

"Because I'm mad at Mommy. She said I couldn't go swimming right now."

I glanced at the thunderstorm brewing outside and silently agreed with my sister that going swimming was not a wise idea. Just then my sister slammed into the house, with a look of terror on her face. "I can't find Beth!"

I pointed to the unicorn backpack huddling behind the stairs. While they live just down the street from us, Beth had never walked to my house by herself. My sister had spent a frantic ten minutes searching for her daughter before running down to my house to enlist my help.

My sister bent down and pulled Beth to her, hugging her tightly, tears falling down her cheeks. The anger she felt at Beth for storming off was replaced by the intense relief she felt that she had found her daughter safe and sound.

And so it is with our God. Our sin angers Him, but His love for us is so strong that even when we have run far from His arms, He anxiously gathers us back to Him.

Father God, thank You for pursuing me even when I am running away. I'm so grateful that nothing and no one on this earth can ever pull me away from Your presence. —Erin MacPherson

Digging Deeper: Jonah 2:1–10; Romans 8:35–39

Tuesday, August 10

Be careful not to practice your righteousness in front of others to be seen by them. If you do, you will have no reward from your Father in heaven. —Matthew 6:1 (NIV)

From the time I was a small child, my family has been involved in the Martha O'Bryan Center, so when I was asked to serve on their board, I jumped at the chance. Soon, I found myself serving as board chairman of this ever-expanding organization that serves a large number of Nashville's underprivileged children.

The near-impossible project of organizing and building a school within the center became our focus. Over the next years I became deeply involved in raising funds to build a new school from the ground up.

All along, my thoughts kept flying to that grand day when I would be asked to be a primary participant in the groundbreaking ceremony. The mayor of Nashville would be there, and of course there would be a giant pair of scissors to cut the ribbon—not to mention golden shovels and special hard hats for important people like me to wear.

I'll have to admit, my importance expanded by the day.

And then the date was announced. Somehow no one had checked with me. The day was right in the middle of our scheduled family vacation. I would miss the whole thing.

Remembering my vision of cutting the ribbon with the giant scissors, I felt more than a bit sheepish. I stepped back and remembered why I had worked my heart out on the project. It was never for my glory. It was to build better lives for children in need.

Dear Lord, thank You for all the opportunities I've had. Help me to be content with the rewards You give.
—Brock Kidd

Digging Deeper: Proverbs 25:27; 1 Corinthians 3:18

Wednesday, August 11

For by grace you have been saved through faith. And this is not your own doing; it is the gift of God. —Ephesians 2:8 (ESV)

One of my best friends wishes that he had faith. He wants to believe in God, but doesn't. He has been arguing with God, and against God, since he was a teenager. Now he's talking with me about it all.

"I went to church last month, every Sunday," he says to me one morning.

"You did?" I reply, surprised.

"Yes. I even cried."

"When? Or...I mean...what in the service made you cry?" I ask.

"Some children were being baptized. It was so beautiful," he says.

My friend was raised in the church. He was, in fact, baptized as a young person, but then a few years later he left in anger.

When he says to me, "I want to believe, Jon," it confuses me. I mean, if someone wants to believe, doesn't that mean they, at least, in part, already do believe? I'm unsure. But I know that the Holy Spirit is at work in my honest, God-wrestling friend, in ways that only God fully knows.

Lord, today I bring before You those who do not yet know You. They are Yours to love. —Jon M. Sweeney

Digging Deeper: 2 Corinthians 5:17–18

Thursday, August 12

My Presence will go with you, and I will give you rest. —Exodus 33:14 (NIV)

Sunrise, my golden retriever, paced the concrete floor. I groaned and pulled the sleeping bag over my shoulders. I hadn't gotten a good night's sleep in months. Every night my mind whirled like a tornado over the details of having a cottage built on my farm. Tonight I'd decided to get away by having a "campout" in the tack room of my barn. But Sunrise refused to lie down and sleep.

A blinding flash of lightning pierced the dark night, followed by grumbling thunder. Shaking with fear, Sunrise nuzzled me. I stroked her head. This freak lightning storm had come out of nowhere, and it rumbled for hours. *God, I need some sleep.* Sunrise bumped me with her nose. I flipped the light and slipped on my shoes. "Okay, I'll take you out."

I grabbed a flashlight as Sunrise bounded out the door, raced to my Subaru, and stared at the hatch, as if to say, "I'm ready to go home now."

I rubbed my forehead. "Sunrise, we are home. This is where we're going to live. C'mon, let's go to bed." Sunrise sulked behind me.

I pulled my sleeping bag and pad off the cot and onto the floor. Sunrise wiggled next to me as I crawled into my floor-bed. As soon as I draped my arm over her, I felt her body quit quaking. Suddenly, it didn't matter where on earth she was. She quit fretting because she was in my presence. *Hmmm, that's my answer too.* While in the middle of life's storms, I needed to rest in His presence. We both slept peacefully the rest of the night.

Lord, thank You for being with me every moment of every day—and every night. Amen.
—Rebecca Ondov

Digging Deeper: Hebrews 4:1; Matthew 11:28; 1 John 3:19

Friday, August 13

Behold I have awaited your words; I have hearkened for your reasons, until you search out the words.
—Job 32:11 (CHABAD)

The rabbi was going out of town and asked me to sub for him and give the Friday night d'var Torah. I'd done it before. I enjoyed teaching, and although public speaking still made me nervous, any shakiness never reached my voice.

Usually when I do a d'var Torah, something in the weekly portion leaps out at me and demands to be talked about. This particular week, however, nothing grabbed me. It felt like losing my taste for a food I'd always loved. Digging into the commentaries didn't help. I was tempted to tell the rabbi that I'd like to skip this time, and I knew he'd understand, but I kept thinking that there had to be something that would speak to me, that the repetitions, the contradictions, the seemingly obsolete laws had to have meaning for me. But I kept not seeing anything I could use.

Finally I gave up and went to see the rabbi, expecting him to say he'd find someone else to speak that week.

Instead, he smiled at me and said, "You're waiting for inspiration. That's the wrong way to approach this. We can't get out of our obligations by saying, 'I don't feel like it.' You know that."

It was clear that I had to come up with something or the congregation wouldn't have a sermon at the service. As I was driving home, I went past a church whose sign read simply: "God knows." I laughed, and said aloud, "Okay, God. Want to share it with me?"

By the time I got home, I'd figured it out. I talked about finding ways to do the right thing, even if we don't think we can.

Dear God, searching out Your meaning is a task I don't want to avoid, even if it seems impossible.
—Rhoda Blecker

Digging Deeper: Deuteronomy 4:10; 1 Samuel 3:17

Saturday, August 14

For as the earth brings forth its sprouts, and as a garden causes what is sown in it to sprout up, so the Lord God will cause righteousness and praise to sprout up before all the nations. —Isaiah 61:11 (ESV)

I've never had a green thumb, but for my daughter who loves cherry tomatoes, I decided to give growing my own vine a try.

Though I'd done nothing but buy a seedling at the store, I felt strangely proud as I put the tender plant in the ground with good soil. I carefully watched it grow outside my window, watering it and spraying for insects as needed.

All was well for several weeks, until our dog ran backward into it while chasing a Frisbee. In less than a second, my little plant was snapped at the base of the stem. If only I could repair the stem, my plant would still grow, I reasoned. I went inside and got some tape (feel free to laugh, all you gardeners). I just couldn't bear to let it go.

Days went by and I saw that my efforts had failed. *Of course,* I thought. *I have no idea what I'm doing!* But soon, another seedling sprouted next to the damaged one. I felt silly. How could I have thought God needed my help? He doesn't need tape; He can create a whole new vine!

But still a few days later, I found little green tomatoes on the vine I'd thought was a goner. God had not only given me a new plant, He'd even made the damaged one fruitful! Perhaps He appreciated my pitiful little effort after all.

Lord, You don't need my help, but all the same, I thank You for valuing my feeble efforts…and for making broken things (like me) fruitful when we think all hope is gone. You are so good to us!
—Ginger Rue

Digging Deeper: Genesis 1:11–12; 1 Corinthians 3:6

Sunday, August 15

Through Jesus, therefore, let us continually offer to God a sacrifice of praise—the fruit of lips that openly profess his name. —Hebrews 13:15 (NIV)

Eyes closed, lips crimped in resolve, I sat in Sunday morning service listening to the music offered by a team of praise leaders likely as physically spent as I. Though a lifelong music lover, I could summon no music in that moment. Instead, congratulating myself for having managed to place my body in that seat, I determined to let the songs wash over me while I remained closemouthed. *Just for today.*

One of the songs we sing in my church speaks of "praising [our] way through." But aren't fatigue and praise natural opposites? I reasoned. And isn't it logical to praise when we feel good and remain silent when we don't?

Such might be true of those with no hope, but for those who lay claim on an eternal relationship with God, praise is owed. Though sometimes it feels a bit foreign, praise is a mandate, and unlike in ancient culture where animals—and sometimes even humans—were mandated as sacrifice, the sacrifice called for in Hebrews 13:15 is only "the fruit of lips" openly professing His sovereignty from a sincere heart. Little thanks to ask in exchange for eternal life, I was reminded, as I subsequently joined the praise that morning.

At times, a mere whisper might be all our souls can muster. Yet as Christ followers we praise our way through: when we lose jobs, when a friend's harsh words prick our hearts—even, mixed with tears and stabbing emotions, through the suffocating loss of a loved one. And often we discover, to our delight, that praise gently releases the Savior's power to heal.

Holy Spirit, thank You for reminding me that praise is not just a feel-good exercise; it is a cleansing of the heart and a lifting of the soul.
—Jacqueline F. Wheelock

Digging Deeper: Jonah 2:9; Ephesians 5:19; Revelation 4:8–11

Monday, August 16

Physical training is of some value, but godliness has value for all things.... —1 Timothy 4:8 (NIV)

My daughter Emily found the perfect saying for me: "Every time I say the word *exercise* I wash my mouth out with chocolate!"

I convince myself to exercise, most days, by meeting my friends to walk: Karen, early weekday mornings, and Joyce, late Sunday afternoons. We talk as we weave through our suburban neighborhood, so the hour passes quickly. But whenever one of them leaves on vacation, I count that as my vacation, too!

Then I found something even more boring than exercise. Stretches.

I'd asked a physical therapist to look at my painful shoulder. She diagnosed the problem. "These muscles are extremely tight!" She gave me four different shoulder stretches that I am to do every day. Hold each for thirty seconds, then repeat the process. Bo-ring.

Maybe I could convince myself to do them if I had an end point. "How long do I need to do the stretches?" She responded with a question, "How long do you need to change the oil in your car?" Ouch.

Okay ... is there something else I could do while counting out all those thirty seconds?

I remember the people who asked me to pray for them. Of course I have been praying ... when I think of it. I name the friend caring for her elderly parents, the cousin whose best friend is dying, Emily's frustrating work situation, the friend who is traveling.

Hmm. Four prayers, four exercises, then repeat. I bet the time will pass quickly. That sounds like a commitment, with no excuse to take a vacation.

Thank You, Lord, for nudging me to keep my body and spirit healthy. And for not giving up, especially when I want to. —Leanne Jackson

Digging Deeper: 1 Thessalonians 5:17; Hebrews 12:1

Tuesday, August 17

For the Lord gives wisdom; from his mouth come knowledge and understanding. —Proverbs 2:6 (ESV)

Very recently I had a huge mishap at work; a colleague and I dropped an entire gallon of yellow paint near the entrance of the military chapel I call home. As I was lamenting to Nanny on my way home after the incident and figuring out how to clean the yellow mess, she suggested I call maintenance to clean it. I caught myself smiling.

I smiled because my thoughts on calling maintenance were summed up with the unspoken response "This is the army; we clean our own messes." When did I come to understand and speak army so readily? Truth is, after devoting twenty-two years as a civilian to this institution called the army, I've changed. My time serving with the army has changed my resolve, my knowledge, my perspective, my faith, and my discipline, and for good measure, I can speak army acronyms with the best. It is often I find myself surprised by my words or actions that have been influenced by army culture.

We are changed for the better or for the worse by influences. The institutions, environments, and causes we become part of influence us in abiding ways. We often have to discern how we have been changed. Much to my chagrin, I have caught myself more than once over the years speaking tougher than I want to—a side effect of the army. Mentally, I must make changes when that happens and remember who the Lord calls me to be.

Lord, may I judiciously recognize the influences that help develop my character and my life in You, and may I make necessary adjustments. Amen.
—Jolynda Strandberg

Digging Deeper: Genesis 26:4; 2 Chronicles 34:1–7; Nehemiah 4

Wednesday, August 18

Two are better than one, because they have a good reward for their toil. For if they fall, one will lift up his fellow. —Ecclesiastes 4:9–10 (ESV)

Anxiety gripped my stomach as I trudged along a walking trail in the small Montana town where we spend our summers. My husband, Jim, was temporarily stuck at McMurdo Station, Antarctica, where he'd been servicing the base's microscopes. He should've been home already, but his flight out had been delayed again and again by turbulent weather. In a couple of weeks, our family would be making our annual journey north to our winter home in Fairbanks, Alaska. It was becoming clear that the overwhelming job of packing up the house would be mine alone. I sighed. I didn't see how it'd all get done.

Honk, honk, honk. I looked up. A V of geese was visible overhead, heading south. I remembered reading how geese travel in formation to conserve energy. The bird in front pulls the geese behind in its slipstream. And the uplift of the wings of the birds following creates a draft that pushes the group forward. The overall effect of this aerial push-pull is dramatic, allowing geese who travel together to go up to 80 percent farther than a solitary goose, flying alone.

I thought about the friends who knew our situation and had offered to help. One had said she'd watch our six-year-old as I packed. Another volunteered to help put the garden to bed for the winter. Still someone else had said she'd help me can the mountains of garden produce piled in the kitchen. It was true Jim was delayed, but I was hardly alone. I had a flock of friends ready to lift me up and move me forward. Together, we'd get done what I couldn't accomplish alone.

Thank You, God, for the encouragement and beautiful blessings my friendships bring to my life.
—Erin Janoso

Digging Deeper: Ruth 1:16; Ephesians 4:16

Thursday, August 19

We work hard with our own hands. When we are cursed, we bless; when we are persecuted, we endure it. —1 Corinthians 4:12 (NIV)

I've started a part-time hobby remaking furniture. I remake tabletops with used toboggans, rebuild discarded desks with old basketball flooring, and make lamps fashioned out of church organ pipes. I make everything except money.

When I discovered this new pursuit (or it discovered me), I was excited by the challenge of remaking something in a different way, of experimenting with new materials and methods, the endless fun of the new. Then reality gnawed away at the novelty, and the honeymoon was over. Now I'm learning the patience of a good hitter in baseball: with hard work, practice, and tenacity, one day I will earn the honor of failing in just seven out of every ten tries.

My biggest obstacle (other than money—see above) is engineering. I have trouble connecting the heavy gym floor to the repurposed desk. I have trouble connecting the awkward, unbalanced toboggan to the reused hairpin legs. I have trouble connecting my vision with the unforgiving laws of physics.

I have trouble connecting where I am with where I want to be. I have trouble connecting.

There's probably a metaphor in there somewhere—about the nobility of hard work, of trying to rebuild something using the materials that one has available, of striving to overcome the unrelenting laws of nature, about having the faith to pursue something you don't understand and can't yet envision. But you'll have to excuse me because I think I just figured out how to connect the rickety top to the solid foundation.

Bless the work of our hands, Lord, as we labor to find You. —Mark Collins

Digging Deeper: James 1:22–25

Friday, August 20

STRUGGLING TO PRAY
Do I Really Care about Others' Problems?

Sometimes it takes a painful experience to make us change our ways. —Proverbs 20:30 (GNT)

I've always been so physically healthy—and self-centered—that prayer requests about others' pain barely register in my mind. That all changed this summer while my husband and I were in California visiting our daughters.

The day before flying, I shopped for birdseed. That's what I always do—about to leave town, I embark on a massive cleaning project or must have some nonessential household item. Seeing no staff to help me and in a hurry to get home and pack, I pulled a forty-pound bag onto my shoulder and lurched to the line at the register.

The next day I woke in agony from my neck to my fingertips. Cervical radiculopathy. The common term, a pinched nerve, understates the torture. During our trip, I couldn't sit comfortably, turn to chat with the girls in the backseat, look up at birds in the wildlife refuge beside our hotel, or sleep.

I watched TV all night, and a painkiller ad kept coming on with an endless list of dire side effects that had previously seemed hilarious.

Now, though, I cried sincere tears for the ad's probably fictional fibromyalgia sufferer. Some people, I abruptly realized, endure this misery constantly! Even now, finally over my pinched nerve, I feel genuine empathy when someone requests prayer for pain.

Use my suffering, God, to improve me. —Patty Kirk

Digging Deeper: Romans 8:18–34

Saturday, August 21

For it is by grace you have been saved....
—Ephesians 2:8 (NIV)

"Ladies, tennis is a game of grace," our tennis instructor said.

I was doomed. I'd never really played sports, and learning to play tennis at middle age was a new challenge for my unathletic body. It was tough enough to learn the mechanics of the game. But graceful? In my mind, I tromped across the court like an elephant instead of a gazelle.

But I'd wanted to learn how to play tennis my whole life, and now that my children were grown, I was pursuing that dream.

When my game improved, I joined a team, excited to be a "real" tennis player. But instead of fun, I witnessed how competition can change the atmosphere.

One day, after one of our doubles' pairs lost their match, Susan stomped off the court and walked up to the captain. "Trish made too many errors today. And when she missed that overhead shot, it made us lose the game! Please don't pair me with her again."

I had watched the game, and although Trish did miss some shots, so did Susan. In fact, everyone makes mistakes, whether in tennis or in life. But blaming someone else for their mistakes doesn't solve anything.

Instead, what we need is grace—not the kind that describes our movement but the kind that God shows us by forgiving us. Just as I want to play tennis with someone who shows me grace by not holding my mistakes against me, I need to be the same way and show grace to others. After all, none of us is perfect.

Thank You, Lord, for showing us grace and not holding our wrongs against us. —Marilyn Turk

Digging Deeper: Matthew 7:3–5; Romans 3:23; Ephesians 1:7

Sunday, August 22

And when you pray, do not keep on babbling like pagans, for they think they will be heard because of their many words. Do not be like them, for your Father knows what you need before you ask him. —Matthew 6:7–8 (NIV)

I've always been in awe of my brothers and sisters in Christ who are able to pray in front of others. It's a gift that I thought I didn't have or wouldn't be able to acquire. While I am comfortable praying on my own, I didn't think my prayers in front of others were fervent enough, passionate enough, nor did they include the *right* words to be shared with a group. Or so I thought.

I became a part of a triad at my church—groups of three members who meet weekly to discuss the previous week's sermon and to share thoughts and life with each other. Our triads are meant to be comfortable and encouraging and operate without leaders, sharing the opening and closing prayer duties. I fretted about this, and then I did one better: I prayed for the courage to lead our group's devotions.

It wasn't easy for me. I didn't have the Bible lingo down, I didn't raise my voice, and I didn't speak with great passion. I thought that my words weren't powerful or moving. My triad sisters, both more experienced corporate pray-ers than me, seemed moved by my prayer. And then I realized that prayers aren't a performance but an expression of what is in and on your heart.

"Good pray-ers" are simply those who seek to follow God's Word and to hear His voice. That's far more important than choosing the right words, the pitch, or a righteous tone.

Father, I thank You for the ability to come to You and to speak to You in the presence of others.
—Gayle T. Williams

Digging Deeper: Job 22:27; 33:26

Monday, August 23

BECOMING JUST ME AGAIN
Turning Downs into Ups

And the Lord God said, "It isn't good for man to be alone; I will make a companion for him, a helper suited to his needs." —Genesis 2:18 (TLB)

When Jack was sick with metastatic melanoma, that entire year was filled with a lot more downs than ups. After he died I was determined to reverse that. And so I began. I got rid of my thirtysomething-year-old bed and bought a brand-new bed with plenty of room to flip from side to side and fling my arms and legs hither and yon.

Learning to live completely alone brought interesting dilemmas, like how was I going to get the sunscreen rubbed onto my back? One day in the hardware store I saw a long-handled wooden bamboo spatula. At home I smeared sunscreen lotion all over it and rubbed it successfully all over my back.

The third thing I did to enhance my uphill climb was to say yes to every single invitation I received from friends, relatives, and neighbors whenever they asked me to join them for an event or adventure. Within the first five weeks of Jack's death I went to a couple of movies, a dinner theater, three boat rides, hikes in various parks, and lunches and dinners with friends.

One thing I didn't do right was the time I was at a big box store with my friend Paula, who suggested

I buy the house-brand toilet paper because it was soft, strong, and a great bargain. So I picked up the big package. When I got home and realized I'd purchased forty-five rolls of toilet paper, it took me an hour just to find places to store the five nine-roll packages. As I laughed myself to sleep that night I learned that sometimes it takes a while to adjust to living alone.

Lord, give me big doses of courage, strength, wisdom, and laughter as I navigate this single lifestyle.
—Patricia Lorenz

Digging Deeper: Psalm 90:10–12; Hebrews 11:13–16

Tuesday, August 24

Each of you should use whatever gift you have received to serve others, as faithful stewards of God's grace in its various forms. —1 Peter 4:10 (NIV)

"Life doesn't frighten me." I painted these words on the side of my son's painting for his teacher Alison. He beautifully replicated an abstract, crown-wearing dinosaur by her favorite artist, Jean-Michel Basquiat. I added the quote by her favorite poet, Maya Angelou.

I explained the significance of the quote in a letter that accompanied the gift. "Before you came into our life, school was a frightening experience. It's not scary anymore."

School was the place where my son was torn down. Even after his ADHD diagnosis and a pricey private school, teachers continued to focus only on his struggles.

I knew this school would be different when Alison's first words about my son were "Brandon has the most beautiful soul." I was right. His love for learning and confidence blossomed under her tutelage. How could our painting ever compare to the life-changing gift she'd given us?

Soon after we gave her the painting, Alison was attacked by a stranger. During her recovery, she said the painting and quote were an emotional focal point during the tough times. "I'd look at his painting and calm myself down," she said. "Brandon helped me get back up on my feet daily."

When we share our gifts with someone, we can never fathom how great an impact we will have on that person's life. Alison did that for Brandon, and I'm so touched he was able to do that for her as well.

Lord, thank You for the gifts You've placed in my heart to give. May they be a blessing to this world and a testament of Your love. —Karen Valentin

Digging Deeper: Matthew 5:14

Wednesday, August 25

They shall still bear fruit in old age.
—Psalm 92:14 (NKJV)

I was feeling old and worthless when my granddaughter Hannah called with a request.

"Grandpa, I wonder if you could grow some zinnias for my upcoming wedding reception. They are my favorite flower, and no one can grow things like you can."

I went right to work, planting large zinnias everywhere: around the foundation of the house, in raised beds, even in plastic pots. Enough, I figured, to produce about five hundred blooms.

They were growing well when a fungus turned some of them gray, and I had to cull those out. Then came the Japanese beetles, who turned the leaves into lace doilies. The final insult was a storm that blew the tall plants to the ground. It took me a day to stake them back upright.

As the reception drew near, I counted only about a hundred and fifty blooms left.

Then I fell ill, with a vicious case of vertigo, and I spent the day of the reception in bed. My daughter, Natalie, picked up the zinnias and took them to the reception.

As I lay in bed, my head spinning, I felt as if I had failed my granddaughter. Zinnias are the easiest flowers in the world to grow, but somehow I failed.

The next day, however, Hannah called to say, "The flowers were perfect, Grandpa, just enough for the small reception area. Everyone raved about the large, bright blooms, and some of the guests took flowers home with them. I'm sending you some pictures." She sounded very happy.

I have decided that I am not always the best judge of my worth. I have a tendency to be too hard on myself. Sometimes I just need someone to call me and say, "Grandpa, we still need you."

Help me to recognize my worth, Lord, even when I don't feel it. —Daniel Schantz

Digging Deeper: Isaiah 40:8; Matthew 6:28–30

Thursday, August 26

And if I go and prepare a place for you, I will come again and receive you to Myself; that where I am, there you may be also. —John 14:3 (NKJV)

Late last night when our house grew quiet, I sat alone in the den thinking about a new school year beginning soon. My thoughts floated back to 1957 when I was six years old and starting first grade at Brent International School in Baguio City, Philippines. I can still glimpse each of my classmates' faces, recall most of their names, laugh at our frequent misbehavior, and relive our joys and fears. I also remember my patient teacher, Mrs. Ocsenia, who taught us the vital and fundamental skills of reading and writing. I could not write this story today without her love and care.

As I reflected, I realized that I do not know where any of my old classmates live now. Scattered all over the world as they must be, there is no way to track them down, telephone them, or even send an email. Sixty-two years ago seems locked in the past and secluded in a "different world."

Turning off the last light in our house, I sat in a gentle darkness and suddenly thought, *I can at least pray for them.*

So, for the next twenty minutes, I "called the roll," saw their young faces in my memory's reflection, and uttered a prayer for each of my long-lost friends. Somehow I sensed a spiritual reconnection. And I intuited that all of life is moving toward "sweet reunion" in a dimension that our physical eyes cannot see and our minds cannot comprehend. Death is but a doorway to deeper love and laughter.

Dear Father, may I trust that love and friendship is separated only for a moment. Amen. —Scott Walker

Digging Deeper: Proverbs 17:17; John 15:12–14

Friday, August 27

Take delight in the LORD and he will give you the desires of your heart. —Psalm 37:4 (NIV)

A recent writing exercise asked me to list everything I loved.

Here are some of that list: *Chocolate, of course. The smell of cut grass. The relaxed, quiet pleasure of a job well done. Laughter around the dinner table at the end of a meal. Red barns at summer twilight. My cat's head butt against my shin. My husband's greeting as I walk through the door.*

I delight in these things. Do I delight, in the same way, in God? Where is He on that list?

The way my mom folds me up in her arms when she hugs me. My dad's patience. The sparkly way the air feels before a thunderstorm. Being all alone in a dark, cool church.

I look at the list again. God is there, suffusing every single thing on that list with grace and holiness and joy. I delight in Him by delighting in them. This perfect world! My perfect life! I am blessed to be alive.

Indeed, He gives me the desires of my heart.

God, no matter what happens today, my life is good. You make it so. —Amy Eddings

Digging Deeper: 2 Chronicles 11:12; 1 Samuel 15:22; Psalm 35:9; Isaiah 42:1

Saturday, August 28

Therefore, if anyone is in Christ, he is a new creation; old things have passed away; behold, all things have become new. —2 Corinthians 5:17 (NKJV)

My teenage son was washing and waxing his new-to-him car for the very first time. It was his dream car—an older muscle car—and he had worked hard to earn it. Now I got to show him how to wash and wax it. We did this in the triple-digit heat of our Northern California town. I explained how to take care of his chamois. How to apply the wax and buff it to a high gloss. But Jonathan insisted on doing all the work. After some sweat and strain, he stepped back, folded his arms, and admired the mirrorlike finish. A big smile spread across his face. "Dad, it looks like a brand-new car! That shine makes all the work worth it!"

I was surprised at how choked up I became. Memories flashed through my mind—teaching him to ride a bike, to catch a ball, to write, to swim, to pray, and now to wash and wax his very own car. Though he stood a good six inches taller than me, he still found joy in showing me the results of his labor. My heart as a father was full.

In my heart, another truth bubbled up. Because of His love, God's own Son made me His personal project. He Himself did all the work to forgive me and polish me up. He then presented me as a gift to His Father. In that moment, I realized a fraction of the satisfaction that must have welled up in the Father's heart when His precious Son showed Him me, the grace-filled result of His sacrifice and grace. In the eyes of heaven, my Savior created a brand-new me, and I am grateful forever.

Gracious Father, I can never fully express my thankfulness for Your transforming work of grace in my life. Amen. —Bill Giovannetti

Digging Deeper: Jude 24

Sunday, August 29

Religion that God our Father accepts as pure and faultless is this: to look after orphans and widows in their distress. —James 1:27 (NIV)

Through my role at church I support adoptive and foster parents. So it came as no surprise when a foster mom from church announced that she and her husband were taking in a large sibling group the next day. I was shocked, however, when this mom of five young children revealed the exact number of foster children in this sibling group—seven in total, ranging from newborn to seventeen.

After receiving my friend's text, I quickly drove to her home to help. Expecting to enter total pandemonium, I was amazed to witness the most organized chaos I had ever seen. Children were playing quietly, teenagers were watching an animated movie, and adult helpers were changing diapers, cuddling babies, and managing a lunch-making assembly line.

I exhaled, relieved at the peace I felt. After a quick check-in and encouraging word to my friend, I joined the child-care assembly line. I spent much of my weekend in her home, braiding girls' hair, making up feeding bottles, and rocking babies to sleep.

By the end of the weekend I could feel my heart attaching to these children. On the day they were scheduled to leave my friend's home, I entered her house feeling sad and conflicted. I knew the children needed a more permanent placement, but I also knew my friend would miss and worry about them. As they rode away in their social workers' cars, I wiped tears from my cheeks.

My heart was heavy, but grateful for my friend who stepped in to care for these kids and also for the opportunity to share a little help, too.

Lord, thank You for the opportunity to care for
vulnerable children and orphans in their despair.
—Carla Hendricks

Digging Deeper: Psalm 146:9; Isaiah 1:17;
Matthew 25:40–45

Monday, August 30

I love the LORD, for he heard my voice.
—Psalm 116:1 (NIV)

"I've lost my Jerusalem cross necklace," I texted
my friend Joyce because we'd spent the weekend
with them at their mountain cabin. After searching
everywhere at home, I hoped they might find it.

This was no ordinary necklace. My pastor's
wife got it for me on their recent trip to the Holy
Land because I kept their dog while they led a
large group from our church on this two-week trip.
They gave it to me over lunch, a time to thank
me and my husband, Lynn, and share stories from
their trip.

I held the necklace as they described their faith-
deepening experiences—praying in Gethsemane,
baptizing people in the Dead Sea, walking the paths
Jesus walked. A trip to the Holy Land was on our
bucket list, but because of health issues, I knew the
necklace and what it represented was the closest I'd
come. Other women who'd been on the trip had
gotten the same necklace. I felt like one of them
when I wore mine and saw them wearing theirs.

Now, after months of wearing it often, I'd lost it and felt I'd lost more than a necklace.

Joyce texted back: "I've looked everywhere but can't find it. I'm so sorry."

Again, I looked in all the places I'd already looked. But I didn't want to give up hope.

A couple of days later, I was putting on my shoes in our closet and looked up to see...my Jerusalem cross necklace, hanging from a hook where I keep my favorite necklaces!

Was it there all along? I certainly didn't see it. All I know is that my necklace now represents my own holy experience. "Lost, now found."

Lord, I am grateful for the unique ways You reveal Yourself to each of Your children. —Carol Kuykendall

Digging Deeper: Matthew 18:12–14; Luke 15:24

Tuesday, August 31

Blessed is the one who fears the Lord always, but whoever hardens his heart will fall into calamity. —Proverbs 28:14 (ESV)

"Are you okay, Asa?" I asked my nephew as I handed him a plate of pancakes. He kept moving around, as if he couldn't find a comfortable position.

"Yes, just fine, Auntie." He poured syrup all over his pancakes; just as was about to take a drippy bite, he twitched again and the pancakes fell to the floor.

"Asa! What's wrong?" I was worried. Maybe he was injured? Sick?

He smiled at me. "Nothing, the frogs just keep moving."

"The frogs?"

He stood up and pulled not one, not two, but *four* big bullfrogs out of his pockets. That was the moment that I made a new rule, one that I never imagined I would have to make: "No frogs at the breakfast table."

Two days later, Asa came over again. Just as he sat down at the table, he jumped up and raced back outside. He emptied his pockets, this time full of two frogs and a tiny lizard.

"Sorry, Auntie, I forgot the rule."

Sweet Asa. He wants to do the right thing, he really does, but the temptation to scoop up a frog, a lizard, a tiny garter snake is just too much to resist. And so we have instigated a door check policy— before Asa enters my house, he stops and checks his pockets and reports to me that they are, indeed, empty.

I wonder if a similar policy would be good for each of us. A "door check" if you will. Just pause for a few minutes. Check your heart. Make sure all of the frogs and lizards and snakes are left outside. And then enter into the presence of your God.

My Lord, I know that I often make the same mistakes over and over. Please forgive me and keep my heart soft toward You. —Erin MacPherson

Digging Deeper: Psalm 51:2–4; 1 John 1:9

JOYFUL IN HOPE

1 _____

2 _____

3 _____

4 _____

5 _____

6 _____

7 _____

8 _____

9 _____

10 _____

11 _____

12 _____

13 _____

14 _____

15 _____

16 _____

17 _____

18 _____

19 _____

20 _____

21 _____

22 _____

23 _____

24 _____

25 _____

26 _____

27 _____

28 _____

29 _____

30 _____

31 _____

SEPTEMBER

In the same way, the Spirit helps us in our weakness. We do not know what we ought to pray for, but the Spirit himself intercedes for us through wordless groans.

—Romans 8:26 (NIV)

Wednesday, September 1

The houses will be full of good things which you did not put in them, and there will be wells that you did not dig, and vineyards and olive orchards that you did not plant. —Deuteronomy 6:11 (GNT)

A song they often play on the classic rock station invites us to consider this question: where might we be without love? (I've modified the words because reprinting lyrics in a book can be expensive, but perhaps you know the one.)

Whenever I hear this song, I think of my family. My whip-smart mom would've made an outstanding doctor, but back then, the career choices for most women were teacher or nurse. Had she not been one of nine children, perhaps she would've had the opportunity to buck tradition, but a scholarship to nursing school was not something she could pass up. After serving in the US Navy, Daddy went to college on the GI Bill and later worked in law enforcement. Mother and Daddy took turns taking care of my brother and me between their shifts at work and their classes, both of them eventually earning master's degrees. Before them, my grandparents worked in factories or farmed or picked up the occasional lifeline from President Roosevelt's infrastructure program that created jobs for Americans during the Great Depression.

These are things I never forgot when I had the opportunity to go to college right out of high school and study literature. Some of my classmates skipped class frequently or didn't read the assigned books. Me? Front row, every single day. Once, a professor of mine asked me to stop answering questions so that he could hear from the other students! But how could I not give 100 percent when my parents and grandparents had worked so hard to clear this beautiful path?

Father, I drink daily from wells I did not dig. Where would I be without my loving family? —Ginger Rue

Digging Deeper: Exodus 20:12; 1 John 4:19

Thursday, September 2

Follow my example, as I follow the example of Christ. —1 Corinthians 11:1 (NIV)

"*Sit down,*" I said, putting on my best Mom Voice. You know the voice—we all have one. It's firm, commanding, and definitely "done with your nonsense."

James has always been my delightful wiggle worm. Unless he's asleep, he's up and dancing, moving and bumping around the house to the songs he asks Alexa to play for him. I normally let him enjoy his personal dance party so long as his feet are on the ground, no food is in his mouth, and he's not hurting anyone.

So when he hopped up on the bench and started dancing, I knew I had to put a stop to it, especially because Beau, eighteen months, does exactly what his big brother does. Sure enough, before I could break out the Mom Voice, Beau was also up and dancing, giggling wildly, certain he looked just like his big brother.

"James, you have to remember that Mom's number-one job is to keep you safe," I reminded him sternly. "Plus, Beau is watching, so let's show him what's safe and how to behave."

I've often struggled with whether putting the weight of being an example is healthy for my kids. They're young, still learning themselves. Was it too much to ask?

But then I remember that I'm their example, and my mom is mine, so it's really never too early to remember, or learn, that your actions impact and influence others.

I don't ask my kids to be perfect, but I do ask them to try their hardest and act in love, even if that means we have to take a break at dinner and move the dance party to the kitchen floor.

Lord, help me be an example to those around me today, one worth emulating. —Ashley Kappel

Digging Deeper: Matthew 5:16; 1 Timothy 4:12; Titus 2:7

Friday, September 3

Then Jesus told his disciples a parable to show them that they should always pray and not give up. —Luke 18:1 (NIV)

I keep a God Box. It's a round black cardboard box. I think it was the gift packaging for a necklace. I place in my God Box folded bits of paper with written prayers for help with some of my biggest or most intractable problems. It's a tangible act of turning them over to God.

I've lifted the lid from time to time and have opened the little notes.

Here, a prayer for my marriage. It's undated, as I suppose it should be. We always are in need of God as the divine third in our relationship. I like to think of Him sitting on the couch with us, listening as we talk about feeling hurt or angry or ignored. That prayer gets answered every time an argument ends with both of us laughing.

On this piece of paper, a prayer to have a baby. That must have been written in 2003, when we were going through fertility treatments. We were not successful. But I consider this prayer answered because of the deep peace I feel about my life, our lives, as they are. The infertility I sought with such zeal to negate is something I accept with a cheerfulness that, at the time, I hadn't thought possible.

What I learn again and again from this exercise is that the problems that twist me up so tightly and painfully today will unwind. The mere, mundane passage of time has a softening effect, yes. But the wiping away of every tear, the bracing wind of forgiveness, and the joyful acceptance of my life as He wills it come from God.

God, when I stop to think about it, You always answer my prayers. Thank You. —Amy Eddings

Digging Deeper: 1 John 5:14–15; Philippians 4:6

Saturday, September 4

He is not afraid of bad news; his heart is firm, trusting in the Lord. —Psalm 112:7 (ESV)

It's outdoor swim meet day, and the community pool is thick with activity. The sun is strong and the air is humid-heavy. It's loud. My heart beats fast as I look for my family under one of the colorful pop-up tents that make the lawn look like a midway at the county fair.

My twelve-year-old Gabriel switched teams—a result of our recent move. He's quiet. Reserved. Once he makes a friend it will be forever, but today I worry I'll find him sitting alone.

I walk along the poolside searching, and someone calls my name from under a gold canopy. A former teammate friend asks about Gabe, and for a moment everything feels comfortable. Then the image in my head returns—my boy by himself while others laugh and talk, sitting pretzel-legged on beach towels.

The announcer calls an event and I look to the head of the pool where teams begin to form lines. That's when I see my boy standing to the side of a sea of swimmers. I recognize how he holds his shoulders and the blue cap we bought at the sport store last night.

Only Gabriel is not alone.

He's in the center of a cluster of boys. He's laughing. His hands move in gestures. Silly? He's being silly? He's by nature a serious boy, and this cutting loose makes me cry joy.

I take a moment to watch.

The still water breaks with rhythm as swimmers dive in. People press close, but I want to hold this picture. I'm reminded once again that the Lord is with my children. Always.

When I finally find my husband and new team, I know that as my children grow and stretch and reach new places, it's an opportunity for my faith to do the same.

Lord, help me to trust. You are worthy. Amen.
—Shawnelle Eliasen

Digging Deeper: Psalm 20:7; Isaiah 26:3

Sunday, September 5

Now to him who is able to do immeasurably more than all we ask or imagine, according to his power that is at work within us. —Ephesians 3:20 (NIV)

Should we turn around? I asked my husband in the car. We'd been at a standstill, waiting for a train to start moving, for twenty minutes. I kept anticipating it would move every few seconds, but it didn't budge.

I looked at the clock and let out a sigh. We still needed to eat dinner, put the groceries away, finish the laundry, and get our six-month-old to bed. We had a routine on Sunday nights. Yet something had started to feel like sandpaper to my insides about the routines that had subtly begun to accumulate in our lives. They had actually caused me to forget about dreaming bigger.

I'd had a deep sense in my spirit for some time about there being so much more to life than getting up, going to work, coming home, and repeating. Yet there were still so many unanswered questions about it: What did that look like? How does a family survive if we lived any differently right now? All I knew was I felt stuck like this train. And that awareness made the days and weeks feel longer than ever before. Waiting does that to you.

My eyes shifted above the brim of the train. I always find Jesus in the vastness there. *Don't turn around on this road less traveled,* I felt Him say. *I've planted a seed in you to chase after this. There's more to life than this. You'll be uncovering it soon as long as you keep your eyes on Me and not the part that feels stuck.*

Jesus, what am I looking for that only You can fulfill? Please lead me day by day and help me to follow.
—Desiree Cole

Digging Deeper: Lamentations 3:25; Jeremiah 29:11

Labor Day, Monday, September 6

BECOMING JUST ME AGAIN
Finding My Purpose

These were his instructions to them: "Plead with
the Lord of the harvest to send out more laborers
to help you, for the harvest is so plentiful and the
workers so few." —Luke 10:2 (TLB)

After Jack died I stumbled through the myriad tasks
every widow must face. The paperwork is mind-
boggling. Dividing mementos among his children
and grandchildren. Cleaning out his desk. Donating
his clothes. It was work—lots and lots of work.

But when that was all finished, I worried, *Now
what? There's nobody I have to cook for, shop for,
vacation with, do laundry for, encourage, swim and
play cards with, discuss life's happenings with. What is
my purpose now?*

As the weeks unfolded, my purpose became
clear. It was all about work. As a senior citizen I
knew my days of actually going out into the world
cranking out a forty-hour workweek were over. So
I started a little volunteer business, driving friends
and neighbors to the Tampa or St. Pete airports or to
doctor visits. I became more active at church. Started
some writing projects. Wrote more letters to my kids
and grandkids. Organized my closets. The more I
worked, the happier I became.

The first Labor Day was celebrated 139 years
ago in 1882, when ten thousand workers marched
in the streets of Manhattan. Back then the average

dedicated American worked six days a week, twelve hours a day. Thank goodness my workdays are much less than twelve hours! But I sure do feel blessed because of my labor. I've learned that real honest-to-goodness work is the one thing that gives me purpose. And purpose is the one thing that makes me feel whole, happy, fulfilled, and ready to tackle the world. Happy Labor Day!

Father, You are the boss of my labor. Guide me, enable me, give me strength, courage, and stamina to work every day to Your glory. —Patricia Lorenz

Digging Deeper: 2 Thessalonians 3:7–13; 1 Timothy 5:17–18

Tuesday, September 7

"Have I not commanded you? Be strong and courageous. Do not be afraid; do not be discouraged, for the Lord your God will be with you wherever you go." —Joshua 1:9 (NIV)

Our Bible study leader was diagnosed with thyroid cancer as we began a new study in the book of Joshua. That first week, she solicited prayer. She claimed Joshua 1:9 as her mantra.

We who taught the children ordered T-shirts to encourage her. Soft forest green with white script letters proclaimed Be Strong and Courageous. We'd wear them each Tuesday to show her we were praying.

When mine arrived, it was too large. Maybe a washing would shrink it. I threw it on the laundry room floor to remind myself to add it to the next load.

I forgot about the shirt until Monday night. When I picked it up, a nearby bottle of bleach was tipped on its side. On the back right corner of my brand-new, too-big T-shirt was a white stain the size of a quarter. Ugh.

At Bible study the next morning, I sat against the wall near the door of the toddler room. Once everyone arrived, I pushed the door shut from my spot on the carpet. Sitting too close to the door, with a too-big shirt on, I felt material near my left shoulder get stuck between the door and frame. I pulled. A pencil-size rip joined the bleach mark. *I can't wear this the next eight months!* I thought.

That evening, I logged online to order a new shirt. A quiet knowing fell over me. Strong and courageous is a battle cry for a difficult mission that could bring wounds and scars. I proudly wore my too-big, bleach-stained, torn T-shirt the rest of the year, for both our leader and me.

Dear Lord, thank You for reminding me to remain strong in prayer no matter what.
—Stephanie Thompson

Digging Deeper: Deuteronomy 31:8; Galatians 6:2

Wednesday, September 8

May the God of hope fill you with all joy and
peace as you trust in him, so that you may overflow
with hope by the power of the Holy Spirit.
—Romans 15:13 (NIV)

It was one of the hardest decisions of our thirty-
three-year marriage. We'd both avoided it, especially
Julee, but her suffering had grown unbearable,
the disks in her spinal column being crushed by
damaged vertebrae. Finally, she was willing to take a
chance on surgery.

She'd injured her back during years as a singer and
actress. Once, performing a concert in Bucharest, she
tripped over a cable as she was coming onstage and
nearly had to cancel the performance. As it was, she
could barely move during that show. In a crazy off-
Broadway musical when we were first married, her
role required her to be hoisted aloft to escape a space
monster (I kid you not). The hoist operator was new
and wrenched Julee's back out of alignment.

She'd tried everything for relief: injections, pills,
physical therapy, yoga, massage, meditation, rest—
lots and lots of rest. Finally, reluctantly, she had
agreed to surgery, even if it would have to wait a bit
due to a flare-up of her lupus.

"Edward, I'm scared."

"I know, baby, but the doctor says the risks are
minimal. The worst-case scenario is you stay the same."

"That's what scares me. Staying the same. That's the same as losing hope, and I can't lose hope."

She was right. What outcome could be worse than the loss of hope? Of knowing nothing will change? I'm not sure I could face that risk. But Julee will. She told me, "There's only one way I can do this: with God. I don't ask Him to take away the fear, just to go through it with me."

I'll be there, too, for Julee, asking God to be there for both of us.

Father in heaven, in our deepest pain we turn to You for hope. —Edward Grinnan

Digging Deeper: Romans 5:2–5; 8:25

Thursday, September 9

The Lord does not look at the things people look at. People look at the outward appearance, but the Lord looks at the heart. —1 Samuel 16:7 (NIV)

Logan stomped into the house from school and slammed his book bag on the floor.

"What's wrong?" I asked.

"I'm going to change my name! Everyone makes fun of me and calls me "little Logan!"

Logan was dealing with the same thing my three older sons had endured, having the last name of Little. It didn't help that Logan was smaller than average. Kids like to tease each other, and it was

Logan's misfortune to have a last name that matched his stature.

"Your father was teased the same way when he was your age," I offered.

He responded with a frown.

Outside, I saw a hummingbird at the feeder and pointed. "Logan, look how fast his wings move." Beside the lake near our house, a four-foot-tall blue heron stalked a fish. "And see that heron? Isn't he huge? You see, God didn't make all birds the same size and He didn't make all people the same size, either. But each of them is special and important, just like you are."

Logan glanced from the heron to the hummingbird. "Little birds are faster. I'm fast, too."

Satisfied, he switched his attention to a video game.

I was reminded of the story in the Bible about how David was chosen to be the future king of Israel. David was the youngest and smallest of his brothers, so no one expected God to appoint him to be king. But God surprised everyone and did just that, showing us that He sees us differently than people do.

Lord, help us to appreciate and accept each other for the unique persons You created us to be.
—Marilyn Turk

Digging Deeper: 1 Samuel 16:1–7

Friday, September 10

When I am afraid, I put my trust in you.
—Psalm 56:3 (NASB)

My daughter got a new kitten. His name is Jimmy. He's absolutely adorable—white and fluffy with big green eyes and a tiny pink nose. He's also tiny—he weighed in at 1.8 pounds at his first appointment. Picture a white fuzzy fluff ball about the size of a can of soda.

Keep that picture in your mind as I describe to you my dog. His name is Zeke. He's a great big golden retriever who clocks in at just under a hundred pounds. He's also adorable, in a big, floppy giant dog sort of way.

Now that you have those pictures in your mind, you'll laugh when you hear that Zeke is absolutely terrified of Jimmy. If Jimmy walks into the room, Zeke cowers in the corner. He hides behind me, whimpers, and will only come out when Jimmy is safely removed from his view. The mere sound of Jimmy's tiny meow causes Zeke to tremble.

It's so funny.

Poor Zeke doesn't seem to realize that Jimmy is absolutely no threat to him. Even if Jimmy came at Zeke with claws out, Jimmy wouldn't even be able to reach Zeke's nose to bat at him. Zeke doesn't realize his own size and strength (not to mention the fact that I wouldn't bring anything into our house that would harm him), so he spends his days hiding from the scary monster kitten.

Aren't we the same way? Hiding from the "terrifying" kittens in our lives when we have a God who is so much bigger, stronger, and more trustworthy than anything that causes us to lose courage?

Lord, help me to trust You when I am afraid. Help me to know that there is nothing that can keep me from the safety of Your arms. —Erin MacPherson

Digging Deeper: Philippians 4:6; 2 Timothy 1:7

Saturday, September 11

To you I lift up my eyes.... —Psalm 123:1 (NRSV)

This is a true story from the time of the Holocaust—one that feels relevant for today.

Several women and men were hiding in the same basement in a city in Europe that had been overrun already by the Nazis. These Jewish survivors had each lost spouses, friends, and children. They were angry with God. While they hid, they decided to put God "on trial."

They began to talk in the early evening, making arguments for how God must not exist, why God cannot possibly be loving toward us, how God had abandoned them—they who had been faithful to Him. These survivors argued into the night. They cried and yelled, and they often disagreed with each other.

After several hours had passed, it looked—through the thin basement window where they all were hiding—that the sun would soon be coming up. One of the assembly turned to the others and said, "It is almost morning. We should prepare for our morning prayers." And they did.

> **Even when I cannot understand how something so bad can happen to me, or to those I love, God, I will praise You.** —Jon M. Sweeney

> Digging Deeper: Psalm 123:2–3

Sunday, September 12

With my mouth I will make your faithfulness known through all generations. —Psalm 89:1 (NIV)

Early this morning, as usual, I walked out our front door and picked up the newspaper on the steps. I laid it out on the kitchen counter, checked the front-page headlines, and then turned to the obituaries. I'm in the age group that's commonly represented on that page, which means I might know someone whose name appears there.

Even when I don't know anyone, I'm intrigued by the information chosen to sum up the important legacies of one's life. I try to imagine who wrote the words and under what circumstances. I've heard families talk about the difficulty of that task, sometimes arguing about what and what not to include. Some people write their own obituaries. Even my father did that.

Many obits read like mini memoirs, starting with when and where someone was born. "In the backseat of a '64 Chevy" was one of my recent favorites. The most interesting ones reveal unique personalities. Amid the résumé of educational degrees earned and jobs held are descriptions of personal passions...for the ocean, mountain climbing, fishing, or cooking. And what will be missed: her chocolate chip cookies, his banjo playing, their Fourth of July picnic, her laughter.

Obituaries not only honor a loved one's life, but they also inspire those of us who read them. When a wife is described as "the love of his life," it makes me want to be that for my husband. "Faith has been the center of her life" makes me yearn to be known that way. This morning I read, "He went to be with the Lord with thanksgiving and great expectations." I want to follow in those footsteps.

Lord, I want to live as many who have gone before me, so others may know You through me.
—Carol Kuykendall

Digging Deeper: Psalm 22:26; Ecclesiastes 5:4; John 17:3–5

Monday, September 13

He is the one you praise; he is your God, who performed for you those great and awesome wonders you saw with your own eyes.
—Deuteronomy 10:21 (NIV)

"Can you drive Glenda's husband, Shack, to the hospital in Payson?" a friend asked on the phone. "There's been an accident."

We pieced together the details after we picked up Shack for the ninety-minute ride from our home in Chandler, Arizona. Glenda and her friend Barb had been T-boned at sixty-five miles per hour. Rolled twice. Concussions. Glenda—one broken rib. Barb—an injured arm from the air bag. Bangs and bruises.

A normally quiet man, Shack repeated the details over and over, along with the questions. *How did they survive? Why weren't the injuries worse? Do we know anything else?*

In the emergency room, the doctor talked over the details of the pain medication he was sending home with Glenda while Shack gave her sips of water and gripped her hand.

A bit muddled, Glenda assured the doctor she didn't need the prescription, that the most over-the-counter pain meds she took for anything was half a pill. The doctor looked at her chart, fingered her swollen right eye with its multiple shades of purple and blue, and said, "Of all the days in your life, I think this is a full-pain-pill day."

Our drive was quiet on the way home, as the nausea from the concussion hit Glenda. She gulped fresh air from an open window while Shack patted her shoulder.

Silently, we each mulled over the earlier question. *How did they survive?* Not yet spoken, the answer wrapped around our hearts as solid and as reassuring as the entwined fingers of our two friends.

A miracle. We were living a miracle.

Jesus, even full-pain-pill days can contain Your miraculous presence in our lives. —Lynne Hartke

Digging Deeper: Job 5:9; Jeremiah 32:27; Luke 18:27

Tuesday, September 14

But Jesus called the children to him and said, "Let the little children come to me, and do not hinder them, for the kingdom of God belongs to such as these." —Luke 18:16 (NIV)

My wife, Sandee, still runs twelve miles a week despite the fact that her knees are shot. Well, *shot* might be too strong a word. Her knees are…um…shot. I was right the first time. They are shot.

My in-laws have whispered to me that I should tell Sandee to stop running. I have myself a good chuckle, then whisper back two questions: "Have you ever met my wife? Do you think that would work?" The silence that follows is the answer.

Several therapies have been tried: stretches, anti-inflammatory drugs, needles. Some things worked for a while, but nothing long-term. So my wife has stuck to her homemade remedy: a heady mixture of tenacity and denial, plus a knee brace. Sandee says this concoction works fine. Then again, that could be her homemade remedy speaking.

Recently, someone else noticed Sandee's struggles. A little girl was happily skipping in the other direction, then turned around to catch up with Sandee.

"I saw you running," she said, breathless and earnest. "I'll pray for your knee."

From Sandee's description of the encounter, the girl might be a little "touched," as my sainted mother used to say. Then again, maybe not. Maybe genuine compassion is in such short supply that when we see it offered so freely, we assume that something must be wrong.

I will say this: Sandee's knee did feel better, almost instantly. I don't know what proportions make up Sandee's homegrown recipe—how much tenacity, how much denial—but I do know that it takes only a pinch of unsolicited mercy to go a very long way.

Lord, thank You for sending Your small angels to repair the world, one knee at a time. —Mark Collins

Digging Deeper: Mark 10:15–16; Hebrews 13:1–3

Wednesday, September 15

My Father will love them, and we will come to them and make our home with them.
—John 14:23 (NRSV)

My wife, Kate, and I stopped by our local Dunkin' Donuts to get some "fuel for the road" prior to driving fifty-five miles to see her cardiologist.

Three weeks prior, Kate underwent open-heart surgery. By all indications, her healing was progressing well. Yet any visit to a heart doctor is a visit that includes unease and concern.

After I received my two decaf coffees and a few munchies, I headed for the door.

"Hi, Ken," came a friendly voice from the line of early-morning patrons. "How's Kate?"

I glanced to see Ginny, a longtime resident of our town and backbone member of our church. In the moment I saw her, I immediately experienced a tangible sense of calm, assurance, and promise.

We briefly discussed the doctor's trip Kate and I were taking, and how well she seemed to be doing. "Tell her we're asking for her... and having her in our thoughts," remarked Ginny as I departed.

After thirty years in the army, and some seventeen different changes of address, we moved to the Hudson Highlands five and a half years ago. Although we did not know a soul here prior, we'd experienced a deep sense of church community, acceptance, and shared spiritual care from the start.

As I walked to the car with Dunkin' Donut snacks in hand, I was energized. I knew not only were Ginny's thoughts with us as we drove off, but the prayers of an entire congregation were also being raised on our behalf.

Loving God, we thank You for houses of worship where we are sustained by Your camaraderie, grace, and presence, through the lives of Your people.
—Ken Sampson

Digging Deeper: Acts 18:22; Philippians 1:3

Thursday, September 16

Therefore we do not lose heart. Though outwardly we are wasting away, yet inwardly we are being renewed day by day. —2 Corinthians 4:16 (NIV)

Early morning at the gym, I started my workout on the elliptical. My plan was to go early and get it over with. The gym was crowded, everyone else probably having the same intention.

An older man, nearing ninety, pushed his walker to the cycle beside me. His daughter helped him make the transition from the walker to the cycle, cradling his arms as he inched to the bike.

Once settled, the man pedaled slowly in purposeful circles.

"Okay, Dad," his daughter said. "You're doing great! Wow. Look at how great you're doing."

Every now and then his daughter patted his shoulder and said, "You got this, Dad."

Head down, sweat around his temple, the man kept at it. Once our eyes met and he smiled the most beautiful smile, a smile that seemed to say, "I'm happy to be here."

I looked at the clock and then at the controls on the elliptical, hoping no one would notice the tear that ran down my face.

Dear Lord, I am in awe of the human spirit that grows stronger and more beautiful with life's challenges.
—Sabra Ciancanelli

Digging Deeper: Psalm 71:9; Isaiah 40:29

Where there is no guidance, a people falls, but
in an abundance of counselors there is safety.
—Proverbs 11:14 (ESV)

"So I'm a tennis player, not a golfer." My teenage
son, Jonathan, laughed out loud as he swung and
missed the golf ball for a second time. We were
enjoying a family vacation in Hawaii when I
suggested we hit a bucket of balls. I hadn't golfed in
a decade, and he had never held a golf club in his
life. The prospects for comedy were high.

We got set up at the driving range. Manicured
fairways rose to amber mountains against a crystal-
blue sky. A gentle Hawaiian breeze made the scene
magical. I showed him how to tee up a ball. I helped
him grip the club the way my dad helped me long
ago. He was eager and had at it. Like most first-time
golfers', his swing was too hard and too fast. He
didn't keep his balance, and took his eye off the ball.

Strike one. We both laughed. Strike two. More
laughter.

"Slow down," I said. "Let the club do the work."

That's when he made his comment about his
section-winning high-school tennis team. Then he
added, "Nobody's good at everything."

As he drew back carefully for his third swing, his
comment took hold. There were too many items on
my plate. Too many ideas crowding out things that
mattered most. Books to write. Websites to build.
Sermons to craft. A church to run. Landscaping to

fix. Home repairs to finish. The list was exhausting, and I was straining to do it all. Was God saying to let some things go?

Jonathan's third swing rocketed the ball with a satisfying *crack*. His smile said it all. "Dad, you're supposed to let the club do the work."

Yes, comedy. Meaningful comedy.

Lord, keep me from trying to do it all, that I might rest and walk in Your grace. Amen.
—Bill Giovannetti

Digging Deeper: 1 Corinthians 12:21

Saturday, September 18

I will lift up mine eyes unto the hills, from whence cometh my help. —Psalm 121:1 (KJV)

One rainy Saturday I received a text from my son Harrison, who is in DC for his first year of college: "Dad, hope all is well at home. My freshman year is flying by. I'm thinking about you and 'Ithaca' today. Enjoy the ride. Love you!"

Written by Greek Poet Constantine Cavafy, "Ithaca" reminds us that the journey is even more important than our destination and that experiencing each day as it comes is actually what "life" is all about. The poem was a favorite of my father's and mine as I was growing up. Back then, he and I shared a love for poetry and music in much the same way Harrison and I do now.

I was texting Harrison back when Mary Katherine burst into my office. "Daddy, Mommy got us a hundred-piece mermaid puzzle! Would you pleeeeasssse come work it with us?"

There was no way on God's earth I could possibly have said no to that. Ella Grace, six, was standing over the box waiting for us, and two-and-a-half-year-old David was running around the table in circles. The girls radiated enthusiasm as we fitted the puzzle pieces together.

As we placed the last piece, I considered framing it so we could enjoy it forever. The girls were ecstatic. "Mama! Come see." As we met Corinne at the top of the stairs, I noticed David hadn't followed us. I looked over my shoulder and there he was, gleefully tossing the puzzle pieces into the air. The girls were disappointed, but then because there was nothing else to do, we laughed and then laughed some more.

Later I texted Harrison, "Thanks for the reminder, Harrison, it came at just the right time... and I love you too."

Father, as I journey forward, set my eyes on all that's good, each day that I live. —Brock Kidd

Digging Deeper: Psalm 25:1; Philippians 3:13–14

Sunday, September 19

Set me as a seal upon your heart, as a seal upon your arm; for love is strong as death. —Song of Songs 8:6 (ESV)

What an incredible honor. Our older son, William, asked me to perform the wedding ceremony for him and his bride, Karen. I couldn't say no, but I was sure worried about being able to rise to the occasion. It was almost like wondering if I could ever rise to the role of fatherhood. What would I say about marriage to my son and future daughter-in-law and how would I do it without bursting into tears?

The ceremony was on a hilltop in Northern California on a luminous September day, the bride and groom surrounded by friends and family. I stood in the front of our gathering, waiting with the groom and best man—our younger son, Tim—as the wedding party approached. I was fine until I saw my own bride, Carol, coming down the aisle, remembering how we had gone through a similar ceremony thirty-some years earlier. And here we were all these years later, "for richer, for poorer, in sickness, and in health."

What I wanted to say about marriage—what I did say—was that we wouldn't have been able to do it without the support, care, and affection of countless loved ones, people like the very ones who were witnessing this ceremony. If there's any reason to do a wedding in front of a lot of people (instead of sneaking off to a justice of the peace), it's to say to them: Thanks for being here. Stick with us. We'll need you. We'll depend on you. Till death us do part.

The bride and groom said their vows and I pronounced them husband and wife, not without noticing my son, like his dad, shedding a tear or two.

Lord of all, may my heart be filled with love, love to spread and give away. —Rick Hamlin

Digging Deeper: Proverbs 18:22; 1 Corinthians 13:1

STRUGGLING TO PRAY: Caring about Faraway Strangers

If you really keep the royal law found in Scripture, "Love your neighbor as yourself," you are doing right. —James 2:8 (NIV)

Whenever someone at church prays a "big prayer"—for world peace, say, or an end to poverty or the victims of some faraway disaster—I feel rebuked. *Here you are praying about your own petty problems,* I mentally admonish myself, *when people out there are facing real problems. War. Starvation. Tsunamis.*

Then I remember a writing student I had once who'd grown up in Kenya and was always getting mad at our class for not knowing or caring about the problems there that animated her.

"Y'all need to look past your own experience!" she raged.

She and I talked a lot that semester.

"You're right," I said. "But you care about Kenyans because you lived there. It's hard to care about what's going on far away to people you've never met. People care about what's around them. That's just how it is."

That's how it is in Scripture, too, we discussed. Throughout the Bible, we're commanded to love our "neighbors."

We can, maybe should, expand "neighbor" to include everyone, and the story of the good Samaritan—Jesus's answer to a Scripture expert's sanctimonious question, "Who *is* my neighbor?"—is often read that way.

But the characters in Jesus's story—the beaten man, the priest and the Levite who walk around him, and the Samaritan who helps him—are all travelers far from home, among foreigners. They become neighbors in the moment of encounter, when they're close enough to see one another's needs.

For the rest of the semester, my student made it her cause to bring Kenya close to us through her wonderful writing, thereby enabling us, at least momentarily, to care past our own experience into hers.

Father, help us love those we encounter every day and not walk around them. —Patty Kirk

Digging Deeper: Luke 10:25–37

Tuesday, September 21

Now to him who is able to do far more abundantly beyond all that we ask or think, according to the power that works within us... —Ephesians 3:20 (NIV)

On my first visit to a friend who'd moved several hours away, I got the grand tour of her quaint little rental home. I remarked on an "interesting old battered suitcase" sitting on a window bench in her dining area.

"Actually, that's a trumpet case. My son doesn't play anymore and he wants me to donate it."

I reacted instantly. "Well, if you're donating, my grandson plays trumpet in both marching and jazz band at his high school. He borrows the school's instrument, which has drawbacks. He would love a trumpet of his own."

My friend promised to check with her son soon. He agreed the trumpet could go to Josh. A couple of weeks later she brought it with her on a trip our way.

When I called to tell Josh I'd found him a trumpet, he couldn't believe it. But when I said it was purchased new in the 1980s, he wasn't quite as excited. Forty years earlier was antiquity to a fifteen-year-old!

After the trumpet was delivered by another family member—Josh lived sixty miles away—I was eager to hear how he liked it. He phoned to say he hadn't known what to expect, but it looked better than he'd thought. One of the valves was sticking and he was going to have the music store check it over.

When the trumpet was cleaned and ready to play, we learned it was valued at fifteen hundred dollars! An old "suitcase" had proven to contain "abundantly beyond" all that we could "ask or think."

You are the God of rich supply! Giver of every good gift. Accept my offering of thanks. —Carol Knapp

Digging Deeper: 1 Chronicles 13:8; Psalm 20:4; 81:10

Wednesday, September 22

O Lord, You have brought my soul from the grave.
—Psalm 30:4 (CHABAD)

Shortly before he died, Keith told me he knew
what he wanted to get me for my next birthday.
He had seen me eagerly using Michael Carasik's
The Commentators' Bible volumes as each became
available, often years apart. So far, I had the books
on Exodus, Leviticus, and Numbers. He said, "I
want to pay for the last two for you, in case I'm not
around when they come out."

Two years later, I got the volume on
Deuteronomy and wept over it, thanking Keith
for it as if he were there. More years went by, and
my relationship with my local "family" (which I
called my "here" family to differentiate them from
the "there" family in California I'd gained from
Keith) was created and blossomed. For Mother's
Day this year, they gave me a gift card for the online
bookseller I ordered from.

When the volume on Genesis was finally
available, I ordered it, ready to take the last of the
money Keith had given me to pay for it—only to
realize that the gift card had automatically kicked in;
the book was paid for.

I was upset. This gift was supposed to have come
from Keith, the last thing he would ever give me. I
shared my feelings with a friend, who looked at me
as if I were crazy. "What you're not seeing," she said,
"is that it's like Keith is telling you he gave you the

'here' family just like he gave you the 'there' family."
I realized I had been wrong. Keith would never be
done with giving to me—and the books were only
one of his many gifts.

**You know how much I love the husband you gave me,
God. Thank You for teaching me more about him
every day I still live.** —Rhoda Blecker

Digging Deeper: 1 Chronicles 16:8;
Proverbs 1:5

Thursday, September 23

**He has delivered us from such a deadly peril, and he
will deliver us again. On him we have set our hope
that he will continue to deliver us, as you help us by
your prayers. Then many will give thanks on our
behalf for the gracious favor granted us in answer to
the prayers of many.** —2 Corinthians 1:10–11 (NIV)

My husband received some disturbing news while
our oldest daughter was out of the country for two
weeks on a business trip. We shared the news with
our other two adult children but decided to wait
until our daughter returned home to tell her. After
all, we reasoned, why worry her when she was so
far from home and there was nothing she could do
about the situation anyway?

When she did find out, she was upset, not by the
news as much as by the fact that we had not shared it
with her right away.

"Number one, we do not keep secrets in this family," she said. "Number two, your not telling me meant less prayer!"

She was right on both counts. We should not have kept the situation from her, even temporarily. And had we told her, she could have prayed. Prayer was what we'd needed, the more the better. How short-sighted of us to forget the one thing that can make all the difference.

Father, thank You for our amazing children, from whom we learn so much, and thank You for our family of pray-ers. —Kim Taylor Henry

Digging Deeper: Psalm 65:5; 1 Thessalonians 3:10

Friday, September 24

Start children off on the way they should go, and even when they are old they will not turn from it. —Proverbs 22:6 (NIV)

Right from the start, my daughter Katie needed surprisingly little sleep. She rarely cried, mostly cooed and kicked, but was awake every single hour I was. I learned to carry her infant seat from room to room as I did laundry, showered, cooked. Her first sentence was "No nap."

I tried to return to my B-K (Before Katie) habit of time alone each day to read the Bible. Nothing worked until the summer Katie turned two, when she began to sleep later than I did in the mornings. That hour, or even a half hour, spent reading and meditating gave me more patience throughout the day.

As fall arrived, Katie woke earlier each day, until my time alone whittled to nothing. If I set my alarm earlier, her internal alarm kept pace. I became frustrated, and our days became tense.

Finally, I decided on a new approach. The next morning Katie ran into my room grinning. "Good morning!" I opened one eye. I hugged her. I patted the bed next to me. "We are going to read together!"

Katie snuggled close. She watched my face as I read the lectionary aloud, recited the suggested Bible verses, then prayed silently. Once again, our days became smoother.

One morning, as I finished the reading, Katie reached for my Bible. "Now it's my turn. Where is the bookmark?" I handed her the long, narrow lectionary.

She scanned the lectionary. She announced the reading, "Thirty-eight pounds." She turned a few pages of the Bible, studied it, then intoned, "I love you."

Dear Lord, You have a soft heart for little children —and tired mothers. —Leanne Jackson

Digging Deeper: Deuteronomy 11:19; 1 Corinthians 13:13

Saturday, September 25

Declaring the end from the beginning...
I will accomplish all My good pleasure.
—Isaiah 46:10 (NASB)

My wife, Michelle, and I had been on the road awhile. And two weeks of concert dates in Hawaii sounded more like a vacation than work. By the end I was wiped out. To add to all that, the airline decided it would be a fun idea to reroute us to San Diego instead of flying us back to our car in Portland. By the time we'd landed, it was well past midnight and the airport was closed. With an early flight out, there was no use getting a hotel. Hungry, tired, and fifteen hundred miles away from where I needed to be, I was less than happy.

We finally found a large couch that would accommodate a few hours' sleep. A girl sat there, clicking away on a laptop. We said hello to her and settled down.

"Where are you guys coming from?" she said.

"Hawaii. How about you?" Michelle replied.

"Oh, I've been here. At a conference. Learning how to astral-project myself through wormholes...." She went on for a bit, a rambling tangle of New Age catchphrases, then turned back to the blue glow of her screen.

"She needs Jesus," Michelle whispered to me.

I cast a bloodshot eye toward heaven. *Really, God? Now?*

And I think God smiled.

Because, as is His way, our beautiful, eternal Travel Agent had planned an appointment between two travel-dazed pilgrims and a precious daughter. A daughter He loved even before He laid the foundations of the earth.

No, we didn't sleep that night. But thanks to the gentle work of God, we now have a new friend who couldn't care less about wormholes, but is excited about her Father.

And you know what? I'm learning not to grumble when my heavenly Friend decides to change my travel plans.

Lord, teach me to trust You in every detour.
—Buck Storm

Digging Deeper: Romans 8:37–39; Galatians 2:20; James 4:14

Sunday, September 26

To all who mourn in Israel, he will give a crown of beauty for ashes, a joyous blessing instead of mourning, festive praise instead of despair. In their righteousness, they will be like great oaks that the Lord has planted for his own glory.
—Isaiah 61:3 (NLT)

"Serene," "beautiful," and "breathtaking" just didn't do it justice. Margi and I joined another couple to explore the most wonderful botanical gardens I had ever experienced. Hawaii is home to spectacular flora, and the rainforest gardens we visited that day were over-the-top. Multihued orchids clung to the trunks of verdant trees. The towering canopy of coolness sheltered a grandeur unlike anything I had seen before. A brook ran down the rocky hillside to the sapphire sea, creating its own falling-water music. Clear pools and an explosion of flowers traced the rocky stream down the gorge. One of our group compared it to the Garden of Eden.

We were even more impressed when we heard the origin story. A century-old abandoned sugar plantation, the place had been used as a garbage dump. Decades of rusted cars and appliances dotted the overgrown hillside. But fifty years ago, a husband-and-wife team saw the potential. They bought the property and went to work. With machetes and elbow grease, they pulled out the trash, chopped away the overgrowth, uncovered the beauty, and planted an abundance of native species in the fertile soil. The result was a rare treat for the senses.

"It's like what God did for us," said my friend Dave. "He forgave us, bought us, cleaned us up, and showed off our true beauty."

His offhand comment wound its way into my heart. As we followed the trail to the sea, I offered a silent prayer of thanks for God's forgiveness and grace.

Dear Savior, though words alone can never do justice to the grace You have shown to me, I want to say thank You for Your great salvation and love. Amen.
—Bill Giovannetti

Digging Deeper: Titus 3:5

But whoever has the world's goods, and sees his brother in need and closes his heart against him, how does the love of God abide in him? Little children, let us not love with word or with tongue, but in deed and truth. —1 John 3:17–18 (NASB)

This morning as I prepared to teach a freshman class at Mercer University on the subject of international relations and world peace, I reviewed an intriguing book by Karen Armstrong that focuses on ancient wisdom and its application to our modern world. Armstrong observed how our world is radically more interwoven and interconnected than even a decade ago. This factor creates an international dynamic that is both promising and exciting, and yet dangerous. She concludes: "You cannot confine your benevolence to your own people; your concern must somehow extend to the entire world."[*]

My missionary father once told me that the future welfare of the United States depends far more on how much we love the world than how well we defend ourselves. Of course, this is a delicate balance. But it is a balance that each generation must measure and adjust.

As I look out my office window, I see dozens of lampposts across our campus. On each lamppost is a large canvas banner permanently suspended that

---

[*]Karen Armstrong, *The Great Transformation* (New York: Alfred A. Knopf, 2006), p. xiv.

states our university motto: "At Mercer Everyone Majors in Changing the World."

The most important dynamic that positively changes the world is love. And you can love the world through chemistry, biology, psychology, religion, mathematics, engineering, sociology, art, music, military science, political science—any academic major taught on a college campus. But the goal of all education and global endeavors must be to love the world.

Dear God, may I do my part to love and change the world. Amen. —Scott Walker

Digging Deeper: John 3:16; 15:12–13

Tuesday, September 28

Let's have a feast and celebrate. —Luke 15:23b (NIV)

My husband Don's birthday, September 28, is almost always during harvest, a time when farm families like ours are overwhelmed with work. He'd had only one birthday party as a child. Adult celebrations usually meant cake after a late supper, although after he retired we sometimes went out for dinner.

Months before Don turned 80 our children decided to surprise him with a reception and birthday party in Denver, since several family members live in Colorado. They sent invitations and reserved rooms. But how could we get Don there without suspecting anything? There was an ice rink near the hotel, so I told Don we'd be watching grandson Caden play in an off-season hockey tournament.

There were some close calls. Grandson Ryan entered the hotel just before we did, but quickly ducked into a hall. Grandson Caleb distracted Don while I shushed the desk clerk who asked if we were party guests. The TV in our room displayed the words "Welcome Schwab Birthday Party"; I hit the off button before Don saw it. We got him to the reception room by pretending to stop at a traveling art exhibit before going to the game.

The look on Don's face when family and friends yelled "Surprise!" was one of pure joy! He had a wonderful time visiting, eating, and listening to the youngest girls' impromptu karaoke concert. The next day we visited a butterfly garden, then concluded the weekend with a birthday celebration that included more friends, a picture display of Don's life, and a huge cake.

"My second party was my most wonderful time ever," Don said as he blew out the candles.

Lord, You attended a wedding, ate with tax collectors and friends, and even prepared breakfast for Your disciples. May I cherish the memory of Don's party and, like You, be ever ready to celebrate.
—Penney Schwab

Digging Deeper: Luke 5:29–32; John 2:1–2; John 12:1–3; John 21:10–14

Wednesday, September 29

Rejoice with those who rejoice; mourn with those
who mourn. —Romans 12:15 (NIV)

I sat in the movie theater filled with emotion as
I watched one of the most intense films about
drug addiction. I had known the young actor
who played the main character when he was just
a little boy. His performance was so believable
that I had to constantly remind myself that
the adorable little boy I had known was now a
successful actor, not a struggling addict on the
brink of death.

I thought of my own children, and my heart
ached at the very thought of them walking this
painful journey. My life has never been touched
by addiction personally, yet by the final scene my
spirit felt crushed. As the credits rolled, an agonizing
sound filled the theater.

An older gentleman sitting alone in the front
row was openly bawling. The pain as he wept was
so palpable that it rendered me motionless in my
seat. Eventually, he quieted down. I took a deep
breath and stood up to leave, but as I walked I felt an
incredible need to hug this man. I sat back down and
struggled between my fear of approaching him and
this deep pull to console him.

"Can I give you a hug?" I quietly asked as I finally
stood in front of him. He smiled and reached out his
arms to me. I knelt down and we embraced—it was

one of the most beautiful moments I'd experienced in a long time.

The pain of our experiences can hold so much power over our lives. But the incredible power of human connection is undeniable, if we are willing to give it away and receive.

In a world that is filled will so much pain, Father, continue to tug at my heart so I can be used as an expression of Your love and compassion.
—Karen Valentin

Digging Deeper: 1 Corinthians 12:26

Thursday, September 30

Indeed, he who watches over Israel never slumbers or sleeps. —Psalm 121:4 (NLT)

I'd been going through a season of struggle, wondering about unanswered prayers and why God took so long to work in my life. That's when we met an unexpected friend from the sea.

Our family had visited our favorite beach in Hawaii. The sand was silky smooth, the waters crystal blue, and the crashing waves perfect for boogie boarding. As we walked the shoreline to find a place to set up our umbrella and chairs, a dark shape followed us about fifteen feet offshore. It swam up onshore and then scooted along the sand to stop about ten feet away from my wife.

It was a seal. A big one, a five-hundred-pound visitor. Later, an expert on these things told us it was an endangered monk seal and an extremely rare sight.

As a confirmed city slicker, I didn't know whether to laugh or to run. Margi, however, thoroughly enjoyed the moment. Our new friend seemed to smile at her. She smiled back. A crowd formed a respectful distance away, phones out, recording everything. The seal waved its flipper. Margi waved back. With big black eyes, whiskers, and an endearing smile, the animal looked like a toy. But it was a wild creature, a sweet example of God's abundant creation.

A moment later, the seal scooted back into the waters and swam away. The encounter became a highlight of our trip. Later Margi commented on the serendipity of the moment. "If we had arrived just a minute earlier or later, we would not have enjoyed that experience. The timing was perfect."

Just like everything God does, I thought. His timing is as perfect as His provision. It was time for me to quit fretting and start resting in Him.

Father, You never forget me, never lose me, and never fail to provide for me. Please help me trust Your wisdom and Your timing. Amen.
—Bill Giovannetti
Digging Deeper: Psalm 31:15

JOYFUL IN HOPE

1 _____

2 _____

3 _____

4 _____

5 _____

6 _____

7 _____

8 _____

9 _____

10 _____

11 _____

12 _____

13 _____

14 _____

15 _____

16 _____

17 _____

18 _____

19 _____

20 _____

21 _____

22 _____

23 _____

24 _____

25 _____

26 _____

27 _____

28 _____

29 _____

30 _____

OCTOBER

I will remember the deeds of the Lord;
yes, I will remember your miracles of long
ago. I will consider all your works and
meditate on all your mighty deeds.

—Psalm 77:11-12 (NIV)

Friday, October 1

Remember today that your children were not the ones who saw and experienced the discipline of the Lord your God: his majesty, his mighty hand, his outstretched arm; the signs he performed and the things he did in the heart of Egypt.... Teach them to your children, talking about them when you sit at home and when you walk along the road, when you lie down and when you get up.
—Deuteronomy 11:2–3, 19 (NIV)

I have written books set in the time of slavery, conducted years of research on American slavery, and taught children in schools. So I was surprised when my daughter looked at me earnestly and said, "It was humiliating when my teacher pointed to me and told me that people like me had once been slaves."

Lanea is right. Her comments pricked me and reminded me that I need to continue writing, studying, and sharing the history, even when it is uncomfortable.

The descendants of the enslaved are often shamed or terrified of sharing their stories; there are few, if any, monuments to slaves or what they accomplished. My grandparents didn't talk about it, even though they were the first generation of my family not born in the shackles of slavery. Maybe the memory was too close, too bitter.

No one told me, when we sat around the dinner table, so I didn't think to tell my own children that our ancestors carved roads, farmed, erected buildings, and planned cities. I told Lanea and my son, Chase, "I should have told you that all of the enslaved people who went ahead of us were heroes—whether they ran to freedom, took up arms to fight slavery, or suffered and survived captivity—millions of heroes who relied on the Lord."

God, give me the courage and space to tell the stories. Help me to remember and encourage others that we have overcome dark days with Your help and guidance.
—Sharon Foster

Digging Deeper: Deuteronomy 11:19; Psalm 126:1; Proverbs 22:6

Saturday, October 2

The Son is the radiance of God's glory and the exact representation of his being... —Hebrews 1:3 (NIV)

On my previous trips to the Holy Land I have yearned to feel the presence of Jesus and the disciples. I have dug my toes in the sands of the Dead Sea and walked the Via Dolorosa. But I finally found that feeling last year at Capernaum.

Yes, Jerusalem itself is breathtaking for its history and culture. You can visit the holiest Christian sites, such as the Church of the Holy Sepulchre and the Mount of Olives. And while there is some evidence that these locations are historically accurate, the fact is most of them were identified by the emperor Constantine's mother, the Christian convert Helen, on a pilgrimage she undertook more than three hundred years after the death of Christ.

At Capernaum, I stood among the sun-blasted ruins of a Jewish synagogue with a small group of travelers, a breeze drifting in off the sea. The site has been extensively excavated and carbon-dated. Some of the columns, felled by earthquakes, have been resurrected. Otherwise it is as it was, the stone floor smoothed by the wear of centuries.

"By reliable biblical and historical accounts, Jesus preached and worshipped in this very building upon these very stones," said our guide.

He came down from Nazareth to the fishing village of Capernaum to reach a new and what He hoped was a more receptive audience for His startling message. Here He met the disciple Matthew, who lived but a few doors away. Here He healed Simon Peter's mother-in-law of fever, among many recorded miracles. Finally, He cursed the town for its rejection of His preaching.

When the feeling came, I felt it in the soles of my feet as well as my heart, a pervasive warmth, a shifting of my soul.

Jesus, I have stood upon Your ancient stones and felt You in the very soles of my feet. Help me today to walk in Your steps. —Edward Grinnan

Digging Deeper: Isaiah 9:6; John 14:6

He said to them, "You are the ones who justify yourselves in the eyes of others, but God knows your hearts. What people value highly is detestable in God's sight." —Luke 16:15 (NIV)

"I wasn't raised that way."

A friend railed at the plans for an upcoming family event that he deemed not suited for his attendance. How could he mingle with people whose lifestyles so blatantly ran afoul of how he'd been reared? In recent years, I'd heard him many times conflate his salvation with his upbringing—the lives of his forebears always the stick by which he measured his righteousness.

I shook my head, my friend's beleaguered measuring stick reminding me of my own legalistic stubbornness. Though my issues were not the same as his, traces of pharisaical works persisted.

Did I pray enough? Did I pray *long* enough? Did I even pray the right way? Would God really listen to somebody with thoughts as disparate as mine? Like my friend, I treasured my godly parents who deposited within me a fierce desire for God. Would I ever measure up to the kind of righteousness I saw in them?

No matter the "right" things we do as Christians, they can only yield a temporary good feeling too often tainted with a little pride, a bit of superiority, a dose of pity rather than compassion. Listening to my friend, I realized I'm just as far from my own righteousness today as I was over fifty years ago when I stood before an altar, hands lifted in the air, giving my life to Christ.

Your genes don't constitute your salvation, the Lord reminded me. *I do. It's My blood, not yours, that prepares you for My table.* I was comforted. I would stand in the righteousness of God.

Jesus, please grant me the foresight to evermore resist self-righteousness. —Jacqueline F. Wheelock

Digging Deeper: Isaiah 64:6; Mark 2:13–17; John 8:3–11

Monday, October 4

Be watchful, and strengthen the things which remain.... —Revelation 3:2 (KJV)

Now that I have passed my "best by" date, I find that aging is a series of losses, but with compensations.

The loss of energy frustrates me, but I still get a lot done, because I work smarter. I'm more organized, rest often, and use a lot of power tools.

This year I experienced my first "silent spring," as I can no longer hear the birds chirping. However, I can still hear the geese that honk their way overhead, making me smile.

I have so many "floaters" in my eyes, it's like looking at life through two bowls of goldfish, but I can still read without glasses.

My teeth have all been crowned, and while these "new" body parts cost a thousand dollars each, at least I can still eat.

I have lost some of my dearest friends, but I have made some wonderful new friends.

My biggest loss is the loss of future. How many more years will I live? Some seniors panic when time runs out, and they do foolish things. On the other hand, some seniors do their best work at the end.

Never did I dream that I would be this happy at my age. Every day I wake up is a kind of Christmas present.

I am trying to live by the John the Apostle's advice, to "strengthen the things that remain." I keep in touch with my children and grandchildren. I exercise and eat right, and I have come to cherish little things, like my morning coffee and newspaper, leisurely bike rides, opening the mail, a hot bath in the evening, followed by a bowl of popcorn and an old Western. And praying myself to sleep at night.

Thank You, Father, for saving some of the best till last.
—Daniel Schantz

Digging Deeper: 2 Corinthians 4:16; 13:3

Tuesday, October 5

From Zion, perfect in beauty, God shines forth.
—Psalm 50:2 (NIV)

"When Colby dies, will he go to heaven?" James asked while petting our (still very much alive) golden retriever.

"I don't know, buddy," I replied.

"Colby doesn't like the car, so he might not like going to heaven. Does heaven have roads? How do you get there? Do you get to bring your lovies? Will you be there? Will you go before me? Do they have ice cream there?" James asked, pausing for a bite of cereal.

I took the opening. "I'm so glad your brain is thinking about heaven," I said. "Do you remember how we get to heaven?"

"Jesus," he replied.

"That's right!" I said. "You need to love Jesus and do what He asks, which is that we love others and help care for them."

"Like Colby?" he asked.

"Yep," I said. "I don't know what heaven will be like. The Bible says no one is sad there, but we don't know much else, so I like to think of heaven as the best place ever. Like maybe it's covered in race car tracks."

James's eyes grew wide. "Really?" he asked.

"I don't know," I told him. "The only thing I really know is that we're going to love it there and be with Jesus forever. How does that sound?"

"Great," James replied. "And I really hope Colby gets to go. Maybe heaven has lots of yards to dig holes in."

"Maybe so, bud," I said, silently thanking God for five minutes amid a nutty morning routine to talk about heaven, and how we get there, with one of my best buddies.

God, grant me more moments to share You and Your glory with those in my life. —Ashley Kappel

Digging Deeper: Revelation 7:13–17; 21:4–8, 19–21

Wednesday, October 6

The thief comes only to steal and kill and destroy. I came that they may have life, and have it abundantly. —John 10:10 (NRSV)

Not today, Satan. I'd seen that odd phrase recently. Now it was on a bumper sticker on the car in front of me. No time to ponder. I was late for exercise class. Again.

I wheeled into the gym parking lot and sprinted to the group room. The body combat class had already begun. I was embarrassingly late nearly every day. Sometimes I talked myself out of coming altogether.

My friend Jenny was in her usual spot in front. She caught my eye in the floor-to-ceiling mirror and smiled. I pushed down my shame and focused on the high-impact routine. Following the instructor's moves, I punched and kicked an imaginary opponent. As usual, once I started moving, I felt terrific—both mentally and physically. Why did the voice in my head try to talk me out of this? Why was it such a battle? Every. Single. Day.

That bumper sticker flashed in my mind.

After class, I walked with Jenny to the parking lot. I confided my internal struggle to come, but couldn't

imagine why the devil minded if I exercised or not.
I worried she'd think I was a nut. We'd not talked
about spiritual things.

"God wants us to care for our bodies," Jenny said
thoughtfully. "He doesn't want temptation to get in
the way of our health."

In the driver's seat, I recalled the bumper sticker.
Maybe the imaginary opponent I fought at the gym
wasn't imaginary. The next day, the voice was silent.

**Lord, help me to stand against the enemy. Give me
discernment to distinguish between my voice and his.**
—Stephanie Thompson

Digging Deeper: Ephesians 6:11–17; 1 Peter 5:8–9

Thursday, October 7

**But you—who are you to judge your neighbor?
—James 4:12 (NIV)**

I went to church the other day for a noontime service
that's designed for people on lunch hour. My church
is in downtown Milwaukee, near many office
buildings. There are usually twenty to thirty people
there at noon.

On this day, the service had begun and the gospel
was being read, when a man carrying two large
overstuffed bags of possessions burst in the door.
He wasn't trying to be quiet as he walked the center
aisle toward the front of the church. At one point,
he turned and gesticulated wildly with his arms,

scowling at a few people, in a way that made it pretty clear he was drunk. But he kept walking toward the front. When he reached the first pew, he loudly tossed the bags down and took off his coat, tossing that down rather dramatically, too. Then he turned around and looked at everyone, saying something that was inarticulate but angrily expressed. We didn't know what he would do next.

He then entered the pew, pulled out the kneeler (we have those in our church), and got down on his knees. He began to pray. That's all I have to say about him.

About *me*, I'll say this: I judged him way too easily.

Forgive me, God, for how I judge everyone around me all the time. Change my heart, mind, and soul.
—Jon M. Sweeney

Digging Deeper: Matthew 7:1–3

Friday, October 8

Set your minds on things above, not on earthly things. —Colossians 3:2 (NIV)

"Come on! Jump up!" I urge. Cookie, my dog, is perfectly capable of jumping up into my SUV so I can take her to the dog park, her favorite place in the entire world. But will she do it? Absolutely not!

I can't understand why she doesn't know the drill by now and jump in willingly. I take her nearly every day to this promised land of other dogs to play with and dog-loving humans who are much more interesting to her than everyday old me. By now you'd think she'd associate hopping in the car with this great reward.

Instead, she tugs at the leash, wanting to walk in the neighborhood. Because the neighborhood, though far less interesting and joy-filled than the dog park, is right now. So every day, I have to pick her up and put her in the car. When she looks at me askance, I remind her that I love her and that I have something wonderful ahead for her. Doesn't she know this by now? Doesn't she know how good I am to her and that everything I do is for her good and not her harm? Doesn't she know I have promised her something far more amazing than what she can see right now, and that I am trustworthy to keep my promises?

Sounds kind of familiar.

My Master has promised me a place far more wonderful than right here, right now, but I spend so much time caught up in the immediate. I ask Him to let me stay here longer, for my children's weddings, my potential grandchildren, cherished days with my beloved husband.

When we arrive at the park, Cookie's pure elation has made her forget all about the neighborhood walk she wanted instead.

Lord, help me fix my mind on heaven. —Ginger Rue

Digging Deeper: Isaiah 25:8–9; Revelation 22:5

Saturday, October 9

For we know in part ... but when the perfect comes, the partial will pass away. —1 Corinthians 13:9–10 (ESV)

I had promised that, come autumn, I'd take a neighbor teenager with special needs to a high-school football game. "Choose which one," I said, hardly knowing the most basic rules of the game.

"Homecoming," she responded, hardly knowing what the word meant beyond "it's a big deal; everybody goes." We went. She thrived. Sitting at the end of a row and later standing at the fence right above the cheerleaders, she rooted for her home team, stomping her feet, clapping her hands, punching the air. "Let's go, Warriors!"

I survived. I was hemmed in by fans on their feet, obstructing my view, shouting their support, waving air-filled tubes. I listened. Teams scored. The marching band played. I looked for the moon. I prayed—for my young friend, her family, her future. For my neighborhood, my household, my church. The clock ran out. Halftime. From my tote, I pulled a neck scarf. I turned to my neighbor student and made a motherly threat: "Put on your jacket or we're going home." We stayed—to the at-long-last bell. The score wasn't close—a double-digit disparity.

"That was fun!" she exclaimed in the car. "Thank you."

"And it was great that your school won."

She hesitated. "Miss Evelyn, we lost. Didn't you know?"

Her answer caught me up short. I could blame much of my ignorance on lack of field knowledge or poor seat selection. But not knowing who trounced whom? What a pathetic, inexcusable gaffe. "Oh dear. I'm sorry. Next year I'll pay better attention. Maybe you can help me keep track."

Lord, my human knowledge is limited by my background, interests, geography, opportunities. But that's no excuse for distraction. Help me be attentive to what is important today. —Evelyn Bence

Digging Deeper: Romans 15:14; 1 Corinthians 8:2–3

Sunday, October 10

The Lord had said to Abram, "Go from your country, your people and your father's household to the land I will show you." —Genesis 12:1 (NIV)

Are you going to sign the lease today?" my mom asked. She and I were repotting plants on my parents' back patio.

"I don't know. It's a nice apartment," I said.

I poured soil into a clay pot. The robust scent of earth filled the air. "But when I sign those papers, I'll officially live three hours away. I know the job I've been offered is a great opportunity. But this move will be difficult."

My mom nodded.

"It will be hard for me, too," she said. "But I know you are stretching into the person you're meant to be. And that gives me peace."

I sifted the soil in the pot until it was level. Then I grabbed a potted fern. It had seen better days. Crinkled brown leaves dropped as I lifted it. I pressed my fingers between the fronds, then flipped the plant over. As I eased the pot upward, removing it from the plant, I revealed an intricate tangle of roots. They were woven so tightly they retained the shape of the removed pot.

"No wonder that little guy has been so sickly," my Mom said. "He's root-bound."

I placed the fern in its new pot. There were several inches of empty space in each direction—space to grow.

Looking at the fern, I understood that this move was my own repotting. If I stayed where I was, I wouldn't be able to stretch and gain new experiences. I wouldn't be able to grow.

I topped off the pot with soil, then dusted off my hands.

"I'll be right back," I told my mom. "I need to fill out some paperwork."

Father, help me to seek opportunities to grow.
—Logan Eliasen

Digging Deeper: 1 Samuel 2:26; 2 Peter 3:18

Monday, October 11

Now therefore ye are no more strangers and foreigners, but fellowcitizens with the saints, and of the household of God. —Ephesians 2:19 (KJV)

The wedding party in white and royal blue poses in front of the church, when the bride frantically motions to me. "Mrs. Schilling! Mrs. Schilling! Get in the picture!"

"But I'm not family...."

"Yes, you *are*! Get in!"

I awkwardly insert myself in a back row and the photographer resumes his work. As I smile for the camera, I reflect how this group of former refugees has adopted me into their family. Why, just last week, I was honored to be included in their traditional Rwandan wedding celebration, even dressing in the traditional *mushanana*: a bunched skirt, low-slung sash, and tank top. By wearing the same clothes as the bride's family, I'd made my identity clear, especially to the bridegroom's family and guests.

I had met the bride and her parents years earlier when all of them attended the college where I taught. As I learned more about their seven-year journey as refugees from the Rwandan genocide, I helped them to share their experience for a local magazine. Their stories of courage, endurance, and faith humble me still. I wrote letters of recommendation so they could continue their education in health care. I love their beautiful spirits.

They love that I listen and embrace them as new American brothers and sisters. Though our faces share no family resemblance, our hearts share love and admiration. Isn't that what family is all about?

Lord of all, You have made us in Your image. Of course we are one! —Gail Thorell Schilling

Digging Deeper: Exodus 2:22; Deuteronomy 10:19; Galatians 3:28

Tuesday, October 12

He awakens Me morning by morning, He awakens My ear to listen as a disciple. —Isaiah 50:4 (NASB)

Acquainted through church, she asked me to be her mentor. Each cadet in Idaho Youth ChalleNGe Academy—a national program for at-risk teenagers run by the National Guard—has a mentor during the residential program and the year following. Cassi, sixteen, felt a pull to improve her life.

IDYCA is reached by a switchback mountain road off the Clearwater River that opens to unexpected tabletop prairie. Then more forest and climbing and finally the tiny historic gold mining town of Pierce.

The trip there is small stuff next to what the cadets have volunteered for. No personal electronics. A strict daily regimen of healthy diet and physical fitness, of high-school classroom studies followed by homework. The teenagers learn life skills and participate in service projects in local communities.

On a Mentor Day visit to Cassi, she and I spread a blanket by the shaded river's edge. I was as ready to be mentored by her as she was eager for my insight. I asked what had been her most valuable lesson in the program. She said, "I have learned self-respect."

She then told of a girl who had recently been expelled from IDYCA after refusing multiple chances for success. Cassi said, "She just wouldn't learn."

Cassi has grabbed hold of her opportunity. Responsible for her behavior. Able to make meaningful changes—to listen—to be humble in heart. To persevere in her goals.

Moses told the Israelites they were to love God and "walk in all His ways" (Deuteronomy 10:12 NASB). He said, "See, I am setting before you today a blessing…if you listen to the commandments of the Lord your God…" (11:26–27 NASB).

Beside the calm river with Cassi, I felt God mentoring us both.

Lord, I choose blessing. —Carol Knapp

Digging Deeper: Proverbs 19:8; Isaiah 50:4–5; Luke 11:28

Wednesday, October 13

And when you pray, do not be like the hypocrites, for they love to pray standing in the synagogues and on the street corners to be seen by others. Truly I tell you, they have received their reward in full. —Matthew 6:5 (NIV)

I had a simple agenda for my fifty-fifth birthday: stay home from work and not cook. But the day ended up including many moments that filled me with more gratitude and happiness than I had imagined.

I decided to share lunch with my ninety-one-year-old dad. As I walked my father to my car, my friend Joe, whom I had not seen in many years, passed by, threw his car into park in the middle of the road, and sprinted to give me a hug. It was a gift of great worth to me, because I always enjoyed my conversations with Joe and missed our chats.

Once my dad got to the car, the sky opened up and the rain fell hard. My dad, who uses a walker, would likely get wet if we decided to eat at a restaurant owned by another friend. To avoid the rain, I picked up a pizza from the restaurant. Wanting to devour the hot pizza immediately, we decided to sit in the car and eat.

The rain teemed, but we were dry. I asked Dad to lead grace before we ate. I don't remember all the words my father prayed, but I know that he asked the Lord to cover my family and me. His prayer felt familiar, as I've been hearing his prayers since I was a child. But this was different, somehow: I am no longer a child, but what a great comfort—and birthday present—it was to hear prayers from my dad offered on my behalf.

Father God, thank You for enabling my father on earth to still seek to cover my family and me with his petitions to You, on my behalf. —Gayle T. Williams

Digging Deeper: James 5:16

Thursday, October 14

I lift up my eyes to the mountains—where does my help come from? My help comes from the Lord, the Maker of heaven and earth. —Psalm 121:1–2 (NIV)

She was trying to do it all by herself. The woman next to me at the grocery self-checkout stations had dropped her container of blueberries. She was dashing around the floor, picking them up one by one and dropping them into a bag, not stopping to ask for help, and not making much progress in ridding the floor of the multitude of rolling berries.

I wanted to help. I considered trying to pick up some berries, then realized there was someone better equipped to assist. I decided my best help was not to join in the cleanup attempt, but to ask that person to help her. I located the attendant assigned to the section and said, "That woman dropped her blueberries. Would you help her please?" The attendant grabbed a wide broom and within less than a minute had cleared the floor of the scattered culprits.

I left the store grateful for this reminder of two important truths: First, when I'm trying all alone to pick up the "dropped blueberries" in my life, God stands ready and equipped to help. I just need to ask. Second, when others are so entangled in their problems they forget to seek His help, I can ask for them.

Lord, how often we try to solve our problems alone.
Thank You for the gift of prayer—and each other.
—Kim Taylor Henry

Digging Deeper: Psalm 46:1; 72:12; Colossians 4:3

Friday, October 15

My health may fail, and my spirit may grow weak, but God remains the strength of my heart; he is mine forever. —Psalm 73:26 (NLT)

Many people live day to day with severe pain. My friend Priscilla, who has had fibromyalgia for over ten years now, is one of them. Three years ago she suffered from a blood clot in her brain, which worsened her condition. Now she experiences extreme amounts of pain daily throughout her whole body. She is unable to work, fly, drive, stand, or sit for long periods of time.

Living with chronic pain is physically and emotionally draining for her, but because of her positive attitude and love for life, you wouldn't know she had the condition from looking at her. At times, she asks the Lord, "Why me?" But then she quickly remembers that no person, including herself, is exempt from pain and suffering. She says, "God sees my tears and hears my cry."

Priscilla doesn't let her pain take away from her love for life or from the small victories that each day brings. Every day she has a number of activities that keep her faith and spirit going. Each morning when she wakes up, she thanks God for the gift of another day. Before she gets out of bed, she reaches for her cell phone to read her daily devotion. And when she is having a hard time getting out of bed, she recites the Scripture "I can do all things through Christ who strengthens me."

When I think of Priscilla, I am encouraged by her faith, courage, and tenacity. She has taught me to count my blessings and make the most out of every day, even the tough ones.

Lord, comfort and sustain those who live daily with physical and emotional pain. —Pablo Diaz

Digging Deeper: Psalm 23; Revelation 21:4

Saturday, October 16

He is the one you praise; he is your God, who performed for you those great and awesome wonders you saw with your own eyes. —Deuteronomy 10:21 (NIV)

Higgins Lake in the center of the Michigan "mitten" is our favorite place. We've come here since our boys' beginnings.

Today we're all together. My husband, Lonny, our five sons, and me. We walk along the spring-fed lake until we find the spot where frigid water bubbles from the sand and foliage yawns to expose a watery, pebbled path.

We walk fast up the stream, the water so cold it needles our skin. One boy slips and another reaches to help. One finds a rock smooth for skipping and hunkers down to retrieve it. Soon, low limbs that behave as bridges hold several sons and they tightrope-walk over the water.

Lonny takes my hand. We stand in moss as lush as carpet, and suddenly my soul opens wide. I'd walked in with plenty of worry. Life is full of uncertainty—from jobs to schools to selling the home we'd recently moved from. But here there is room for none of that. There is only room for worship.

Heaven shines in gold patches through a green canopy. My boys play, and praise flows like water.

Lord, You are kind. You are the giver of good things like the beauty of this secret space. You've brought such healing to my family. You are powerful. You are compassionate.

I've heard it said that the act of worship shouldn't be limited to Sunday mornings, and I understand this because what I feel here can't be bordered by brick.

The creek ripples and rushes. Birds sing. Trees rustle. Brothers laugh and live. And my soul joins this song.

O Lord, how I love You. Amen.
—Shawnelle Eliasen

Digging Deeper: Psalm 75:1; Revelation 14:7

Sunday, October 17

Do not cast me away when I am old; do not forsake me when my strength is gone. —Psalm 71:9 (NIV)

Guess what? I don't like aging. Late fifties is not looking so good on me.

There was a brief and golden time, in my forties, when I didn't scrunch my nose and go "blech!" at my reflection in the mirror. I liked how I looked. I felt fit and pretty. Now I feel pretty old. Dark circles under my eyes. Marionette lines around my mouth. The thin lines like railroad ties across my lips. And let's not talk about bellies or bunions.

Then again, maybe we should. By doing so, I shine some light on my vanity and pride, which likes to hide in the shadows of wellness. There's nothing healthy about my growing reluctance to be photographed.

God, give me some peace about this. After all, there's only one thing for sure about aging, and that is that it will continue apace.

I spent a recent afternoon at my mom's house. We looked through old pictures of our family. They captured pounds gained and lost, bad perms, ill-fitting suits, and acne. The flesh changed, but the animating spirit that made my mom Mom and my dad Dad and my five silly siblings so indispensably *them* was what sparked their smiles and fueled the light in their eyes.

I looked at my eighty-year-old mom. She was voted "Most Likely to Succeed" by her finishing-school classmates. She was pretty then. She's beautiful now, in a way beauty schools can't teach. She, like my dad, will die, and I will only think of her knobby hands and her time-kissed face with the desire to behold them one more time.

God, the only one scowling at my aging body is me. Grant me the wisdom that's supposed to come with old age, so I can see myself anew. —Amy Eddings

Digging Deeper: Psalm 73:26; 2 Corinthians 4:16; James 4:14

Monday, October 18

If we are faithless, He remains faithful....
—2 Timothy 2:13 (NASB)

Altitude sickness, they told me.

I lay, shaking, in a remote cabin wrestling with God. After weeks of concert ministry, my wife and I were worn to a frazzle. To make it worse, honorariums had been almost nonexistent.

"God, I'm done. If you're still in this, I *really* need to hear your voice."

I heard wind in the trees, but heaven stayed silent.

A tiny church the next morning... Still weak, I sat on a folding chair in front of exactly thirteen people. Our hosts had told us the church could barely keep the lights on and hoped we wouldn't expect much in the way of compensation. "Don't worry, we travel by faith," we said. But, honestly, inside I was struggling.

I'd seen the man look in the window a couple of times, but barely when he came in. I *did* notice, later, when he stood up right in the middle of the service and surrendered his life to Jesus. The little church was so excited. They'd been praying for him—a troublemaking ex-convict—for years.

Later, the church passed a shoe around for an offering plate. We knew it wouldn't be much but took it thankfully.

But God is God. That night we were amazed to see that He, through that little gathering, had provided enough to make up for every night of the entire tour.

Our Father *always* keeps His appointments. And He certainly had one that morning with a broken man and thirteen people in a little church.

And He had one with me.

I'm so glad God is strong in our weakness. Faithful when we're faithless. Aren't you?

Heaven hadn't been silent after all.

Thank You, Lord, for strength on the journey.
—Buck Storm

Digging Deeper: Exodus 15:2; Isaiah 41:10

Tuesday, October 19

"What no eye has seen, what no ear has heard, and what no human mind has conceived"—the things God has prepared for those who love him.
—1 Corinthians 2:9 (NIV)

Years ago, when I was diagnosed with stage IV ovarian cancer and given a two-year life expectancy, I began to wonder more about heaven, with both fear and fascination. Heaven used to be a faraway place, but it suddenly seemed closer, and I wanted to know more about the journey from here to there.

Stacks of books have been written on the subject, so I did some reading, talked to people, and asked lots of questions. I felt overwhelmed by all the information and have to admit I still feared the unknowns. Especially the fact that I had to die in order to get to heaven, and dying scared me.

Well, guess what? I didn't die. In fact, I have outlived that life expectancy by fifteen years, but many of my questions still live within me, and I still wonder what the process of getting to heaven will be like.

Just a few weeks ago, a friend told me something that is reshaping my thoughts. He and his wife had gone to visit a dear friend who was dying. They went to say goodbye and sat together with the family in her last moments. She had not spoken for hours and her breathing was slowing down. In her final moment she uttered a single word. Her last as she journeyed from here to there. Loud and clear, the word was heard.

"Wow!" she said. And took her final breath.

Lord, what a perfect response to the first glimpse of heaven...living up to all Your promises. Wow!
—Carol Kuykendall

Digging Deeper: Romans 8:11; Philippians 3:20

Wednesday, October 20

The Lord will perfect that which concerns me; Your mercy, O Lord, endures forever; Do not forsake the works of Your hands. —Psalm 138:8 (NKJV)

"I'm so hungry and thirsty that my energy is all zapped out," my daughter whined, falling into the car like her legs were too weak to carry her. She riffled through my tote bag, which usually held a refreshing drink and fruit. But not today. "And no snack, either?" she asked. "This is terrible."

"I'm sorry, Reagan. I've been so busy I must have forgotten to pack a snack."

I sighed. Being overwhelmed with a hectic schedule had become my norm. Too much to do, too little time. I could already foresee an evening just as chaotic as the others had been. The stress affected my mental and physical health, plaguing me with headaches and sometimes an upset stomach.

Later that night, I was catching up on work emails when my daughter came in for her routine good-night kiss. "Mommy, you should take a break," she said. "You always tell us to talk to God and things will work out the way they're supposed to." I hugged her tighter and promised to heed the advice I'd shared with my children countless times.

Like my daughter earlier that day, I was hungry and thirsty, yet in a different way. My spirit needed to feed from God's Word, and I was thirsty for His presence. Before I drifted to sleep, I reminded myself of God's faithfulness—no matter how big or small my problem. And then I carried my worries and obligations to the feet of Jesus and left them there.

God, help me to trust Your plan for my life. I can lean on You for help, because You do all things well.
—Tia McCollors

Digging Deeper: Joshua 1:8–9; Proverbs 3:5; John 4:14

Thursday, October 21

The Lord is close to the brokenhearted and saves those who are crushed in spirit. —Psalm 34:18 (NIV)

I explored the map of Hudson, New York, on my computer, zooming in on the address of my appointment. I'd purposely stayed away from Hudson because it had been my nephew's home and driving through triggered my grief.

Switching the setting from the illustrated map to street view, I looked for a good place to park. Street view is amazing. A moment captured—with people on the street, cars traveling, people walking dogs—a frozen piece of time that can be zoomed in and explored. On the corner, I noticed a blurry figure in the distance. For a second, the posture, the height, I thought, *Wait. Is that him? My nephew, Jeremy.*

Jeremy had lived only a block or two away. It was entirely possible that it was him. Closer zooming didn't help, the figure was too blurred to tell, but then it occurred to me, *If this isn't him, his picture could still be here.*

For a few hours that day, crazy as it sounds, I found peace virtually zooming up and down streets looking for my nephew in the panoramic photos that were taken years ago. I think it was the possibility that I might see him again, and that feeling was beautiful and exactly what I needed.

Grief has many stages—five that have been widely documented—but I believe there are an infinite number, as unique as each relationship, some as odd and fleeting as searching for a loved one on virtual maps. Yet somehow by the grace of God, healing happens. One step at a time, peace comes.

Heavenly Father, grief is complicated and different for everyone. Help me and all those struggling through the process. Help us find peace.
—Sabra Ciancanelli

Digging Deeper: Psalm 55:22; Revelation 21:4

Friday, October 22

I am the light of the world.... —John 8:12 (NIV)

There was a switch problem at Canal, so the trains were backed up and unbearably crowded. As we grumbled our way south, I weighed my options: walk through the park in the rain or slog through the long underground tunnel at Forty-second Street amid hordes of sweaty, disgruntled people. I chose to escape as soon as possible.

A pool of people stood by the subway exit, warily eyeing a cascade tumbling down the stairs. I popped open my umbrella and headed out.

Within a block I was soaked to the ankles. By the time I reached the entrance I use to enter Central Park, I was wet to the knees. There was no flow of bicyclists or morning congregations of dog walkers. Rivers of runoff poured down the pathways. Then, with a clash, the skies opened up with increased ferocity, rain hammering so hard I could not hear the squish of my shoes.

I shivered and put my head down, pulling the umbrella tight to ensure maximum body coverage. All I could see was the pavement. Diverting my attention from my misery, I turned my thoughts to how to find God in the rain. *It's just me and You here this morning, Lord,* I prayed. *Will You help me see You?*

The huge drops attacking the asphalt bounced two and even three inches upon impact. I leaped over a four-foot swirling puddle next to a leaf-clogged drain, and then noticed that each of the hammering raindrops created a momentary flash as it rebounded. In this cold and wet moment, in the midst of discomfort, there was light. Not the kind of light and comfort I craved, but light all the same.

Thank You, Father, for focusing my eyes on Your light when I am tempted to see only darkness.
—Julia Attaway
Digging Deeper: John 1:5; 1 John 1:5–7

Saturday, October 23

Therefore encourage one another and build
each other up, just as in fact you are doing.
—1 Thessalonians 5:11 (NIV)

I set up tables in my church and hung up signs for
my first "Free Kids' Clothing Swap." Tables were
labeled for boys on one side and girls on the other,
from infant to teenage.

Moms arrived in droves, dropping off their
children's outgrown clothes and browsing through
piles on the other tables for bigger sizes. I answered
questions, folded, and did my best to organize the
growing tables spilling over with clothing. Other
moms jumped in to help as more and more people
arrived.

Although I was surprised by the amazing turnout,
I knew this was a big need. I could see it in the
posts of the single moms' group I had created on
social media. Isolation was another, something
many moms experience when their children are very
young. So, soon after the clothing swap I organized a
"Mom Speed Dating" night, a fun way to meet other
moms. Shortly after, moms were contacting me in
anticipation for the next "Mom Event."

During my personal hardships in motherhood,
I struggled to understand why life was so hard. I
longed for community and for my needs to be met
when I felt powerless to meet them myself. And
yet these are the experiences that gave me such a
heart for mothers, especially single moms. I didn't

always get that sense of community I ached for as a struggling mom, but now that I'm in a better place in motherhood, my passion and purpose are clear. I can create for others the villages I yearned for so many years ago.

Lord, thank You for turning our past miseries into present ministries. —Karen Valentin

Digging Deeper: Matthew 25:40

Sunday, October 24

Let us not become weary in doing good, for at the proper time we will reap a harvest if we do not give up. —Galatians 6:9 (NIV)

During a recent visit to my hometown in Maryland, my family and I attended our former church for Sunday morning service. I attended this church during my college years, and my family's history there is rich. This is the church where my husband and I exchanged wedding vows, where we had our firstborn son's child dedication, and where God built my spiritual foundation.

During the service we enjoyed a lively worship set, singing along and raising our hands in praise to gospel music that uplifted God and honored our African-American heritage. We listened to a challenging sermon. We also reconnected with old friends who have known us since we were twentysomething youth-ministry leaders.

A young woman approached our pew. She reached over to embrace me and remarked, "You might not remember me, but the first time I visited this church, you were the first person to share how to begin a relationship with God."

As she spoke, my mind transported back to the outreach ministry I had served many years ago. At the end of service each Sunday our team would connect with anyone needing prayer, and occasionally someone would step forward wanting to begin a faith walk with Christ. Suddenly, I remembered sharing Scripture and praying with this young woman over two decades ago.

Visiting our old church gave me a small glimpse into the impact I have had in this woman's life. It also encouraged me to continue seeking opportunities to affect others' lives even today, whether or not I am blessed to witness the impact or results.

Lord, help me continue to do good in others' lives, knowing that You are planting and watering a beautiful harvest. —Carla Hendricks

Digging Deeper: Proverbs 11:18; 1 Corinthians 15:58; 2 Thessalonians 3:13

Monday, October 25

O Lord, how many are Your works! In wisdom You have made them all . . . animals both small and great. —Psalm 104:24–25 (NASB)

Over the past forty-five years of marriage, Beth and I have enjoyed and nurtured four generations of golden retrievers. Ten years ago when we moved from Waco, Texas, to Macon, Georgia, we had four golden retrievers "bedded down" in the back of our Suburban... Beau, Muffy, and their two puppies, Bear and Buddy. It was hard to find a motel that would accept all of us!

Time passes quickly and last month, our last Texas golden retriever, Buddy, died of pleasant old age. Beth and I are still grieving. However, last week, we adopted another beautiful golden retriever puppy. Her name is Lexi and she is a free-spirited young lady. She is chewing up anything she can fit in her little mouth. However, she is bringing great joy to us, and we are again experiencing the spiritual gift of nurture.

As I left home this morning, I knelt down and gave Lexi a big hug. While driving to work I spontaneously began to sing an arrangement of verses based on Psalm 104: "All things bright and beautiful, all creatures great and small, all things wise and wonderful, the Lord God made them all." In that moment I realized that joy and perspective were returning to me. The grief of the loss of Buddy was lifting. And a profound experience of the goodness of God was glimpsed through the rearview mirror of sweet memories.

Thank you, Lexi! And thank You, God, for "all things bright and beautiful." —Scott Walker

Digging Deeper: Psalm 8; 23; 50:11

Tuesday, October 26

Therefore do not be anxious about tomorrow, for tomorrow will be anxious for itself. Sufficient for the day is its own trouble. —Matthew 6:34 (ESV)

I look down when I run. I know it's not the greatest form. I've heard you're supposed to keep your head erect, staring far off into the distance, bounding over hill and dale. But when I run I'm often checking for potholes or rocks or any surprises left on the sidewalk or trail. Looking for what's at my feet.

I don't go very fast anyway—I seem to get slower by the day—and I don't go very far. Just a half-hour jog up and around the park. If the weather's really rotten I can go to the gym and do it on a treadmill, but I find that boring. I'd rather be outside, under the trees, admiring the view, catching the breeze, even if the push up the hill takes my breath away. (Is it possible that the hill has gotten higher over the years?)

Here's what I'd say about looking down as I run: the long view can be really scary in life. I can imagine all sorts of mishaps coming along the way, sorrows, struggles, disappointments. Worries can get the worst of me. But didn't Jesus say, as it goes in the old King James language, "Sufficient unto the day...?"

So I focus on what's immediately in front of me, that puddle I should leap over, the pothole I should skip, the branch I don't want to trip over. God willing, I'll make it home in one piece, ready to face the challenges of the day.

Lord, give me the strength, courage, foresight, and
wisdom to do what I need to do this day.
—Rick Hamlin

Digging Deeper: 2 Timothy 4:7; Isaiah 40:31

Wednesday, October 27

The end of a matter is better than its beginning, and
patience is better than pride. —Ecclesiastes 7:8 (NIV)

"I want to completely declutter the basement before
Thanksgiving," my wife, Pat, said while we were out
for a walk.

"I have a lot of stuff going on.... Why do we need
to do that now?" I questioned. Pat and I had decided
to downsize to a smaller home. Earlier that afternoon
we had signed the final drawings for a new house.
Construction wasn't scheduled to start for another
six weeks, and Thanksgiving was less than a month
away. "So, when do you want to start decluttering?"
Pat asked. "In the winter—maybe after New Year's.
We won't even be moving until late spring," I
replied. "But the time will go really fast," she said.

A few days later my friend Jim asked me how
everything was going. I shared that I thought Pat
was moving too fast with decluttering. "Just get
out of the way and let her run with it," he said.
Jim's words cycled through my mind. The next
morning, I suggested to Pat that we pick a week,
clear our schedules, and dedicate the time to

totally declutter the basement. We agreed, selected a week, worked together, and got it done. Weeks before Thanksgiving, the basement was practically empty.

Finishing the decluttering freed us to handle all the unexpected things that popped up along the way. And when the builder sent a text saying the house would be ready a month early, our timeline dramatically accelerated—selling our current house, packing for the move, handling both closings. It was good Pat had a plan. What I had resisted at the start became a blessing.

Dear God, thank You for friends who help us see when we are the roadblock to something that needs to be done! —John Dilworth

Digging Deeper: Matthew 5:41; Philippians 2:3–4

Thursday, October 28

Jesus said, "Let the little children come to Me."
—Matthew 19:14 (NKJV)

What's trending on social media in Aurangabad, India? Apparently, me. In the last hour I've been stopped more than a dozen times by random people, all asking for a selfie with me. I feel a bit like a celebrity who's famous for absolutely nothing. Our guide explains that my pale, freckled skin is exotic. So is where I come from—a mythical land where everyone supposedly has running water and a car. Taking a photo with me is like mugging with a unicorn. I smile for the camera, shake hands, offer a cursory "happy to meet you," and then scurry off to rejoin my tour group.

Three elderly women with mahogany-colored, deeply lined, weathered skin grab my shoulder, pleading for a quick photo. Hurriedly, I put my arms around them and pull them in close, so we'll all fit into the frame. In the cell phone image reflected back at me, I see a rather plain, middle-aged, white woman, flanked by three huge grins, sporting few remaining teeth. The women's gold-bordered saris in sapphire and ruby hues put my T-shirt to shame. My tour group is on the move, so I offer a quick goodbye and leave.

Back on the bus, I wonder why I didn't honor these sweet women by asking for a photo in return. The answer was simple. They weren't on my personal agenda. I was so busy taking pictures of a historical monument that I didn't really see the priceless treasures walking right beside me. If Jesus took time to hold children in His lap, I can certainly take a moment to acknowledge and honor those whom God allows to cross my path.

Father, remind me daily that every individual I meet is worthy of Your love and Your time—and mine.
—Vicki Kuyper

Digging Deeper: John 3:16; 1 John 3:1; 4:7–8

Friday, October 29

Commit to the Lord whatever you do, and He will establish your plans. —Proverbs 16:3 (NIV)

"We don't have enough help!" my son complained to me one day after work. My son gets so frustrated because other employees he works with at the restaurant often don't come to work or just quit. Being shorthanded creates more work for everyone else and a stressful environment. Unfortunately, this lack of commitment is common in other areas as well.

I've noticed the same lack of commitment in team sports. As a parent, then grandparent of children on teams, I've seen how a player's lack of commitment to play the game, or even show up, affects others negatively and hurts the team's overall performance.

Commitment seems to be a bad word for many people in jobs, relationships, school, and family.

I'm thankful my parents instilled in me the importance of commitment. I'm also thankful my husband, Chuck, has the same principles. Recently, one of my sons commended Chuck on his devotion to our family and for all he's done for my children. In the ten years we've been married, we've had our trials, but we've pushed through together, whether it was difficult or not. Commitment isn't always easy. Yet God tells us to press forward, to finish the race, to commit our work to Him. Even Jesus kept his commitment to God the Father by doing the work

God sent Him to do. Shouldn't we be as faithful to our own commitments?

Father, please keep me committed to the tasks before me, even when the going is difficult. —Marilyn Turk

Digging Deeper: Psalm 37:5; John 6:38

Saturday, October 30

**Your word is a lamp to my feet and a light to my path.
—Psalm 119:105 (NASB)**

My daughter gave me an iPhone so we could keep in better touch through texting. But I found myself checking my phone more and reading my Bible less. The habit had snuck up on me.

Then someone close to me found herself in a hard place. Praying for her one morning, I got the distinct impression I should text her encouragement in a daily Bible verse. No reply required. I began with just the verse—later adding a thought on the passage.

My first text in November read, "May Your loving kindness comfort me, according to Your word to Your servant" (Psalm 119:76 NASB).

About two weeks in I sent, "Behold, God is my salvation, I will trust and not be afraid; For the Lord God is my strength and song, And He has become my salvation." (Isaiah 12:2 NASB). I added, "We each have our own words, but faith is a love song."

In January, "…you appear as lights in the world, holding fast the word of life" (Philippians 2:15 NASB). I explained, "The literal meaning of 'appear as lights' is 'shine like stars.' We've got star power!"

Also in January, "'Am I a God who is near,' declares the Lord, 'And not a God far off?'" (Jeremiah 23:23 NASB). I said, "The nearness of God is with us every day. Such comfort."

February brought, "He gives strength to the weary, and to him who lacks might He increases power" (Isaiah 40:29 NASB). I wrote, "This verse is my mile marker in life."

Something extraordinary happened in my daily texting. I was still on my phone, but I was back where I belong—in the Word of God.

I missed You, Lord. There is no substitute for You and Your words of life! —Carol Knapp

Digging Deeper: Deuteronomy 32:18; Psalm 119:30–32

Sunday, October 31

Sanctify them by the truth; your word is truth. —**John 17:17 (NIV)**

Spaghetti and eyeballs.

Apparently, that's my culinary specialty. It all started when my kids were little and I happened to make spaghetti and meatballs on Halloween night. I spotted a can of sliced olives in the pantry and in a moment of whimsy, put an olive slice on each meatball.

My kids (obviously) loved it. So much so, in fact, that the next year, it was almost expected that spaghetti and eyeballs would grace our dinner table on Halloween night. And so a tradition was born, one that even my teenage son says he looks forward to.

It's funny that this simple recipe has morphed into a tradition, but it has. I love it. I love that my kids know that as part of our family, there are certain things that make us *us*. Christmas caroling and eggnog on Christmas Eve's eve. The neighborhood parade on our bikes on the Fourth of July. A giant egg hunt on Easter. And yes, spaghetti and eyeballs for Halloween.

But I want more for my family. I want us to be a family that is known for praying unceasingly. A family that studies truth and clings to it. A family that actively seeks those things that are good, true, and beautiful in a way that honors Jesus.

And so this year, when I serve up my big plate of spaghetti and eyeballs, I plan to sprinkle our meal with heaps of Parmesan cheese, yes, but also with prayer for the many families who will celebrate Halloween without knowing *Him*. With gratitude for the season that is upon us. And with a yearning for Jesus that goes beyond just physical hunger.

Jesus, give me the insight to seek You and Your truth.
—Erin MacPherson

Digging Deeper: Mark 7:9; John 16:13

JOYFUL IN HOPE

1 _____

2 _____

3 _____

4 _____

5 _____

6 _____

7 _____

8 _____

9 _____

10 _____

11 _____

12 _____

13 _____

14 _____

15 _____

16 _____

17 _____

18 _____

19 _____

20 _____

21 _____

22 _____

23 _____

24 _____

25 _____

26 _____

27 _____

28 _____

29 _____

30 _____

31 _____

NOVEMBER

So I say to you: Ask and it will be given to you; seek and you will find; knock and the door will be opened to you.

—Luke 11:9 (NIV)

Monday, November 1

Since we are surrounded by such a great cloud of witnesses...let us run with perseverance the race marked out for us. —Hebrews 12:1 (NIV)

I grew up in a church tradition that kept All Saints' Day off its calendar. I now appreciate the feast day and its commemoration of faithful members of the family of God who have died. Not that I fully understand its meaning. Ditto for an adolescent neighbor who comes over often, sometimes raising questions about my parents, deceased for decades. Recently, when we were making a recipe from my mother's file box, she asked, "Does your mom see us?"

"The Bible says there are 'witnesses' in heaven. I think that means yes, but we don't know exactly."

"Well, tell your mother in heaven about me, okay? That I'm your neighbor friend." And, "When I get to heaven, how will your mom know me?" Questions, questions, trying to find a tethered place between two households and two realms.

This afternoon she noticed a picture of my dad and placed herself in the family lineup. "He's my great-grandfather. And you're my grandmother."

"I'm like an *extra* grandmother," I corrected. Her imagination kept looking for connections. "If you and I were both the same age, we could be 'old' friends." And then a futuristic setup: earth requesting help from heaven. "If you die, will you pray for me? Will your father pray for me, too?"

I gave hopeful answers. I suggested we pray—gratefully asking God for grace for us today, here and now, and for our families, here and beyond. Amen. With her spirit settled, her focus moved to the mundane—the October wall calendar. "Miss Evelyn, you forgot to turn the page."

November 1. All Saints. Without even trying, we'd noted the day.

God of all generations, we may not understand the interplay between heaven and earth, but we entrust our todays and tomorrows to You. —Evelyn Bence

Digging Deeper: Ephesians 1:15–21

Tuesday, November 2

Be hospitable to one another without grumbling. —1 Peter 4:9 (NKJV)

Throughout my long college teaching career, my wife has taken care of the house: cooking, cleaning, caring for the children. Now she is not strong enough to do some things alone. Retired, I am able to help with the hard jobs: mopping floors, cleaning tubs and sinks, unclogging drains. Everything except dusting, because, she says, "Men can't see dust."

My favorite domestic duty is cleaning up the dirty dishes. After every meal, we have a "date" at the kitchen sink. She washes, I dry. We don't have—or want—a dishwasher. We enjoy working together as a team. I do the heavy pots and pans that she can't lift.

I scrape the encrusted skillet with a metal spatula, and I enjoy showing off my strength.

As we work, we rehearse the day's events: "There was a famous author signing books at the library."

"Oh? Anyone I know?"

"Naw, never heard of him."

"There was a big accident at the convenience store. A man drove right through the door."

"I guess parking wasn't convenient enough?"

Standing close to my redhead, I can smell the fragrance of her perfume and see the freckles under her smiling Irish eyes. When she laughs at one of my corny lines, her eyes sparkle.

Done, I head for the TV room to catch the news.

"Thanks for helping out, Danny."

"Well, thank you for that delicious meal."

I am thankful to have found a small way of giving back, for all the years she has given to me.

It would be a very lonely world, Lord, without my Sharon. —Daniel Schantz

Digging Deeper: Ecclesiastes 4:9; Ephesians 5:21

Wednesday, November 3

Then shall thy light rise in obscurity.
—Isaiah: 58:10 (KJV)

During the sixteen years I've been a tour guide at the Shaker Village in Canterbury, New Hampshire,

I've learned a lot about this religious group's faith as reflected in their lifestyle and design. One hallmark feature that I especially admire appears in every building: "borrowed light." This simple architectural detail lets ambient light enter indirectly into a space otherwise blocked. These openings might include panes of glass set in an interior door, a full-size window set into an interior wall beside a stairwell, or small panes of glass set into closet walls. Sunlight enters a window from the outside of a building, travels through a room—then penetrates farther through the borrowed light feature.

Back in the eighteenth and nineteenth centuries when these buildings were built, folks depended upon candles—a perpetual fire hazard. Borrowed light reduced the necessity for candles. Yet, even after the advent of electricity, the antique interior windows still allow the gift of light to be used more efficiently to brighten dim places.

So I wonder... do I live my life as a borrowed light feature? Do God's light and love pass through me to beam upon others? Or by my stubbornness and indifference am I a wall blocking God's grace?

Light of the world, may I always be a window to share the radiance straight from You.
—Gail Thorell Schilling

Digging Deeper: Isaiah 58:8; Matthew 5:14–16; 2 Peter 1:19

And God said unto Moses, I Am That I Am: and
he said, Thus shalt thou say unto the children of
Israel, I Am hath sent me unto you.
—Exodus 3:14 (KJV)

I sit on my deck listening to the flow of traffic
along what was once a quiet country road, traffic
that was practically nonexistent thirty years ago
when this deck was constructed. To my surprise, the
intoxicating hum of morning traffic is a pleasant
complement to the potted plants bursting into a
haphazard rainbow along the deck's edges. A blend
of the old and the new, I reflect. A striking snapshot
of life itself. I smile through a sigh as I think of the
one constant among all the vicissitudes of my life,
the Great I Am.

I love that while God the Father answers Moses's
uncertainty with a direct "I Am That I Am," leaving
it at that, God the Son—ever-mediating Lord
that He is—offers a list of "I Am" metaphors to
strengthen us throughout the ages. In the Gospel of
John, Jesus lays out a smorgasbord of comforts to
those willing to put their trust in Him, declaring, "I
Am the Bread," "the Light," "the Door," "the Good
Shepherd," "the Resurrection," "the Way, the Truth,
and the Life," and "the Vine." As often stated in
the African-American community to describe the
excellence of something, He's "all that *and* a bag of
chips."

No matter the increase in the traffic of our earthly ups and downs, Jesus is that everlasting, never-too-busy friend—always there, sustaining us when life's changes overwhelm us. What more can we ask? While we can't control time's inexorability, we are blessed with the stability of eternity through the Great I Am.

Lord, no matter the climate, weather, or traffic, I'm so grateful for the beauty of this day and Your indelible stamp of hope upon it. —Jacqueline F. Wheelock

Digging Deeper: John 6:35; 8:12; 10:9; 10:11; 15:5; Revelation 1:8

Friday, November 5

Now faith is confidence in what we hope for and assurance about what we do not see. —Hebrews 11:1 (NIV)

My sister-in-law recently noted the nearly identical traits I share with my oldest daughter. "Faith talks like you," Laura said. "She doesn't have your sarcastic drawl, but the words are the same."

The "sarcastic drawl" description would be wrong if it weren't completely accurate. And yes, my daughter Faith and I are very much alike. This has led to a deep and abiding love, a good deal of confusion, and some remarkable spats. Our relationship, thank God, is much better now, because Faith has become a better person. (Me? Well, ah…still some work to be done there.) But I well remember how we would argue into the night, both using the same strategy and tactics. Invariably, our matches would end in frustrating draws, like playing chess against a mirror.

This, too, is my struggle with faith—the concept, not the daughter. There is a deep and abiding love, some spectacular fallouts, and all accompanied by confusion. This time it's more like shadowboxing: I am truly fighting myself, and wondering why I'm not winning and wondering why it feels so fruitless. Luckily, faith—both the concept *and* the daughter— are far more forgiving and merciful than me, and choose to use arms to embrace rather than to fight.

Huh, I think in my sarcastic drawl. *Seems like a strange and unorthodox strategy. Perhaps I should try it sometime.*

Lord, in faith, I pray to You; in humility, I seek You.
—Mark Collins

Digging Deeper: Psalm 69:13–15

Saturday, November 6

So do not fear, for I am with you; do not be dismayed, for I am your God. I will strengthen you and help you; I will uphold you with my righteous right hand. **—Isaiah 41:10 (NIV)**

My golden retriever, Gracie, loves to hike Monument Mountain in the Berkshires of western Massachusetts—

about five hundred acres of wooded trails leading to a seventeen-hundred-foot peak. Me, too.

Gracie is a wonderful, sensitive girl. But sometimes her nose gets the better of her and off she goes into the woods, streaking through the underbrush. Usually, she finds her way back to the trail in a few minutes or so. Any longer than that, I blow a whistle and call her name. That gets her attention, along with a treat.

So that sun-wrapped day I wasn't worried when she tore off after some maddening scent or the other. I sat on a rock and waited. Five minutes. Ten. I blew the whistle. Still no Gracie.

After twenty minutes I started hiking. I hiked up to Devil's Pulpit and still no Gracie. I hiked up to Squaw Peak and down a loop trail, breathless with panic. It was going on two hours and I would have to call Julee soon and tell her. Just then my phone rang. "Edward, did you lose Gracie?" Julee asked. In response I did my best stammering Ralph Kramden impersonation. "Some nice guys found her," Julee interrupted. "They called our number on her tag. They'll meet you in the parking area. Hurry."

I nearly collapsed with relief, yet I was so mad at Gracie! But when she came running to me, it was clear she was as frantic and hysterical as I was, panting and whining. "We found her at the peak, just sitting all by herself waiting." My heart swallowed my anger in one gulp. Gracie was an answer to prayer. How could I be angry at that? I knelt beside her. "It's okay," I said. "Have a treat."

Father, how many times have I strayed from You, lost and frantic? May I always find my way back into Your loving arms. —Edward Grinnan

Digging Deeper: Luke 19:10; Ephesians 2:8–9

Sunday, November 7

Above all, love each other deeply, because love covers over a multitude of sins. —1 Peter 4:8 (NIV)

"The house looks nice, Mom," I said. I sat down on the couch in my parents' new living room.

"Really?" my mom asked. Her eyes were earnest. It had been difficult for her to leave her 1860s home and move to a modern house.

"This room looks nothing like the listing pictures. You've put your mark on it."

I looked around me. The walls were lined with bookshelves. Potted ferns tempered the trendy fireplace. The old grandfather clock ticked in a new corner.

"The one thing that feels out of place is the TV," I said. My eyes were drawn to the massive flat-screen mounted on the wall—a remnant of the home's previous owners. Its dark screen was dominating.

"That's the next thing to go," my mom said. "I've never had a TV in my living room. I want the focus of the room to be people, not a television."

Her words hit me hard. My mom centered her home on people. More than that, she focused her life on sharing Christ's love with others.

Sitting in her living room, I questioned the focus of my own life. I'd spent a lot of my time wrapped up in my own wants and concerns. My education. My career. My aspirations.

I wanted to mirror my mom's love for others. I wanted to mirror her love for Christ.

So I made a silent promise to myself to remove the television screens from my life—to shift my focus from myself to others.

"I'm glad you think the house is coming together," my mom said.

It was. Because her focus was in the right place.

Lord, help me to use my life to share Your love with others. —Logan Eliasen

Digging Deeper: 1 Thessalonians 3:12; Hebrews 13:1–2

Monday, November 8

Let thine ear now be attentive, and thine eyes open, that thou mayest hear the prayer of thy servant, which I pray before thee now, day and night, for the children of Israel thy servants, and confess the sins of the children of Israel, which we have sinned against thee: both I and my father's house have sinned. We have dealt very corruptly against thee. —Nehemiah 1:6–7 (KJV)

My mother and my two aunts had a lot in common: they were smart, beautiful, older than my father, and opinionated—they hated each other. As a child, I didn't know why my mother and aunts disliked each other so. In fact, I still don't know.

But their dislike kept us from sharing meals, holidays, or hugs; it survived two of them—more than half a century later. The hate spilled into the next generation. My cousin and I never played together, talked, shared presents. Now only one aunt remains, and she has dementia.

I occasionally reached out to my eldest aunt in letters, cards, and a phone call here or there. But mostly, I was silent, trying to avoid the family rift. They were grown folks, I thought; they wouldn't listen to me. But in retrospect, I could have been braver.

Rather than letting childish fears keep me silent, I could have talked to my mother, encouraged her to settle whatever dispute kept them apart. I could have urged my father to be a peacemaker between them. I could have prayed for the courage to love my aunts more and reach out to them. I could have tried to talk to them, so they could learn to love me, rather than despising who they thought I was.

Today, I will start anew and reach out to my cousin.

God, You are the one who turns hearts of stone to flesh. Give me the courage to love and to have faith that You will intervene and sow love and peace where it does not exist. —Sharon Foster

Digging Deeper: Nehemiah 1

Tuesday, November 9

"Do not work for the food that perishes, but for the food that endures to eternal life, which the Son of Man will give to you. For on him God the Father has set his seal." —John 6:27 (ESV)

We have a beautiful family of next-door neighbors with five little girls, all of whom bless us. One afternoon I was looking after the neighbor girls when the eldest, Avery, came home from kindergarten. I asked her what her favorite subjects in school were. I truly expected her response to be "Recess!" Proving me wrong, Avery said, "Cleaning up and helping out." I chuckled and told her she has an open invitation to visit my home whenever she likes.

After thinking more intently on her response, I found Avery's answer is really quite profound. Of all the knowledge and skills she is learning in kindergarten, helping others and caring for the world will positively affect her family and community for the rest of her life. In a world where our children are expected to learn more content at a much quicker pace than previous generations, the importance of helping and serving sometimes can be lost in a busy school day.

We should all be careful about what is prioritized in our own lives. Avery's favorite subjects are also the tangible deeds that speak important truths about respect, honor, compassion, and service. It is inspiring that at a young age, Avery enjoys the core Christian principle of loving and serving your neighbor. May we all be so blessed to follow her example.

Lord, help us to remember in a world where there is much to gain that our service to others is paramount. May we seek You first in all things and through all things, and may we know the joy of helping out and cleaning up. Amen. —Jolynda Strandberg

Digging Deeper: Matthew 14:17–19; Luke 9:13; John 13

Wednesday, November 10

For am I now seeking the favor of men, or of God? . . . —Galatians 1:10 (ASV)

My daughter's music lessons were held in an obscure practice room at the local university's music school. Judging from the many filing cabinets crammed into such a small space, it appeared that the room was used mostly for storage and that the occasional private lesson held there was an afterthought.

As I waited quietly one afternoon, my eye was drawn to a trophy sitting atop a pile of cardboard boxes in the corner. I went over to investigate. And what do you know? Some students had won second place in their division at a college jazz band festival, held at another, lesser-known university, in 1976.

I tried to imagine how the students who'd been presented this trophy must've felt that day. Were they proud? Or disappointed to have come in second?

Where were they now? And did any of them even remember the competition anymore?

The trophy, apparently long forgotten and now covered in dust, seemed a reminder of Solomon's repeated declaration in Ecclesiastes that "all is vanity." Likely, these students had worked hard on their music, but what did it matter now? It wasn't as though their grandchildren were telling their friends, "Hey, my grandpa's ensemble came in second in their division at a competition forty-five years ago."

I thought of the things taking up space in my attic at home. Hundreds of copies of magazines with one page containing my tiny byline. Copies of books I've written, many now out of print. Things that my children will probably feel bad about throwing away when I'm gone but have nowhere—and no real reason—to keep. And yet wasn't I so proud of myself at the time?

Lord God, help me remember that only the things I do in Your Name will endure. —Ginger Rue

Digging Deeper: Psalm 103:14; Ecclesiastes 1:2

Veterans Day, Thursday, November 11

The greatest among you shall be your servant.
—Matthew 23:11 (NASB)

Today I presided at the funeral of a United States Air Force veteran, Chief Master Sergeant Allan Penrod. Born in Kentucky in 1920, he was the son of a poor sharecropper, and his family moved frequently. His mother died when Allan was seven years old and he matured quickly.

As a boy, Allan discovered he had mechanical gifts and could "fix anything." During the Great Depression he often repaired the worn-out shoes of his school classmates. He was brilliant and could compute math problems in his head without notation. As a child, he worked in tobacco fields pulling worms off the leafy plants. Later, he participated in the Civilian Conservation Corps to assist his family and serve his country.

When Allan was eighteen, he proudly joined the United States Army Air Corps and became a flight mechanic and an armament specialist. He served in World War II, the Korean War, and the Vietnam War. Retiring from the air force, he held perhaps the most respected rank: Chief Master Sergeant.

Following his military career, Allan again served his country as a mail carrier for the United States Postal Service for nineteen years. Upon full retirement, he became a carport engineer, repairing anything his neighbors needed fixing.

This morning an Air Force Honor Guard carried Allan's coffin to his grave. Soon, a twelve-gun salute resounded, a bugle taps solo played, and his family was presented the folded flag of the United States of America. There was not a dry eye among family and friends.

Allan Penrod lived a life of service above self. And, to echo his favorite maxim, he always "left things better than you found them."

Father, on this Veterans Day, we thank You for the
sacrifice of those who serve their country.
—Scott Walker

Digging Deeper: Mark 10:45; John 15:13;
1 Corinthians 10:24

Friday, November 12

A new command I give you: Love one another. As
I have loved you, so you must love one another. By
this everyone will know that you are my disciples,
if you love one another. —John 13:34–35 (NIV)

Over the years I've attended many funerals. My
grandparents, parents, aunts, and uncles have all
passed on. Friends and neighbors have died, some
tragically. As a church organist I've participated
in funerals for people I didn't know. Most of the
services were a blessing and many included some
humorous moments. When Don's uncle died,
the pastor chuckled and said, "He was an ornery
old guy!" before reading the obituary that
summarized his life accomplishments.

Recently, though, I attended a service that
was different. The woman's obituary listed
surviving family members but didn't mention any
educational attainments, activities, memberships,
or achievements. I wondered what her life had been
like. How did she spend her time? Was she bored?
Did she know Jesus?

My questions were answered when the pastor asked if anyone would like to make remarks. Person after person stood to speak. "She opened her home and heart to me when we lost our house." "She took me in when I was pregnant and unmarried." "She bailed me out of jail and helped me get a job I still have." "Without her pushing me, I wouldn't have finished high school." When the pastor asked how many people present had been touched by her kindness, almost everyone stood up.

No activities or accomplishments? Only the most crucial one of all. She loved. She loved in word and action, and she loved without judgment or condemnation. And isn't that all Jesus asks of us, too?

Holy Savior, keep my focus on the one thing You have commanded: that I love others as You have loved me.
—Penney Schwab

Digging Deeper: Romans 12:9–13; Ephesians 5:1; 1 John 4:7–11

Saturday, November 13

May the Lord answer you when you are in distress; may the name of the God of Jacob protect you.
—Psalm 20:1 (NIV)

Around here, we talk about guardian angels, if they're real and what we think they do. I tell my kids that I absolutely believe in angels because, while I haven't seen one, I've seen their work firsthand.

The kids got the chance to experience it one night when our glass shower wall, an L-shaped piece so heavy that I can't lift it alone, came crashing down while they were in the bathroom. When I ran in, I saw Olivia, six, in the now-open shower mid-suds, and James, four, cowering beside the sink, howling in fear.

The wall had not only fallen, it had fallen on James. Once I had triple- checked that he was scraped and bruised but not seriously injured, I turned to the wall, which was precariously balanced on both the edge of our bathtub and a plush stool, which sat a good four inches below the lip of the tub.

The installers agreed when they came to make the repairs: there's no way that wall shouldn't have shattered. There was no logical reason why it had remained perfectly intact, except for angels.

Without something, or someone, holding up that glass wall, James would've been surrounded by shattered glass or, worse, pinned to the floor by a wall I couldn't lift. Instead of being in the ER, he was on our couch with an ice pack on his scrapes and a cup of milk in his hands.

I don't know how my kids will remember that night, but I hope that their minds grow to understand that sometimes you can only explain the unexplainable with the unseen.

Jesus, thank You for being there in moments that I am not, to love and comfort those around me.
—Ashley Kappel

Digging Deeper: Daniel 12:1; Acts 12:15; Hebrews 1:14

Oh, the depth of the riches and wisdom and knowledge of God! How unsearchable are his judgments and how inscrutable his ways!
—Romans 11:33 (ESV)

"Hi, Grandpa," I said cheerfully as I walked into the room, resting my hand on his shoulder in greeting as I passed. He startled, jumping enough that he spilled the coffee in the mug he was holding.

"Oh, Erin! I didn't notice you come in!" he said, as I bent to wipe up the mess. Concern prickled. I'd approached him in what should've been full view, yet he hadn't seen me.

Grandpa had just turned ninety-four, and glaucoma and macular degeneration were taking their toll on his eyesight. The doctor said he saw only a small pinhole tunnel of what was directly in front of him. Lately, though, things seemed to be getting even worse. Not that you could persuade Grandpa of that. "I see good enough," he'd tell you if you asked. It seemed an impossible declaration, given how much I watched him miss, but—I'd realized—it made sense. If you can't see what you're missing, how would you ever know it was there?

It must be what it's like for God, watching us, I thought as I poured Grandpa another cup of coffee. God's creation surrounds us all, but my finite human senses will never see or comprehend most of it. How much God must watch me miss every day! Yet He doesn't condemn me for my poor eyesight. He

467

calls me His beloved child. He tells me that, in His perfect eyes, I am acceptable, "good enough," to use Grandpa's words, exactly as I am. How startling. How wonderful.

Even though I can never understand all that You are, God, I praise Your ways that are higher than my ways, and Your thoughts that are higher than my thoughts. Thank You for Your perfect, incomprehensible love.
—Erin Janoso

Digging Deeper: Job 26:14; Romans 5:8

Monday, November 15

The LORD loves righteousness and justice; the earth is full of his unfailing love. —Psalm 33:5 (NIV)

A British comedian recently passed through Cleveland on a tour that will take him around the world. He said his goal was to encourage people to be positive and to be a force for good against the darkness he saw in the world.

I knew that darkness. As a newscaster, I talked about it every day. Political divisions were becoming more entrenched, mass shootings more frequent, and heroin overdoses so common that officials were advising the public to carry overdose reversal kits.

The crowd cheered for his message of hope, and so did I.

The comedian was quick to add that this hope was not rooted in God. He said he didn't believe in "the floaty man," as others did, because he could not understand why an all-powerful being who supposedly loved us would stand idly by and watch as children died of cancer or Nazi soldiers gassed six million Jews.

The crowd roared in agreement. I did not.

He didn't tell the whole story, I thought. He didn't talk about the more than twenty-six thousand people who risked their lives to save thousands of Jews during the Holocaust. Or the many charities that provide financial and emotional support for the families of kids with cancer. The firefighters who started up a hundred and ten flights of stairs after hijacked airplanes plowed into the World Trade Center in 2001. The surviving firefighters who comforted the wives and children of the firefighters who did not return.

God isn't standing idly by at all. The earth is full of His unfailing love.

God, open my eyes today to all the ways You've been lovingly faithful to me and to all Your creation.
—Amy Eddings

Digging Deeper: Psalm 10:12–14; Lamentations 3:22–23; John 16:33

Tuesday, November 16

You, then, why do you judge your brother or sister? Or why do you treat them with contempt? For we will all stand before God's judgment seat.
—Romans 14:10 (NIV)

I'm not a fan of our homeowners' association Facebook page. It's morphed into a place to judge others and post complaints. One neighbor, I'll call her Alice, seems to be always looking out her windows, admonishing online those whose dogs roam off leash, reporting unfamiliar cars, and reprimanding those who drive too fast (me included). We're beyond the city limits on two-acre lots, after all.

Late one evening when my husband was away, our shih tzu mix bolted to the front door, barking and growling. A man walked to our porch.

"I'm a little lost and can't get out of here," he said loudly. "Can I come in and use your phone?"

My heartbeat raced. Our house was at the back of the neighborhood. Why didn't he stop at the others he passed? Everyone had a cell phone these days. Why would he want to come in?

"One minute." I held up a finger, hurried into the kitchen, and called 911. The police were dispatched and arrived just as the man walked back to his car.

Relief swept over me, but it was short-lived. *What if he goes to a neighbor's house, they open the door, and something bad happens?*

I tapped the Facebook app on my phone, found the HOA page, and alerted the neighborhood. No sooner had I finished typing than a message chimed from Alice. Her husband was on his way to my house.

Later she posted: "Three neighbor men headed your way to help as soon as I saw the message. Here's our number. Call anytime!"

Lord, thank You for my nosy neighbor who turned out to be a guardian angel. Help me not be so quick to judge the intentions of others.
—Stephanie Thompson

Digging Deeper: 1 Corinthians 10:24; James 4:11–12; 1 Peter 3:8–12

Wednesday, November 17

LOSING JOHN: All the Moments
... let me first say farewell.... —Luke 9:61 (RSV)

I often engaged in a sentimental little fantasy, imagining John's and my last moment together. It was always just the two of us, speaking such moving words of love that I would actually weep.

Our actual parting was very different. In 2017, John had two operations for an abdominal blockage. The third time we made that trip to the hospital, ambulance siren wailing, John declined a third surgery. At ninety-four he opted to return home, with hospice care.

What I chiefly remember of those last few weeks is a continuous stream of people passing through our apartment. The hospital bed came with a team of technicians. A work crew removed the sliding doors from the shower, another installed a floor-to-ceiling post. There was an oxygen tank and a heart monitor and a blood pressure machine, each requiring a covey of consultants. There were nurses and aides and two men to assist John in the reconfigured shower.

And I? In the midst of all this end-of-life activity, I managed to deny to myself that John was dying, racing across the room to readjust his oxygen mask. How could he get better if he didn't breathe?

I went to bed, that final night, before the late shift came on, so I'd never met the nurse who woke me at 4:00 a.m. to tell me that John had died in his sleep. After all the fantasies, I'd failed in the end to speak those words of love.

At last I was granted a few moments alone with John. And in that silent room I heard God say, *Of course you spoke them! You did and John did—spoke your love over and over in a thousand ways through seventy years. It's not the final moment that matters to Me, but all the moments that come before.*

Lord, let me pass up no chance today to speak love.
—Elizabeth Sherrill

Digging Deeper: Ecclesiastes 3:1–15; Numbers 6:24–26

Thursday, November 18

Work willingly at whatever you do, as though you were working for the Lord rather than for people.
—Colossians 3:23 (NLT)

One morning, as I prepared to begin my workshop, Don't Let Limitations Stop You, I looked out at the audience and noticed it was made up of younger and older male inmates. These men came from different religious, economic, and social backgrounds but were all eager to learn how to reach their goals.

This wasn't my first training session at this federal correction institute. The first time I volunteered there was for a job and career fair to help inmates prepare to reenter society. After the event, a few of the inmates requested that I return to the prison to lead personal growth programs. This was a surprise to me, but I happily accepted the offer to continue my work to help the inmates gain different life skills.

When I hold these training sessions, the men are engaged, ask great questions, and share their insight on the topic at hand. And my heart is filled with joy. I have been blessed with an opportunity to help people who need a chance to rebuild their lives.

I never envisioned myself conducting workshops within a prison, but God did. We never know how and where God is going to use us to serve others. I'm just grateful that He knows where we are needed and how to get us there. When I first came to this prison, I thought I would be volunteering for one day. Now, a few years later—and thanks to God—I am still helping this population and truly enjoying the experience.

Lord, position us where we are needed even in those places we don't envision ourselves. —Pablo Diaz

Digging Deeper: Matthew 25:35–36; Acts 9:13–15

Friday, November 19

Look to the Lord and his strength; seek his face always. —1 Chronicles 16:11 (NIV)

I sat in my car in front of Anne's house. The engine hum was comforting. I watched digital numbers on my display change and change again. "Lord, be with me," I whispered. Then I pulled keys from the ignition and dropped them into my bag.

Anne was mama to two young sons and a newborn, and a few minutes later I sat at her table while she served chicken salad. Recently, Anne asked me to be her mentor after I'd been on a panel of experienced mothers at a brunch she and her friends organized. I didn't know Anne well, but I liked what I did know. She was a gifted teacher. A boy mama. Her love for the Lord was tender-fierce.

But a mentor? I had one—an older, wiser woman I'd walked miles of life with. But be one? I wasn't sold.

I wore worry like a sweater. I dragged my feet through life change. My husband and I had mountain-size parenting issues. My spiritual shortcomings were a long list.

Anne and I began to talk as her toddlers napped and her babe-in- bassinet slept near a crackling fire. Conversation was polite and easy—the gentle flow of hopeful friendship. But it didn't take long for things to go deep as we shared about our marriages. Our families. Our hearts and our homes.

"I appreciate your transparency," Anne said later as I rooted through my bag for keys. "You're honest and real. You love the Lord, and you lean into Him with your life."

Anne wasn't drawn to a story without struggle. Or to flawless faith. She was drawn to His perfection in my imperfection. To His might in my mess.

"Thank you, Lord," I whispered. I smiled all the way home.

Lord, when I am weak You are strong. Amen.
—Shawnelle Eliasen
Digging Deeper: Psalm 121:3; 138:3

Saturday, November 20

To the praise of the glory of His grace, by which He has made us accepted in the Beloved.
—Ephesians 1:6 (NKJV)

"Are we sure we want to do this?" Margi and I examined the paint sprayer one last time before committing. Rather than buying new furniture, we decided to just paint our old stuff.

The experts at the paint store suggested the correct sprayer. My wife and I read the directions, poured in the paint, and prepared to spray. Big blue tarps protected our driveway. Dark wooden dressers, flanked by their drawers, stood in rows like soldiers, awaiting our amateur efforts.

"Once we start, we can't go back," I said.

Margi smiled. "Let's do it! It doesn't have to be perfect."

I gulped. Perfectionism lurks in the corners of my heart, always ready to pounce. The fear of making mistakes nags at me. It makes me question my worth. But Margi's encouragement was enough. With the rumble of an air compressor filling our ears, I triggered the sprayer.

It was working. Our freshly painted furniture actually looked good. The color was beautiful and the sheen was great, because—following directions from the experts at the paint store—we kept it wet. "Wet enough to shine, but not wet enough to run." After a few hours, everything was finished.

That's when I made a fatal mistake. I suggested another coat. "I'll just make it a light mist." That light mist turned into a dull finish. I didn't keep it wet enough, and the shine was gone. So was the paint, so was our energy, and so was my self-worth. Margi must have seen it in my eyes. "Don't worry, honey. It's still beautiful," she said. And it hit me—my worth before both God and those I love doesn't depend on me being perfect. It just depends on me being me.

God, You alone are perfect. Help me to be good with that. Amen. —Bill Giovannetti

Digging Deeper: Colossians 3:17

Sunday, November 21

He told those who were selling the doves, "Take these things out of here! Stop making my Father's house a marketplace!" His disciples remembered that it was written, "Zeal for Your house will consume me." —John 2:16–17 (NRSV)

I love words. Every once in a while, a new word crops up that interests me. *Disruptor* is my latest fascination. It appears in business reporting to describe an up-and-coming person or company seeking to disrupt an existing market or system. Often, it refers to a new technology or individual with a "big" innovation designed to wreak havoc on, and eventually replace, a current industry. Disruptor is a buzzword, meant to generate excitement and even a little fear about what is to come.

When reading one of my favorite Gospel passages about our Lord cleansing the temple with what must have seemed like violent zeal to the people of the time, I realized that Jesus was a Disruptor.

He may not have been marketing a new iPhone or cloud-based technology, but He was introducing a brand-new way to communicate with God. Like today's disruptors, He was offering a faster, more efficient, more direct path to the Almighty. In Himself, He presented the kind of mega-gigabyte network that even our technology-obsessed world will never see. He was eradicating the spam, clearing out the detritus, and demonstrating a new way for us to "do" faith. Jesus offered Himself as the ultimate CEO: His only interest in profit was for us.

Jesus, help me to welcome Your disruption of my life and routines, to the profit of my soul.
—Marci Alborghetti

Digging Deeper: Matthew 1:18–2:15; John 14

Monday, November 22

She sets about her work vigorously; her arms are strong for her tasks. —Proverbs 31:17 (NIV)

My wife, Pat, and I were spending Thanksgiving week at our son's home. Soon after we arrived, we talked about where we would go for Thanksgiving dinner. Johnny said, "What I would really like is for Mom to cook the things we've always had on Thanksgiving and eat here at my place." Pat said she would, and it sounded great to me.

Johnny had recently moved into his first house and eats most meals out. His kitchen was not equipped for cooking a big meal. But Pat gamely planned the meal and we all looked forward to spending Thanksgiving together in Johnny's new home. The day arrived, and Pat was busy in the kitchen; the many wonderful aromas heightened our appetites throughout the afternoon.

Shortly before time to eat, we talked about how we would spend the next day. Each of us wanted to spend Friday differently, which led to some noticeable disappointment and family tension. Before the meal, as we joined hands to give thanks, Pat said, "Hey, let's just have fun this evening—I cooked this whole dinner with only a teaspoon!" We all laughed and the tension in the room melted away.

Wow... *with only a teaspoon*—words that added just the needed humor to recenter us. Words that also made me realize I had taken for granted what Pat had done to make our family's favorite

Thanksgiving meal in a kitchen equipped to prepare snacks.

Dear Lord, help us cherish the efforts made in love by family and friends that create the beautiful moments in our lives. And guide us to rise above trivial annoyances that get in the way. Amen.
—John Dilworth

Digging Deeper: Proverbs 31:10–31;
1 Corinthians 13:4–5

Tuesday, November 23

LOSING JOHN: Becoming a Widow
I have yet many things to say to you, but you cannot bear them now. —John 16:12 (RSV)

It didn't come all at once, the realization that John was dead. It hit me in small, unexpected little jabs of awareness.

Making an entry on the wall calendar in the kitchen: Dr. Tam, with a T in parentheses (for me, nicknamed Tib) to distinguish it from John's appointments (J). Suddenly knowing—really knowing—that this calendar records only one person's dates now. Automatically stopping at John's desk before running the dishwasher; coffee cups tended to accumulate there. But the only thing on his desk is the moon cactus he tended so patiently. Reaching in my own desk for an envelope and finding a nearly full box of stationery on beautiful pearl-gray paper with raised lettering: Mr. & Mrs. John Sherrill. Unusable, of course, but somehow impossible to toss in the trash.

You can't prepare yourself for these little stabs of pain. You can't steel yourself as you do for, say, a dinner party, when you know ahead of time how hard it will be. I've come to think of them as part of God's gracious provision for handling a loss that would otherwise overwhelm us. If we had to take in a death immediately, had to let the full extent of the loneliness ahead sweep over us from the start, I know I, for one, couldn't have handled it.

And so it was only step by little step that I became a widow. I think in God's infinite compassion, He allows this buffer zone of denial, for a while. But of course He who said, *I am the truth* will not let us evade reality for long. With these sudden small wrenches of the heart He brings us to acceptance, at a pace even reluctant learners like me can maintain.

Lord, help me always to embrace the real, for only there will I find You. —Elizabeth Sherrill

Digging Deeper: John 14:1–7

Wednesday, November 24

STRUGGLING TO PRAY: Recognizing Answered Prayer

And Jesus increased in wisdom and in stature and in favor with God and man. —Luke 2:52 (ESV)

As a lifelong cook, I've always loved Thanksgiving. At twelve, I proudly took over from my dad the cooking of our traditional meal: turkey with bread stuffing, mashed potatoes, giblet gravy, cranberry-orange-apple-walnut relish, a gratin of little onions, the weird marshmallow yams, rolls, and pies.

My Thanksgiving prayer is one I pray all year—that my girls will grow up to love others and God.

Cooking bored the girls as kids, but when they turned twelve I assigned each a task: Charlotte the stuffing and Lulu the cranberry relish. As they got older, they took charge of the pies, first just deciding what kinds but eventually weaving dough lattices and making leaf-shaped decorations gritty with sugar sparkles. Last Thanksgiving, we bought six-inch pans so they could make six different pies without any going to waste.

This year only Lulu came home, though. Charlotte had gotten a puppy and immediately became its mom. She arranged her days around Milo's nap times and meals and toted everywhere a bag holding kibble, bowls, toys, treats, and poop bags. Mid-November she texted she couldn't leave Milo, so she wasn't coming home.

Thanksgiving with just Lulu was enjoyable but not the same. Lulu made her cranberry relish—opting for less sugar, a good move—but I made everything else.

This is how it'll be now, I lamented. *The girls off somewhere, working, raising kids, cooking their own Thanksgiving meals.*

Then I realized that, too, would answer my Thanksgiving prayer: my girls grown up, nurturing others.

Thank You, Father, for making us in Your image, so we can grow, love, and become more like You.
—Patty Kirk

Digging Deeper: Hebrews 5:12–14

Thanksgiving, Thursday, November 25

Let us come before him with thanksgiving....
—Psalm 95:2 (NIV)

It was our first Thanksgiving, and the first time all our children—Chuck's and mine—were assembled under our roof for a family meal.

Wanting everything to be perfect, I had scoured magazines and Pinterest for ideas and decorations. The house was adorned with fall colors, the pumpkin spice candles were lit, and the guest bathroom had Thanksgiving-themed towels.

The dining room chairs were festooned with gold fabric that tied in the back, accented with a sprig of fall leaves. Coordinating napkins complemented each place setting. The festive centerpiece was a colorful ceramic turkey accompanied by candles and pilgrim salt and pepper shakers.

I'd chosen a variety of foods, hoping everyone would find them tasty.

As I rushed back and forth to get everything prepared on time, our family began arriving. I barely had time to acknowledge them because I was so focused on preparations.

Soon, the meal was ready, and we began carrying dishes to the table. Although my table was large enough to seat everyone, it was difficult to find enough room for the food. As I was carrying in the turkey platter, my stepdaughter reached to remove the centerpiece from the table to make room. I gasped, and everyone looked at me. Then my daughter-in-law seized the awkward moment by saying, "Step away from the turkey!"

Everyone burst out laughing, and I realized how foolish I was to be so preoccupied with perfection that there wasn't enough room for the food. As I looked around at the smiling faces, I saw the whole reason for the celebration—to be thankful, not just for food, but for people to enjoy it with.

Thank You, Lord, for blessing us in so many ways. Help us to appreciate each other. —Marilyn Turk

Digging Deeper: Luke 10:41

Friday, November 26

Whatever good anyone does, this he will receive back from the Lord.... **—Ephesians 6:8 (ESV)**

Eight-thirty yesterday morning, Thanksgiving. How many times had I done this before—standing at the kitchen sink, addressing a cold, bald turkey that would by the day's end feed my holiday guests? I cut and tugged at the tight packaging. I reached for the bag of organs tucked down deep. It was still icy; I had to yank it free, and my fingers froze. Following Martha Stewart's advice, I ran tap water over and through the ins and outs. Suddenly, I was rassling twelve pounds of slippery flesh that felt like forty. "This is the last time," I said to myself, as I seasoned with salt and herbs and pinned back wings. "The last turkey I'm ever roasting." Too much hassle, and the day had hardly begun.

I peeled potatoes, replicated my mom's bread stuffing, set a festive table, and after noon I welcomed friends, who filled out the menu with sides and pies. One of them carved the bird to the bone. We gathered around the table and blessed the meal. Two guests, strangers to each other, had more in common than I knew. Conversation flowed, from the serious—every culture has its feast days; why do humans celebrate?—to the humorous. The visitors stayed longer than they had planned.

Over dessert, I admitted my morning meltdown— never again—and my softening stance. "You've given me such a good day, I'm ready to reconsider."

"No need," a friend cut in. "Next year, everyone, our house!" Will we gather again next year? Will their offer stand? Time will tell. But if need be, I'm set to go, ready to grapple and roast, renewed by the memory of a communal feast.

Lord, thank You for memories of positive outcomes
that ease the burden of a heavy workload.
—Evelyn Bence

Digging Deeper: Matthew 11:28–30; Acts 10:38

Saturday, November 27

*Or suppose a woman has ten silver coins and loses
one. Doesn't she light a lamp, sweep the house and
search carefully until she finds it?* —Luke 15:8 (NIV)

Where was my money clip? I looked everywhere
for it. Turned the house upside down. Not in my
top drawer, not on my dresser, not in my briefcase.
"Have you seen my money clip?" I asked Carol.
Nope. She hadn't seen it anywhere.

Maybe I'd been pickpocketed. Maybe the money
fell out of the pocket and somebody grabbed it
without my knowing. Maybe I left it at some store.

I seemed to have become the Absentminded
Professor with a specialty in Lost Things. First it was
my passkey to the gym, then it was the keys to our
house, now the money clip. Okay, the keys showed
up (in the *back* of the drawer) as did my passkey (in
my coat pocket—of course). But the money clip was
gone. I was sure of it.

I replayed every move I'd made in the past few
days, looking for some answer. "It'll show up,"
Carol said. But I doubted it. That felt like trusting
some godly advice when you *know* the worst has
happened. "Help Rick find his money clip," Carol

said at grace that night, almost as an aside. Of all impossible prayers.

Was it only the next day when I was doing the laundry and taking my pants out of the washing machine that I felt that lump in my front pocket? Yes, the eternally lost money clip and three damp twenties. "Laundering money," a friend of mine said wryly when I told him the story. Maybe just coming clean. Sometimes things *do* turn up. Sometimes the worst things you fear don't happen.

In the meantime, it doesn't hurt to add a prayer.

When I'm lost, Lord, let me be found.
—Rick Hamlin

Digging Deeper: 1 Samuel 9:20; Matthew 7:7

First Sunday of Advent, November 28

THE TRUE LIGHT THAT GIVES LIGHT
Making Room for Him in Our Hearts
Faith is the substance of things hoped for....
—Hebrews 11:1 (KJV)

"Oh, Mama," five-year-old Keri gushes as she dances into the kitchen, where I'm on my knees, scrubbing the floor. "I didn't know Pa and Bebe were coming!"

Equating housecleaning and grandparent visits as she does, her face is radiant with expectation.

On this first Sunday of Advent, I laugh as I relive that bygone moment.

Somebody's coming, I think. I smile as I unpack the crystal Advent wreath and place it in the middle of the table. I remember Keri's glow of anticipation, as I fit four tall candles around the circle and set the larger Christ candle in the middle.

In our family, we light a candle on each Sunday of Advent, and for us, the first candle represents expectation, the second peace, the third joy, and the fourth love.

This first candle takes us all the way back to Isaiah and the promise of the child who would come: the one called *wonderful.*

I think again of Keri's certainty that a clean house prepared the way for a visit from her beloved Bebe and Pa.

Our preparation for the Christmas season is not that different. Somewhere between too many parties and too much food, hours of shopping, and the laughter, the giving, and the receiving, surely we will find Him again. We hope to recognize Him in the eyes of those we meet—the weary salesperson, the harried mailman, the rushing shoppers. And we promise ourselves that we will remember to make room for Him at our table and most especially in our hearts.

Oh Father, Your greatest gift is at hand. Let us look past the complications and wait for Him with great expectation. —Pam Kidd

Digging Deeper: Proverbs 16:1; Isaiah 9:6;
Luke 2:10

Monday, November 29

Your word is a lamp to my feet and a light to my path. —Psalm 119:105 (ESV)

"Here you go!" my twenty-two-year-old son, John, said cheerfully, handing me a stack of hundred-dollar bills. Since he began working he has also begun paying me rent. He prefers to pay in cash, I think because it is concrete evidence he is contributing to the family. We both enjoy the monthly ritual.

This has been a long, long time coming. There were the years in which John's anxiety triggered rages, then the years when he was depressed and didn't leave the house except to walk the dog or go to therapy. There were long stretches of time when there seemed to be no path forward. Through those I learned that my inability to see how life could improve meant only one thing: that I couldn't see the way through.

Oddly, in retrospect, I can't see the path we took, either. I think that's because John's progress was so incremental, each step forward so infinitely small as to be almost unnoticeable. It may also have something to do with the fact that the "lamp to my feet" that lit my path was much like the handheld oil lamps of biblical times, casting only enough light to illuminate my next stumbling step.

Yet now my son is gainfully employed, a taxpaying citizen. He does not earn a lot, but he works hard and his boss likes him. Someday, I think, he will probably be able to afford his own apartment. I'm not worried about when that happens. There are those who might argue John "should" be doing X or Y or Z. For me, those "shoulds" don't matter: I've learned we can't move forward from where we wish we were. We can only move forward from where we are now.

Lord, let Your word illuminate my next step. And then the one after. And the one after that.
—Julia Attaway

Digging Deeper: Psalm 44:18

Tuesday, November 30

Men ought always to pray.... —Luke 18:1 (KJV)

As I thread my way through the early-morning traffic, the little robotic voice in my car's dashboard is telling me every turn to take and predicting the exact time I will arrive at my office.

Thanks to modern-day technology, I can simply request an address and the voice in the dash will give me exact directions to the place I want to go. If the traffic snarls or there's an accident ahead, the voice redirects me and guides me to another route.

Now, remembering the takeaway from last Sunday's sermon, "pray often and listen for God's response," I suddenly see this app in a new way. Or maybe I should say, in an ancient way.

Prayer, I know, is mentioned 132 times in the Bible. We are reminded over and over to pray, to talk to God, and then, just as importantly, to listen to how He answers.

How many cars, I wonder, in this morning traffic are equipped with those magical voices in the dashboard? And that's not considering the vast numbers of people across the world who don't own cars, or phones, or any of the crazy GPS apps so many of us depend on.

And yet we all have access to the greatest "direction giver" imaginable. In fact, I acknowledge, He is riding right beside me in this car, ready to guide me though my day.

I turn off the app. The robotic voice is silenced.

"Hey, God," I say out loud. "There's a long day ahead for me, people to help, decisions to make. I sure would appreciate your sticking with me through the day, pointing me in the wisest directions, and taking me exactly where you want me to go."

Father, hear my prayers, and take me where I'm supposed to go. —Brock Kidd

Digging Deeper: Psalm 55:17; James 5:16

JOYFUL IN HOPE

1 _____

2 _____

3 _____

4 _____

5 _____

6 _____

7 _____

8 _____

9 _____

10 _____

11 _____

12 _____

13 _____

14 _____

15 _____

16 _____

17 _____

18 _____

19 _____

20 _____

21 _____

22 _____

23 _____

24 _____

25 _____

26 _____

27 _____

28 _____

29 _____

30 _____

DECEMBER

He that dwelleth in the secret place
of the most High shall abide under
the shadow of the Almighty.

—Psalm 91:1 (KJV)

Wednesday, December 1

And he shall besiege thee in all thy gates, until thy high and fenced walls come down, wherein thou trustedst, throughout all thy land: and he shall besiege thee in all thy gates throughout all thy land, which the Lord thy God hath given thee.
—Deuteronomy 28:52 (KJV)

It is hard to trust God, to relax and go off duty.

All of us have challenges, but it is amazing that my friend Kimberly can still function. She is a competent, dependable person— ultra-competent, ultra-dependable.

She works full-time, and she is a newlywed; she struggles with the recent loss of her eldest daughter, and her surviving daughter is away in college. She often complains about all of her responsibilities and stress and feels overwhelmed. I can feel how tired she is. "Take a day or two each week and tell everyone you're off duty. You won't be Old Faithful for them on your days off." I say to myself, "*Let God step in.*"

She sighs in response, but I know her expression really says, "No way. I can't." I encourage/nag her some more, only to be met with more sighs.

As I recount this conversation to my daughter, Lanea, she says maybe I would be wise to take my own advice and institute my prescription for Kimberly in my own life.

Take days off? Tell my loved ones I'm not available? Lanea often asks me to look over some project that she is working on. And there are urgent family matters that need my attention. *What will happen if I let go?* I sigh. It is hard to go off duty, but I'm reminded of my conversation with Kimberly and decide it's time to let God step in.

Lord, I trust You. Thank You for overwhelming me, tearing my fences down, and teaching me to trust You. Let my trust not just be in word or thought, but in my heart and in my bones, and let it be my first instinct.
—Sharon Foster

Digging Deeper: Proverbs 3:5–6; Hebrews 4:12

Thursday, December 2

The Lord will fight for you, and you have only to be silent. —Exodus 14:14 (ESV)

I was at the airport and the line through security was over an hour and a half long.

You're feeling anxious for me just reading those words, aren't you? I'm sure you can imagine how I felt, standing there checking and rechecking my watch, knowing that my plane was taking off in twenty, ten, five minutes.

Well, spoiler alert: I missed my plane. I sprinted through the airport only to find that the plane had left ten minutes early. There wasn't even a gate agent there anymore for me to yell at.

So I did what any completely rational traveler would do at 5:45 a.m. after she missed her flight: I found the nearest gate and yelled at that agent.

Okay, so it wasn't my best moment.

But it certainly was one of his. He smiled and said, "I'm so sorry you're so frustrated. Why don't you head over across the hall and get yourself a cup of coffee and I'll figure this out for you?"

I stared at him. I had really unloaded on him, and he was saying he'd take care of it.

And so I did. Twenty minutes later, I returned with a double latte to find the gate agent standing with a new set of tickets in his hand. He had forwarded my bags, reprinted boarding passes, and gotten me to my destination at approximately the same time.

"Thank you." It was all I could manage. That and a teary handshake as I walked to my gate, realizing that he had fought what was certainly a treacherous battle for me. All I had to do was get a cup of coffee and trust him enough not to interfere.

Father God, help me to learn to sit back and trust instead of trying to force my own way.
—Erin MacPherson

Digging Deeper: Ephesians 6:10–18; James 4:7

Friday, December 3

LOSING JOHN: The Joy of Heaven
I will turn their mourning into joy....
—Jeremiah 31:13 (RSV)

We held the funeral a week after John's death. The family came from Florida and Oregon,

Tennessee and Maine and Georgia: children and grandchildren—even our eldest great-grandchild. How wonderful, friends said, that they could all be there, since flights were so hard to book in December. But they'd all made their reservations months before; this was the day we were to celebrate John's and my seventieth anniversary.

And indeed it was a celebration, as a funeral should be, an occasion to share favorite memories of "Papa John." It was snowing as we drove to the church that evening. Only the family, I thought, would venture out on a stormy Saturday night. It wasn't as if we were at the church in New York where we'd gone for fifty years; we'd lived here in Massachusetts only eight years. But John could not walk half a block without making a friend, and as we filed in from a door near the front, I saw that the church was full.

For me the most unforgettable moment came at the end of the service, when the congregation followed the acolytes bearing tall processional candles out into the falling snow and down the steps to the memorial garden. Father Tim cleared the snow from a little patch of earth, dug a small hole, and— as he'd done for how many others—poured John's ashes into the ground, a symbolic return to the soil from which God formed us.

That night, though, the disposal of physical remains seemed as unimportant as of course it is in the wondrous story of our redemption. In the darkness, a mantle of snow covering every bush and twig, sparks from the candles flying upward in the night sky, it seemed that the joy of heaven came very close.

Lord, John is rejoicing in Your kingdom and I am homesick to be there. —Elizabeth Sherrill

Digging Deeper: 1 Corinthians 2:9; Hebrews 13:14

Saturday, December 4

In him we have redemption through his blood, the forgiveness of sins, in accordance with the riches of God's grace. —Ephesians 1:7 (NIV)

The morning was still newborn. My son Logan was home, and he and I sat at the table while the rest of the family slumbered.

"Look at these, Mom," Logan said. He handed me the local newspaper. It was December, and there were letters to Santa from the early 1900s. We live in Iowa, and these children were from farm families—strong, persevering, good-souled people who broke the ground to break their bread.

"Santa, will you please bring me an orange?" one letter read. "My sister would like to have a picture book. Please remember me."

Logan and I read letter after letter. Once in a while, a child asked for something fanciful like a piano or an alligator, but most of the wants were meager. A hair ribbon. A kettle for Mama. A new coat. This raw simplicity made my chest tight.

"It's striking," I said, "that almost every letter ends with 'please remember me.'"

Logan nodded.

While I sipped coffee and watched the sky wake, I thought about this common cry of the human heart—of all who draw breath. Please remember me. Don't forget me. Don't abandon me, leave me out, or let me go unnoticed.

Oh, what a gift it is that God the Father did not!

Sin separated me from Him, but the Lord made a way for me. God Most High sent His Son, a flesh-and-bone, beating-heart, Savior-baby, because He would not, could not, forget or overlook me.

That morning at the table, Christmas just around the corner, I rejoiced. We don't have to worry and wonder like those children. We're remembered.

O Lord, You saw my sin and You were compassionate. Thank You, Father. Amen. —Shawnelle Eliasen

Digging Deeper: John 5:24; Acts 4:12

Second Sunday of Advent, December 5

THE TRUE LIGHT THAT GIVES LIGHT
Experiencing the Peace of Christ

And, lo, the star, which they saw in the east, went before them.... —Matthew 2:9 (KJV)

On this second Sunday of Advent, David and I are in our favorite early-morning spot in our living room, drinking coffee. "Guess it's about time for

T. S. Eliot," I say, handing him a book dog-eared for our annual read of Eliot's *Journey of the Magi*.

"'A cold coming we had of it...,'" he begins.

I sit back cupping my mug of hot coffee, following the long, difficult trek of these wealthy kings who, led by a star, ventured into an unknown and desolate land. How completely surprised they must have been to find God born in a stable, as a poor baby.

The birth of Jesus, one Magi lamented, was the death of his old life, as he returned to his palace where he was no longer at ease.

Let's be honest. The journey to Christmas is difficult for many of us. Beyond the work, there are sacrifices that we struggle to make, both financial and personal. Do I really have time to buy a coat for the poor child, or spend an entire day preparing a party for refugee families? Who can help me scrub the kitchen at the temporary homeless shelter?

Tonight we will light the peace candle on our Advent wreath. And hearing the poem, I know I don't want to end up like the Magi, longing for a different way. Instead, I want to meet the child where He is waiting... with the homeless, the needy, the stranger in a foreign land.

Join me on the journey. Sure, we'd rather stay in our comfort zone. We'd rather hang on to our money. We'd rather not get our hands dirty. But something precious, profound, and very real waits: the peace of Christ.

Father, point the way for each of us, to the place where we will find the Christ. —Pam Kidd

Digging Deeper: Matthew 2:1–12; 6:33

Monday, December 6

Turn away mine eyes from beholding vanity.
—Psalm 119:37 (KJV)

Well, I didn't exactly come here for a beauty makeover! I grumble, and steer away from the Department of Motor Vehicles, where I've just renewed my driver's license. Though I had groomed myself a bit more than usual, the photo is ghastly. In fact, I am so startled by the picture of the baggy-eyed woman with unkempt hair that when the clerk asks if the image is okay, I nod. I can't speak. Now I'm stuck with this frumpy photo for another five years.

I know, God. I know. I'm being very vain. On the scale of life's real tragedies, a bum photo doesn't even register. I know it's not important...just a minor disappointment. I'm being foolish. Yes, I can see with these eyes despite the eye bags. Yes, I have hair. Friends having chemo aren't so lucky. Right, the car still runs well and I'm competent enough to drive it....

And my friends and family still beam when they see this face. And all of it works: eyes, nose, mouth, ears. No paralysis. No cancer. All these wrinkles prove I've had plenty to smile about.... God, I'm sorry for complaining. Honest.

By the time I arrive home, I've hidden the offending photo in my purse and made peace, yet again, with God and my tendency toward vanity. Almost.

A few days later, a bank teller needs an ID for a transaction. She looks at my driver's license, looks at me, then says, "You know, you're a lot prettier than this photo!"

Lord, do I feel You winking at me?
—Gail Thorell Schilling

Digging Deeper: Psalm 4:2; Proverbs 30:8; Ecclesiastes 1:2

Tuesday, December 7

When Jesus then saw His mother, and the disciple whom He loved standing nearby, He said to His mother, "Woman, behold, your son!" Then He said to the disciple, "Behold, your mother!" From that hour the disciple took her into his own household. —John 19:26–27 (NASB)

My mother, Dorothy Walker, is ninety-eight years old and living in a nursing home near our house. She has had an interesting and challenging life. Shortly after World War II, she met and married a Colorado cowboy, Al Walker. The cowboy became a Baptist minister and my parents spent eight years as missionaries and teachers in the Philippines. When my father was forty-six years old, he died suddenly from a heart attack. Our family returned from the

Philippines to my mother's hometown in Georgia. Mother became an elementary-school teacher, struggling to raise my sister and me. Now, years later, we are faithfully trying to support our mother.

Mother is confined to her bed in a nursing home due to physical health and hip replacement surgery. She cannot walk, she is deaf and often confused, and dementia is encroaching. But through it all she is gentle, sweet, and cooperative. Life has a way of "reversing roles" between generation to generation. And I am trying to adapt to my new role.

This scenario is so true for most families, and it takes courage, faith, and strength to persevere. Jesus experienced this, too. On the day of His crucifixion at age thirty-three, Jesus asked the apostle John to take care of His mother. This was His final concern.

One of my mentors used to say that the challenge of adulthood is "adapting to life amid the inevitability of decline." He is correct. However, the journey is fulfilling and well worth the cost!

Father, may each generation be faithful to each other. Amen. —Scott Walker

Digging Deeper: Proverbs 23:22; Matthew 19:19

Wednesday, December 8

LOSING JOHN: Taking God's Hand
Where I am going, you cannot follow me now....
—John 13:36 (RSV)

For all my fantasizing about the moment of death, I'd never let my thoughts venture even a day further. There are many widows here in this retirement community, and each of us has handled bereavement in her own way.

Some tell me they got hyperactive, went back to work, volunteered for half a dozen causes. One friend who with her husband led a busy social life is now a near recluse. Another who spent years as her spouse's caretaker turned into a social butterfly.

My reaction was to run—from Portland, Oregon, to Miami, Florida, Washington, DC, to Buenos Aires, Argentina. At the end of that first year, I realized I'd been at a different airport every month. There were reasons for each trip, of course: a visit to far-flung family, a meeting, research for a story. But even as I walked down yet another boarding ramp, I knew I was mostly just running.

I thought at first that I was running away from that empty apartment, where never again would a deep voice call out to greet me as I came in. I was in Uruguay when I suddenly knew that no, I wasn't running *from* as much as *to*. I was traveling in a frenetic, mindless search for my husband. John and I had spent so much of our lives on the move. Even if we weren't living overseas, there were many years when we spent more than half the time away from home. Surely, my subconscious must have insisted, if I went far enough, fast enough, I would catch up with him!

And if I cannot overtake John on his current journey? When out of sheer exhaustion I slowed down enough to listen, I seemed to hear God ask if I was willing to take His hand and walk, not run, into this new stage of life.

Lord, Your pace is best for my faltering steps.
—Elizabeth Sherrill

Digging Deeper: Psalm 9:10; 46:10

Thursday, December 9

And behold, I am with you always, to the end of the age. —Matthew 28:20 (ESV)

It's late on a Thursday night. I feel exhausted. This week has worn me thin. I'm sitting at my kitchen table, spinning my cell phone on the tabletop.

I desperately want to call Rachel. To tell her how much I miss her. To hear just a few syllables of her voice. She used to answer on the first ring. Now I don't even know if she would pick up.

I struggled when Rachel and I decided to go our separate ways. Lately, I've been doing better. I'm finally healing. But sometimes, when I'm tired and empty, I start to look back. I pick at emotional stitches until my wound is red again.

I can think of several friends I could talk with right now. But I only want to talk with one person. Rachel understands me. She knows how I think and how I feel. But she's the one person I can't call.

I slide my phone across the table in frustration. It collides with a pile of books. My Bible is at the bottom. I haven't opened it this week. That strikes me as significant.

I'm mourning the loss of my best friend. My confidante. But I've pushed away the One who is always there for me. The One who will never stop listening. No wonder I feel empty inside.

I pull my Bible out from under the pile of books. A bookmark leads me back to where I left off. But before I start to read, I turn off my phone. Tonight, instead of miring in what I've lost, I'm moving toward what I can never lose.

Jesus, thank You for being a constant in my life.
—Logan Eliasen

Digging Deeper: Deuteronomy 31:6; Joshua 1:9;
Romans 8:38–39

Friday, December 10

Let the message of Christ dwell among you richly as you teach and admonish one another with all wisdom through psalms, hymns, and songs from the Spirit. —Colossians 3:16 (NIV)

Years ago I sadly set aside a book proposal for an inspirational compilation I'd titled *The Power of Song*. But this morning I think of pulling it out of the file, after recent encounters with a neighbor adolescent girl with special needs—and fears.

I've accompanied her, and her mom who struggles with English, to many medical appointments, few as foreboding as last week's root canal. Assurances of sedation—you'll be asleep—weren't tempering her terrors. Her mother held her hands. My grip on her ankles failed to control her frantic kicks. To calm her cries, I sang a soothing prayer we'd learned at vacation Bible school. A repeating petition, "Hear us as we pray," checked my own anxieties. When she finally quit fighting, I wept with relief. Others had taken notice. The song had piqued the interest of the anesthesiologist, whose turban designated a faith tradition different from mine. He asked who I was, why I was helping this family. "From their church?"

"A neighbor," I replied. "Like an extra grandmother."

Which seemed the case again last evening, when the phone rang at 8:55. It was the neighbor girl whispering a request I'd never heard from her. "I can't get to sleep. Will you sing me a lullaby?"—a word she knew only from storybooks. Yes. Quickly improvising, I turned the same prayer into a nighttime tune: "Give us sleepy hearts . . ." Then quietly a final "hear us as we pray." The song sufficed. Sleep tight.

I think I'll tweak the title of the book proposal. In this season of life, *The Gift of Song* seems more personal.

Giver of all good gifts, fill our hearts and voices with songs that strengthen me—and others.
—Evelyn Bence

Digging Deeper: Psalm 77:1–6

Saturday, December 11

"Martha, Martha," the Lord answered, "you are worried and upset about many things, but few things are needed.... Mary has chosen what is better." —Luke 10:41–42 (NIV)

My mind churned with my never-ending to-do list. At the very top was that insatiable chore called grocery shopping. Not thinking of the many souls who would love to have the means to buy a fraction of what I would purchase that day, I asked myself, "Didn't I just do this?" When would it ever end?

Coming dangerously close to resentment, I wondered, *Where is the rest God promised?* On that wintry morning, my endless scroll of duties—grocery shopping, phone calls, even mission work—seemingly defied what I longed for from God, but that same God quickly admonished me with a lesson I'd learned before. Chores went more smoothly when I was at peace. True rest rose and fell with my peace quotient.

Martha's complaint to Jesus about the domestic duties she carried while her sister, Mary, sat at His feet surfaced in my thoughts. "Upset by many things," Martha, too, needed that "better part" of rest called peace, "not as the world gives"—not that recliner, novel-reading rest I craved—but inner peace that causes us to count our blessings even as we fight supermarket-aisle traffic, the kind of rest that descended during the 2018 holidays when I crocheted caps for the homeless and ended each day of it feeling blessed, not spent.

The rest God promises has less to do with our physical bodies and more to do with His eternal love. Godly women both, Mary understood this while Martha was still learning. Yet no matter which sister we identify with, the key is listening to the Lord who reveals to us what is truly needed and what it takes to obtain rest.

Dear Savior, please sharpen my hearing toward the better part. —Jacqueline F. Wheelock

Digging Deeper: Matthew 11:28–29; Hebrews 4:9–11

Third Sunday of Advent, December 12

THE TRUE LIGHT THAT GIVES LIGHT
Receiving Christmas Joy
Many, O Lord my God, are thy wonderful works... they are more than can be numbered.
—Psalm 40:5 (KJV)

I'm out for an early walk on the third Sunday of Advent. Back home, the den is filled with Christmas cards that need to be addressed. There are boxes of wire ornaments waiting to be wrapped and sent to those who help with our Zimbabwe project. There's a pan of burned cookies on the kitchen counter and three piles of color-coded laundry.

I need a place to hide.

In the park, the day is cold and dark. Ahead the huge cedar tree is surrounded by a ring of dirty snow.

I'd like to cover the tree with tiny white lights to surprise those who pass by. Okay, it's an improbable fantasy, but it makes me smile.

As I get closer, the sweet smell of cedar surrounds me. I step up to the tree and spread its branches; it would be nice to crawl inside. A bunny scurries out, and a bird takes flight from a high limb.

Suddenly, I am struck with a revelation. This giant cedar is a God-sent sanctuary. Birds nest here, chipmunks burrow, squirrels curl in the branches. At night deer surely come here to snuggle close together and sleep.

Okay, I burned the cookies, and I'll be up half the night addressing cards, but I can't wait to get back home, to my own sanctuary. A place God, in His abundance, has given me. A place where I can find happiness in clean laundry and stamped cards and ornaments wrapped and ready to mail. Even the burned cookies, crumbled on the deck, will make some bird happy.

Tonight, as we light the Advent candle of joy, I'll be wondering how our house would look wrapped in twinkling lights.

Father, on our way to Bethlehem, remind us of the joy You scatter along the way. —Pam Kidd

Digging Deeper: Psalm 107:9; Isaiah 26:3

Monday, December 13

LOSING JOHN: Rich in Christ
This poor widow has put in more than all....
—Mark 12:43 (RSV)

A year after John died, I took the longest trip of all as part of a mission to South Africa. We visited schools and orphanages and churches and the prison where Nelson Mandela spent twenty-one years breaking rocks. We walked through ultramodern cities and vast "townships" without electricity or running water.

I turned out to be something of an attraction, with my walker and white hair. I learned that *How old are you?* was asked respectfully. When I answered that I was ninety-one, an awestruck little circle would form around me; life expectancy for most of these beautiful people is half that.

We witnessed what to me seemed hopeless problems of poverty. And what did we find wherever we went? Hope! A nation focused not on its needs, but on its strengths.

I saw a wonderful example at the Eternal Flame church. The congregation, as at other churches we visited, was black and "colored" and white— fellowship that under apartheid was illegal. For years they'd been struggling to raise money to move from a tent to a permanent structure. The Sunday we were there, the pastor and his wife had just returned from a mission trip of their own—to Sweden. I didn't think of Sweden as a particularly needy place, but apparently this congregation had been moved by the plight of Christians in that very secular country.

Sweden is also a wealthy country. While there, the pastor said, they'd been given a check for a great deal of money—more than enough to fund the church building that was still years out of reach with their own resources. But he'd handed the check back. "We were there to give, not take. We didn't want to focus on need when we're so rich in Christ!"

Father, I am rich in years. Show me how much I have to give. —Elizabeth Sherrill

Digging Deeper: Psalm 92:12–14; Proverbs 20:29

Tuesday, December 14

He will wipe away every tear from their eyes, and death shall be no more, neither shall there be mourning, nor crying, nor pain anymore, for the former things have passed away. —Revelation 21:4 (ESV)

From the kitchen, I heard Jacques say, "PawPaw, do you want to buy a rock?"

"Let me see," said PawPaw.

Over the course of PawPaw's last year, this was a common exchange between my four-year-old, Jacques, and PawPaw, which revolved around PawPaw's impressive rock collection from around the country; they often played "rock store." My heart always melted during these exchanges, because my own childhood was filled with the same memories. Inevitably, we always seemed to bring home a few rocks after each visit.

Not long after this exchange and on the sad day PawPaw died, I suggested to JoElla, my daughter, and Jacques they paint one of PawPaw's rocks to place in his casket. When I returned from work that day, I found an oval rock with two sides painted; one side had a very detectable nine-year-old rainbow, and the other side had a four-year-old abstract rainbow. I was surprised that both children chose to paint the symbol of God's fidelity and covenant, a rainbow. It was just a simple rock, but it exuded promise and hope.

As the rock was placed in my grandfather's hands for burial, I knew my children's gesture was without doubt the work of our Lord in their hearts. On a day marred in grief, sorrow, and tears, two little children brought the generosity, peace, and hope of the Lord's love and promise to a family who was grieving and struggling.

Lord of comfort, help us to recognize You in those around us—in their deeds, words, and love. Amen.
—Jolynda Strandberg

Digging Deeper: Lamentations 3:51;
Matthew 5:4; 2 Corinthians 7:10

Wednesday, December 15

Bear with each other and forgive one another if any of you has a grievance against someone. Forgive as the Lord forgave you. —Colossians 3:13 (NIV)

My feelings were hurt. A friend, at least I thought we were friends, deleted me from her friends list on Facebook. The only reason I could figure was that we didn't share the same political views. It seemed she felt I was no longer worthy to be her friend. That stung. I strive to be fair and unbiased, willing to listen to both sides and make my own judgments.

Wayne and I don't always agree on matters, either. My husband enjoys reading science fiction, and I prefer regency romances or historicals. This doesn't mean the end of our marriage. It's the same when it comes to choosing television programs. He likes viewing the more suspenseful dramas, while I tend to like documentaries and romantic comedies. Sure, books and television programs might be lower stakes than political convictions, but our mutual respect allows us to disagree on matters big and small.

As I mulled over my former friend's rejection, my pride snapped into place. I didn't need her as a friend anyway. I had plenty of people I preferred who were fair-minded. Then I thought about what Paul had written about doing our best to get along with everyone. Swallowing my natural tendency to write her off as well, I knew what I needed to do. I sent her a private message and apologized for anything I might have said that offended her. I didn't expect to hear back and was surprised when I did. We will probably never agree politically, but that's fine as long as we can respect each other's opinion.

Father, like in the prayer of St. Francis, let me be an instrument of Your peace. Where there is hatred, let me sow love. —Debbie Macomber

Digging Deeper: Ephesians 4:31–32

Thursday, December 16

Then He who sat on the throne said, "Behold, I make all things new." And He said to me, "Write, for these words are true and faithful."
—Revelation 21:5 (NKJV)

I was sipping coffee in the morning with my daughter, Josie, who was home from college. The world we saw was beautiful—verdant hills with trees waving in the gentle breeze. Birds chirping. A hummingbird flitting from flower to flower.

"Dad, do you remember the orange glow in the sky?"

I set down my mug and sighed. "I'll never forget it." She was not referring to a sunset or sunrise. She was referring to the beginnings of a wildland fire that swept through our town several years ago.

Fire season is a way of life in rugged Northern California. The orange glow had been there for over a week, and we thought nothing of it. There were miles of wilderness and hills and valleys between us and the fire. We'd seen over the years how the firefighting agencies were experts at keeping the fires out of towns like ours. But on the morning after Josie asked about that "orange glow," we were evacuated from our home, and would be out of it for almost a month. Thankfully, our home and those of our neighbors in our little valley were spared, but others were not. We returned to an intact home, a heartbroken community, and a blackened landscape.

Josie smiled as she scanned the beautiful field stretching into the distance behind our home. "I thought it would never come back, but it mostly did."

She was right. There were still scars, not only on the land but in our hearts, too. Yet our world was still beautiful. Our family was whole. Our home was a place of love. We'll never forget the heartbreak of living through a fire. But we know better than ever before that our God makes all things new.

Lord, I believe Your mercies are new every morning. Amen. —Bill Giovannetti

Digging Deeper: Lamentations 3:23

Friday, December 17

For we walk by faith, not by sight. —2 Corinthians 5:7 (NKJV)

"How do you like my office?" Allison asked. Surrounded by the freshness of a newly painted room, I said, "I like it a lot." I love blue, and the walls were a soothing shade of my favorite color. Allison and her husband are eye doctors. I was there to help with a business issue.

My eyes were quickly drawn to the words on a new wall hanging behind Allison's desk, For We Walk by Faith, Not by Sight. I especially liked how the words were arranged like an eye chart, with a very large font at the top progressing to smaller fonts on each subsequent line. I first wondered why she didn't choose Matthew 6:22, "The lamp of the body is the eye. If therefore your eye is good, your whole body will be full of light" (NKJV)—words that emphasize the importance of proper eye care. Then the deeper truth of 2 Corinthians 5:7 struck me. Think about how much of our lives we live in the darkness of the unknown—times when we are dealing with a career change, health issue, financial struggle, or relocation, times when even with perfect physical vision, we can't see the outcome.

As my wife, Pat, and I downsized to a smaller home this year, we faced many unknowns and unexpected developments. With each new encounter we did our best to make the right choice. We wouldn't know how it worked out until we began living with our choices. The words in Allison's office from 2 Corinthians 5:7 had inspired me to seek God's guidance in making each decision and leave the results to Him.

Dear God, thank You for being our eyes through stretches of life where human eyes are not enough. Teach us to surrender the outcome and trust that You are working for our good. Amen. —John Dilworth

Digging Deeper: Matthew 6:22–23;
Romans 8:24–25

Saturday, December 18

And in the same region there were shepherds out in the field, keeping watch over their flock by night.
—Luke 2:8 (ESV)

I was heading to church the day of the Christmas pageant. I had that sweet sense of anticipation, thinking of what fun it would be. It always is. Mary and Joseph, the baby in a manger, the kids dressed as shepherds and wise men and angels—some of them decked out in floppy ears with fluffy tails to take their roles as sheep, *baaing* their way down the center aisle.

I stepped onto the subway, glad to get a seat—there seemed to be several empty seats right around me. As soon as I sat down I realized why. The scruffy-looking homeless guy opposite me, hunched down beneath a black parka, a bag at his feet, and a certain stench coming my way. *Great,* I thought. *The perfect thing to kill my Christmas cheer.* I could have used a little frankincense and myrrh right then to sweeten the air.

Then I thought again of that first Christmas. What would the shepherds have looked like or smelled like? After all, they spent their days and nights watching sheep. How often did they get to bathe? They wouldn't have been dressed in fancy clothes. And yet they were the first, among the chosen few, to hear the good news, called to the baby's side. Like me. Like all of us.

The guy looked up from his hoodie and we exchanged a few glances. "Merry Christmas," I said. "God bless," he said. I gave him a buck before I got off the train.

This year's pageant was surely the best one ever... until next year.

Lord, there is a part for all of us to play in Your story. Shepherds, wise men, Mary, Joseph, we're all called to honor You. Show us how. —Rick Hamlin

Digging Deeper: Matthew 1:21; John 1:14

Fourth Sunday of Advent, December 19

THE TRUE LIGHT THAT GIVES LIGHT
Traveling in Love

For he shall give his angels charge over thee, to keep thee in all thy ways. —Psalm 91:11 (KJV)

I hold the cedar box in wonder on this fourth Sunday of Advent. It holds the story of another journey, one with all the Advent elements of expectation, peace, joy.

It's my mother's story.

It begins with a brilliant young girl with few opportunities. As a senior in high school she was a top student. As graduation neared, a furniture store in Chattanooga gave all the girls a small cedar chest as a promotional, to encourage parents to purchase large chests for their daughters. Except the free chest was my mother's only present.

The day after graduation, my mother caught a bus to town, to find a job. With boundless potential, she ended up behind the candy counter in F. W. Woolworth. She never complained. That's where she met my father. I smile, remembering my daddy singing, "I Found a Million Dollar Baby (in a Five and Ten Cent Store)."

They married, struggled, became successful, traveled, and lived a good life.

Until now, the little cedar chest has made me sad, thinking of the abundant life my mother gave me, when hers had been so difficult.

But there's something about lighting this candle of love, sometimes called the angel candle, that makes everything different tonight. I see a young girl boarding a city bus, with an unseen angel by her side. It was the first leg of a journey that took her around the world, to places she never imagined, and to a life that stretched beyond her dreams.

On this last Sunday of Advent, as we journey toward the Christ Child, let's travel in expectation, believing that a similar angel of love is ever by our side.

Father, embolden us with Your great love. —Pam Kidd

Digging Deeper: Isaiah 43:19; Luke 2:10; Philippians 3:13

Monday, December 20

But he said to me, "My grace is sufficient for you, for my power is made perfect in weakness." Therefore I will boast all the more gladly about my weaknesses, so that Christ's power may rest on me. —2 Corinthians 12:9 (NIV)

Picking up the frame from its place on my parents' bookshelf, I leaned in for a closer look. I remembered the taking of this picture. What a drama it had been, trying to get fourteen people, including a number of small children, assembled in one place, looking in the correct direction, with two open eyes and pleasant expressions on their faces. It hadn't gone exactly smoothly, but Mom had insisted it was the only thing she wanted for Christmas that year—a picture of the whole family gathered together for the holiday. So, for her, we'd powered through the chaos and gotten it done. This photo had been the best of the dozen we'd taken, and at the time, I remembered feeling disappointed by its imperfections.

Now, though—years later—it was specifically the photograph's quirks and flaws that drew my eyes and made my heart smile. Dad had been caught midword. "Cheese!" I recalled him saying just as the camera's self-timer flashed. My daughter, barely more than a toddler that Christmas, was turned sideways, attempting to entertain her baby cousin. My sister's eyes were closed. And my grandmother, who'd passed away a couple of years ago, was sitting in her chair, looking down at her hands, a serene smile on her face.

We'd thought we wanted a perfectly posed and polished holiday photo. What we'd gotten instead was an authentic snapshot of our clamorous, rollicking family, just as it really was. What could be more perfect than that?

Thank You, God, for the reminder that it is the authentic and vulnerable sharing of our inner hearts, our human quirks, flaws, and foibles, that opens the door for God's grace to shine through. —Erin Janoso

Digging Deeper: 1 Samuel 16:7; Psalm 139:1

Tuesday, December 21

LOSING JOHN: A Community of Caring
He will wipe away every tear from their eyes....
—Revelation 21:4 (RSV)

Condolence cards! Every time I returned from my restless roaming, they awaited me. I placed them, with their lovely depictions of flowers, birds, rainbows, on the too-bare surfaces: John's desk, his place at the breakfast table.

Friends' messages were helpful. Philip, who knew us well, wrote: "Losing John must feel more like an amputation than a death." And I understood better my feeling of not only grief, but brokenness.

Betsy knew I'd need these words of Dietrich Bonhoeffer: "It is nonsense to say that God fills the gap [left by a loss.] He keeps it empty so that the communion with another may be kept alive, even at the cost of pain." And I stopped wanting the heartache to cease.

Curiously, though, it was messages from strangers that meant the most. John and I were just names in print somewhere to these folks, yet they'd reached out to console someone they didn't know. It said to me that there is more goodwill—more love—in the world than we imagine.

As the months passed, fewer messages came. Time heals; Tib must be doing fine. Actually, as the anniversary of John's death approached, I was anything but fine. And then, wondrously, a new stream of condolences began! Because *Daily Guideposts 2017* was already in the mail by December, news of his passing wasn't reported there until the 2018 edition. Readers just learning about it sent their condolences. Long after the first outpouring of concern, I experienced the grace of renewed caring.

It's given me a new routine. When an acquaintance dies—a sadly frequent occurrence in this retirement community—I send a note. But then I mark the date on next year's calendar, when someone will be needing a little pen-and-paper hug.

Lord, today let me be part of Your boundless community of caring. —Elizabeth Sherrill

Digging Deeper: 2 Corinthians 1:3–4; Galatians 6:2

Wednesday, December 22

BECOMING JUST ME AGAIN
Spontaneous Joy
**Praise him with tambourine and dancing.
—Psalm 150:4 (NIV)**

The Christmas before Jack died, he was in a rehabilitation center in between hospital stays. This certainly wasn't the traditional Christmas celebration I'd come to expect over the years. There were no presents exchanged, no Christmas Eve Mass, no huge Christmas Eve party at Jack's son's house.

The only Christmasy event that day happened when a woman came into Jack's room with a Santa hat and a keyboard. She played a few Christmas songs and serenaded us with holiday gusto. But the best part was two technicians from the rehab staff who, when they walked past the lively keyboard music, grabbed on to each other and started dancing right there in the hallway. Karen and Shaun, who were wearing bright red scrubs for Christmas, lifted my heart and boosted my spirits so much that we three laughed over their spontaneous dancing antics every day for the rest of Jack's stay.

I began to wonder if I ever did anything spontaneous that brought joy to the hearts of those around me. The next Sunday I gave Sister Lucia a big hug when I saw her in the gathering space at our church. A few days later when I'd been swimming alone in our community pool early in the morning, I was so overjoyed to see my friend Lois show up that I jumped up and down in the pool, arms waving, yelling, "Yes! I was praying you'd show up!"

I may not be dancing in the hallways, but I can tell my more enthusiastic demeanor is making a hit with my friends.

Lord, encourage me to be more spontaneous and to show affection to those I love every day and in many ways. —Patricia Lorenz

Digging Deeper: 2 Samuel 6:12–15; Psalm 30:1–12

Thursday, December 23

So do not fear, for I am with you: do not be dismayed, for I am your God. I will strengthen you and help you: I will uphold you with my righteous right hand. —Isaiah 41:10 (NIV)

It was a few days before Christmas and I had a houseful of family and delicious Puerto Rican food. I lifted my phone out and over my head to take a selfie with my loved ones smiling in the background. My lips were painted red and my smile was full and bright. There was a sparkle in my eyes, and joy exuded from my face.

The next day, a memory popped up on my social media page. It was a picture of my sister and me eight years ago. My face was angled in the same direction as in my Christmas photo, and my hair was pulled back in my usual ponytail. But there was a clear difference in these two photographs. The one with my sister was a week after my husband and I had separated. This was the beginning of my journey as a single mom.

I placed the two images side by side. On the left, the weight of the world was so heavy on my face, not even my smile could disguise it. To the right, I was a woman full of light and life. I ached for this hollow person on the left, recalling so clearly her pain. Even now I wish I could go back and encourage her, tell her that she'll find joy once more, and that her heart will heal.

I want to let her know that although the process of grief is long and painful, it's completely worth it on the other side. I wish I could tell her that she's stronger than she thinks or feels, and she'll accomplish more than she's ever dreamed. And in her darkest moments, when all she wants to do is give up, I want to tell her to hold on! But that is something I can never do. All I can do is be grateful that she did.

Thank You, Lord, for giving me the inner strength to get through the storms, even when it seems like they will never end. —Karen Valentin

Digging Deeper: Psalm 46:1

Christmas Eve, Friday, December 24

THE TRUE LIGHT THAT GIVES LIGHT
Anticipating Your Greatest Gift
Neglect not the gift that is in thee....
—1 Timothy 4:14 (KJV)

Christmas Eve. We made it once again. Now, suddenly, I want time to stop. I want to fly back and feel the expectation of lighting the first Advent candle, and sit snuggled in the living room as David reads about the Magi. I want to lean my face into the scratchy cedar tree and then realize the blessing of my mother's long life.

Christmas Eve. It's come too soon.

Oh well, there's nothing to do now but pull my Santa hat from the top closet shelf and get ready to laugh. Our tradition is to open our gifts to each other on Christmas Eve. Santa comes later.

Brock and Keri and their giggling tribes will arrive shortly, unloading presents until there's a sea of bright boxes piled all around the tree. There will be much hurrying as we eat bowls of hot vegetable soup and devour homemade pimento cheese sandwiches.

And then the Santa hat! It was a splurge some years back, this red velvet hat with a foot-high bouncy, twirly thing, complete with a bell on the top.

When I don the hat, everyone knows it's time. I drag in my big red Santa bag, and peek inside. The room grows quiet.

"Now, what have we here?" I say.

I pull out a gift for each person. I've been working toward this moment for months. Saving up, searching the Internet, poring through catalogues, and walking the malls until I find the most perfect gift possible for each of the people I treasure.

Some, I know, call this conspicuous consumption. I call it love.

Father, thank You for creating me to laugh, for the delight I can take in giving gifts, for the joy and anticipation of Your ultimate gift! —Pam Kidd

Digging Deeper: Matthew 7:11; James 1:17

Christmas, Saturday, December 25

THE TRUE LIGHT THAT GIVES LIGHT
The Christ Child Is Born!
For unto you is born this day in the city of David a Saviour, which is Christ the Lord.
—Luke 2:11 (KJV)

On Christmas morning, I arise early. I turn on the ovens and set the cheese grits, the egg casseroles, and the sweet breads out on the counter. Then, in the quiet house, I light the middle candle on the Advent wreath and wait for the Christ.

I study the crèche, handmade in Zimbabwe. A stream of animals wait in line to see the baby. There's a donkey and a camel, sheep and goats. There's also a hippo, a lion, a warthog, a giraffe, a leopard, and a rhino.

A baby destined to be the most important religious figure this world has ever known. Buddhism calls Him enlightened, Hinduism calls Him the Incarnation of God, Islam considers Him a true prophet of God, and the Jewish faith considers Him a great teacher. We call Him the Son of God.

Later, we welcome guests of different races and religions into our home on this holiest morning. David reads the Christmas story as we gather at the table. Sure, it means varying things to each person gathered there. But together we are like the improbable hoard of animals waiting for a glimpse of a Zimbabwean crèche. Even though we are all very different, we find ourselves in a simple place, where each heart humbly longs for love.

Now I pass the cheese grits around the table, and then the eggs. I see people laughing, trading stories, getting to know each other. I look deeply, really deeply, into the eyes of each person I serve, and for one moment a radiant light bursts around me, and I stand at the manger and smell the hay.

Father, unrecognized at first, You come. —Pam Kidd

Digging Deeper: Isaiah 40:5; Luke 2:13–14

Sunday, December 26

Cast all your anxiety on him because he cares for you. —1 Peter 5:7 (NIV)

God knew what I needed when he sent me Beau. Since he was born, Beau has been even-tempered, quick to good humor, and (thank you, Jesus) a good sleeper. So it surprised me when he was eighteen months old and bedtime shifted from a sweet snuggle, prayer, and song to an hour-long cry fest.

New teeth weren't the culprit; neither were tummy troubles, pj mishaps, or diaper maladies. He wasn't even mad so much as sad.

One night, we rocked and snuggled, and then Beau pointed to his bed. Once tucked in, he pointed to his rocker and I had the most vivid flashback to James at his age saying, "Sit, sit."

"Do you want me to sit in the chair, buddy?" I asked. "Yah," he said, grabbing his blanket and rolling onto his tummy.

He peeked over his shoulder a few times to be sure I was in the chair, and each time I'd reassure him, saying, "I'm still here, buddy. You can go to sleep."

Soon enough, he was snoozing soundly, snoring his awesome baby snore that both makes my mama heart soar and reminds me that he's probably going to need his tonsils out someday.

But we're not borrowing trouble tonight. Tonight, I'm going to sit and be his safe space so that he can drift off to sleep. While he dozes, I sing him songs, pray over his growing hands and feet, and remind him that he's never really alone. Even when Mommy goes downstairs, he's got Jesus with him, sitting in that same rocker, all night long.

Jesus, when anxiety creeps into my heart, allow me to find comfort in the folds of Your love.
—Ashley Kappel

Digging Deeper: 2 Corinthians 1:3–4; Colossians 3:15

Monday, December 27

"The heart of man plans his way, but the Lord establishes his steps." —Proverbs 16:9 (ESV)

I often pray for the future readers of a Daily Guideposts post as I write it.

So right now I'm praying for you. Praying that the words I write will resonate with you right now, in the place where you are, and in the way that you need it.

The amazing thing is that God, in His omnipotence, answers this prayer.

A few years ago, I got a letter from a reader who told me that a story I shared about kids being mean to my daughter had shown up on her bedside table on the exact day when she faced a similar situation.

Another time, a reader wrote me to tell me how my stories about my youngest son reminded her of her own son John. She told me about how John had grown into a man after God's own heart, a father of six who pastored a church. (I'm sure you can imagine how reassuring it was for me to hear that even the most rough-and-tumble kids grow up into men and women of God.)

And just last year when my grandmother was struggling in her dying days, every single time I opened up my *Daily Guideposts*, I read something that seemed to speak to me exactly where I was at that moment.

It's mind-boggling to think about how God is working right now to establish my steps, so that in time, He can reveal to you how He established yours. I can't fathom it, but I do treasure it. I treasure the fact that today, right now, you will read these words that I wrote months ago and know that God has plans for you today.

I pray that today is wonderful.

Father, thank You for establishing Your plan for my life long ago. Help me to follow Your will today. Amen. —Erin MacPherson

Digging Deeper: Jeremiah 29:11, Esther 4:14

Tuesday, December 28

LOSING JOHN: Held Safe by God's Love
A father to the fatherless, a defender of widows, is God in his holy dwelling. —Psalm 68:5 (NIV)

My challenges as a widow were minor compared with a younger woman's. My mother was fifty-three when my father died, and remained a widow for thirty years. Our daughter, Liz, was fifty-four when her first husband passed away. I have a friend who lost her husband when they were both twenty-four. John's death at ninety-four was not a tragedy like theirs, but a normal, natural occurrence. To lose a husband in one's own old age, however, poses a special set of problems.

Six months after John died, the macular degeneration I'd been battling made my eyesight so poor that I made the ever-dreaded decision to stop driving. Along with the loss of independence comes a shift in relationships from giver to receiver, endlessly thanking the thoughtful friends for whom it's "no trouble at all" to transport me to church, to the dry cleaner, to the supermarket. Of course it's trouble! Especially since my bulky walker has to go in the trunk (and then where do the groceries go?).

Worse was to come, when a year later my "better" eye failed, too, leaving me groping through a formless, gray world, unable to recognize faces, read, or write except in gigantic letters on my word processor. Bizarrely, ridiculously, I've reacted by being angry—at John. Doesn't he know how frightened I am? Doesn't he realize how I count on him? Why in this crisis has he abandoned me?

I'm told that it's not unusual to feel anger at a partner who's missing when needed most. I also know that when I confessed the anger to God, He gave me words to cling to: *I am holding you in My arms, as I am holding John: safe, protected, beloved, now and forever.*

As the outer world grows dark, Lord, grant me the
inner light to see more clearly Your love for us both.
—Elizabeth Sherrill

Digging Deeper: Psalm 32:7, 91:1–2

Wednesday, December 29

**Neither shall they say, Lo here! or, lo there! for,
behold, the kingdom of God is within you.**
—Luke 17:21 (KJV)

Two weeks, and my scarf was still missing. Punctured
with holes the size of a pencil eraser, it was a favorite
I had clung to for years. It had become a Linus
blanket for me, so I plundered my bedroom until
one day, among all the other articles of like size and
color, I found it—right where it had always been.

Sometimes we overlook the God working inside
us in favor of talented spiritual singers or inspiring
speakers at large rallies or experienced mission
workers come to share, all of whom are often
worthy. But in Luke 17, the Lord says, "Behold, the
kingdom of God is within you." Each smile at the
gas pump at the end of a trying day, each hospital
visit and hug, every gift ushered forth from a steady
committed heart is a picture of the kingdom that lies
within believers. If we follow Jesus's teachings, we
need look no further for the kingdom than what we
carry inside. Everywhere, all the time.

Frantic to find that old scarf, I'd been looking for
what was in plain sight. Problem was, my focus was

skewed. Only when I retraced the steps of my search did I find that cherished piece of cloth lying where it had always been.

What if today we all used what is within us to magnify our God? What a glorious impact we could leverage! And perhaps, as we humbly refocus, our spiritual chests would expand a bit as mine did at the discovery of my scarf in plain sight.

Thank You, Lord, for the treasure You have placed within. Help me never to overlook it.
—Jacqueline F. Wheelock

Digging Deeper: John 14:17; 1 John 4:4

Thursday, December 30

Your love, Lord, reaches to the heavens, your faithfulness to the skies. —Psalm 36:5 (NIV)

For decades I've valued the friendship of a poet who lives in the city but writes nostalgically about country living. A few years ago she gave me a three-dimensional eighteen-pointed star that encases a small lightbulb. Its shiny Mexican tin is punched with myriad decorative holes that leak light. In the daytime, it blends in with my living room décor. Before going to bed some evenings, I turn off the large lamps and let the starlight speak. Settle in. Quiet down. God is faithful. God is here.

I also live in—and love—the city. But sometimes I'm a little homesick for open spaces, including the nocturnal grandeur I remember from childhood, when my family vacationed at a rural church campground. On clear nights, we kids slept on army cots set up on the ballfield. Someone pointed out the North Star, the Dippers, Ursa Major—Big Bear. In the thousand points of light were we looking for God? For a divine message? Longfellow called stars "the forget-me-nots of the angels."

Last week I closed up my house, preparing to drive to the countryside for a few days. I anticipated a nighttime recap, gazing at the heavens. But the skies remained cloudy, and I returned home disappointed, that is, until I saw the tin star, which I'd forgotten to unplug. My friend's gift spoke for the grand Maker of heaven and earth: *God is faithful. God is here. Welcome home.*

God, Creator and Sustainer, thank You for signs and symbols that assure me of Your steadfast love.
—Evelyn Bence

Digging Deeper: Psalm 136; John 8:12

New Year's Eve, Friday, December 31

I am the Alpha and the Omega, the First and the Last, the Beginning and the End.
—**Revelation 22:13** (NIV)

I'm sipping my first cup of coffee on the last day of the year. It's still dark, and I nudge the curtain to catch the first glimpse of light. It's an odd personal tradition, a secret I've kept until now—to watch the sunrise on both the last day and first day of the year.

My ritual started eighteen years ago. I was pregnant with my oldest and had been up early that New Year's Eve morning quite by accident. I was struck by the beauty of the sunrise when it occurred to me that this might be a wonderful way to commemorate this special time. I knew I'd be too tired to stay up to midnight, so I thought, *I may not see the ball drop, but I'll watch it rise!*

The Japanese have a word that means welcoming the first sunrise of the new year, *hatsuhinode.* I zipper my winter coat over my bathrobe, find my favorite hat and knitted mittens, and go to our side porch, which faces east.

The first hint of light gives shape to the darkness. From the sheer silence, it seems I am the only one awake. Perfect. Just God and me, and I'm taken by the mystery of it all—the passage of time and the challenges and blessings that will unfold in the days to come. My thoughts shift to loved ones. I pray for good fortune and health and then I let go of thinking. I lose myself in the holiness of the moment, the Alpha and the Omega, the First and the Last, the grace of God shining right now.

Heavenly Father, You are the beginning and the end, the Light of my life. I trust You with my days and I praise You for Your glory. —Sabra Ciancanelli

Digging Deeper: 2 Corinthians 5:17; Jeremiah 29:11

JOYFUL IN HOPE

1 _____

2 _____

3 _____

4 _____

5 _____

6 _____

7 _____

8 _____

9 _____

10 _____

11 _____

12 _____

13 _____

14 _____

15 _____

16 _____

17 _____

18 _____

19 _____

20 _____

21 _____

22 _____

23 _____

24 _____

25 _____

26 _____

27 _____

28 _____

29 _____

30 _____

31 _____

FELLOWSHIP CORNER

 **Marci Alborghetti** and her husband, Charlie, are doing less traveling and sticking closer to home this year as they are both enjoying God's many blessings, including a wonderful new apartment that looks out over the Thames River and onto Long Island Sound and fun times with their godsons; they are also dealing with health and financial challenges. In other words, as Marci says, "Life!" She is learning more about what it means to be faithful in prayer "just about every day. I have discovered that if I focus only on asking the Lord to help with the challenges, I can easily forget about all He has already done for us, and that is a long and gratifying list. I feel that He is also leading me more into prayer time that is quiet and even restful for me, more like a time of refuge and respite. And that's been both a revelation and a gift!"

 "This has been a better year for my family," writes **Julia Attaway** of New York City. With her two youngest children in high school and her husband, Andrew, auditing college classes, Julia is enjoying the "solitude" of taking the subway to a new job, walking through Central Park,

and using a different part of her brain. "I have no way of knowing if our woes are gone for good or just for now," Julia admits, "so I focus on being thankful each and every day we have stability."

"I've enjoyed a quiet year, generally close to home in northern Virginia," writes **Evelyn Bence.** "My small church community is vital to my spiritual growth. In concern for neighbors, family, friends, and woes of the wider world, I more intently turn to prayer, asking for—and grateful for—guidance and strength, mercy and grace. I'm also trying to memorize a few favorite hymns, most recently 'Surely It Is God Who Saves Me,' based on lines from Isaiah 12. I host occasional dinner parties, welcoming guests to my table."

Even as **Erika Bentsen** of Sprague River, Oregon, was writing this year's series about losing her father, her father-in-law also passed away. "My husband went up to be with his family and spent the final day with his dad." Seeing the power of Christ's salvation at her dad's bedside brought a changed perspective of this world. "I put too much value on meaningless things that perish. I saw real wealth—Dad being personally welcomed to heaven by Christ Himself." That moment will never leave her for the rest of her life. "Jesus was with us through it all. Heaven really is real." Erika's sadness is tempered with a lifelong game she played with her dad. "I folded laundry as a kid. Dad found dryer sheets in his socks and thought I'd done it on purpose, so he hid dryer sheets in my lunch box." The game went on for years. "I thought I'd won when I put a dryer sheet into his pocket after he passed away, but I was wrong." Ever since then she has been finding a ridiculous amount of dryer sheets in her clothes. "I'm finding them in the oddest places. When one turns up I say, 'I love you, too, Dad.'"

"I've learned that excitement is highly overrated," says **Rhoda Blecker.** "This has been a year where all the heightened emotion was not welcome. I know that at my age you experience losses, but it would be better if they didn't come in bunches. I have blessed the quiet times, when there is music and reading and going to movies with a friend.

"Dog Halle and cat L. E. are healthy, and I stay busy serving on six committees at the synagogue, teaching classes at the community college, walking with spiritual directees, and editing some very good manuscripts. Those are the kinds of challenges I welcome.

"I am grateful for the blessings of every day—friends, work, the birdsong that comes in from the feeders and the tangles of blackberry bushes, my supportive synagogue community, and the wild bunny who visits the backyard every day, much to Halle's delight."

 **Sabra Ciancanelli** of Tivoli, New York, says, "Some days I look at my sons—now taller than me—and wonder, where did the time go? How on earth did they grow so fast? Maybe that longing explains why I recently made the decision to get two rescue kittens, adorable orange tabbies, one long haired, one short, siblings that came all the way from a shelter in Georgia. Thank heaven our dog and other cats are working through the kinks of having energetic fur babies zooming around our house. For now, our new additions to the family, Nova and Gillie, have reminded me of the joy I feel when I open my heart and home to love."

 **Desiree Cole** of Olathe, Kansas, shares, "I started walking on the road less traveled with Jesus a few years ago, and I've never been able to return to anything ordinary after that." Desiree

is on a passionate pursuit for God's heart. The longing began when she lived in New York City and worked as an in-house writer and editor for many publications, including *Guideposts*. Since then, she relocated back home to Kansas to be closer to family.

Blessed with the spiritual gift of prophecy, she uses words to reach into places in the heart that we often feel but many can't describe. As she leans more into her prophetic gifting, she also is on a search to find the bigger dreams Jesus believes we are meant to live outside of the ordinary life. Desiree lives with her husband, Zachary, son, Oliver, and their golden retriever, Charlie Brown. "I don't always know what He has in mind, but I've always believed He's good."

"Here's a sure sign of aging," says **Mark Collins** of Pittsburgh, Pennsylvania. "I added tiny electronic tags to my keys, my wallet, and my glasses. If I lose one, I can find it through an app on my phone. Problem is, I can't find my phone." Mark admits his crooked route through the last few years has meant other losses, too—including, briefly, his faith. ("I lost my faith the old-fashioned way—the traditional mixture of hubris, self-pity, and self-importance.") His journey back was helped immensely by the steady stream of notes and prayers he received from *Guideposts*

readers. "You will never know what a difference you made in this pilgrim's journey. I'm sorry I couldn't respond to every note I received, but I treasure them all. What a holy, wholly generous gift."

Pablo Diaz writes, "This year, my wife, Elba, and I will celebrate our fortieth wedding anniversary. It seems like it was just a few years ago that we met at a youth retreat in upstate New York. Over the past thirty-nine years, Elba's partnership, love, and companionship have greatly enriched my life. God's faithful presence has sustained us through this amazing journey, providing a safe shelter during life's storms. We plan to celebrate this milestone with family and friends, who have surrounded us with prayer and love. Our prayer is that God will grant us the health, strength, and energy to continue to be there for our family and friends, and always be available to serve others."

Several of **John Dilworth's** devotions mention some aspect of moving. "Moving became a big part of my life this year," he says, "because my wife, Pat, and I decided, after twenty-five years, to downsize from the two-story home we loved to a more efficient one-level home for the years ahead. Deciding, signing, building, decluttering, selling, buying, packing, moving, and unpacking turned into a ten-month process. Although quite time-consuming, the process went amazingly smooth—our new home was ready a month early and our existing home sold within a day.

"We thanked God daily for guiding and helping us complete the day's projects. We were blessed with people throughout the undertaking who helped smooth our way and even made the experience mostly fun! Just as we were doing the final decluttering pass-through of our house, our pastors did a sermon series on decluttering our spiritual lives. What we learned in one certainly helps with the other!"

 **Amy Eddings** is a writer and a journalist. She is the local anchor of NPR's "Morning Edition" on 90.3 WCPN in Cleveland. "The work is exciting; the hours, not so much," she says. She grew up in the Cleveland area and is getting to know the city as an adult with a driver's license and a car. She and her husband, Mark, live in an apartment in a converted warehouse in downtown Cleveland.

"This year has been an exciting one," says **Logan Eliasen.** "I took and passed the bar exam. I moved across Iowa. I started my first job as an attorney. And through each of these changes, I've learned to more fully trust in the Lord. I've claimed His promises and relied on His faithfulness. And He has shown Himself to be worthy of my trust. I can't wait to see what He has planned next."

"The past year brought many changes for our family," says **Shawnelle Eliasen** of LeClaire, Iowa. "The sweetest of which was healing. We've experienced rich, deep healing in our relationships, and from it comes the deepest kind of joy." Shawnelle, her husband, Lonny, and four of their sons moved across the Mississippi River to be closer to the school the boys will attend as high school students. "We experienced weeks of subzero temperatures and seemingly endless snow in the Midwest this winter. Everything was closed or canceled. Our family spent many winter days together in our new home—in closer, cozy quarters. We're used to a home built in the 1800s where the wind blows inside! This was our first warm winter, and I'll hold the days we shared as treasure. God heard our prayers and met us with love and grace."

 **Sharon Foster** is working on a new book and grateful that the Lord keeps her family in His hands. Sharon says they talk and pray together, regularly.

"The last few summers," Sharon writes, "my son, Chase, has been in Nome, Alaska, learning to dive in the Bering Sea, a long way from the opera career he has studied for. But recently Chase made his debut at the Metropolitan Opera in New York City. What a gift God has given him, and what a blessing that He keeps opening doors for Chase to use his gift.

"It is the same with my daughter, Lanea, who uses her gift of administration to help others—often the poor and homeless, though now she's helping police departments work with issues of racial equity; she has so much compassion for them.

"When I am tempted to give up, Lanea and Chase inspire me, so I am writing almost every day. They are reminders of God's faithfulness to me."

 With two kids now in college and the growing Pathway Church to pastor, **Bill Giovannetti** continually finds joy in the little things with his wife, Margi. He's gotten back into bass fishing with a friend across the street, and he's playing tennis with people half his age. Bill is excited

that his discipleship course, called the Grace Pathway, is blessing ministries across the country. He is also privileged to speak at numerous events each year. You can keep in touch with Bill on social media and at his website, www.MaxGrace.com.

"Last year I wrote about my brother's recent kidney transplant," says **Edward Grinnan** of New York City. "What a joy it is to tell you that he is doing fine and requires no more treatment. Julee's lupus has improved enough for her to have long-delayed back surgery. Two big prayer requests answered!"

As for golden retriever Gracie? "As you can tell from my devotions, she is an endless source of interest, inspiration, and comfort—and occasionally exasperation. The lessons we learn from each other!"

Edward is Editor-in-Chief of *Guideposts* and Vice President of Guideposts Publications. "My work today is focused on helping *Guideposts* prepare for the future and keeping it relevant to the national conversation with content that speaks to people in their daily struggles and triumphs. That is what Dr. Peale intended when he founded the organization seventy-six years ago."

Edward is currently working on a book about Alzheimer's and the toll the brain disease has taken on generations of his family. He has written two previous books, *The Promise of Hope* and *Always By My Side: Life Lessons from Millie and All the Dogs I've Loved*. Both books are available from Guideposts.

 "Every year life changes in countless ways, and every year some things stay the same," **Rick Hamlin** says. He still prays on the subway train on his way to work, he still works for *Guideposts*, he is still married to his writer wife, Carol Wallace (whose book *To Marry an English Lord* was the inspiration for the TV series Downton Abbey), and they both still sing in their church choir. But now he has two married sons, and the younger one, Tim, recently moved back to the East Coast with his wife, Henle, to attend seminary; the older one, William, lives and works in San Francisco. If they want to reminisce about their childhood he tells them to look at back copies of *Daily Guideposts*. He's still looking ahead.

 **Lynne Hartke** has spent more than three decades exploring desert trails with her husband, Kevin, and rust-colored mutt Mollie, encountering the beauty found in barren places, a beauty enjoyed by the couple's four grown children

and four grandchildren. A pastor's wife and breast cancer survivor, Lynne receives inspiration from other survivors at the cancer organizations where she volunteers. She is the author of *Under a Desert Sky: Redefining Hope, Beauty, and Faith in the Hardest Places*. Connect with her at www.lynnehartke.com.

"This year has been one of embracing change and growth," says **Carla Hendricks** of Franklin, Tennessee. As the wife and mom of four celebrated four family graduations this year, including her oldest son's college graduation, she has experienced the bittersweet emotions of her children growing up. After eighteen years of PTO meetings, back-to-school bashes, and holiday parties at her kids' elementary school, she felt a rush of nostalgia during her baby girl's elementary school graduation. At the same time, she and her husband, Anthony, are enjoying her children's increased independence and the physical, emotional, and spiritual growth that has become more evident each year.

Kim Taylor Henry writes, "The ache of the loss of our exuberant, faithful Aussie, Montana. The excitement of the engagement of our daughter Rachel to her wonderful boyfriend, David. The joy of the birth of our sixth grandchild, fourth granddaughter, Charley Makenna Jones, to daughter Lauren and son-in-law Chris. The adventure of a month in Australia. The blessing of time spent with family. The gratitude for readers joining me in the journey of my book, *Making God Smile, Living the Fruit of the Spirit One Day at a Time*. The grace of our loving God through it all. It was quite a year! Please visit me at www.KimTaylorHenry.com."

 **Leanne Jackson** of Fishers, Indiana, echoes Patricia Lorenz that "Life is short, let's do it now." "My husband Dave's retirement threatened to be overshadowed by his diagnosis of pancreatic cancer. It turned out to be the chronic kind (who knew?). We plan around Dave's monthly injections, and brace for his random, exhausting pain attacks that send him to the couch for a few hours. But we toured Scandinavia with our church choir; he rested in the bus when the pain hit. He biked the Empire State Ride, twice, to support cancer research; he found unexpected support from the other riders. To feed his soul, he regularly plays violin and volunteers at the cancer center.

"I manage our new, large binder called Medical Expenses. I wait anxiously with Dave after each CT scan, exhaling when the oncologist announces 'stable.' But every single day I 'do it now'—at least one activity that feeds my soul—pray with a friend, dig in the garden, text our grown daughters, inhale the sunset. And I savor every blessing that comes my way, including writing for *Daily Guideposts*."

"Last year," says **Erin Janoso,** "my husband, Jim, daughter, Aurora (six), and I split time between two places: Fairbanks, Alaska—our winter home— and Roundup, Montana—where we've been spending our summers. Our south/north migrations are opposite those of many creatures, but we've found it's what works best for our little microscope sales and service company. Plus, it's nice being able to grow tomatoes and peppers outside, something that's easier to do in Montana than in Fairbanks.

"This year has been a rich one, full of travel, deepening relationships with new friends, and fresh adventures—such as homeschool kindergarten. I've also been able to continue to work on both my writing and my trumpet in both places. It all leaves me feeling so very grateful."

Ashley Kappel lives in Alabama with her husband, three kids, and golden retriever rescue. This year has been a blur of dance recitals, dinosaur museums, and baby milestones, and she's savoring every minute. She asks your prayers that God renews her patience and strength daily as she mothers three adorable souls and continues her own walk with Jesus.

This past year, **Brock Kidd** and his wife, Corinne, took all four kids on an adventure to Spain. "When I say adventure, I'm referring to the wonderful country that Spain is, as well as having four of my children ranging in age from twenty down to three in tow! While we enjoyed the architecture, food, and festive culture, it was the diverse religious history around Madrid, Seville, and Barcelona that reminded us of the importance of accepting others who may not agree with exactly everything we believe." Brock reports, "Jesus's greatest commandment of love must stay front of mind in these times of divisiveness."

In addition to a great summer vacation, Brock and Corinne continue to work with the Martha O'Bryan Center, which is Nashville's second oldest nonprofit serving Nashville's "least of these."

A few years back, a powerful fad took root in England. People wore simple safety pins to tell those being discriminated against, "I am a safe place." **Pam Kidd** writes, "I took to the idea and still sport safety pins on most of my clothes. Occasionally, people come up and thank me, but most have no idea what the pin means. But I do. It reminds me daily that a bit of God travels within me, so how can I not stand strong for those who are vulnerable, how can I not spread kindness and reach out to those in need?

"On the home front, I try to remember to look deep into my husband David's eyes each day. It makes me happy to see God there, looking back. I try to laugh over spilt milk, listen carefully to what our grandchildren say, and take joy in children Brock's and Keri's lives. I hope that David and I, hand in hand, can always be their safe place—and if they look very closely into our eyes, they might see a bit of God looking back."

 There were lots of developments in **Patty Kirk's** life this year. Her husband, Kris, survived a heart attack and quadruple bypass surgery. They got a silver Labrahound puppy named Karl, who keeps their beagle, Sawyer, company. Daughter Charlotte completed her PhD in chemical engineering and became a data scientist for an online craft store, a first step toward her career dream of owning a yarn store. She also got engaged and plans a "destination wedding" at a ski resort. Charl will

wear a home-sewn wedding dress, guests will wear flannel shirts "or whatever," and the reception will feature ordered-in pizza and cupcakes. Daughter Lulu passed her qualifying exams and is now at work on a dissertation about medieval translations from Latin into German vernaculars and vice versa. Patty got a point-and-shoot digital camera for Christmas to take with her on her birding jogs and has begun amazing herself and followers with her regular #birdoftheday pics on Instagram.

In sad news, Patty's newfound love, the Oklahoma Thunder, lost star players Russell Westbrook and Paul George to enemy teams, so her first foray into sports fandom may be ending after one thrilling season, alas.

 "I have a raggedy strip of crocheting—a prayer scarf—I keep near," says **Carol Knapp**. "I tell my grandchildren, 'All my prayers are in that.' Corrie Ten Boom said, 'The wonderful thing about praying is you leave a world of not being able to do something and enter God's realm where everything is possible. This is why every Tuesday I write a family 'Pray Day' email. We rely on the 'realm of the possible.'"

Carol and her husband, Terry, continue to love life on the mountain in Idaho. "Between a road trip to Phoenix, a train trip to Minneapolis, and a plane ride to Anchorage, we've covered the bases—seeing our four children and twenty grands. A number we couldn't envision on our wedding day fifty years ago!"

 **Carol Kuykendall** writes, "We're entering a family milestone this year as our oldest grand-girl begins her senior year in high school and our youngest enters first grade. The reality emphasizes the message of my revised book released last year, *Give Them Wings,* so we are making the most of opportunities to get ten cousins together while we still can. Lynn and I are also busy attending the grandkids' school performances and sporting events, while recognizing the blessing of being close enough to do so.

"In other news, I visited the Mexico–Texas border with a group of evangelical women so I can understand the needs of immigrant families. At home, Zeke, the golden retriever puppy we got last year, recently celebrated his first birthday, which we hope means less chewing our shoes and more coming when called. I'm still actively involved in MOPS as a mentor at our church, and also part of an active prayer team, learning to be faithful in prayer by praying for people on Sundays after church."

Vicki Kuyper has been a freelance writer for over thiry years, having written over fifty books, including *Wonderlust: A Spiritual Travelogue for the Adventurous Soul* and *A Tale of Two Biddies (A New Wrinkle on Aging with Grace).* She's also written countless greeting cards, devotions, crossword puzzles, video scripts, book reviews, and one sheep pun calendar. Vicki committed her life to Christ at the age of eighteen at a Young Life camp. Since then, she's discovered that the closer she draws to God, the bigger she realizes He is, and the less about Him she fully understands. Thankfully, this doesn't make her nervous—just more curious.

Although Vicki calls Colorado Springs, Colorado, home, she's just as likely to be found in some remote corner of the world, hiking, taking photos, and exploring God's glorious gallery of creation. In between writing, travel, and playing peek-a-boo with her four amazing grandchildren, she'd love to connect with you at www.vickikuyper.net or on Facebook at vickikuyper@1wittybiddy.

Living the single life in her seventies is not what **Patricia Lorenz** had in mind when she married Jack in her sixties. "But when he died in 2019," she says, "I remembered what he told me when we first started dating in 2004, not long after his beloved wife of forty-three years had died. He said, 'Jane would not want me to sit around feeling sorry for myself.' So that became my motto after Jack passed away. Shortly after he died I became a volunteer ambassador at the Tampa airport. I also love to travel, so I started taking more trips, some by myself, some with friends and relatives. I started writing another book, this one about living a full life after a spouse dies or a divorce occurs. I'm painting with my alcohol inks and still painting jars to sell or give to my loved ones. And of course I'm at the pool working out for at least an hour and a half every morning. This year, as I celebrate my thirtieth year of writing for *Daily Guideposts*, I am overjoyed that it's a life filled with blessings too numerous to count, thanks to Jack and his philosophy of moving on with grit, gusto, and grace."

 **Debbie Macomber** is a #1 *New York Times* bestselling author and one of today's most popular writers, with more than two hundred million copies of her books in print worldwide. In her novels, Macomber brings to life compelling relationships that embrace family and enduring friendships, uplifting her readers with stories of connection and hope.

She serves on the Guideposts National Advisory Cabinet, is a YFC National Ambassador, and is

World Vision's international spokesperson for their Knit for Kids charity initiative. A devoted grandmother, Debbie and her husband, Wayne, live in Port Orchard, Washington, the town that inspired Guideposts' Cedar Cove series.

"I had always assumed that my years parenting teenagers would grow my patience in affliction," says **Erin MacPherson** of Austin, Texas, "but instead I've found them full of hope. Yes, we have our moments where angst overpowers joy, but I am hopeful in the many ways God is working in my family. And so between soccer practice and football games, volleyball matches and swim meets, I'm trying to take quiet moments to just take it all in and to see the hope that is unraveling around me in my seemingly ordinary life."

Tia McCollors loves bringing uplifting stories and messages of faith to the hearts of women, whether it be through speaking or through her inspirational novels and devotionals.

One of her greatest joys is raising her three children along with her husband, Wayne. She decided to set aside the unnecessary hustle and bustle of life so that she could be intentional about instilling faith, making memories, and building a legacy with her family. Born and bred in North Carolina, she can now usually be found wrapped in her favorite blanket on the couch, pecking away behind a keyboard, or discovering hidden treasures in the surrounding cities of the Atlanta, Georgia, area. You can connect with Tia online at www. TiaMcCollors.com, through her Facebook pages, or on Instagram@TMcCollors.

 When **Roberta Messner** returned home after her harrowing withdrawal from medically prescribed opiate pain medication, the divine enigma of her miraculous recovery was solved. As she played her voice mail, read email, and collected a tall stack of colorful envelopes and packages from her rural mailbox, she at long last understood.

"I hadn't confided in a single soul outside of my tight inner circle about what was happening," Roberta admits. "And yet, precisely when I was at my lowest, folks mysteriously sensed something terrible was wrong and prayed for me. Friends all across the country. Fellow writers. Beloved readers from the *Guideposts* family of publications who never, ever gave up on me."

Roberta is thrilled to report there has been another miracle. Doctors believe that with the change in her medication, her brain pain pathways have changed.

She is no longer on medication and is experiencing *no pain*, the first time in over fifty years.

"It's been an exciting year and a half as I had a little cottage and barn built on my farm," says **Rebecca Ondov** of Hamilton, Montana. In evenings and on weekends she loves going on adventures, oftentimes kayaking mountain lakes or horseback riding rocky trails with Sunrise, her golden retriever, trotting by her side. Rebecca sums up this last year by saying, "Some mornings as I sip coffee from my deck and watch the sun rise over the snowcapped peaks, I have to pinch myself. I see how God has given me priceless friends, my treasured animals, and a beautiful place to live. God really does answer our prayers and give us our dreams." She invites you to connect with her on her website, RebeccaOndov.com, and on her Facebook author page, where nearly every day she posts a quote to inspire you, which she calls a "Morning Pondering."

Ginger Rue has spent the past couple of years studying STEM (science, technology, mathematics, and engineering) for her new book, *Wonder Women of Science*, co-authored with rocket scientist Tiera Fletcher, an MIT graduate who is working with NASA on the Mars mission. "The more I've learned about physics, microbiology, and the like, the more in awe I've been of God," Ginger says. "The intricacies of His creation are truly mind-blowing." The book highlights the outstanding work of a dozen women who, Ginger says, are "rock stars in their respective STEM fields." Her favorite part of the book? "My co-author, Tiera. She's as faith-filled as she is smart, so that's saying a lot!"

Ken Sampson voices gratitude for his wife Kate's continuing recovery and healing from open-heart surgery. He has renewed appreciation for the daily responsibilities of homemaking—meal planning and cooking, laundry, housecleaning. The Sampsons continue to enjoy and take delight in their grown children and granddaughter, Chanel. Additionally, the recent posting of one-minute *Guideposts* encouraging videos on American Forces Network is cause for joy as these "inspirational commercials" can be seen by military members around the globe.

Since retiring from the classroom, **Daniel Schantz** has spoken at a greater variety of situations: He entertained the local Rotary club with a talk on "The Pleasure of Planting

Trees." He performed at granddaughter Rossetti's wedding under a tree in a park. The Missouri "Young At Heart" seniors group had him speak on "Graceful Aging." And since Sharon's Bible study group is starting the book of Ecclesiastes, they invited Dan to introduce the book, which he taught at the college for many years. Dan is experimenting with new breeds of raspberries and tomatoes in his garden, and Sharon revels in her quilting clubs. Dan and Sharon have been together since 1963.

Gail Thorell Schilling of Concord, New Hampshire, reflects: "One sultry day last summer, I began re-reading the forty journals I'd written since 2000. In the very first, I was surprised to find myself yearning to teach outside a traditional classroom and write without being solitary. The subsequent journals include many prayers to find my way. I've now been mentoring lifelong learners in memoir writing since 2015, have taught spiritual writing, and even published my own memoir (*Do Not Go Gentle. Go to Paris*). Though it took many years, my prayers were answered in ways I could not have foreseen. Now I watch with wonder and gratitude as my little granddaughter learns to say her own prayers and a new generation of faithful prayer takes root."

"My first *Daily Guideposts* devotional appeared September 9, 1978," writes **Penney Schwab** of Copeland, Kansas. "It was about the sad faces and smiley faces my oldest son Patrick's kindergarten teacher used to help her students learn. Now my children are grown, two grandchildren are married, and the youngest grandchild is a teenager. My husband, Don, and I still live on our farm seven miles from the nearest town. Highlights include weddings, grandchildren's hockey games and livestock shows, gatherings with family and friends, and renewal of our small church under the leadership of a dedicated pastor. We also enjoyed attending the Chickasaw Elder's Conference in Oklahoma. Romans 12:12, 'Be joyful in hope, patient in affliction, faithful in prayer,' has sustained me through changing life situations. And I am in awe of God's goodness in allowing me to be a *Daily Guideposts* writer for over forty years. Throughout those years, I have been wonderfully blessed by other writers, editors and staff, and the readers."

Last year **Elizabeth (Tib) Sherrill** planned a trip to France with her daughter, wanting Liz to see the places where her father and mother had lived. Six weeks before their scheduled flight, however, Tib lost most of her vision, her world reduced to a cloudy four-foot radius surrounded by a bewildering fog. They decided to go on the trip anyway. "It was a new kind of travel," Tib says, "seeing places and people through Liz's eyes, learning to listen with new intensity. Appreciating scents and tactile impressions I'd otherwise have missed."

Buck Storm is a critically acclaimed author and musician. Because of his novels *The List, Truck Stop Jesus*, and *The Miracle Man*, as well as nonfiction work *Finding Jesus in Israel*, he has made friends around the world. Buck and his wife, Michelle, have been married for thirty years and have two married children. Visit him at www.buckstorm.com.

Jolynda Strandberg has spent twenty-two years as a civilian with the military, serving as a director of religious education. She and her family have returned from an assignment in Europe to Clarksville, Tennessee. She is also a proud wife and mom to three children ages twenty-six, nine, and five. This past year the Lord has spoken hope for the future with two important graduations; her oldest child graduated from LSU

Health Sciences Center, and the youngest child graduated from preschool.

 **Jon M. Sweeney** and his wife adopted a teenage daughter two years ago. They also moved back to the Midwest. "It's been a year of challenges and change," Jon says. He's the author of thirty-five books, including *St. Francis of Assisi,* published by St. Martin's Press, and the fourth book in his series for children, *The Pope's Cat.* He's a busy father of four, a husband, and also the editor-in-chief at Paraclete Press.

 This year's *Daily Guideposts* theme "Faithful in Prayer" is close to **Stephanie Thompson's** heart. Once her daughter, Micah, started high school, Stephanie and husband, Michael, upped their nightly prayers for her safety, development, and decision-making abilities. "With social media and the Internet, this generation carries access to the world in the palms of their hands. They face a higher degree of temptations and challenges than we did as youth."

Stephanie also found a Moms In Prayer International group that consisted of other mothers with students at Micah's high school. "Every Friday morning after drop-off, five or six of us prayed specific prayers for the school, staff, and students," she explained. "Then we'd break into groups and pour out the personal needs and concerns we had for our children and pray over them. It was a sacred time. Praying with those women for an hour a week bonded us as lifelong friends."

Stephanie and her family live in an Oklahoma City suburb with a pug named Princess, a schweenie (shih tzu/dachshund mix) named Missy, and a tuxedo cat named Mr. Whiskers.

"Parenting never ends," says **Marilyn Turk.** "This past year, Chuck and I have learned to be faithful in prayer, because once children are adults, there's often nothing else you can do for them but pray, especially when they live far away. We now have four wonderful grandsons but keep hoping someday we'll add a granddaughter to the family. During the summer, we've been visiting more parks in our travel trailer, and this year, our grandson Logan got his own kayak, so one of us doesn't have to tow him anymore.

"I've been blessed to have more opportunities to write inspirational historical fiction and pray that readers will be blessed by my books as well. I've also learned that my role in life seems to be as a human extension cord. I'm always connecting people to whoever or whatever they need, and I'm happy to be a part of their journey."

"Rest. This is something I'm learning to do after years of keeping myself busy with my boys," **Karen Valentin** shares. "The responsibility of raising them on my own was a role I took very seriously. No ball could be dropped, no opportunity missed that could better their future, no fun activity too exhausting to ensure a happy and memorable childhood. Yet after an especially exhausting and financially demanding year, I decided to take a break. Less spending on activities and sports, less traveling here and there chasing new and fun experiences. This summer was our first taste of what it means to rest. We enjoyed lazy days full of snuggles and real conversations. As I slowed down, I could fully breathe in the blessings of each day and be thankful to God for every simple moment. My prayer is that I continue to rest in Him, remembering that I am not raising my children on my own. He is with me every step of the way."

"Ten years ago," says **Scott Walker**, "I concluded a thirty-two-year chapter of being a pastor and returned to my alma mater, Mercer University, to teach and direct the Institute of Life Purpose. Today as I completed teaching my class of college freshmen and walked across the lovely campus, I felt a deep feeling of happiness and fulfillment. I was reminded that in every chapter of life God has a unique and important task for us to fulfill.

"Beth and I have also just adopted our fourth generation of golden retriever. 'Miss Lexi' has come to live with us and be the new puppy for our three grandchildren to help raise. We just can't live without a dog!

"The Guideposts family has also become such an enduring part of my life. There is a spiritual sense of living and working together with so many people I have seldom met but feel related to. We are connected by a common purpose to be the presence of God in the lives of all our brothers and sisters. I am glad that we are family!"

 **Jacqueline F. Wheelock** writes, "Having grown up in a tiny community in coastal Mississippi, I recall the numerous summer nights spent staring at bits of the moon through the leaves of live oak trees. Though I was always a dreamer, the possibility of becoming a published author never entered my thoughts. Yet through what could appear to the human eye as a maze of circumstances, in 2014 I published my first novel. Now, years later, I cannot help but remember

with humility that God's thoughts are not mine; neither are His ways, evidenced in the sweet memories He forged for me last Christmas as every member of my immediate family gathered in West Palm Beach, Florida—no small feat for my busy children, their spouses, and their children. Another reminder that, with Him, possibilities are limitless." The mother of two adult children and the grandmother of two granddaughters, Jacqueline treasures her years spent enjoying the company of her husband.

Gayle T. Williams is a native New Yorker, now living in the city's suburbs with her husband and two sons. She is a faithful member of New York Covenant Church in New Rochelle and has been a reporter, writer, and editor for the past thirty years. In addition to reading and writing, she enjoys listening to a wide variety of music, ranging from New Wave to '70s pop to classic jazz. She is honored to be able to share God's direction in her life with the readers of *Daily Guideposts*.

SCRIPTURE REFERENCE INDEX

AUTHORS, TITLES, AND SUBJECTS INDEX

A NOTE FROM THE EDITORS

We hope you enjoyed *Daily Guideposts 2021*, published by the Books and Inspirational Media Division of Guideposts, a nonprofit organization that touches millions of lives every day through products and services that inspire, encourage, help you grow in your faith, and celebrate God's love.

Thank you for making a difference with your purchase of this book, which helps fund our many outreach programs to military personnel, prisons, hospitals, nursing homes, and educational institutions.

We also create many useful and uplifting online resources. Visit Guideposts.org to read true stories of hope and inspiration, access Guideposts OurPrayer community, sign up for free newsletters, download free e-books, join our Facebook community, and follow our stimulating blogs. To delve more deeply into *Daily Guideposts*, be sure to visit DailyGuideposts.org.

You may purchase the 2021 edition of *Daily Guideposts* anytime after July 2020. To order, visit Guideposts.org/DG2021, call (800) 932-2145, or write to Guideposts, PO Box 5815, Harlan, Iowa 51593.